A PLUME BOOK

A YEAR UP

GERALD CHERTAVIAN is the founder and CEO of Year Up. He serves on the boards of Bowdoin College, the Boston Foundation, the Harvard Business School Social Enterprise Initiative, and the Massachusetts State Board of Elementary and Secondary Education. A graduate of Bowdoin College and Harvard Business School, he lives in Boston with his wife and three children.

Praise for *A Year Up*

"Read it—and be inspired."
>—Marc Benioff, chairman and CEO, Salesforce.com

"An incredibly engaging, powerful story that brings to life the amazing potential of urban youth and what we must do to empower them to succeed."
>—Wendy Kopp, CEO and founder, Teach for America

"An inspiring tale of headstrong young people who beat the odds and their journeys from the inner city to college to corporate America."
>—Kenneth Chernault, chairman and CEO, American Express

A Year Up

**HELPING YOUNG ADULTS MOVE FROM POVERTY
TO PROFESSIONAL CAREERS IN A SINGLE YEAR**

Gerald Chertavian

P

A PLUME BOOK

PLUME
Published by the Penguin Group
Penguin Group (USA) Inc., 375 Hudson Street,
New York, New York 10014, USA

USA | Canada | UK | Ireland | Australia | New Zealand | India | South Africa | China
Penguin Books Ltd, Registered Offices: 80 Strand, London WC2R 0RL, England
For more information about the Penguin Group visit penguin.com

First published in the United States of America by Viking,
a member of Penguin Group (USA) Inc., 2012
First Plume Printing 2013

℗ REGISTERED TRADEMARK—MARCA REGISTRADA

THE LIBRARY OF CONGRESS HAS CATALOGED THE VIKING EDITION AS FOLLOWS:

Chertavian, Gerald.
A Year Up : how a pioneering program teaches young adults real skills for real jobs—with real
success / Gerald Chertavian.
p. cm.
Includes index.
ISBN 978-0-670-02377-6 (hc.)
ISBN 978-0-14-312370-5 (pbk.)
1. Year Up (Organization). 2. Occupational training—United States. 3. Young adults—
Vocational education—United States. 4. Young adults—Employment—United States.
5. Internship programs—United States. 6. Internship programs—New York (State). 7. Poor
youth—Vocational education—New York (State). 8. Poor Youth—Employment—New York
(State). 9. Poor youth—Education, Higher—New York (State). I. Title.
HD5715.2.c47 2012
331.25'920973—dc23   2012000606

Printed in the United States of America
10 9 8 7 6 5 4 3 2 1

Set in Janson MT Std with DIN
Original hardcover design by Daniel Lagin

For my wife, Kate, and our three children, Cameron, Casey, and Callum;
For David Heredia, my best teacher;
And for our students and graduates.

Contents

A Year Up

Honk for Opportunity

I **'M NOT A BULLHORN KIND OF GUY.**

Even when explaining my life's passion, I speak softly and carry a portfolio full of powerful statistics. Besides, Harvard Business School grads don't march. Bankers don't march. Typically, they are the ones being marched against. But on May 13, 2010, this HBS alum was excited and a little bit anxious to be taking it to the Boston streets—with some prominent bankers in tow. It wasn't a protest. It was a moving public recognition of a workforce development program that actually puts people into good jobs. Plenty of Americans would take to the streets to cheer that kind of good news.

Just before 11:00 a.m., I pushed back from my desk on Federal Street in the heart of the financial district and pulled a white T-shirt over my standard work clothes: an oxford cloth button-down shirt and tie. The T-shirt was stamped with the words "Walk for Opportunity" and the logo for Year Up, the nonprofit workforce development program for urban young adults that I founded in 2000.

We first opened our classroom doors around the corner on Summer Street in July 2001 with twenty-two students drawn from tough inner-city neighborhoods such as Dorchester, East Boston, and Roxbury. They were part of a growing and vastly underserved population, a category that has since been labeled America's "disconnected youth"—now an estimated 5.2 million young adults ages eighteen to twenty-four nationwide who are not employed and do not have more than a high school diploma. Lacking

affordable college or technical training, their career paths might peak somewhere around "You want fries with that?"

By that spring morning nearly a decade later, Year Up had served more
than three thousand students nationwide, teaching them marketable job and
professional skills and placing 100 percent of those who qualified in their
training period into internships with the best American companies. On the
march that day, one of my favorite signs was carried by a proud information
technology student: I CAN PUT A SERVER TOGETHER IN 42 SECONDS. CAN YOU?

Walk for Opportunity marches were being held in all six cities where
we had opened Year Up programs: Boston, Providence, Atlanta, Washington,
D.C., New York, and San Francisco. We took to the streets to remind Americans of the deep inequalities in opportunity in this country and to raise
awareness of Year Up's success in bridging that divide. We're not exactly a
household name, so it's also a means to introduce ourselves. For our students and graduates, the walk is a loud, spirited expression of pride in their
accomplishments. If I could hustle to Logan Airport and catch the shuttle
to New York on time, I'd be trekking and hoisting a bullhorn in both cities
that day. In hindsight, I probably shouldn't have worn the wingtips.

When I got outside to Summer Street, Year Up staff members were
registering walkers by the hundreds. It was a great coalition: students, staff,
corporate employees whose firms take our interns, students' families and
friends, civic leaders. Homemade signs bobbed along the sidewalk:

WE TAKE THE ROAD NOT TAKEN

WE WANT CAREERS

A HAND UP, NOT A HANDOUT

Near the mouth of a busy ramp funneling suburban traffic into downtown, marchers held up signs that urged HONK YOUR HORN FOR OPPORTUNITY.
Our high-spirited Boston drivers obliged, and the noise began to build. We
lined up behind a big yellow Year Up banner and started walking up Summer
Street. Police cars stopped traffic and escorted our T-shirted throng, which
had grown to several hundred.

Our reception was gratifying and rather sweet. After ten years, Year Up
was a known quantity downtown, recognizable beyond our modest blue and
white banner flying at Ninety-three Summer Street. Nearly a thousand of

our students and graduates had distinguished themselves interning in local businesses. Hundreds had become permanent employees in offices all around us. On a sunny, seventy-degree day, the emerging downtown lunch crowd was upbeat and amiable, offering handshakes, high fives, and thumbs-ups along our way. Office workers waved and hollered from balconies and windows. We were headed for that venerable front lawn of American democracy, Boston Common. Our mission, as one sign put it: WALKING TOGETHER TO CLOSE THE OPPORTUNITY DIVIDE.

Together we were, from both sides of the divide. Year Up students and graduates include some of the poorest, most disenfranchised and talented young people this country has long overlooked. They are low-income urban young adults, eighteen to twenty-four. Year Up's student body is 61 percent male, 39 percent female. They are mainly of color: 59 percent black or African American, 21 percent Hispanic or Latino, 5 percent Asian, 5 percent white, and 10 percent other or mixed; 83 percent have earned a high school diploma and the other 17 percent a GED; 34 percent live in public or subsidized housing; 16 percent are parents.

Cheering them on that day were some of the oldest, largest, and most powerful financial institutions in America: JPMorgan Chase, Bank of America, BNY Mellon, SunTrust. They lent their logos, their resources, and some enthusiastic foot soldiers. In Boston, State Street Corporation's executive vice president, George Russell, came out and walked with us. Serving as grand marshal for the march in New York: Jim Cochran, managing director at JPMorgan Chase. Two days shy of my forty-fifth birthday, the hope—and the justice—in that improbable coalition seemed a magnificent gift. We had all worked so very hard to build it. And after a decade's efforts, life had teed us up a perfect day. Boston Common was green and blooming and teeming with young energy and enterprise. My wife, Kate, and two of our three children, Casey and Callum, were right there with us, as they have been all along. It felt good and right. And from my vantage point in the middle of the bright, energized crowd, it also looked and felt like something much bigger than what we had first envisioned.

The PA system proved inadequate for the size of the crowd, and I had to yell my short speech. I'm not used to hollering, but I even ventured a little call and response:

"What is Year Up?"

"A movement!"

Bakari Barrett, a Year Up student, was a more poised and polished speaker. He stepped up and told some undeniable truths in a bit of slam poetry:

Lack of money gets less education
No jobs, and further degradation
It's getting devastatin'
And I walk both sides of the tracks
So who better to provide you the facts?

Although Bakari had attended Roxbury Community College, he still needed a job and more professional and technical skills. He had heard that Year Up could provide all of that, plus a direct connection to the job market, so he decided to apply. On the day of the walk, Bakari was three months from graduating, interning at JPMorgan Chase. He did so well that he was hired permanently and is now a fund accountant specialist there, with a bright future ahead.

Across the country, all the Year Up marchers—graduates and current students—had worked impossibly hard during our yearlong program, earning coveted internships at top-tier corporations: Bloomberg, Bank of America, UBS, Google, Citi, Wells Fargo, Kaiser Permanente, American Express, and more. Some would have those internships extended; others would be hired permanently. Some would go on to college. Their striving and success have been taught as a case study in "social entrepreneurship" at Harvard Business School.

Though most Americans may not have heard of Year Up, we have interns and graduates succeeding beautifully, if unseen, in high-profile workplaces. They're in the high-tech, ultrasecure NOC, or network operations center, for AOL outside Washington's Dulles Airport. They're tackling software glitches for professors and researchers at MIT, tracking stock trades for JPMorgan Chase and State Street, managing the help desk for thousands of Wells Fargo employees.

As I write this, our nation is in the grip of an economic crisis unprecedented in the modern age. Yet in the midst of record joblessness, Year Up has been able to place our students in good jobs in terrific companies, and we have some pretty audacious plans for expansion. How come? And what's it to you?

The stakes are high here. Our future as a viable, competitive economy is at risk. We had no crystal ball to predict the current job market woes; I started Year Up by looking backward at long-term systemic failures that have only grown worse. Our program is the response to an Opportunity Divide that, as it gets more acute, makes our mission more compelling and our methods more acutely needed. Putting underserved and marginalized young adults to work in real career paths isn't a miracle. It's an achievable reality if you give them access to opportunity. What we provide is good, job-focused education to enter a market starving for skilled workers. How basic is that?

Seeing is believing. By the time you have heard our story and seen exactly how our program works, I'll have demonstrated a few encouraging truths.

There's reason for hope: As our nation's demand for skilled labor increases and its pipeline for high-quality entry-level workers runs dry, Year Up is building a dynamic new workforce specifically trained for those jobs. For ten years, over four hundred leading organizations have found added value in our students as interns and as permanent hires. We've expanded our program across the nation and we've proven our model works.

Hope rests on a simple but critical change in perception: Year Up's talented, successful workforce is made up of individuals too many of us have long been conditioned to see as liabilities. I am going to convince you that this is flat-out wrong. Our young adults are huge assets to an ailing economy once they're given an opportunity. I am going to show you how the adversity of their beginnings can make them stronger, more motivated employees. Far from being a drag on our economic engine, these skilled new workers will be the key to its future.

All of us can benefit: Depending on your circumstances, there are different ways to hear Year Up's story and process its lessons.

If you're an employer, look to these pages for new ways to build a vital, sustainable workforce, one that can leverage your HR expenditures, improve employee retention, and make a greater contribution to the communities where you operate.

If you're well employed, please read this with an eye toward how you can help ease this nation's painful job crisis with even the smallest contribution of word and deed. Our corporate partners, volunteers, and working alumni will show you how it's done.

If you need a job or a new start in life, look to these young people—challenged in ways you might not dream of—for the inspiration to find your own way.

If you grew up in a challenged urban community with abundant risks and scant resources, as our students have, if you understand their struggles all too well, take heart and some practical survival tips from their astonishing journeys.

If you have never had the opportunity and good fortune to meet or truly *know* a single one of the over five million young people labeled "disconnected" in America today—if your only images of our urban young adults are on street corners, in mug shots, or as stereotyped movie characters—listen closely to their voices here and see who they really are. Our students are my heroes; get to know them and you'll find yourself wishing that you—or your children—had their determination and courage.

My name is Gerald Chertavian, and I'm a successful businessman and a social entrepreneur.

At least that's how they'd probably script my introduction on that classic quiz show *What's My Line?*

Back in the freewheeling eighties, I was a somewhat naive and very hopeful emergent capitalist. I hit Wall Street fresh out of the whispering pines of Bowdoin College in Maine, yellow power tie snapping in the breeze, and I was always in a hurry. As a $21,000-a-year credit trainee at Chemical Bank, this Armenian dentist's son from the former mill town of Lowell, Massachusetts, was there to make a name for myself—and, I hoped, some money.

I was frugal, driven, and ambitious, and I had a plan. I left the bank to get my MBA and used what I learned in business school to help build a multimillion-dollar Internet consulting company. My partners and I sold the firm to great advantage on the cusp of the dot-com bust. It gave me the means to begin my next career—the one I'd wanted all along.

These days, "social entrepreneur" is a term used to describe a newer breed of nonprofit executives who tackle stubborn social problems with workable business strategies. Change makers with business-inspired methods, compelling metrics, and better-built mousetraps are making headway on problems that have resisted floods of money and good intentions in the past. Op-ed columns debate social entrepreneurship; Bill Gates and

Michael Bloomberg fund it; two recent Nobel Prizes went to social entrepreneurs tackling environmental, health, and economic problems in developing nations.

It is a growing field of endeavor, and it's now attracting some of the keenest, most innovative minds. It has always been the right fit for me, and selfishly so. I've needed to do this sort of work since I was a college student working on summer youth programs back in Lowell. In the early nineties, when I was studying at Harvard Business School, I was one of just a handful of people to join the Nonprofit Club.

Today it is called the Social Enterprise Club, and it is one of the largest clubs on campus. In 2010, 12 percent of Ivy League graduates applied to Teach for America on graduation. Fixing what's broken in this country is the right thing to do. More and more of our nation's most promising young people are discovering that it's also a great and satisfying career. Some move back and forth between corporate and nonprofit work as opportunities and their own interests change and intersect. The idea for Year Up, albeit in rudimentary form, first appeared in an essay on my application to Harvard Business School in 1989. Its inspiration came from my experience toggling between my work in the privileged financial district and my weekends as Big Brother to David Heredia, a ten-year-old Dominican boy living in the Rutgers Houses, then one of the toughest crime- and crack-ridden projects in lower Manhattan. David was and is a gifted artist; given his circumstances, his best outlet might have been tagging subway trains with graffiti.

Mission statement? Year Up is committed to closing the ever-widening Opportunity Divide in this country. You'll hear that phrase a lot from me, but it's hardly my invention. No doubt you see evidence of it wherever you live. For the first time since the nation's founding, successive generations of Americans are less upwardly mobile. Our children may not do better than we have. Or even as well.

The historic and widening gap between the haves and have-nots is tearing our country apart; you can see the growing fault lines in a succession of recent headlines in the *New York Times* and the *Washington Post:*

THE NEW INEQUALITY

THE COSTS OF RISING ECONOMIC INEQUALITY

NO CHILD LAW IS NOT CLOSING RACIAL GAP

PROFICIENCY OF BLACK STUDENTS IS FOUND
TO BE FAR LOWER THAN EXPECTED

5 MYTHS ABOUT OUR LAND OF OPPORTUNITY

More recent figures on the racial differences in wealth show our students' generation to be comparatively worse off than their parents. In the years 1984 to 2007, as they were growing up, the racial wealth gap *quadrupled*. A recent Pew study found that as of 2009, the average Caucasian had twenty times the wealth of the average Latino and eighteen times the wealth of the average African American.

Yet against this stark landscape, Year Up gets results. Within four months of completing the program, 80 percent of our graduates are employed or in school full time. They are resolutely on their way up. Employed graduates earn about fifteen dollars an hour—more than double minimum wage in some areas.

They leave our classrooms with considerable advantages. Year Up graduates enter the workforce with a half year's on-the-job experience and a solid set of professional skills, from drafting a proper e-mail to workplace etiquette and teamwork dynamics. By contrast, 40 percent of employers rate high school graduates as underprepared for entry-level jobs, lacking basic skills such as math, written communication, and professionalism.

Where does that land much of America's "disconnected youth" in this economy? The 2010 federal poverty guideline for a single person was $10,830. Alternative career paths—such as drug dealing—can yield big money and pricier consequences. In New York State, the average expense to house a prisoner for one year is $36,835—a waste from any perspective.

This kind of comparative math can be numbing and disheartening. But sometimes, if you turn it around, it's excellent food for thought—if a little tough to digest.

Come to dinner with me for a moment, in a sleek corporate dining room on the Microsoft campus overlooking the Charles River in Cambridge; Harvard rowers are making their last runs as the lights come on along the riverbanks. The evening is being hosted by New Profit, one of the nation's leading venture philanthropy organizations. New Profit invests significant capital in programs run by social entrepreneurs. Along with three other heads of successful nonprofits, I'm once again singing for my supper in a room full of very wealthy potential donors. We need them. The fees paid by corporations for our interns cover about half of our expenses for each student. Less than 10 percent of our funding is from the government. The rest must be raised at tables like this one. The food is superb, the talk earnest and civil. Until I get the question that always kills my appetite.

"Gerald, at $25,000, isn't your model pretty expensive on a cost-per-head basis?"

"That's a great question. Let me ask you, sir, do you have children?"

"Yes, I do, two children."

"That's wonderful. And I'm guessing they're about college age."

"One is finished; the other is in her junior year."

"That's great. And I'm also guessing that your kids were fortunate enough to go to a great private school."

"Yes, they did go to private colleges."

"Congratulations, that's great. Now, the top-notch private schools today cost about $52,000 a year—but the school's endowment generally kicks in another $13,000 to cover what it really costs, making that a total of $65,000 a year. Four years of that comes to $260,000, which we willingly, lovingly spend. I hope my own kids will go to such institutions."

My questioner is nodding cautiously and the room has gotten very quiet.

"Why, then, do we think that spending one-tenth that amount on a young adult who has had no opportunities or advantages is somehow expensive? Why is one person worth ten times the investment of another?"

The gentleman absorbed it well. Pointing out inequity doesn't have to make you the skunk at the garden party. It also helps if you can finish with a little more applied math, in terms of investment impact. A 2009 study by an economic consulting firm found that Year Up Boston graduates showed more than a one-million-dollar increase in lifetime earnings. They will contribute commensurate taxes.

In so many ways, they're just what our economy needs. Despite the nation's high unemployment rate, jobs are going begging—the very jobs our graduates learn the skills for. They can help correct an alarming structural mismatch: With fourteen million Americans unemployed, three million jobs remain unfilled. Research by the labor economists Anthony P. Carnevale and Donna M. Desrochers shows that the United States is facing a shortage of fourteen million college-educated workers in the next ten years. Consider a second skein of *New York Times* headlines that describe a critical and growing shortage of skilled labor for American business:

DESPITE SIGNS OF RECOVERY, CHRONIC JOBLESSNESS RISES

ONCE A LEADER, U.S. LAGS IN COLLEGE DEGREES

IN JOB MARKET SHIFT, SOME WORKERS ARE LEFT BEHIND

The title of a 2010 report on National Public Radio stated the problem succinctly: *The Skills Gap: Holding Back the Labor Market.*

There are plenty of jobs out there now, many of them information based, that don't require college degrees. But they demand skills not taught in high schools. Year Up teaches technical and professional skills that change with the job market; the program is flexible enough to meet needs in different locales and markets. In Boston we began teaching Web design and dropped it when the demand dipped; we added financial operations and quality assurance after listening to what local employers said they needed—badly and right away.

It's not rocket science. We do what the very best for-profit organizations do: Stay lean, hungry, and flexible. Grow a loyal, resilient, and engaged workforce on high support and high expectations. A popular sign that appeared in most marches that day in May simply quoted a Year Up core value: WORK HARD AND HAVE FUN.

That ethic—and our measurable results—have solidified and expanded our ties with the business community. JPMorgan Chase, a financial institution over two hundred years old with global assets of over two trillion dollars, has become a deeply committed corporate partner, involved now in six Year Up sites nationwide. Having bought the skills and energy of nearly one hundred of our interns from the New York City sites alone, managing director John Galante—chief information officer for Chase Wealth Management— says he has found a steady source of young talent applicable to many positions at Chase. Though the bank has been generous with everything from office space to seed money for new sites, its hiring of our interns is not seen as charity. That investment keeps paying dividends. "The interns' success is very measurable for us," Galante says. "When we look at how much it costs to bring them in, knowing that they have good basic training and how much they contribute, the corporate end sees it as a good investment."

Sometimes, at a business lunch in the financial district, Galante finds himself recommending Year Up interns to CIOs and COOs at other firms. "I'll say we've had some great experience with a terrific program. It's a source of young, ambitious, smart labor. It's worked out very well for us in terms of being an excellent business case for certain skill sets. It's a great way to reach out to close the divide. It's also a great energizer for the employees around the interns as they come in. I tell anyone—there's not a big risk here. Add it up: a great business case, great for the community, an energizer for your staff—it's really a win-win."

Our admissions and community outreach staffs have heard it all:

For real?

Are you playin' me here?

I think y'all might be lying.

Even potential applicants, many of whom have been through other job programs without results, are understandably skeptical when they first hear—through guidance counselors, community outreach programs, relatives, and friends—what Year Up can do in eleven intense months. Very often we hear them say, "I thought it was just another . . . *program.*" They have no reason to believe we can deliver what so many others have not. The U.S. Government Accountability Office reports that the United States spends eighteen billion federal dollars on forty-seven different workforce development programs. Only *five* have been formally evaluated. The majority of these programs fund efforts rather than results and don't require a clear connection to employers. The industry itself is fragmented and unregulated, with thousands of mom-and-pop training organizations that aren't being held accountable for ensuring their clients are getting jobs. Few have undergone scientific evaluation to prove that they are effective. Add it all together and you get a workforce development system that doesn't really work. Given all the disappointments they have already absorbed by age eighteen, it's no surprise that young adults entertain serious doubts when they read our ads and handouts that sound like the ultimate late-night infomercial: *Earn while you learn.*

But it's true. Students in the Year Up program don't pay any tuition or fees. They earn a daily stipend while they study and intern; graduates also attain up to twenty-three college credits. We encourage and help facilitate college study during and after our program, so that graduates can continue their career growth.

Briefly, this is how it works: After a rigorous admissions process, the next five months are spent in our classrooms learning marketable skills in areas such as information technology, financial operations, and quality assurance. In addition, students have a deep immersion in professional skills—everything from dressing and communicating professionally to managing their own finances. They learn how these soft skills and positive attitudes will help them succeed in the workplace. Students spend the next six months in full-time internships, applying what they have learned with our corporate partners. Each site graduates two classes a year; when one class of students begins their internships, a new class takes their place in the learning and development phase of the program.

We're banking on them to succeed—literally. As I mentioned, the fees companies contribute to have Year Up interns cover half of our expenses. And if our interns don't meet expectations, we don't expect our corporate partners to pay us. Year Up's solvency depends upon our interns doing well. I've never lost a night's sleep worrying about that. I am not a particularly religious man, but I have boundless faith in these young souls.

Listen to Carlos, a New York student three months into the program, as he greeted a young man waiting in the student lounge for an admissions interview. The nervous applicant got a firm handshake, a big smile, and a friendly warning: "I'm not gonna lie, some days it's gonna beat up on you. If you think you can dog it here, there's the door—get out while you can. But if you really want it, if you can stay focused, a lot of people have your back here. I'll have your back. Just remember, the ones who come poppin' in here saying, 'No problem, I'm gonna kill this,' they're the ones gone after a week."

The reporting in our book draws from all of our learning communities across the nation and is collaborative, consensual, and well documented. The students speaking in this book are all real; we don't do composites. Some of their stories are painful, tragic, and outrageous. A few absolutely defy belief. Names and a few identifying details have been changed in some cases to ensure the safety and privacy of students and their families—as well as their futures. When a pseudonym is used for the first time, it is noted by an asterisk. We undertake this book with the same guiding principle that powers Year Up: respect.

On average, close to 70 percent of our incoming students graduate. Compare that with community colleges, where almost half of college students seek postsecondary education. Despite a fivefold increase in enrollment over the past forty years, only 34 percent of students entering community colleges complete any degree program—within eight years after high school.

At Year Up, there is no tolerance for what's been called the soft bigotry of low expectations. We expect a lot from our students because we respect them. We are not a charity operation. Each student signs a contract agreeing to adhere to Year Up's rigorous and nonnegotiable expectations and core values; infractions of the contract requirements—from lateness to missed assignments—result in the loss of a portion of that week's stipend. Performance is also assessed with our point system. Each student begins the program with two hundred points. They earn more points for meeting all expectations and lose them for infractions. We never expel, but any student who loses all points effectively "fires" him- or herself from the program.

We cut no slack, we accept no excuses, and the classroom door will be closed in your face—resulting in an infraction—if you are one second late. We insist on proper business attire, no T-shirts, no sneakers, no street slang— no fooling.

But it's not just another version of "tough love." Along with those high expectations for their performance, students draw on a deep and well-honed support system. Each of our sites employs mental health professionals to help students cope with the persistent challenges they encounter in their lives. Students are assigned on-site advisers who check in often—daily, if necessary—to ensure that "outside noise" is not keeping them from doing their best. They are also partnered with mentors drawn from the business community who provide more support, role modeling, and networking opportunities.

All of these professionals are skilled and dedicated. But their efforts would be of limited use without the students' most valuable asset: peer support. They learn to rely on one another for a hand up, whether it's help with an IT assignment or a six-thirty wake-up call. Students are organized into small (up to forty-person) learning communities known as LCs. Orientation week for any Year Up class is dedicated to creating bonds that often last far beyond the program; a decade after graduation, five graduates from our first Boston class of twenty-two still get together regularly for love, laughs, and support.

Why was Marisol,* a twenty-one-year-old single mother, tearful on the last day of her learning and development phase in Brooklyn as her LC prepared to head out on its internships? "Well, I'm really happy—I can't wait to start my internship. But I can't believe I won't be coming here every day anymore. We started out not talking to each other much, just looking down at our feet. Now we are so tight. We're family. Everybody here has your back. I never had this in my life—people you can call anywhere, anytime. And they're there for you, no matter what."

Why and how Year Up works—and the hope it holds for America's future—are what this book is about. I don't expect you to believe in its viability unless I show you, in the trenches, day to day. See how our students come in—watch them struggle, take risks, and excel. Take a hard look, too, at the ones we lose and the forces that conspire against them. This is our students' book, just as Year Up is their success. Ours is a tight, collaborative organization built on constant feedback, mutual trust, and six core values that make ours a safe, caring, and uplifting community. It's hardly my story; it's the story of our astoundingly committed staff, corporate partners, mentors, donors, volunteers, and my wife, Kate, who has been a full and dedicated partner for each step of this meaningful journey. Of course we also need the voice of my Little Brother from the Lower East Side, David Heredia, now an artist, husband, and father living outside Los Angeles.

In all of our locations across the country, Year Up hallways are noisy with excitement and promise in so many young voices. In staying true to that atmosphere—and our culture of really listening, to everyone—this narrative may get a bit boisterous sometimes, and as loud and insistent as some of our students' vivid slam poetry. In 2012 Year Up expects to serve just over fifteen hundred students from San Francisco to Atlanta and points in between. I travel constantly between sites to check in and see what's on their minds. I hear from students and alumni every day in e-mails and phone calls; Kate is always setting extra places for graduates and mentees amid our children at the dinner table. And my BlackBerry is still set to ping every time a student—no matter where or when—fires him- or herself from the program. There's always time to reflect on how we might have served someone better.

Finally, before we jump in: If there is one thing that gets this mild-mannered social entrepreneur into a decidedly unsociable state, it's the suggestion that our graduates are so exceptional, our success rates so above the curve, that we must "cream" our admissions pool and accept those most likely to make it through. Nothing could be further from the truth.

As you hear their stories, know this: Our students come into their admissions interviews with an average of three challenges each, ranging from homelessness to domestic violence to lack of child care to past interactions with the justice system. You can't go into a single Year Up classroom anywhere in the nation without finding young people who have been touched by violence at home or in their neighborhoods.

Even if they haven't studied Nietzsche, Year Up students have an instinctive understanding of his famous maxim: *That which doesn't kill us makes us stronger.* They know how to hammer their toughest challenges into a set of strengths any employer would be glad to have. As one Brooklyn student put it: "I figure if I've survived my own life so far, I can knock this thing out of the park."

We have asked for a special assist from students in Class Nine of the Manhattan and Brooklyn sites to take us through the Year Up journey from beginning through internship and on to graduation. The young men and women you are about to meet are typical of the applicants who show up every weekday, in greater and greater numbers, at all of our sites—if anything about their lives can be called typical.

Among them: Malik,* a former special education student trying to escape the fate of his brother, murdered in street violence; Taleisha,* consigned to foster care at age eleven and back living in public housing with her three-year-old son; Cassandra,* homeless, self-supported since her midteens, and astonishingly resourceful. These students were invited to help narrate our story with no prescreening of their test scores or grades. If anything stood out about them during their first week with us, it was the sheer determination they showed in just getting themselves to our door.

The New York Walk for Opportunity was scheduled for late afternoon, and I made the shuttle with just minutes to spare. I wanted to be there. If Boston is home, New York is where this movement found its inspiration. The marchers were already gathering on Manhattan's Lower East Side as my taxi sped along. I'm probably one of the few ex-commuters who still loves the jarring, potholed ride along the East River down the FDR Drive.

As a young banker, I used to ante seven dollars a day to carpool in a packed van from the Upper East Side down the Drive to Wall Street. David Heredia's public housing complex is located just off that ever-clogged artery, right by the Manhattan Bridge. My home and Year Up's national headquarters are in Boston, and when I come to visit Year Up NYC, I always ask the airport taxi to take the Drive so that I can see the windows of the Heredias' apartment and remind myself where this all began.

The afternoon of the march, the cab dropped me right outside the Rutgers Houses. David's mother, Cornelia, still lives in the same apartment, and after the greetings and hugs I could tell she was apprehensive and a bit unclear about the growing crowd downstairs. In my barely adequate Spanish I tried to explain to her what we were doing.

"Caminar por la oportunidad."

I'm not sure I got my point across, although after over twenty years, I'm sure that Cornelia trusted me. But she seemed apprehensive when I introduced her—through a bullhorn—to the marchers who gathered outside the project and they cheered her loudly. David looms large in Year Up lore; nearly all students have seen an orientation video outlining his story. Cornelia, who raised five sons alone in the Rutgers Houses, is a heroine—and Year Up's proud *abuela*.

"Ay, Geraldo . . ."

My "second mother" apologized that a bad back prevented her from walking with us. She waved us off down Madison Street toward Pearl and the steep granite canyons of the financial district. The echo effect was terrific.

The feeling in the financial district is so different from what I remember when I started my work life there. And in the area near the stock exchange, it looks more like a K-9–patrolled pedestrian mall, owing to the post-9/11 security issues. I'm always surprised by the number of tourists who now pour out of the Wall Street subway stations at all hours. Are they there to check the pulse of American capitalism in these difficult economic times? Or is it just a quick detour on the way to peer at Ground Zero?

Whatever the draw, they were out in force along our route, looking puzzled but pleased at catching the modest spectacle. Just as we reached the heart of the financial district on Broad Street, my cell phone rang. It was Mike O'Brien, a friend and fellow social entrepreneur, calling from an office above.

"Hey, Gerald, is that you down there?"

Yep. Same guy, same suit, more meaningful job description.

We finished the march in front of the iconic Federal Hall at Fifty-five Wall Street, beneath the supersized bronze statue of George Washington.

His hand was raised out toward us—I'd like to think in benediction. The founding father took his presidential oath of office on a platform there in the spring of 1789, kissed the Bible he had sworn on, and received a booming thirteen-cannon salute. We figured it was a fitting place to hold America to its promise of social and economic justice for all.

CHAPTER ONE

"Yo, God. What Are You Doing?"

"**W**HO ARE THEY?" A WOMAN AIMING HER TURQUOISE POINT-AND-shoot camera asked no one in particular.

September 10, 2010, was another bright, warm day. Class Nine of Year Up New York City, eighty-seven strong, had assembled on the steps of Federal Hall behind a Year Up banner for the class picture taken there at the start of each term. The New York staff jokes about how many tourists have found the sight worth capturing for their click-and-save digital scrapbooks, peering at them later in Beijing or Berlin and wondering, "Who is Year Up?"

The students in those class portraits are mostly of color: African American and Hispanic, several Asian, a few Caucasian faces. For them, Wall Street had been as distant and irrelevant to their lives as the Great Wall of China. They had traveled there from some of the poorest, most neglected, and crime-ridden neighborhoods in Brooklyn, Harlem, lower Manhattan, the Bronx, and Queens. The majority of them—over 90 percent—came from households eligible for public benefits; if they had any employment it was in a numbing succession of minimum-wage jobs that netted an average yearly salary of just over six thousand dollars.

Since we opened the facility in September 2006, enrolling a new class every six months, Year Up New York City had graduated seven classes while an eighth was completing the internship phase. Class Nine also included thirty-nine students in our new Brooklyn site. All of them had graduated from high school or obtained a GED, a Year Up admissions requirement. Here are a few of the nonacademic skills some of Class Nine had found it useful to learn along the way:

How to find space in your heart and in your cramped apartment for young cousins whose parents died of AIDS.

How to stay clean and nourished and navigate your Bronx high school without anyone knowing you're homeless, penniless, and on your own at sixteen.

How to calmly and effectively seek a transfer when your English teacher calls you the most unspeakable of racial epithets.

How to get a good night's rest when the other foster teenager in your room sleeps with razors under her pillow.

How to use Facebook to save your own life—literally.

———

Like the New York City classes before them, they started life abundantly rich in what social workers call "risk factors." More than 40 percent had some sort of financial hardship—low income, lack of medical insurance, scant or no resources for college or job training. A third had significant challenges at home: They had been in foster care, acted as the primary caregiver for other family members at a very young age, or were confronting some other sort of family crisis—drug abuse, domestic violence. Some were already parents themselves, struggling with limited resources and child-care issues. Others were homeless or transient. Most had been severely short-changed by substandard or "failing" public schools.

If you just read the papers, most of what's reported is fairly grim data. The New York State Education Department reported that in New York City, only 21 percent of students entering city high schools in 2006 (as many of Class Nine did) graduated with high enough scores on state math and English tests to be deemed ready for higher education or well-paying careers. Broken down along racial and ethnic lines, the stats were even worse: Only 13 percent of African American students and 15 percent of Hispanics qualified in that "readiness" category.

Motivation is not measured in those statistical surveys, but that is a key factor in Year Up's admissions process. We look for students who are willing and eager to make a significant change in their lives. That day in New York, the eighty-four looked anything but disconnected, disaffected, or hopeless. They were wearing suits and ties, business-appropriate skirts and dresses, shined shoes, and two-hundred-watt smiles. A cheer went up among them, loud enough to startle the security dogs outside the stock exchange into alert mode.

Once the photos were taken and the banner was rolled up, the students and their instructors walked a block and a half and around the corner to a suite of crisp blue and white Year Up classrooms at Fifty-five Exchange Place. The eighty-four were divided into two learning communities ("LCs" in program vernacular) under the guidance of site leaders Massomeh Muhammad (LCM) and Linzey Jones (LCL). Separately, each LC was to close out an intense orientation week with a group exercise known as Milestones.

Not all sites use it, but in most cities the staff has created some form of group exercise that helps an incoming class gel. Growing a supportive community is crucial in a program that relies on intense peer support and feedback. These students need to care about one another—and quickly.

At the Year Up New York site, Milestones is high input and low tech; it requires courage, some mural paper, and a plastic bin containing marker pens and a box of tissues. Dates, in increments of five years, are written across wide mural paper taped to the walls. Students are invited to walk up and jot down significant moments in their lives near the appropriate dates. And if they choose to, they may stand up front and talk about their individual entries.

First up was LCM. Already the group was vocal and high energy, not unlike its leader. Massomeh is a lively woman given to wrapping herself in vivid, cheery colors that telegraph her background in teaching and running arts programs. Through stylish round glasses, she was watching her new charges intently as they chose markers and ambled toward their blank canvas.

In ten minutes they had covered the paper in brightly colored scrawls and meticulous script. Viewed together, their entries' shorthand took in joy, sorrow—and plenty in between:

I was born!
Father was killed
My little bro was born (person who keeps me together)
In a shelter with mother and brothers

Moved into first house
Foster care
I took care of Mommy
Dad stops drinking
Started playing football
Kicked out of house by mother (homeless)
Mommy passed, lost all my motivation
Lost my twin babies
Got accepted to Year Up!!!!

It may be sufficient for some students to just list their milestones. All are invited to stand up and talk about them if they wish to do so; nothing is mandatory. Staff members also write their milestones, and they stand up to speak about their experiences first. This helps break the ice and give students guidelines for speaking. Andres Gomez, a perceptive and experienced MSW and our student services manager, was running the exercise. It was his first time, but he seemed confident and calm as he ceded the floor to the woman who had hired him. Lisette Nieves, executive director of Year Up New York City—which also includes our new learning community in Brooklyn—stepped up to the front, grabbed a marker, and exhaled.

Lisette's milestones held their attention straightaway. Born 1968: "You couldn't get a more contentious year, but you couldn't get a greater year of hope either." Second daughter of a too-young Puerto Rican couple who lived on a California commune, came back to Brooklyn, and split up. In 1972, put into foster care, owing to her teenage mother's drug addiction. Four months later, mother, full of love and promise, was found dead of an overdose. Raised by grandmothers and aunts until her father returned, found her, and took her home. Brooklyn College. Joyous wedding. Father's death. In 2005, "Had my son."

There are a few other impressive milestones that Lisette generally keeps to herself in these exercises: Former chief of staff of the New York City Department of Youth and Community Development. Overseer of Ameri-Corps projects for the entire Northeast. First Puerto Rican Rhodes Scholar at Oxford University and graduate of the Woodrow Wilson School of Public and International Affairs at Princeton.

That day, she simply wished LCM to understand that the daughter of a drug-addicted mother consigned to foster care had made it through just fine, thank you.

"Happy ending," Lisette concluded. "Think about that."

It was Lisette who instituted Milestones in the New York site, fashioning it after a community-building training exercise she had been taught to facilitate years earlier. "The idea," she explained, "is that you ground everyone in experiences that may have seemed challenging to them. But you use that as a metaphor for hope and resiliency—rather than increase the sense of being a victim."

Lisette knew there would be no shortage of difficult entries on the wall charts. Just to get started, Year Up students need so much more than a student ID card and subway fare. A staff of dedicated professionals—educators, MSWs, advisers—provides daily, steady support to help students cope with what is called "outside noise." They may shine in class during the school week, but our instructors have come to dread Mondays. They have seen the damage a weekend back in the neighborhood or in a difficult home life can inflict.

Andres was scanning the rows for more volunteers. "Anyone else? No pressure. Only if you want to."

Taleisha, the twenty-one-year-old single mother of a toddler son, pointed to her first entry—a ten-year separation from her two dearly loved younger brothers. She had never talked about it—not with the social workers who removed all three children from her mother's home when her brothers were just two and four, not with her loving, tenacious foster mother, and certainly not with the succession of therapists assigned to her case. Taleisha always stonewalled; they just stared at the clock and each other until the mandated appointments were up.

Taleisha didn't talk, period. She could not remember when she had had a friend and was only thankful that no one knew her business in her public housing complex in East Harlem. The first week she had brought her infant son, Jared,* to live there, a fourteen-year-old boy shot directly at them with a handgun on their way in—not aiming, just playing. He missed. And she had cupped the baby's downy head: Welcome home, little man.

Talk about it? It was all just so . . . unspeakable. So what was she doing up in front of everyone? How did her legs even get her there? Tears rolled down her face and Andres, who had been a caseworker at the social services agency that had shepherded Taleisha's teen years, said quietly, "Take your time. And it's okay if you can't right now."

"I'm okay. I think. My brothers were so young when they took us all out of my mother's house. I love them so much and they hardly remember me today. I was the oldest. When they took us, I was eleven, and the social services people had just talked to me. They took us while my mother was at work. I had to call a few relatives about who could take us in, because they were telling us that we were going to sleep there and I didn't want my brothers to do that.

"They asked me would I want my brothers to stay with me in foster care, and I told them no because they had nothing to do with why I had to go into protective custody. They took them back to my mother when I told them that I would just go into foster care. Alone."

Taleisha's choice. Made in the fourth grade with harrowing maturity, that sacrifice set her adrift from all that she loved. Soon after, her mother and her new husband took the boys away to Chicago. No wonder that the rest of Taleisha's short narrative was halting and hard to follow. There was so much more she could not address. But Andres was nodding at her. It was all good, a victory. Taleisha spoke. And as she made her way back to her seat, LCM murmured support.

"I had something like that too. I hear you."

"Thank you. That had to be hard."

Andres nodded next to twenty-one-year-old Cassandra, a tall, stylish young woman with only a trace of her native Jamaican accent. She seemed nervous as she took her place at the front of the room, but determined to speak. She was wearing a slim beige pencil skirt cinched by a wide belt. Hair, nails, lipstick—she's always so perfectly groomed that an instructor had just told her, "You look like you stepped out of *Vogue*." Cassandra had laughed at that. "You have no idea. . . ."

Pointing at the chart, she began with the notation of her birth in Jamaica in 1989.

"My mother left for the United States in 1990, my father in 1992. When my mother left, I was with my uncle. I was seven months old. My uncle raised me; I had no contact with my parents. My uncle grew me so hard. I never knew why he was so rough on me. Now I realize that if he didn't grow me the way he did, I would not be able to make it out of any of my . . . circumstances. He knew my parents well, how they were.

"Him and his wife, they have seven kids. He taught me how to do everything. Let Cassandra do it. I was washing my clothes at six. I learned how to cook at six. I do everything, I'm a hands-on person. When I was eight, I started receiving calls from my father once a year."

Charmaine Peart-HoSang, director of outreach and social services for both Brooklyn and Manhattan, was standing along the side of the room, listening carefully. She is a tall, thoughtful woman with wise eyes and a keen instinct for impending crises. It would be Charmaine's job, along with Andres, to be extra vigilant with this new student, whose privations had been extraordinary right from birth and had only grown worse. Charmaine was also born in Jamaica, though she immigrated to Toronto at age two and grew up there before she came to New York to earn her MSW at Hunter College.

With seven years' experience in counseling New York City youth and a lifelong immersion in West Indian culture, she recognized Cassandra as a "barrel child," the product of "stepwise" migration. Barrel children are left behind with relatives in the West Indies when their parents immigrate to the United States. They have little connection save the occasional cardboard shipping barrel of clothing and supplies sent back to the islands for support. Often children are not sent for until years later; family adjustments are not always smooth.

Cassandra glanced back at the chart and continued.

"So. Another milestone. In 2001, when I was twelve, I came here to live with my parents in Camden, New Jersey. My father had his own floor refinishing company, so they're okay, they're doing great. I had two brothers and a sister. I lived with my parents pretty much for five years. I ran away in 2006 to come to New York. It was an abusive situation."

Charmaine wondered how far Cassandra would take it. From Cassandra's candid admissions interviews Charmaine knew that the abuse was so abominable, recurrent, and apparent that court officers sent Cassandra straight to therapy and to a judge, who instructed her how to legally "divorce" her parents, a process called child emancipation in some states. She got through the legal proceedings with the help of a sympathetic aunt. But afterward, threats of reprisal terrified her. When Cassandra fled her parents' home, she had no identification, no birth certificate, no immigration papers, and no idea how to begin life anew and on her own. She found her way to New York, where a series of relatives grudgingly took her in, then turned her out.

"And I'm sleeping in the park in the winter. It's a park in the Bronx called Haffen Park, one of the worst. But I survive it. I do. In the daytime I go and look around. Where am I going to be? Where did the snow fall the most? In the evening when everyone clears out of the park, I would clear off the snow and just be there for a while, watching. Then I would go by my school friend's house and sit there. They'd ask me, 'You want dinner?' Sometimes I refused, not making it look like I never ate anything. She and her mother never knew. They thought I was staying with a friend.

"I would go back to the park around eleven, walk around first to see if anyone is there. Bad people stay by there. And if I don't see anyone I would go up on the slide and just curl up on the little platform. On the top where nobody could see me. It was one of the high ones. I have all my clothes, my jacket, and my boots, and I would just curl up in a ball to keep myself warm.

"When it's getting too cold, what I do, four in the morning, some-times five, I walk to the train station and sit there, and if anybody, the police or station people, ask me a question, I'd tell them I left my house too early so I'm just sitting waiting. Sometimes, I'm not proud to say, I wouldn't have a Metro card to ride the train to school, so I would climb over the bar to get in. . . .

"School was a relief. It was good for me because they provide breakfast and lunch. I would get an extra breakfast or an extra milk or cereal and make sure I eat lunch and I would be okay 'til the next day. Every afternoon, I'd be one of the last ones to leave. No one really knew what was going on until I decided I couldn't deal with it anymore."

LCM was riveted. A few female students were hunched over, arms folded as if they could feel the desolation and cold. The room grew quieter still as Cassandra discussed her brief stay in a shelter, the difficulties of transporting one's belongings in flimsy, slippery trash bags, finding places to stash them, and working three minimum-wage jobs to secure the lifeline she felt could save her.

"I bought the laptop when I was working. That's the best thing I ever did. It was a present to me from me. It was twelve hundred dollars for the laptop and printer. I said, 'I have to get myself something tangible.' I said, 'I need a serious warranty because I'm constantly on the move.' And I got a five-year one. At an early age I had to think on a higher level.

"I had no one. No. One. But I found huge family on Facebook. And we met up in Harlem, by Applebee's. They said, 'You have to meet everyone else; there's so much of us. Yes, Cassandra, your grandfather and grandmother have a lot of kids.' Huh? Turns out my grandfather had twenty kids alto-gether. In different places.

"This is why I say I'll never close my Facebook account—you never know what's happening. I met my cousins from D.C. They heard about me and they came up to meet me. It feels great. You come all the way to meet me? Me? And with them getting to know who I am, I get so much support from them. What I love is that they're all educated. Nurses, doctors, teachers, counselors. With them, education is the key."

Charmaine watched closely as Cassandra took her seat amid expressions of sympathy and utter shock from her classmates. Her resiliency was just short of miraculous, her coping skills savvy beyond her years. But any stability she managed was a very fragile thing—and balanced on a knife edge. Charmaine and Andres were already bracing for a potential crisis just a week into the program.

Upon leaving the shelter, Cassandra was lodged temporarily with a relative who had become unpredictable and menacing. Even charging the battery of her precious laptop was forbidden to Cassandra. She expected to be homeless again, and soon. But she had promised Charmaine—and herself— that she would absolutely make it to class on time, every day—and hang tough until the situation exploded. Again. She had just explained: "It can get hectic where I stay now. I leave that place every day at first light. But I'm so happy when I'm here."

That same morning, across the East River in Brooklyn, another Milestones session was getting under way in a double-sized classroom, recently painted and carpeted. Year Up's newest space has been carved from the old Dime Savings Bank building; its venerable dome overlooks the hustle and honk of Flatbush Avenue. The learning community of thirty-nine students arrives mainly by subway from Williamsburg, Fort Greene, Bushwick, and Queens.

The space is made available to us at minimal cost—no rent, just operating expenses—by its owner, JPMorgan Chase, a Year Up corporate partner. It is in a weary old part of Brooklyn's downtown undergoing its own year up, with new high-rise condos and office buildings, mixed-use art and enterprise co-ops, and the sprawling Fulton Mall renovation. Even rapper/entrepreneur Jay-Z has sought a piece of the action, investing in Buffalo Boss, a barbecued-wing joint owned by his cousin. This is a construction zone so active that Year Up's temporary backdoor entrance has a secure but speakeasy feel. Watching the procession of well-dressed students navigate the mud and barricades that morning, a deliveryman wondered: "They got a modeling agency or something up there? What's with all these kids in suits?"

Delivery man number two: "Naw, man. I'm guessing a parole office."

Upstairs, Milestones was being led by LCW site leader Wilfrid "Wil" Velazquez. Wil has a voice soothing as aloe and a set of professional tools that let him contain and direct a charged situation with firmness and compassion. He would have his work cut out for him that morning.

First he took the group through his own milestones, startling his co-workers with a revelation they hadn't heard in previous sessions: the devastation caused by the cancer diagnosis of a former girlfriend and his seeking help to cope with it. "I've never talked about that before," Wil would confess later. "You can't ever predict where these things will take you."

LCW got busy. Along two paper-covered walls, the students' bright marker entries ranged as widely as those of their colleagues across the river:

Found God, got baptized

Drope outta HS

Grandmother died, I got arrested

My little bro born! Yeah!

June 18, Mommy dies

Got kicked out of high school

Father went to Iraq, was shot

Finished High School!

Malik, an energetic, somewhat fidgety eighteen-year-old, loped up to the front and pointed out his own entries on the chart. They were easy to find; he had chosen a neon green marker. He pointed to his notation for 2006: "Brother killed."

"I was at my eighth-grade prom. That's when I got the news. I had just got my dance on. The next day was graduation. And I was prom king. My brother Amadou* came into the dance. He told me the news, that our older brother Bakary* was dead. At that time my mind was almost blank. I went back to my home and I could see everybody crying and everything, but I still couldn't believe it. I knew my brother was in the streets and all, but it didn't sink in.

"Then they were telling me how he died. They said that he got set up. He was strangled. They stuffed his body in a trunk, drove it to a Dumpster, and wrapped him in a trash bag. They put him in the Dumpster and set it on fire. And that's when it clicked—those details—and I'm like, 'Nah, you're not serious.' Then they told me the people that did it. We're all in the same project.

"So the day after, I went to the spot where they all hang out. My friend gave me a gun. He didn't even give it to me; I got it from him forcefully. I went to that block and I didn't see anybody. So I was like, 'Wow, either it wasn't meant for it to happen or . . . something.' Because I know if any one of them was out there, something bad would have happened. I would have tried to get revenge—that was my mind-set.

"My mother. Oh, it was bad, bad. My mother had the call, she was at the morgue or wherever you go, to identify the body. I didn't see her that whole night. The next day, you could tell something just broke. I never seen her like that. She's a strong woman, but when I seen her like that, real sad, cryin' her eyes out . . . The next day was my graduation and she didn't come. It was too much for her.

"I had a focused mind-set once I finished eighth grade 'cause I barely made it out. I knew my other option was if I don't get my stuff together, I'm going to be in the streets—like Bakary. And being in the streets would just put more worries on my mother. That's when I knew I just had to get myself together. I felt the only way I could really make her feel happy again or have some type of joy is by me focusing, not being in the streets, just trying to get my schoolwork together. That was my battle. I was going to graduate high school for my mother. I could not take the sadness in her face. No."

There were some stifled sobs in the room, mainly from the mothers on the staff. Charmaine fanned herself with her hand. Tissues bloomed. One young woman hurried out into the hallway, whispering, "It's too close, too close for me." Other students urged Malik to keep going.

"That's all right. You tell it."

"My brother was in the streets and it killed him," Malik went on. "And I seen that everybody my brother was hanging around with, they all was getting locked up and everything. I knew that I had to have another option."

Malik threw his arms wide and grinned.

"So I'm here now. We're all here. Let's do this!"

Malik took his seat amid a flurry of cheers, back slaps, and high fives. Having volunteered next, a heavyset young woman walked to the front, then abruptly bent double and let out a shriek. Her classmates jerked in their chairs at the loud, sudden sound. Through tears, she apologized: "I thought I could, but I'm not ready."

As she was comforted and led away to recover, Wil called on a handsome twenty-one-year-old named Devon,* who had kept his hand raised high for some time. Clearly he was determined to share. Early on in LCW, Devon had established himself as a wit, a willing helper, and somewhat of a cheerleader ("Ping me, man, if you need me to call and wake you up!").

His brother Damien* was a student in the Manhattan site. They were identical twins and close, yet very different. Manhattan classmates often heard Damien before they saw him; having been raised on church praise song and his mother's gorgeous alto, he just loved and needed to sing. Devon played the drums in church, and early on, when he was dreamily getting lost in a beat at his computer terminal during tech class, his new friend Shante* would have to reel him in. "Focus, Dev! Turn the beat down in your head and get back into things."

That day, not yet knowing of their cross-borough duet, both brothers told their classmates of the milestone that almost unhinged their large Haitian family. Theirs is an extended clan solidly anchored by the Queens church where their grandfather is bishop. Devon explained a bit about his family. The twins, born prematurely and six minutes apart, were the first two of four sons; their mother, Odette,* gave birth to them at age nineteen. She and her husband had two more sons and took in their niece and nephew when their parents died of AIDS; she would often cook for the entire floor of their apartment building. All the women, sisters and cousins, aunties and church ladies, older and younger, came to confide in Odette.

Devon pointed to his brown marker scrawl: "October 12, 2004, Mother RIP."

"She was thirty-six. My family had a lot of issues with cancer. It just creeps up in the family. The youngest aunt, when she was about twenty. Then my mom three years later got gastric cancer. She never knew she had it. It was when she fell down in the street, faint 'cause she couldn't eat. People kept saying she's going to pass away. She had half her stomach cut out. The doctors said she had no more cancer, but for some reason it came back.

"When my mom passed away I got in my mind that I don't care anymore. I was depressed, I would cry in my room, in my closet. I didn't want anybody to see me. We used to have my mother's stuff, for two years, it was out all over the room; my father wouldn't let nobody touch it. We didn't know what to do. We were like in really heavy mourning.

"I would say it hurt my dad to the point where he didn't know how to take care of us, meaning emotionally. He was always coming in the house, pay the bills, work, sleep, eat. He had to be the mom and the dad. It was harder for us talking to him.

"I did have a tough talk with God about my mother. I was upset since I didn't understand. I used to read my Bible at a young age. And I'm like, 'Yo, God. What are you doing? Ain't you supposed to be healing her? You said you're a healing God. What you doin'? Why?'

"I should not have ever questioned Him. I should have thanked Him. 'Cause you have to thank God for the good and the bad. But I was just upset. I was fourteen. I wanted my mother. She was the only one we could talk to. And she loved us so."

Devon stood talking over the students' heads, looking out the window at a very blue sky. His stance had grown almost rigid, and his voice dropped as he got to what he calls his darkest place—the moment when he pulled the plug on a computer Skype conversation with a friend and began to heat the blade of a knife until it glowed red, then laid it against his wrist. As he spoke, both arms were out in front of him, with the tender part of his wrists turned upward.

"Half of me is like, 'You got nothing to lose. Just cut yourself. Just end it all now, let it all slip away. Just let it go.' And something else said, 'Don't do it. Why miss out on the great opportunity of life? What would your whole family think?' I wanted to kill myself way before that, but not to such an extreme."

Devon's earth angels pulled him from the brink; the friend he had been talking with on Skype called his spiritual mentor, a man from church, who called and thundered at Devon, "You are *not* going to kill yourself. You *know* where that will land your soul!" His father, a church deacon, was stern when the crisis was over, reaching for his Bible, booming that they didn't even have to look inside its covers—Devon knew what it said. "Life is a gift. So why would you dare throw away such a gift?" His twin was terrified—and furious. "You have the audacity to leave me here alone? How could you?"

"But it was my little brother saved me for the long run," Devon continued. "He got me here. Put me right here in this room today. Jean-Luc,* who was born on our mother's birthday . . ."

Devon's fingers fluttered over his chest. And for the only time during the painful recitation, his voice wavered.

"Damien is my rock, but the little guy, he is my heart. Damien and I were doing nothing after high school. Not working, nothing. Not caring about family or church. Going down was all. Our brother heard about Year Up through his mentor, who works for the city or something. Jean-Luc said, 'You've gotta do this.' It was just a week to the application deadline, and he said, 'You just got to. Pull yourself up, Devon. Pull yourself up.'"

Wil was moving slowly through the big room with a box of tissues. As he leaned into the rows, it almost looked as though he was giving communion. A few students and staff were crying audibly. But as he made his way back to his seat, Devon was okay, smiling, looking a bit like he'd run uphill in a rainstorm—yet visibly relieved: So now everybody knows. Let's move on. . . .

Wil delivered a deft wrap-up, acknowledging the seriousness of the testimony and announcing the day's final activity, a session with Year Up alums—all out in the workplace, doing great. They had done this exercise, too, as new students and were now making new milestones—better, bolder, shaped not by fate or birth but by their own hands and minds. The Milestones exercise is never intended as therapy and never forced. Site leaders are trained to intervene should the recitations get too emotional or inappropriate for a group setting. That rarely happens. In choosing to share their experiences, students are simply getting to know one another better, on their way to becoming a community of learners.

Marisol, the only student parent in LCW, hung back as the room began to empty, a bit stunned by the proceedings. She had never in her twenty-one years been a talker, and never, ever would she stand up there like Devon and the others. Her close friend Jonathan—they'd been devoted to each other since grade school—had told her a lot about Year Up: the stipend, the infractions, how hard the whole thing was. Jonathan barely knew his father; his mother died when he was fourteen. He dropped to the bottom of his high school class and never graduated but later got his GED.

Marisol knew him through it all, and he had always been a straight talker. But he hadn't warned her about this sharing stuff when he just plain harassed her to apply to Year Up rather than join the National Guard.

"Mari, you can't go into the military," he told her. "That's crazy. I'm not gonna let you join. You're smart enough. You'll get into Year Up."

When Jonathan was a few weeks into the program in the spring of 2009, everyone in their group of friends wondered what had happened to him. The change was amazing; he chopped the hair that was longer than Marisol's, spoke like a professional, pulled up his sagging pants and his attitude. "I like that," Marisol thought at the time. "I like it a lot."

Jonathan was part of Class Six in New York, and after his internship in the IT department at American Express, he was hired on a date he'll not soon forget: March 8, 2010. He is a desktop support technician, fixing network and software problems, imaging computers, solving problems for a brace of appreciative vice presidents.

Unbelievable. Beautiful. Marisol celebrated with him. But still, she wasn't buying it when she went on the Year Up Web site and saw that "earn while you learn" come-on.

"Jonathan, are you serious? That's gotta be another scam. You sure you got your job through them?"

Marisol's introduction to Year Up was pretty typical: word of mouth. In all of the cities we serve, the majority of successive classes are filled with the siblings, fiancés, spouses, and friends of students who have been through the program. Though we do community outreach and some advertising, we have found that nothing is as powerful as seeing the profound change and success of someone prospective students know and care for. Marisol's friend Jonathan gave her a version of the pep talk thousands of our students have heard from someone they trust: *It works. Look at me. You owe it to yourself to try. And hey—what have you got to lose?*

That's how Marisol felt. Why not? And so far, so good. If she could get herself up on time, she loved coming there, riding the train with two classmates who met her at 137th Street. All those hard, hard stories. Nobody was kidding around. Everybody wanted up and out—like Jonathan. Marisol gathered her notebooks for the long subway ride back to Washington Heights in Manhattan where she, her three-year-old son, and her mother had moved into a new, safer apartment.

Three months earlier, men had broken into their previous place when Marisol was alone there during the day; they stole her laptop. She escaped, unhurt but terrified, out a side door. She and her mother were in McDonald's with a real estate agent signing the new lease when Marisol's cell phone rang with the news that she had been accepted to Year Up. Finally things were breaking right.

Just don't push her on any of this sharing stuff. Marisol could never see herself standing up there telling any of her own milestones: the senior-year pregnancy that prompted her marriage to the boy she had been with since age fourteen, her lonely stint as a military wife and new mother near a remote North Carolina air base. The divorce. Speaking about that still makes her cry—so no way, no thanks. "I'm not much of a talker. I like to soak things in."

Still dabbing at her eyes as students filed out the door, Charmaine thought Devon's determined truth telling a good sign. Admitting him to Year Up had been a hard decision, given his candor about his recent depression in the first interview. The pressures of the program would be intense. But what were his other options? Both brothers had passed the academic tests. Both seemed motivated. And they were very, very close. The Haitian community behind them was stern and ultraconservative but supportive.

Risk and faith, faith and risk. Charmaine knows the dance. And what a long way they all had to go. She held out a hand to Devon as the room emptied. He squeezed it and melted off into the chattering crowd.

Vaya con Dios, Class Nine. No better off and no more challenged than those who had gone before, some blessed with loving parents, some hurt by abuse, full of grace and bowed with grief, either speaking well or bristling with "ain'ts," "yos," and subjects and verbs that simply could not, would not agree. They had five months to learn to respect—even love—one another and themselves, draft a perfect e-mail, knot a tie, navigate a business lunch and its multiple forks, shoot the rapids of financial software, server hardware, and "corporate anthropology."

Charmaine's cell phone called her back to the future; the Manhattan site was dense with new applicants waiting there with birth certificates, diplomas, and that persistent if unspoken doubt: *Seriously?*

Notice: Town Hall Meeting: Year Up founder and CEO Gerald Chertavian will speak to all LCs on Tuesday, October 12.

Malik, Cassandra, Damien and Devon, Marisol, and Taleisha were all still in the program, working hard despite a range of challenges, when I arrived in Brooklyn to address the whole New York City learning community six weeks into the fall term. Damien had dissolved into tears earlier in the morning but recovered himself; it was the anniversary of their mother's death. Of the 126 who had started on September 6, 4 had either fired themselves or decided the program was not for them.

The Manhattan students took the subway to the larger meeting space in Brooklyn. It was the first time both groups had met, and everyone was pretty hyped, chattering away and scarfing the last of dozens of pizzas brought in for the occasion. I downed a slice with them, standing up. I've learned to eat quickly—to many good cooks' dismay, food is fuel to me—and that morning, as usual, everybody wanted to talk.

There's always a little stir when I show up. The students know my face from some orientation videos and YouTube segments. It can take me half an hour to move down the hall—so many hands extended, everybody with something to say. I travel between sites with a fairly well-honed "stump speech," but I'm always happiest when I just get to spend time listening to what's on students' minds.

How many times now have I stepped into a room full of such open, almost incandescent faces? I wish you could see them. Young hope is blindingly, heartbreakingly handsome. It knocks me out every time to stand up there and take it all in—the pride, the potential—all pent up and ready to go. And I tell them every time, because it's always true: "You look great. Really great."

I love to check out their takes on the required business wear in San Francisco, Atlanta, Providence. Every site has its flavor. That day in Brooklyn: perfectly knotted ties tucked into V-neck cardigans, knife-pleated slacks, ironed by students themselves and often at 5:00 or 6:00 a.m. Some were wearing donated women's pantsuits and men's suit coats, hanging a bit large on skinny shoulders here and there but darn well accessorized. Starched oxford cloth cuffs with just the hint of tattoos peeking out. Clean, polished dress shoes, amazing argyle socks. Impeccable fades, razor cuts, and manicures, and very toned-down bling. Or none at all.

I've heard this from various young men, from Boston to Brooklyn: Often their sudden change to business dress can be baffling or disconcerting to the guys in the neighborhood. They'll stop a student wearing a suit and tie on his way to the bus and offer their condolences: *Sorry, man. Somebody in your family pass?*

Some students have told me that they've found it wise to bring a change of street clothes with them to ensure safe passage back to their neighborhoods. Arriving home in suits and ties they would be harassed—and worse.

I always begin my town hall talks with an exercise that seems to puzzle, amuse, and slightly unnerve them at first.

"Bear with me a minute before I start talking to you. And please . . . give me your eyes."

Giggles, a few murmurs.

"I mean it. I want to walk around the room here and look into all of your eyes. Each and every one of you."

I can almost hear what they're thinking: What's up with this? White guy, graying hair, navy pin-striped suit with the little Year Up pin stuck kind of crooked in the lapel—Mr. Dress for Success himself—laying this X-ray stare on every single face. He's kind looking, not scary. But here, finally, is the guy who got this whole earn-while-you-learn thing going. How come? What's he get out of it? And as one young man in Providence asked me once I'd finished looking into all those faces around the room, "What's with the eye thing? What's it do for you?"

I do try to explain what I should probably call my passion. Here is some of what I told them that day: "It's a huge pleasure and an honor to have a few moments to connect with you and to answer some questions you may have. Also just to look into the eyes of the people who are going to be leading this country. Because with every young adult in this room, all I see is limitless potential. I see talent, I see brains, I see motivation, and I literally see what this country is going to need if we are to have the country we want to have. Because you'll be taking care of a lot of people as you succeed in your lives and your careers.

"What allows us to offer you the seat you're sitting in now? We will invest, happily, $25,000 in each seat. We're so proud to invest in your future. What allows us to do that? Why have hundreds of people chosen to invest in Year Up and in you?"

Hands flew up. One student volunteered, "They knew it would be a good investment."

"How did they know that?"

Someone shouted out that our numbers do the talking.

"You hit the nail right on the head. The numbers speak for themselves. And what's behind the numbers? What?"

Big chorus: "WE ARE!"

"Right. It's you—and the graduates who came before. The reason we can offer you the seat that you're in is that someone was in it before you. They were sitting in these seats, they did well in their internships, and they contributed to those organizations they were working for. And what did those organizations come back and say to us?"

"They want more?"

"That's right, but I'm not sure everyone heard that. . . ."

"WE WANT MORE!"

"*We want more.* Those words—'We want more'—have grown this program from twenty-two students to what will be more than thirteen hundred young adults in 2011. Because of those three words: 'We want more.' You're sitting here today because someone else did a great job. So what's your responsibility?"

"Pay it forward!"

"Again?"

All voices now, and loudly: "Pay it forward!"

"Pay it forward; keep the cycle going. Absolutely right. What a beautiful thing—that if you do well, you have literally created a chance for another human being. Changed someone else's opportunity set, given them a hand up. By helping yourself, you just helped someone else.

"Okay now, let me see hands: How many people here know someone that needs a year up? Look at all those hands. How many of you would like to help them? Guess what, you're helping them right now. Because you chose to get up today, at whatever hour it took to be on time. You chose to look as professional as you do; you chose to bring your whole selves to this environment. You chose to work hard. With those choices you're not only helping yourself, you're helping another person get access to an opportunity that they darn well deserve in this country.

"So when you think about Year Up, I want you think about that ability to impact the lives of others. Not just tens or hundreds, not even just thousands. We should be thinking about hundreds of thousands. And when we think like that, Year Up becomes more than just a training program, doesn't it?

"Tell me, what has it become? What else are we trying to create and build across this nation? What is Year Up really? Imagine in cities across the country, young adults, tens of thousands. What does that start to feel and look like?"

"A movement!"

"Exactly. A movement. If you think back to when Dr. Martin Luther King Jr. was marching on Washington, the buttons on his chest said, 'Freedom and Jobs.' Not just freedom. Freedom and jobs. So recognize that in a smaller way, we are continuing down that path. The path toward civil rights in this country. We're about economic and social justice. We should feel darn good about that. Because a lot of people would be afraid to push forward on those ideals. This group is not afraid."

Did they hear me? Here are a few excerpts from a writing exercise in instructor Randy Moore's business communications class the following day in Manhattan. The assignment: Use some of this week's vocabulary words to comment on Gerald's talk.

His vision of a utopian society is something we should all strive to emulate.

He gives me a feeling that he commiserates with us all.

Gerald was far from disingenuous.

When I travel the country speaking to incoming classes as I did in Brooklyn that day, I am always asked, "What made you decide to start Year Up?" Always, I tell them about a young Dominican boy on the Lower East Side of Manhattan. His name is David.

CHAPTER TWO
Brother from Another Zip Code

"**H**AVE YOU EVER BEEN ARRESTED?"

"No," I answered.

"Have you ever abused a child?"

"No!"

"Have you ever been addicted to drugs?"

"No," I said, wondering when it would stop.

My inquisitor was named Mary, a tiny woman with dull brown hair and a calm, capable way about her; clearly she had spent years keeping vulnerable children out of harm's way.

In 1988, less than a year into my trainee program at Chemical Bank in New York, I was only twenty-three and probably looked all of eighteen, but Mary was eyeballing me as though I were a lifer at Attica. The drab, institutional room looked more like a parole office than the headquarters of a charity dedicated to children. Mary presided from behind a cheap wooden desk with metal sides. I sat in a metal chair saddled next to her desk, the nonprofit equivalent of a conference room. I remember feeling how much power she seemed to have over me at the time. She could say yes or no to what I wanted—a little brother.

I am impossibly impatient by nature. So after repeated busy signals at the number for the Big Brother organization I had worked with in college, I called the next one listed in the Yellow Pages—the Catholic Big Sisters and Big Brothers down on East Second Street. After filling out the requisite forms, I had been summoned for this interview with the organization's social worker. Finally Mary got to the big question.

"Are you Catholic?"

I didn't lie—I just told her that I hadn't been to Mass in a while. Growing up in a largely Irish neighborhood in Lowell, Massachusetts, I had been to enough Masses with my friends. My family had stopped going to their Baptist church by the time I was six. And there were times when it was more fun to hang out with friends in the back pews on Sunday than to stay at home. Mary didn't press it further and I didn't offer anything more.

Two weeks later, Mary and I walked into the Rutgers Houses, a five-acre housing project at Pike and Rutgers Streets on the Lower East Side. The city-built complex, erected in the midsixties, was named for colonial Manhattan's last Dutch-descended farmer and philanthropist, Henry Rutgers, who donated large sections of his farm there to his church. Rutgers was also a captain in the Revolutionary War.

By the mid-1980s, there were skirmishes of a different sort on his paved-over farmland near the base of the Manhattan Bridge. Crack cocaine wars had erupted, and their aftermath would worsen the lives of generations of the inner-city poor nationwide.

Crack first got its foothold on the West Coast. Reporter Sandy Banks, who covered South L.A. for thirty years at the *Los Angeles Times,* summed up the long-term devastation across the nation this way: "Crack steered fathers to jail, lured mothers into the streets and left children to raise themselves in neighborhoods bristling with despair and anger. . . . Crack's reach was made plain in big, public ways: exploding foster care rolls, rising crime, overloaded emergency rooms, skid row's growing underclass."

The scourge barreled east in the mideighties and hit hard. Like the junk bonds that hooked some wheeler-dealers on Wall Street in those days, this new product—invented by drug lords trying to leverage a cocaine oversupply—was cheap, deceptive, and quickly, strongly addictive. In the projects all over New York, crack users were crazier and arguably more dangerous than the classic nodding heroin junkie. They were so creepily strung out that the street name for a combo of crack dipped in PCP was "Beam Me Up Scottie."

Even before the crack wars, Manhattan's Lower East Side—an area bordered by the East River just above the Manhattan Bridge and Canal

Street up to Fourteenth Street—was historically poor and working class. Its tenements were occupied by waves of immigrants—Jewish, Chinese, Italian, Latino. Large public housing complexes like the Heredias' had been built to accommodate the area's mixed and growing population. Bodegas, Chinese grocers, and kosher butchers fed their own from small storefronts and sprawling street markets. It made for a reasonable coexistence until drug dealers began claiming real estate and lives.

By the time I walked into it, parts of the Lower East Side seemed inhabited by tribes of glassy-eyed aliens. In the Rutgers Houses, police crime-scene tape had become common lobby and alleyway decor. On that first trip there with Mary, plastic crack vials littered the gutters and splintered under my shoes. I had no idea what they were.

Mary and I waited for the elevator to clang and groan down to the lobby. The car smelled of urine. There was trash on the grimy floor, and it was dark. We went up, way up. Mary led me to an apartment on an upper floor. There was a sticker on the door that announced, somos católicos ("We are Catholics"), a not-so-subtle attempt to ward off proselytizers of a different faith. There were also quite a few locks. I wondered why so many as I listened to the bolts click and tumble in response to Mary's knock.

A kind but anxious light brown face appeared in the narrow entryway.

"Soy Cornelia, la mamá de David."

Cornelia Heredia led us into her small living room, where I perched nervously on a plastic-covered sofa. Set inside a large wooden hutch adorned with children's photos, an aged TV was playing a Spanish station loudly. Against another wall stood a heavy, treadle-powered industrial sewing machine.

Later, I would learn that Cornelia did "piece work," as it is known in the garment industry, carrying home boxes of precut fabric from an Essex Street company—panels for yarmulkes bound for the devout skulls of the city's Jewish population. She got up at 6:00 a.m. to start pinning and stitching, and sometimes sewed until midnight. For six days' work she earned one hundred dollars, tops. Her sons helped her pack and carry the finished work back to Essex Street and bring home another small mountain of pieces to begin again. Over time, the work ruined her back.

"¿Quieres algo de beber?" Cornelia asked. After twenty years, I still hear that question within seconds of walking in. And my response is always the same.

"Sí, por favor, agua." Thanks to—or in spite of—years of school language requirements and a college semester in Madrid, my Spanish was passable—at least not insulting, I hoped. A small glass of water appeared with a paper napkin under it.

"Gracias, muchas gracias."

"¡Daviiiiiid!" Though normally soft-spoken, Cornelia Heredia had the unsurpassed lung power of the public housing lioness, capable of summoning her cub out of harm's way from eighteen stories up. But no one came.

"¡Daviiiiiiid! ¡Ven aquí!" This said with slightly more authority and slightly less warmth.

A beautiful, almond-eyed, and very skinny ten-year-old appeared from down the narrow hallway. David had a decent Afro and a shy gaze. We shook hands and smiled at each other, both very uncomfortable. I was being introduced to David as his new "big brother." Cornelia would confess years later that she was a bit uneasy about trusting someone looking so wet behind the ears with her youngest angel.

There was ample reason for her to be concerned. Her son wasn't supposed to be alive. David had spent 1977–78, his first year of life, in Bellevue Hospital, recovering from multiple surgeries to correct a congenital intestinal problem. The doctors quoted Cornelia the terrible odds: Of a hundred babies born with David's condition, only two survived. And despite their best efforts, another baby at Bellevue born with it at the time, a girl, had died. At age ten, David must have only weighed sixty-five pounds, and he had a scar across his midsection that looked as if someone had snipped him in two and sewed him back together again.

I knew just the basics about this family: David was one of five sons Cornelia had shepherded between a shelter, run-down apartments, and public housing. She and her husband had married in the Dominican Republic, come to New York, had their children, and come apart. According to Mary, their father was not a regular presence in the boys' lives. The two eldest sons were over a decade older than David and rarely around. But David and his two brothers were still at home and in school. Our first meeting took an interminable half an hour. Here is how David remembers it: "When Gerald walked in the house with Mary, my mother and I were both shocked. Prior to that, the only real close encounter I had with anybody who wasn't Dominican or minority were my schoolteachers. And when you speak to a teacher you're not very open; you make sure you're on your best behavior. So it kind of felt like that in the beginning, really uncomfortable."

Cornelia doesn't speak much English and David answered most of my questions in monosyllables. I wondered what was going through his head. I knew that Cornelia had appealed to a priest at their neighborhood church, St. Theresa's, to help find a mentor for her littlest boy, as she had for his older brothers. The priest sent her to Catholic Charities and ultimately Mary. A couple of candidates of more similar background and skin color had fallen through. But did David want me? No matter. I wanted a little brother, Cornelia wanted adult male support for her boy, Mary seemed to think I'd do, and so it began.

The distance from my work in the financial district to David's home was short. But our experiences were so many zip codes and tax brackets apart. Our paths to that first awkward meeting—and our journey way, way beyond it—really determined my trajectory from banker to social entrepreneur.

David and I were a classic case of Them and Us—on both sides. We got on fine, and I fell hard for this sweet, funny kid. But there were so many issues involving poverty and race between us and so many ingrained preconceptions on both our parts. For one thing, I had a lot to learn about looking at poverty. The Heredias felt fortunate in many ways. After a homeless shelter, three tiny bedrooms were a gift. Walking down those dark hallways, I didn't see it that way at first. Because of his upbringing, David was perfectly fluent in two languages; despite my private college education and studying abroad, I still struggled with Spanish. Which experience delivered a richer grasp of language? I grew up with long summers at our beach house as a matter of course; his family was lucky to have two weeks a year out of their neighborhood at Trinita, a Catholic Charities camp in northwest Connecticut. They looked forward to it all year and settled happily into the communal cabins. Whose summer pleasures were more satisfying? In my much wider world, I never even thought about the color of my skin until I started spending time in David's neighborhood. He was acutely aware of his brown skin every minute we spent outside the Lower East Side. Sure, he was naturally shy. But it took me a while to understand that among my very welcoming friends, David was also more subdued because he was a boy with brown skin.

We were acutely aware of some of these differences from the day we met. But it would take us years to be able to speak about it all honestly, as men. Those conversations are never easy, though we laugh a lot—mostly at our unenlightened selves.

Despite our differences, David and I both had the most precious of resources: extraordinary, strong, compassionate mothers. If Cornelia was wise and strict and protective enough to keep five boys safe and sober during a drug epidemic that was decimating urban families, Joyce Chertavian's boundless empathy and her instinctive need to help people absolutely helped shape the person I became—and the work I do.

Two women, seven sons. I still wish that our mothers could have met. I honor both of them here as David and I look back at childhoods on both sides of the divide.

Picture a young boy in quiet rapture, smiling a bit goofily beneath thick-lashed brown eyes and a shock of dark hair. I am leaning against my mother's knees as she speaks on the phone to a tight circle of friends. She talks for hours, dispensing advice, collecting neighborhood news, and listening—always listening. People always seem to want to confide in her. She strokes my hair as she talks, and as her voice rises and falls, I sit mesmerized and utterly content.

I spent hours with her like that, conditioned at a tender age to becoming a listener myself. Toward the end of her life, Mom's work with fellow cancer survivors would take that skill to its highest level. Her early lesson: You learn the most when your ears are open and your own mouth is closed.

In 1969 I was on the cusp of kindergarten and completely mad about my mother. As Marcus Welby, MD, began to make house calls on ABC-TV and perky Florence Henderson rode herd over the Brady Bunch, Joyce Chertavian outclassed any shirtwaist-and-pearls sitcom mom. She was funny, she was kind, and she was so very beautiful. She looked like a young Grace Kelly: blond, trim, always perfectly, impeccably groomed. It's no wonder my father didn't think he stood a chance with her.

Levon Chertavian—Lev to all—is a small, dapper man with a youthful face that's enviable now, in his mideighties. But it was a drawback for a young man determined to look professional. He admits to feeling a lack of confidence early in life. It didn't help that he suffered through twenty months of chronic, debilitating seasickness aboard a 173-foot steel patrol craft (PC or "sub chaser") in the Atlantic. After Pearl Harbor these small, agile boats were deployed to escort U.S. destroyers and do sonar sweeps for lethal German U-boats. Dad was a sonar operator—when he could manage it.

There is little dignity in being at war with your head over the rail; Dad said that the torment was so relentless, "I almost prayed for a torpedo." Riding out a fierce hurricane off Cuba that took three men overboard to their deaths, he found himself "puking and bailing with the same bucket." State-side, he regained the weight he had lost aboard ship and, with the tuition help of the GI Bill, began college.

He insists he wasn't much of a student, but he survived the academic and practical rigors of the premed program at Tufts University. As a sophomore, he began a dental internship that required living and working in the Sol-diers' Home in Chelsea, Massachusetts. Soon his surgical skills were noticed and very much in demand. Most of the residents were aging World War I veterans facing multiple extractions. Dad looked about fifteen by his reck-oning, but he could ease out a bicuspid with little or no collateral damage. The word went out: *Get the little guy to pull your teeth. He don't hurt.*

Dad figured he always had a fallback if dentistry didn't work out; he and his brother had worked long hours learning the trade in my grandfather's shoe repair shop in Lowell. The third of four children under the close watch of a demanding matriarch, Dad was still living with my grandparents when he began his first dental practice.

It was basic dentistry with long hours and a substantial walk-in clientele. Dentists like Dad left their lights on at night in downtown Lowell, and peo-ple with toothaches would come in, drawn to the sign in his picture window on the second floor above the retail stores. He also worked Saturdays because people got paid on Fridays. This meant that he got paid too—mostly in cash. He got used to people huffing up the stairs and gasping, "*You're* the dentist?" Again, word spread that the young guy was good and gentle at his work, and the practice grew.

My father was ten years older and two inches shorter than Joyce Goudy, the vision from Methuen, Massachusetts, he interviewed at the Forsyth School of Dental Hygiene in Boston. He was there to hire a new hygienist, and she was a top graduate who had won a scholarship there. Miss Goudy accepted the position in Lowell, did her job well, and tolerated Dr. Cherta-vian's unrelenting seriousness in the office—until the day he looked up from a patient's open mouth and saw Joyce looking down at him in a Groucho Marx nose and glasses.

"Your patient is ready for examination, Doctor."

"You damn fool," he thought to himself. He bowed his head and com-posed himself. And finally, the good doctor smiled in his office.

At first they dated on the sly in Boston—Dad felt it wouldn't look profes-sional right there in Lowell. They married in 1956, a year after she had begun working in the office. As they set up housekeeping, they started shoring up one another's shaky areas. Dad could feel shy, and his lovely bride tended to walk with her head down, not making eye contact. She was embarrassed to be so pretty. People stared, and it made her self-conscious.

Over the years, my parents did what partners are supposed to do: They took measure of their insecurities and gently bullied one another toward confidence and self-esteem. Dad is convinced that he reaped the biggest benefit: "Joyce taught me to be who I am today. She taught me more than I ever knew about loving and caring. And about being happy with yourself, that you're good enough."

My older brother, Levon—Lee—was six when I was born in 1965. We shared a room, and he was off to college by the time I was twelve. Growing up, Lee and I were as different as could be. We both had strong competitive streaks and got into our fair share of scrapes. But nothing could diminish the loyalty and caring that persists today; as brothers, we'll always have each other's backs.

Dad installed us in a beige ranch house in what was considered a good part of Lowell: two bedrooms, two baths. The house had those sixties requisites, a den for Dad and a Ping-Pong table in the basement, which also held a family icon: the pinball machine from the shoeshine shop where my Armenian grandfather had his cobbler business. And there were summers at the shore; by 1961 Dad was doing well enough to buy a tiny beach cottage in Seabrook, New Hampshire, about an hour away.

Our mainly Irish neighborhood in Lowell was safe and vigilant; we enjoyed free-range playtime after school until six, when the streetlights came on—the universal signal to get home for dinner. Mom was a housewife and she loved to cook. I can see her, standing over a roast chicken or a fancy beef stew, raising a glass of wine and toasting Julia Child, her kitchen saint, beamed in religiously from WGBH in Boston.

For my mother, food was an outlet for love and creativity. She cooked because she cared, sitting us down to a beautiful dinner and a baked dessert every day. Her culinary enthusiasms were wide ranging. She did some Cordon Bleu training, learned Armenian cooking from my grandmother, and fell so hard for Chinese food that she began assisting Jeannie Tank, a Chinese chef, with her cooking show on Boston TV.

Mom was a calm type B to Dad's tightly wound A, but she was no pushover. Offend her moral code and, kin or stranger, you'd be set straight. During the seventies gas shortage, I remember her outrage when four teenagers cut her off at the pump. She just got out of the car, walked over, and faced them down: "Young men do not do that. I expect you to back your car out of here. That's inappropriate behavior."

Dad was a more distant parent, owing to his total immersion in his practice, which he had modified to specialize in prosthodontics, bridge and crown work. In the summers, when we settled in at the beach, he commuted an hour each way and brooked little nonsense from his sons. He checked our lawn mowing with a ruler and stored hammers and rakes with the same precision he used for his dental tools. Even rare vacations were about work; Dad and other dentists would arrange for professional lectures while the wives chatted and sunned.

Lee and I were schooled early in Dad's uncompromising work ethic. Beginning at twelve or thirteen, we always had summer jobs, and the money went straight to a savings account. The first job I had was bussing tables in Mac's clam bar—a stinky chore that made me rejoice on being promoted to the ice cream counter. At fourteen, I'd get up at 3:00 a.m. and take my place before racks and racks of plain doughnuts—thousands—that we turned into twenty-six varieties between 4:00 a.m. and 7:00 a.m. I worked in convenience stores, at a gas station, and at the golf course, getting there at 4:30 a.m. to line up the carts for the early-bird players.

They were good jobs and pretty carefree summers. Mine was a happy, secure, and loving childhood—until I was old enough to seriously question the standard public education being offered. The less said about high school the better. Some teachers simply phoned it in. Little was expected of us. I read few books to expand my horizons—or my vocabulary. I got straight As doing the bare minimum and hid my grades like dirty secrets from my friends. Anything above a C was not macho, just as playing the piano was, in the ignorant code of fourteen-year-old boys, "faggy."

Lowell raised its fair share of knuckleheads, kids who weren't doing that well in school or at home and channeled their energies into time-honored teen vices. Recreation was inspired by the Friday-night six-pack of beer and a joint. Creativity peaked in dumb stuff like trashing mailboxes and tipping over cars. These guys weren't going places—and anyone who didn't want to stick with that status quo was suspect. My worst memories of that time have to do with peer pressure, with seeing kids forced to do things. I was eager to leave that behind. I endured the static when I graduated fourth in a class of a thousand—then got the heck out of there.

Lee and I had help making a well-chosen exit, thanks to Wyman Trull, a history teacher at Lowell High School. Mr. Trull made time, amid his inspired lectures on Jacksonian democracy and Manifest Destiny, to look to the futures of promising students who came to his attention. He was a kind if single-minded mentor. If you were good enough, you simply had to go to his alma mater, Bowdoin College, which he considered a Valhalla of enlightened education. Lee got the treatment first. Mr. Trull drove him two hours north to coastal Brunswick, Maine, for the irresistible tour and high-minded browbeating. "This is where you will go to college—no question about it."

I didn't have Mr. Trull for history, but I didn't escape his keen radar. And as a current trustee at Bowdoin, I'll always be grateful for the "pay it forward" sort of mentorship he embraced. So I followed Lee to Bowdoin—as I would later on to Wall Street and Harvard Business School.

College held serial epiphanies for a middle-class kid from Lowell—chiefly about achievement and class. I was not a typical applicant; Bowdoin was the choice for many blue-blooded, well-to-do families given to wide-wale corduroy and pastel Shetland sweaters. I showed up in jeans and an Aerosmith T-shirt, and I was guilty of a certain snobbery as well. Fellow freshman dorm mate Richie O'Leary was a policeman's son from scrappy Dorchester. Richie was a city kid who saved every spare penny for a Polo shirt to wear with the collar snapped up like the cool city kids. We both harbored those burbs-versus-'hood stereotypes and loathed each other at first sight. It fell to my freshman roommate, Charlie Ford, to mediate a peace.

Charlie was the quintessential Bowdoin Brahmin, the scion of a well-heeled Cohasset dynasty and so astonishingly handsome that the ladies fell like dominoes at his gaze. But despite his good fortune, Charlie's outlook was steadfastly egalitarian. He brought Richie and me to our senses by reminding us of a new, post–high school truth: Clothes did not make the college man. Having gotten ourselves there, we should have more brains than that.

The last inhibitions of my Lowell adolescence fell away at the end of first semester, when Peter Gross, a blond soccer player, asked me how my grades had ended up. I had gotten three As and a B, but I was loath to admit it. He snatched the paper out of my hand. And to my shock and relief, Peter said, "That's great. That's really great."

This encounter was an eyeblink in time but huge for me. I had an almost physical reaction, as though a dark shade had suddenly rolled up, snapping, and let in the light. And I've since heard the same relief and amazement in many conversations with Year Up students who endured far worse neighborhood mockery when they decided to step up their games. *It doesn't have to be that old way.* Here was a place where working hard and doing well wouldn't count against you. Realizing that academic achievement and social acceptance were not mutually exclusive conditions was one of the turning points of my life. More miraculous: Learning was extravagant, exacting fun.

My first summer back from college, I took a job few people wanted. I drove a group of twelve to fifteen seriously "disadvantaged youths" in a big double van to a work site where they would rake grass cut by the city. These were tough kids, sixteen-year-olds and mostly Latino. It was hot, sweaty work, and they used to break their rakes against a wall in the hope that it would end their workday. I wasn't buying it.

"You break it, you still use it. Bend over and rake with what's left." I'd drop them home at the end of the day, in lousy neighborhoods. Some of their houses didn't have glass in the windows, just cloth. They got paid a little and probably hated the work a lot. But for me there was nothing better than to pull up in the morning and try to energize a group of kids that had had the crap kicked out of them by life.

My college friends thought I was a little crazy to climb into that van full of raging hormones and resentment day after day. I actually looked forward to it. I realized then that I'm a motivator by nature. And not much deters me. They tried to steal my van once, they'd bust up all the equipment, and, as adolescents do, they used up a lot of energy being deeply mean to one another. Drive by our work site and you'd see a bunch of kids swinging rakes trying to hit pigeons. But at the end of the day it was a nice, freshly kept park, and they had a little spending money and less time to get in trouble. I loved it.

I'm not sure what the root cause might be, but I feel alone easily and I've always had a need to connect. So at college I tutored in local schools and signed up with Big Brothers for the first time. I was matched with Larry. He was five and lived with his mom in a trailer park about a mile from Bowdoin. I took him on weekends, and one day his mother asked if I could stay with him for a weekend. She took off, and I tried to bend my frame into a child-sized trailer bunk bed. It was a no go, so Larry came with me to the fraternity house.

In late 1986, as the first semester of senior year drew to a close, we economics majors were looking toward graduation. And we were in awe of the Wall Street types Tom Wolfe famously called "masters of the universe." In those heady, almost-anything-goes days, we all wanted to be investment bankers, though we didn't really know what that meant.

A few of us headed to Manhattan over Christmas break and crashed with Matt Rankowitz's brother, Mike, who was then a hugely successful junk bond trader at Morgan Stanley. In those days, Morgan Stanley ruled junk. And Mike was just like us; he had gone to a good school, come to New York, and joined the investment-banking world. He was living large, making lots of money, and having tremendous fun.

When we weren't gazing in wonder (and some envy) at Mike's apartment and his life, we were trying to set up introductory interviews—anywhere south of Park Row and fat with assets. We hoisted beers and big aspirations: *This is so cool. We're going to be kings of the world too.*

"What the hell are you doing here?" was the gentle encouragement I got from an interviewer at Salomon Brothers, the same high-testosterone firm skewered in Michael Lewis's Wall Street apprentice's tale, *Liar's Poker*. Making the rounds, my friends and I encountered it all: arrogance, disdain, and undisguised sadism. Hazing nervous applicants seemed to be a blood sport. Even New York cabbies dissed me. Lost, late for an appointment, and soaked to the skin from a downpour, I begged one driver to take me to Fifty Broad Street. "It's three blocks away, you moron. F— off."

A series of grim "informational" interviews left me depressed and discouraged. I had zero traction on the job search until I called my brother's wife, Elaine, who offered to check with her former boss about job openings at what was then Chemical Bank. Doug George was kind enough to see me; the interviews went well, I took my drug test, and I got a letter saying I was admitted to the credit training program, making $21,000 a year. I had a job. And it was all because my sister-in-law had hooked me up with Doug, who saw something in me that he wanted to invest in. So let's not forget, Gerald had his year up.

My Bowdoin dorm mate Richie O'Leary got a job in E. F. Hutton's trading program, so we moved to New York together in September 1987, sharing a big, cheap apartment in Brooklyn Heights. I was in a class of about thirty trainees at Chemical Bank, downtown in the financial district. I reported to Fifty-five Water Street, where we took classes in accounting, banking, economics, and credit analysis. If you got below a seventy in any class, you were fired from the program. It was pretty intense.

So was the whole Wall Street scene. Ten- and twelve-hour workdays, Friday-night beer and darts until dawn at the Kettle of Fish. We saw people doing cocaine in the men's room at work and partying harder at night. Tuck in your power tie or risk having a drunken bond trader cut it in half and toss it into the pipes hanging from the ceilings in the waterside bars jammed with our kind: the overworked, underpaid, and oversexed. We had great fun.

Richie was on the trading floor on Black Monday, October 19, 1987, when the big crash hit. When we both dragged home that night, pale and shaken, he described utter panic at the stock exchange; I had still been in class, but there had been meltdowns there as well. Professors kept running into the classroom shouting, "It's down three hundred!" And half an hour later: "It's down five hundred—should we cancel class?"

The devastation hit all levels, but of course the last on board walked the plank first. A few weeks later, Richie lost his job in the fallout, but he managed to get another day job on the exchange and wisely kept studying for his MBA at night. I was safe but sobered. I kept my head down and my share of the rent paid. And once the rigors of the training program were almost behind me, I set out on that search for a little brother that led to the Rutgers Houses.

I didn't realize it until much later, but I needed David. Work was absorbing and exhausting, and I was surviving just fine in the financial gerbil wheel. I loved my friends, but I was missing another kind of connection. Once David and I started spending every Saturday together, the Heredias offered something I craved. I needed to be needed. And I missed family.

Warily but politely, "Geraldo" was welcomed in. Often I would turn up on Sunday afternoons as well, knowing that I could settle in for a hot dinner of arroz con pollo spooned from a family-sized pot that steamed up the windows. We sat elbow to elbow in that compact kitchen, tucking into meals that Cornelia coaxed out of the cheesy little stove that only a landlord could love.

Outside the apartment, David and I just hung out around the neighborhood and playgrounds, got ice cream, and saw movies. And though I was unaware of it, I was a curiosity to the general population. For David, I was a bit of an embarrassment at first: "At that time the community wasn't very diverse. There were some Asian families and us—Latino—that was it. So

I felt a little funny. I thought people figured that I was in trouble, or that Gerald was a cop."

What I also didn't understand at first was how geographically insular David's world was and always had been. I'm often reminded of it now when Year Up students tell us that until they enroll in the program, they have never been in a high-rise office building—or even to their own city's downtown business district. It wasn't a limit David consciously felt as a child: "You have to understand, we just never left the neighborhood. The way I saw a few things outside was with Catholic Charities, bus trips here and there to museums and stuff. And since you didn't leave the neighborhood, it was hard to think about having any plans in the wider world. It just didn't seem to apply."

Not that he was intrigued by the career opportunities close at hand. There were a lot of hard-eyed entrepreneurs on the corners by then, in the lobby, or outside loitering around cars. David remembers it going seriously bad around when he was seven or eight. One night stood out.

"We were in our bedroom with my mother, my brother Willy, and me. She was praying, saying the rosary. We weren't really into it—you know how kids get. And we heard pop! Pop-pop-pop, right under our window. I guess we knew it was gunfire. But we still thought it was some kind of game. Behind my mother, where she couldn't see us, we acted out having a shootout. Big fun. We looked out the window, and there was this guy. He was lying there not moving. The next day we found out. He was a friend of our brother Carlos. And he was dead. That was the first one we knew. We were too young to understand the bigness of it, but Carlos was already a teenager. And a lot of his friends were getting killed."

Cornelia had never let her sons run in the neighborhood after dark. Curfew was 9:00 p.m., and during the daytime they enjoyed some pretty classic urban pastimes—baseball and kick the can. There were summer programs at neighborhood community centers and playgrounds where the boys could spend the day—if they met Cornelia's safety standards. David explains: "My mom and my friend Georgie's mom took us to look at a new community center in Two Bridges housing complex. We were taking the tour and the teacher said, 'You don't want to hang by that side of the playground fence.' She explained that all the junkies and crackheads went there to scrounge around the discarded crack vials on the ground—like a bunch of skinny, raggedy chickens."

In fact, the scavenging was known on the street as "hen picking," done by a scary flock of desperate prostitutes and other users who would get down on hands and knees searching for a smokable fragment of "rock." The two Dominican mothers made tracks out of that scary barnyard; Georgie and David were reenrolled in a center closer to home.

I knew there were dealers in David's building; some floors were notorious and avoided at all costs. There was Maggie, a sad, nonthreatening user with a young son on the Heredias' floor. But I didn't fully understand the acuteness of the situation until I arrived there one Saturday, a bit shaken. It was raining that night, and I had my jacket pulled over my head, not watching where I was going. So I had just walked into the identical-looking building next door by mistake, rung the bell at an apartment with the same number, walked in like I owned the place, and uttered my usual greeting, "Hola, mamá."

An elderly Latina woman opened the door; I figured she was one of Cornelia's many relatives, who visited often. The stunned occupants glared but didn't move as I made a beeline down their hallway toward what should have been David's room. Realizing that this was not David's apartment, I chattered my apologies and hastily withdrew. On hearing my tale, David and Carlos exchanged looks of horror mixed with pity: "Gerald, you're lucky they didn't kill you. Seriously, watch yourself around here."

Though they all knew the dangers that surrounded them, I had to remind myself that the Heredias were glad to have that apartment. They had gotten into the Rutgers Houses in 1980, when David was three. His health had still been fragile, and the hospital had been a much shorter subway ride away than the apartment in Brooklyn that a sympathetic doctor had helped them find.

Before that, Cornelia and her sons had lived for nearly a year in a shelter at the Presidential Hotel in midtown Manhattan. There were no cooking facilities, just three beds in one room for all six of them. The older boys were still in school on the Lower East Side, so after she got them there on the subway, she would go to her mother's apartment nearby on Eldridge Street and cook. The family ate supper there, then took the train back to the shelter. Feeding David was always an exacting chore; his older brothers took turns mixing the bad-smelling milk mixture he had to drink for his compromised stomach.

Despite a long list of forbidden foods, David had a pretty good appetite when we'd go out to eat, and on weekends he often came to the group lunches Richie and I had with friends; at the end of the meal, credit cards were shuffled and fanned out for David, who picked one at random; the lucky winner got to pay. He came to our apartment in Brooklyn, then to the one we moved into on the Upper East Side. But overall David preferred to haunt the art supply stores, like Pearl Paint on Canal Street. He had this beautiful way of looking longingly at something he wanted—a pack of colored pencils, a sketchbook. We'd head back to the Heredias' apartment with a bag of stuff and he would get right down to drawing. Art was his passion. He just wanted to color and draw.

"I picked it up because two of my brothers were heavily into drawing," he says. "When Carlos was out with his friends, I would sneak into his room and trace some of the drawings he had in his notebook, go back into my room, and draw it. My brother Edwin was in the navy. My mother would ask me to write him a letter and draw him something. So I started drawing ships and whatever and mailed it to him. He'd call. 'Oh, man this is great.' It looked terrible to me, but that support I got from him, my brothers, my mother, was what kept me into it."

Street art—graffiti—was the logical outlet. But David's adventures in what was still considered an outlaw genre were not something he shared with me at the time. The work I saw was colorful and upbeat, teeming with strange, cartoony characters and inventive backstories—the things that would later serve David as a professional artist. I knew nothing of the street artists' fraternity and their complicated codes. Carlos Heredia had a graffiti "tag," or signature, a lavishly drawn "DQ." And soon David had one, "AQ."

"It didn't mean anything," David says now. "I just did it because I had really good handwriting. I mimicked Carlos in almost everything he did. I remember him telling me he was going to stop because he didn't want Willy and me to get into it. So he quit. But it was too late, because we were already into it. I had a black book."

A black book was the graffiti artist's portfolio of sorts, but there was a social status attached. These standard black-covered sketchbooks were circulated, admired, pored over, and constantly refined, with a roster of "guest artists." Like the most upscale galleries, participation in another artist's book was by invitation only. It was great for the ego but little else.

David recalls, "The black book was something that only graffiti writers owned. It was not something that you wanted teachers to get hold of, because you're basically ratting out who everybody is in terms of graffiti tags. It's almost like an address book. It's kept hidden. You only get into someone's black book if they feel you have skills, so they can show it off to somebody else, like, 'Oh, this guy did work on my book.' If your skills weren't up to that level, they wouldn't let you do a page in their book. There were all different types of hierarchies.

"So I was spending all this time on it. One day Carlos saw me working on the book and he said, 'You know, D, it's a shame you're wasting so much time working in that stupid little book. You could be putting together a portfolio or work that you can actually keep and be proud of. Use the skills that you have for something that's going to give you a career. Not something that makes you have to hide and run from the cops.'"

I never saw David's black book, which probably showcased some of the best line and color work he was capable of. But it didn't matter. I was already impressed by his creativity—even with playthings. Cornelia explained that when she could not buy the elaborate plastic GI Joe house that David's friend Georgie had, David had built his own out of cardboard boxes and kept adding themed rooms based on episodes he watched of that Saturday-morning cartoon. The construction took up half the living room at its crowning height.

David was fearless, inventive, and totally joyful with a pencil in his hand. But to what end? Who, beyond his loyal family, would encourage him? When Cornelia asked me to take her place on parents' night at David's school right around the corner—her lack of English made it a painful exercise—I was happy to go. But when I stepped up to talk with his teacher, he had no idea who this David Heredia was. Stunned, I made up something to tell Cornelia. And as I took the subway home, I was struck by how basic opportunities were simply closed off to him. It was so damned unfair.

I wanted to make it better any way I could. But what was I thinking when I took this kid to the Hamptons? I had only the best of intentions, recalling my summers in Seabrook. I was religious about seeing David on the weekends, and if I was getting out of the city, why shouldn't I take him along? I was sharing a cheap summer rental with a few people, nothing fancy. Beach, sun, green—I thought it would do David good. But it didn't go well.

Later—much later—David would confess that he had been furious with me for making him "talk to so many white people" during that weekend.

"There were two reasons I was pissed off," he would say later. "One had to do with something that Gerald was trying to teach me. Whenever I would be around strangers, I had a really hard time breaking out of my shell, speaking to them. So when we'd walk into a room with a bunch of his buddies, he'd introduce me to a couple of people and then say, 'Okay, David, I'll be right

back.' And he cuts out. And I'm standing there like, uh, what am I supposed to do? I figured it was just him trying to get me to open up and mingle."

With the best of intentions, I created an excruciating social situation for him. And Southampton really was extraordinarily . . . pale. I should have had a serious clue when we went to the beach and a little kid walked up to David and rubbed his arm to see if the color came off. Neither of us could believe it had happened.

"Oh my God, I felt like the entire visit, I was the only dark-skinned person in the town. I was saying to myself, 'This is New York, not far from where I live. How can this be?' It was just really uncomfortable. I don't think then that I was quite capable of expressing what I really felt. I never directed it toward anyone, but I just had that anger and that uncomfortable feeling."

My work was going well; I rotated through positions in the bank that covered all aspects of lending. For a while I was in middle market lending in the garment trade, threading my way through factories and showrooms. Then Doug George called me and said, "You're working for me now." He explained that he was starting a new group within the financial services division that would assess credit risk on funky things like commercial paper and stock lending. Early on, Doug anticipated the consequences of the investment risks that have so shaken markets globally. He explained, "We need smart people to figure out what that risk is, to try and quantify it and figure out what to do about it."

Since then, Doug George has become an acknowledged sage of risk assessment; he currently leads the Enterprise Risk Management arm of the Depository Trust & Clearing Corporation, which provides settlement and information services for security transactions in the United States and over one hundred countries valued at over $30 quadrillion. Back in 1989, as Doug began to refine his methods, I sat right outside his office in a cubicle. I was the first one in, the guy who turned the lights on every day. The puzzles were intriguing, the economic models elegant and engaging. I loved the work intellectually. But I didn't find it meaningful.

I felt comfortable enough with Doug as a mentor that I confided my restlessness: I told him I wanted to make a lot of money to see what I could do about helping the Davids of the world. Small scale, of course. I knew that Doug saw the full picture; at one point in his life, he had actually been a social worker on the Lower East Side. He understood where my heart was,

but he also—properly—pegged me as a fairly aggressive guy in terms of business.

He felt compelled to issue a stern warning about all the quick money that was being made by smart young people. He cautioned me that my ends, however noble, could not justify questionable means. At that point, most high-powered traders had a very loose grasp of ethics. Ivan Boesky had already gone down in flames; he had implicated Michael Milken, also on his way to the dock—and ultimately prison.

Doug was emphatic: This was a tar pit I should avoid at all costs. "Be careful to maintain an ethical stance—through this and throughout life. You only get one chance to portray your ethics. And if you blow it early on, you're tagged for life."

He was right, of course. Risky business is just that, and it wouldn't do to play Robin Hood, Insider Trader, even if the spoils were earmarked for social and economic justice. And already a few of my financial risks were unwise. Staked initially with a few solid stocks my father had given me early on, I found myself sailing close to the wind as an individual investor, taking some gambles and some stinging losses. But I didn't put another kind of personal investment in strict win/loss categories. At a time I really couldn't afford a glove for the bank's Saturday baseball league, I bought David a computer that cost a month's rent. It was a tangible thing he needed, and credit card debt was so abstract—at least for thirty days.

I also began to consider piling up some serious debt: graduate school. I figured I needed to leverage my position, ramp up my business acumen. Doug was kind enough to write a recommendation to Harvard Business School. And the aspirations I had confided to him I explained in detail in my application. Question 10 on the form was simple: "What are your career plans?" My answer—stripped here of some slightly strained references to Irving Stone's *The Agony and the Ecstasy*—has held up pretty well.

My experiences at Chemical Bank have been both educational and challenging yet I do not feel truly fulfilled. Through my three year involvement with the Big Brothers Society, however, I have begun to realize true satisfaction. I have witnessed the current need to provide guidance and direction for our youth and feel strongly that this need must be addressed. Young, talented minds are being wasted and unless an effort is made

to provide . . . logical, well organized frameworks for these
individuals to pursue their aspirations, a Third World will
begin to develop within our own country. . . .

. . . My goal is to establish a private mentoring program
devoted to bridging the gap between the directionless, yet
talented youth and the productivity conscious corporation.
The program will be designed to help adolescents choose and
attain career goals while simultaneously providing
corporations with a productive entry-level workforce.
Adolescents, age sixteen to eighteen, will be recruited from a
variety of sources, including schools, community centers and
youth programs such as the Big Brothers Society. These
youngsters will take part in a comprehensive vocational and
educational program of workshops, group and individual
counseling, seminars and actual work experiences.

I will target those corporations that recognize and are
willing to address the existent work force problems. By
providing tuition as well as summer and afterschool
employment, corporations will sponsor youngsters throughout
the program and in turn will receive a first-class group of
entry-level employees. Although my goals may appear
idealistic, I have given them a great deal of serious
consideration and see tremendous opportunity in addressing
these needs. . . .

In the twenty-two years since I wrote it, there have been plenty of major
tweaks. But I have never wavered from the basic premise: Youths like David
deserve a chance to fulfill their potential. And American businesses would
be the better for it as well.

In early 1990, when I got my acceptance to HBS, David and I had just
been chosen Big Brother "couple of the year" or some such distinction, and
we were psyched about going to the awards ceremony at Tavern on the
Green. We were sitting on a bench outside David's apartment building when
I explained when and why I'd be leaving for two years. I had already arranged
with my friend Joe Gervais to stand in for me with David when I left for
Cambridge. I got a huge smile and the genuine response I'd come to expect.

"Harvard is a great school, G. That's really good for you."

I was still in a pretty celebratory mood when a friend from Boston called to invite me to a Saint Patrick's Day party at a bowling alley in Cambridge. I flew up on a whim. And at that noisy, beery bash I ran into the greatest good fortune of my life.

Through the smoke and Gaelic mayhem, I saw Kate Smallwood. This was one gorgeous and high-spirited pin buster—bright, British, seductively boho, and clearly no stranger to spontaneous adventure. On being introduced, I found that she had already one-upped me; Kate had flown over from London, where she worked as an art expert for Christie's—on a whim, and just for the weekend.

Though she grew up in London and the British countryside, Kate went to college in Massachusetts, at Wellesley. We had landed at the party by invitation from mutual Boston friends—and in each other's arms by evening's end. When I took her to Logan Airport the following day, it was with a huge grin and the certain knowledge that my world had tilted slightly on its axis.

Kate was so . . . unlikely. Yet something in me said, "Of course." Richie remembers me sounding a bit daft even trying to describe "this amazing girl I met at a party."

I've since been reminded of John Gielgud's line in the comedy *Arthur*. As Hobson, Dudley Moore's long-suffering butler, he says to his employer's kooky new love, Liza Minnelli: "Thank you for a memorable afternoon. Normally, one must go to a bowling alley to meet a woman of your stature."

CHAPTER THREE
Why Is He Doing This?

I QUIT CHEMICAL BANK IN APRIL 1990, JUST A FEW WEEKS AFTER THAT wonderfully fateful bowling party. I figured it was a good idea to put some cultural and geographical distance between my lifetime of East Coast education and my first semester at Harvard Business School. I decided to travel through Southeast Asia until mid-August. I charted an ambling route though Pakistan, Nepal, India, Thailand, Malaysia, Singapore, Borneo, and Indonesia. It would be my first time visiting any third-world country. And my travel plan, I promised myself, would take me completely around the globe.

Before I left, I took another flier. Kate, who had been an art major at Wellesley, was working in the modern British art department of that venerable London auction house, Christie's. I sent a fax to her there: "Would you meet me in Bangkok on June 16th?" Richie O'Leary had a good laugh when I told him. "You really think she'll show up? She's going to be at some bar in London, laughing, thinking some pathetic guy is waiting at the Bangkok airport."

I took off in late April; first stop, Kathmandu via Karachi. I traveled alone for the most part, occasionally joining up with another wanderer, merging paths for a spell, and separating just as effortlessly. I lived on ten dollars a day, ate street food much of the time, got all the bacterial payback I deserved, slept in rooms that the least choosy brothel customer would have rejected, and generally felt as happy and free as I had ever been.

I turned twenty-five on May 15, 1990, in the holiest of Indian cities,

Varanasi. My birthday present to myself was a brief release from pragmatism, a visit to the local palm reader. I looked like a bum—dusty, unshaven, and road worn—when the village seer motioned me to lie down on a mat in his hut for a reading. I gave him minimal background information for his prognostications—just date and time of birth. When I arose, a bit dazed, I scribbled down, verbatim, some of his predictions in my travel diary: "I'll marry a non-US woman before the age of 30, I'll have 3 to 4 children before the age of 36. I will start my own business. Between 36 and 42 I'll undergo a fundamental change in my beliefs, and I'll have some marital problems which will ultimately be resolved. Most pleasing was that I'll progress in my career quite rapidly and be a leader of many men and companies. Also, he said that my luck was well above that of many others and I should trust its positive effects."

More than two decades later, I still shake my head in disbelief at how he got it so right.

On June 16, I headed for the Bangkok airport. I had faith—and a couple of encouraging faxes—to convince me that I would indeed be meeting Kate's plane. Still, the luck aspect of the guru's predictions seemed a bit dubious. Three days earlier, a nasty motorcycle accident on the border of Laos and Thailand had left me badly bruised, on crutches, and gobbling codeine pills against the pain from internal bleeding. I was reading in the arrival lounge when I saw Kate; she blanched when I lowered my newspaper and she took in my injuries. I'll let her explain this six-thousand-mile roll of the dice.

"When I bought the ticket to Thailand, we had known one another for ten hours. I think we both knew there was a real connection. I was very different from what Gerald knew. I was an English girl, incredibly independent. He was very passionate, very keen. He thought I was lovely. I found this surprising and somewhat unbelievable, but I was willing to go for it. He's somebody with remarkable purpose.

"It was the best ten days to get to know someone. We traveled to Koh Samui and the Koh Phangan Islands, spent a lot of time on the beach, talking a lot, eating a lot. Driving around. I just remember talking and talking. It was amazing to meet someone who told you exactly what he thought. There was no game playing with him at all, ever. By the end of it we understood each other emotionally, completely. We knew we were going to be together and make a go of it. He was going to business school and I was going to join him, then we'd go back to England."

I did explain to Kate that I came to her with another deep and important attachment. And a plan.

She recalls: "In Thailand I heard about David Heredia. Gerald was very clear in explaining how important David had to be in our life. He understood that David was as important to him as the other way 'round—he never spoke of himself as helping David. And he was also percolating that workforce idea. It was part of our conversation on who he was and what he valued. He always related his plan directly to his experience with David—always.

"I understood from very early on that he was not a material man. He was a traveler. Experiential. My world is objects—my grandmother's art collection, my work with artists, my own love of fashion. And I met this man who would be perfectly happy with one pair of underwear, one pair of jeans, and a shirt. People were more important to him."

Kate had a very unusual background, although she rarely talked about it. Over the years, I learned that she was a privileged girl of sorts, but not without sadness. Her mother died when she was six and her sister Emma was eight. But the girls had a good deal of love, support, and opportunity. On their maternal great-grandmother's side, there was a wealth and culture that afforded a privileged lifestyle: excellent boarding schools, beautiful homes, and exposure to the finest music, theater, and art.

From her parents' family, Kate inherited a long-standing commitment to no-nonsense, roll-up-your-sleeves-and-*do*-something sort of philanthropy. Their small family foundation was not flashy but highly functional—a quiet tradition that continues to this day. It made perfect sense, then, that Kate would easily understand my experience with David.

London and Lowell . . . Why not? On a bus back to the Koh Samui airport, we planned the next few years: We'd see each other as much as possible during my first year of business school, I'd go to London for the next summer, she'd come back with me for the second year of school, then we'd relocate to London. Done.

At this second airport farewell, I saw my future in the slim little figure walking from the open-air waiting room down the dirt path to the plane. Kate had listened to my dreams as though they were perfectly logical, necessary, and attainable. I realize now: If you are going to do my kind of work, you'd better find a very secure, full-on partner who is just fine with expanded dinners, endless fund-raisers, and an ongoing movable feast—often in your living room—of boisterous, deeply committed coworkers, students, and donors.

You want someone who has no problem with risk—who might actually thrive on it. At twenty-five, I was hardly shopping for those qualities, or even looking for a wife—I simply fell hard. Maybe I was lucky after all.

I headed back on the road, where my vagabond's adventure continued—until one day in Yogyakarta, Indonesia. I was in one of those blissed-out traveler's reveries; I had just finished watching an amazing shadow puppet show with gamelan music—ensemble pieces with drums, gongs, bamboo flutes. The tropical heat was so intense that I was sweating through my money belt—the one you're never supposed to take off. I peeled it off to air it out for a few moments, put it in my day pack, and got into a bicycle rickshaw to return to my hostel. I remember hearing a motorcycle revving loudly, the flash of a hand grabbing my day pack, and then a blur of two helmeted men on a motorcycle racing off in front of me.

Watching the thieves speed away, I realized that I had just lost everything—camera, passport, plane tickets, money, credit cards, identification. I started to hyperventilate. I happened to be near a police station; I went in and started screaming, too panicky and clueless to know that the very last thing someone in Indonesia does is to show visible anger. Such behavior is foreign to their culture. The officers and villagers started laughing nervously. Translation: What's up with this pale, sweaty madman, and what the heck do we do with him?

A man in a civil servant's uniform stepped forward and asked in very broken English why I was so upset. He told me that he would help me and that I could stay with him. We rode on his little Honda motorcycle to a tiny, sparse apartment.

I am still ashamed of my doubts, but I had them: *Why is he doing this? What's the catch? Am I in for some sort of scam on top of a robbery?* Over the next three days, my Indonesian friend took me all over that city, from the American Express office to airline office, from telephone shop to store. He was unfailingly kind and seemed embarrassed that his countrymen had ripped me off.

More amazing: He possessed almost nothing himself, yet he was truly serene. His government wages barely kept him out of poverty, and he gave me everything—support, care, food, shelter. His basic way of life seemed ancient, yet his social conscience was so much more evolved than that of an ambitious Western economics student.

My host reminded me that a lack of material comfort doesn't preclude a richness of spirit—a lesson that would be amplified in Cornelia Heredia's kitchen. Once I had recovered my bearings and a viable credit card, I got moving again, still determined to circumnavigate the globe. I kept in touch with Kate by letter and pay phone. Then, suddenly, she was in Dorset at her parents' home. She had contracted a disease known as Japanese encephalitis—probably from a mosquito bite—and was very ill. Vowing to cross the International Date Line some other time, I folded up my maps and arranged for a flight to London to be with Kate. As she healed, we planned a happy merger of lives, friends, and families.

Within the year, Kate had met my family.

"We've got a bohemian here, Joyce," Dad informed my mother after they met Kate in a Faneuil Hall restaurant on one of her visits to Boston. Dad thought that her "kinda kooky" clothes just screamed boho—though he admitted she looked great in whatever she wore. But what was up with that rubber purse stamped with "Michelin"? Both of my parents loved her right away—and vice versa. Soon Kate and Mom were thick as thieves.

In 1989 Mom had been diagnosed with breast cancer. She had had surgery, and her recovery was going well, though she was unable to tolerate the follow-up tamoxifen therapy that so many women take as a safeguard. She had a job she adored at the Chanel makeup counter at Neiman Marcus in downtown Boston.

I had been the one, in 1992, to goad her into doing some modeling. And she had given it a go with Boston-area photo shoots and appearances for Elizabeth Arden, Chanel, and Christian Dior. But the lights and fussing had brought back that old discomfort at being the center of attention, and she had quit. She was happier wielding her brushes and mascara wands, helping other women feel better about themselves—particularly other cancer survivors coming off the ravages of chemotherapy. Her beauty clinics and makeovers may have been skin deep, but her compassion was bottomless. Mom had a devoted following among her clients and her fellow employees, and she became a welcome and sought-after volunteer at the Dana-Farber Cancer Center. You could always talk to Joyce.

I didn't need my accomplished brother, Lee, who had graduated five years earlier, to warn me that HBS would be a different sort of education than I was used to. Its reputation was daunting, and I made my first trek across the business school campus weighed down by a healthy fear of flunking.

For much of my academic life I had relied on a pretty solid short-term memory; I could memorize pages of text and summon them at will into a blue book. Time after time, this technique had yielded As and A-pluses. At HBS, it wouldn't help me. You're allowed to bring all your notes and texts to take an exam; it's how well you think that's at issue.

My first grade, in a production and operations management course, was a livid, red-inked sixty-four, neatly circled. Lord, I hated that class, crammed with systems, throughput, manufacturing. *Process.* I can barely screw in a light-bulb, let alone run a factory. But over the next two years, I did learn the basic framework of how to run a business. At the time, I was as dismissive as my classmates were of the unsexy "soft courses" in organizational development and management. But the longer you are in business, the more you understand that the basics taught at HBS are what keep the lights on, the bills paid, and the company vital. With the framework an MBA provides, coupled with years of learning on the job, I have come to rely on three guiding principles in both my for-profit and nonprofit ventures. They include (1) authentic leadership based on clearly articulated values; (2) a well-crafted and well-executed strategy; and (3) getting the right people in the right seats.

I probably worked twice as hard as I needed to at HBS, but I've never functioned well in low gear. And I was always looking down the road. Before I graduated, I went to Manhattan in the spring of 1992 to follow up some leads that might help me secure a position in London. Though I had left David Heredia in the capable hands of my friend Joe Gervais, I had really missed him, which was another reason for my trip to New York.

As soon as I could, I took the subway downtown to pick him up. David was agitating to see the latest hot movie, *Juice.* It was an early hip-hop passion play directed by Spike Lee's longtime cinematographer, Ernest Dickerson. The plot centered on four urban young men from striving families as they navigated between conventional career paths and the ghetto job market—one featuring high pay and low life expectancy. David remembers that night as vividly as I do: "The only theater that had it was in Harlem, and I was so excited—I'm in junior high then. And when we get there, everybody was black. Everybody. I'm like, 'Yes, man, I've been wanting to see this movie forever!' Gerald just had this really weird look on his face. There were a couple of scenes in the movie where the guys got really violent. People were laughing and yelling at the screen. Everybody's cheering—'Kill the white guy!' I'm clapping and laughing and I looked at Gerald and I think I actually saw him sweating. He did not enjoy that film one bit. And he never voiced to me what his concerns were, how uncomfortable he felt."

That was a conversation neither of us was ready for. Like the characters in the movie, David was coming of age as a young man of color in a big, tough city. And despite the comic aspects of that night as I squirmed in my seat, it was probably past time to get serious about some pretty basic issues— in black and white. David was beginning to examine and question our relationship in ways that might have made me even more uncomfortable than the movie experience had he voiced them back then.

Following my graduation from business school, Kate and I gave ourselves a six-week holiday traveling through South America before moving to London. As we made plans for our wedding there, I was happy to see my parents looking forward to the trip. For the whole Chertavian clan, our marriage had its fairy-tale aspects. It was held on October 10, 1992, at Spencer House in London—a family home of Lady Diana Spencer—and it was all properly British, right down to the relentless London rain and the double-decker buses that ferried guests between church and reception. We celebrated with champagne, an elegant cake, and Silly String in a can.

We settled into the tiny house in Fulham that Kate had bought after college with an inheritance. For that first year in the UK, I was working for an American-owned direct-marketing firm. My bride took the "for richer or for poorer" part seriously and asked me to hand over my credit cards. I'll confess they were flaming hot with student debt and toxic interest fees, but admitting abject insolvency was just not a guy thing. Besides the plastic meltdown, I'd made some brash investment decisions and lost all my savings on a margin call. Kate had no patience for bruised manly pride. She was simply being practical: "I'd inherited from my mother a bit of a security blanket. Not a vast amount, but helpful. I cut up Gerald's credit cards, which had his school debt on them, about sixty thousand dollars' worth. To clear that debt was important for us to go forward. It was an academic debt, so I didn't feel it was his old girlfriends' dinners. With every penny I earned and could spend I would invest in his new company. There were some very scary periods."

At first, Kate was the main breadwinner as I investigated business possibilities. She started out on her own as an art consultant and gallerist. Having met and hit it off with a wealthy, high-profile collector at a London gallery, Kate was soon buying contemporary British art for him—a collaboration that would last over a decade. I loved to watch her strategize in a stuffy roomful of established dealers. With her client's clout and deep pockets and her own knowledge and nerve, she was a serious player at age twenty-seven. Kate's client was much older, but he had utter confidence in her taste and pricing savvy.

Little was predictable then, and we both loved it that way. Kate would disappear for ten days or three weeks to Montreux, Florence, or New York to buy art or oversee an installation. Her eclectic work brought together artists, musicians and their road crews, potters, gallery workers. They flowed ceaselessly through our house, making their art and doing their laundry. And it was also home to the Kate Chertavian Gallery. It was a pretty fluid, ad hoc operation; more than once I was startled by strangers roaming through our rooms. I relied on Kate to let me know whether I could sit on any new object or only stand back and admire it as a sculptural triumph.

We discussed rewards and risks together, of course. And whenever either of us presented a plan, the other's response was pretty consistent: "Go for it, sweetheart."

In the early summer of 1993, I had just finished a few sets of tennis with my regular partner, Chris Mathias, who explained to me calmly, "Gerald, I just bought two businesses yesterday. One is going to go bankrupt very soon, and I need to focus all of my time on it. The other is a software development and database marketing company that is losing money but has potential. I want you to buy it with me and my partner Martin Gill, and then run it."

I took a deep breath, talked with Kate about investing her money into a struggling, loss-making start-up, and then dove into the expanding world of information technology. Our company was called Conduit Communications. The business press described us this way: "Closely held Conduit provides information technology consulting on marketing and selling over the Internet."

It was almost-virgin territory in 1993, helping corporations develop their databases and online presence. Our eighty-thousand-dollar investment bought us 8 percent of the company with options to buy another 8 percent. I also got the title of managing director and a terrifying learning curve. I had never written a decent line of software code in my life, nor had I managed many people; suddenly I was in charge of six software developers, ten database marketers, and four senior staff. We helped companies step up to the information age, building their e-commerce sites and engines, designing their Web sites, and building customer- and knowledge-management systems.

Things were really shaky at first; we had lost $60,000 in our first month of operation and had $175,000 in the bank. I stopped paying the company phone bill and we plundered our receivables for any available cash. There is nothing like a good cash crisis to clear the mind, though. By February 1994 we had turned a profit of $281, which we promptly spent on champagne. Then every single month for the next forty-six months we delivered increased revenue and increased profit. I applied some of those HBS basics: We hired the best graduates, known as "starred firsts," from Cambridge and Oxford, some of the most brilliant people you could find. We built a strong work hard–play hard culture, and we had the strategic clarity to push hard into the Internet when it was still a hazy vision. We were the cool guys on the street and without a dime of venture capital grew to about eighteen million dollars in revenue with 130 staff and offices in London, Amsterdam, Boston, and New York City.

Everything was going great. Conduit was even able to help design and build the Web site in 1995 when Kate and her client launched an innovative e-gallery that eventually morphed into a commission-free online exhibition space for young, undiscovered artists. David Heredia was still very involved with his own art, working on an impressive portfolio. Kate and I invited him to spend a summer with us. He had never traveled farther from the Rutgers Houses than Camp Trinita, so I was surprised by his initial reaction.

"Well, this is hard to explain," David says. "With grown-ups, you're always suspicious. And you're never used to people being nice to you for no reason at all. Gerald was just like this guardian angel. He would take me to places, get me stuff, never ask for anything in return, and I'd begun to ask myself, 'Why is he doing this? What's he getting out of it?' I know what I'm getting out of it. I would think about that so much that it started to make me feel negative. I started thinking, 'Maybe he wants to make himself look good. Work on his image.' Just sort of thinking real negative thoughts.

"So when he first invited me to London, I said no. I didn't want to take more money; that's an expensive trip. Plus I had to work for the summer. I wasn't going to go on vacation knowing that my mother needs help. Gerald's entreating me: 'Listen, you can come and work for me and I'll pay you at the company.' I hung up and told my mother and she almost hit the roof, she was so upset with me for saying no.

"I unburdened myself to my brother Carlos. I said, 'I don't really understand why he's giving me all this stuff.' Carlos said, 'You can't look at it like that. You have to look at it simply as if you're walking to the building and you see an older lady carrying some grocery bags and you know she's struggling. You're going to help her out and say, "Have a good day," and go home. You didn't do it because you're going to start bragging to your friends about it. It's in your nature to want to help somebody. Everybody can have that in them—even rich people. Somewhere in their life they had help. Some of us happen to get offered this opportunity and are too proud to accept it. You need to get over it. All your life he's been there, taking you around, showing you different things. This is just another experience.'

"I heard what he was saying. God bless the wisdom of Carlos."

As it turned out, David spent most of his time with Kate on that first trip to London. Conduit was all consuming; I was out of the house by 7:00 a.m. and rarely back before nine at night. David did work in the office—somewhat. But mostly he had fun, taking in the London sights and happily gorging himself on strawberries and cream.

Back in New York, David completed an associate degree in art and advertising at a community college, then approached me in 1997 about going to the School for Visual Arts in Manhattan. I told him that if he got in, I would make sure he could pay for it. I wrote his reference letter, he got in, and Kate's parents helped us to pay for his college tuition.

After five years of apparent recovery and good health, things had begun going badly for Mom. Back pain led to tests and the ominous diagnosis; the cancer had recurred and spread to her bones. She went through radiation, chemotherapy, and a series of tough surgeries. As the health crises continued, I flew back and forth to see my parents, who were then living in their Seabrook, New Hampshire, beach house. There was some family joy as well; our son Cameron was born in November 1997. The little house in Fulham was bursting with art, industry, and nappies. Conduit just kept growing. We had been the fifteenth-fastest-growing company in Britain between 1993 and 1998. But just as quickly, the game was changing. Venture capital backed–Internet ventures had gone public, and the market was frothy. Companies like USWeb, Sapient, and Razorfish were being rewarded with billion-dollar valuations. And these companies were doing basically what we had been doing. But they seemed to be doing it better, and they were mobilizing to go global. We decided that we were going to either sell the company or raise a ton of money, go on a buying spree, and go public ourselves. We had eleven offers to buy our company, ranging from $23 million to $83 million. My partners and I looked hard at the situation and at one another; we agreed that selling made more sense. This had been a seven-year run of a crazy, crazy Internet time. Working six days a week, I had been a pretty marginal father for the first two years of Cameron's life, and I never called my friends in America. I worked up to sixteen hours a day and found myself so fried on the weekends that I would wake up on Saturday mornings sick from exhaustion. Weekdays, I often got home at eleven and ate a cold dinner, alone, in a quiet house.

As business grew more stressful, my mother's health went into a steep downward spiral. I felt deeply sad and helpless, and the distance made it worse. On one of my visits to see Mom in 1999, she handed me a copy of an inspirational quote from a Dear Abby article, which I still keep in my wallet, along with Mom's photo. I'm not sure what she was thinking when she gave it to me, though certainly her younger son could profit from some serious risk assessment. There I was, perched on a dot-com limb, soon to be a father for the second time, and wondering whether I dared even think about that non-profit plunge. I read it in my parents' kitchen. A few lines jumped out at me:

> The person who risks nothing does nothing, has nothing, is nothing. He may avoid suffering and sorrow, but cannot learn, feel, change, grow or love. . . . Only a person who takes risks is free.

———

Points all taken.

Back in London, after much soul- and ledger-searching, my partners and I weighed all the offers and decided to sell to a well-run, Cambridge, Massachusetts–based public company called I-Cube. We did the deal. Then, five weeks later, Razorfish swallowed both of us just like one of those animations of the undersea food chain. Suddenly we were part of a company of over a thousand people that defined the Internet bubble and would soon crest at a valuation of $4.6 billion. Everything was about to change; very soon, the dot-com market would crash. But all we knew at the moment was that we were losing control of what we had built.

In late 1999 we recognized that our equity was overvalued in that Wild West dot-com market, and it wasn't a hard decision to cash out. I sold all of my shares in a single trade. As digital numbers and shares crossed in the ether, I instantly had a bank balance that would change my life.

By the time it was done, we sold the company for $55 million in stock and $28 million in options. Eighty-three million. In Conduit's short run, we made about thirty paper millionaires. We had allowed everyone to participate in our stock plan, and even the administrative assistants made five-figure gains, depending on when they cashed in their options. As soon as I was able I sold all of my shares, cashed in my options, paid my taxes, and closed the door on it all.

I felt exhausted and numb, wondering whether it was all really true. Whom do you tell? What do you say? In those few minutes of Wall Street trading activity I had just made more money than both my parents and their parents made in their entire lives. I rode my commuter bike home to Kate and the kids with strangely mixed feelings. I was thirty-five and far from done. But now what?

Mom was barely clinging to life but, thanks to a last-minute decision to try a new surgical procedure, survived to see the new millennium. It only postponed the inevitable a few months—long enough to let her hold her namesake and our new daughter, Casey Joyce, born in November 1999.

Watching someone die is hard. Mom stopped eating and drinking on March 17, and we were told that it would be only a day or two until the end. Thank God. She had suffered plenty. Two days turned into four, and by the sixth excruciatingly painful day, we were all coming unglued. By the early evening of the twenty-third, the house was quiet, as the cadre of visitors and nurses had departed; I went in to be with Mom after hearing what I now know was a "death rattle." It was an ungodly sound for someone so sweet and beautiful. I put my arms around her carefully, in a way that wouldn't hurt her, but it was clear she was past the pain. She took her last breath and exhaled quietly. Devastated as I was to lose her, five years' suffering was over and it was a peaceful moment. My one regret is that I had yet to tell her unequivocally that I would soon start a new chapter in my life called Year Up.

The idea for Year Up had never left me, though it was as yet unnamed. Now, armed with some capital, plenty of time, and all good intentions, I sat down to hammer out a business plan for a new nonprofit. I had settled into

Kate's home office—an incursion that caused some territorial skirmishes—and began doing online research about youth and workforce-development programs and the foundations that funded them.

I started calling people I knew, asking questions. I visited innovative educational programs in northern England, researched vocational education in Germany, and even flew to San Francisco to check out a few programs that were training low-income individuals for Internet jobs. I had a large binder with a section for each aspect of what would become the first business plan: marketing, finances, program, mission, organizational structure, peer organizations, etc.

It was another one of those glorious London spring days when I put a name to years of scheming and dreaming. There was a window behind me, and the sun was flooding the desk. I had a small notebook—the sort I still carry everywhere. I opened up to a blank page and started thinking about what we would call this thing. I thought, "Jumpstart." It was easy to remember, and it evoked what we would be doing—getting folks going. I typed it into the U.S. Patent and Trademark Office trademark database. "Jumpstart" was already taken by a nonprofit—in Boston. Later I'd find that it was on the fourth floor of the very building we'd end up in on Summer Street.

I wrote four more names into the notebook and checked the database for number two: "Year Up." I had always intended it as a yearlong program in which people would rise up—in so many ways. I looked at it on the sunlit page. Yes! To this day I don't recall the other choices I'd scribbled beneath it. I was nervous as I typed "Year Up" into the search box. It wasn't taken. I didn't waste any time registering the name and a Web site.

It was barely two months after my mother's death, and the shock, albeit a pleasant one, of the Conduit sale. I had been doing a lot of thinking. And I had to make my peace with a question that other people—curious students, donors, corporate partners, and friends—still ask me: "Would you have started Year Up if you hadn't sold your company for a lot of money?"

The answer is no. Sure, I would have volunteered a lot and mentored kids on weekends. I'd have been a stellar Big Brother for several other kids. Guiding young people had been an avocation—no, make that a personal need—since I was a college student supervising those sweaty, distracted kids and their flailing rakes in Lowell. And David Heredia is and always will be part of my immediate family.

Given what I had learned with him in the Rutgers Houses, I knew that someday I would need to shift all of my energy to this sort of work, since it was the most meaningful for me. But I also knew the odds of turning that idealistic abstract from my grad school application into a viable vocation. I'd always expected that to take two or three decades to accomplish.

It all happened so fast; the Conduit sale brought forward all of those decisions. But we already had two children. And I have to say that the rightness, the urgent need for the mission would not have won out over the pragmatic realization that I had to provide for my family first and foremost. Sorry if this doesn't sound like the pure motivation of a holy ascetic—but it's honest. I am deeply grateful, every day of my life, that we were able to sell Conduit and gained the means to focus on what I find most meaningful. And finances aside, I was blessed with the ultimate endorsement: "Go for it, sweetheart."

How did I know I was finally, absolutely ready? I knew that the marginal value of money to me was low. Making yet more money just didn't have a strong appeal. If you can't answer the question "What is enough?" then you are living somebody else's expectations. My dad gently helped me to realize that we had been very fortunate to sell our company for what we did and that my hat size ought to stay the same. In his words, "You hit a grand slam. Don't think you can step right back in and do it again." My father-in-law, Guy, always the source of incredibly valuable business advice, helped me to see it from a different angle: "You are young, you are not that far away in age to those that you will be serving, and this venture is going to take a lot of energy. I can't see why waiting another ten years makes sense."

As my research for my nonprofit progressed, Kate noticed me telling more and more people what I was planning. "I know *exactly* what you're doing," she informed me. "You're telling everyone about it so that you have no choice. You'll have to go and make it work now—or look like an empty braggart or a fool."

CHAPTER FOUR
Ping Me . . . Please?

Class Nine, Mid-November

Having hung up his coat with just moments to spare before class, Devon was a trifle breathless but grateful: "Malik is always pinging me, BBMing me. *Wake up, wake up.* He's always on top of me. 'Yo D, you finish your work?'"

Two months in, some students had more than their original two hundred points. Others were steadily losing them. Every Friday, students' weekly point tallies are read aloud by their site leaders. Points gained or lost are indicators of a student's adherence to the terms of the contract that all students sign before they begin the program.

The tally takes in extra points won for conscientious effort and attendance. Points are lost for infractions—everything from missed assignments to lateness to "inappropriate use of electronics" to failure to respect Year Up core values. Lost points also mean dollars lost from a student's weekly stipend. Students earn fifteen extra points for every week without an infraction. Should they fall below one hundred, they are asked to draft a statement of recommitment and share it with their colleagues.

For Class Nine, lateness infractions were still a serious challenge. Weekdays, beginning at around 6:00 a.m., alarm clocks sounded in dark apartments from Washington Heights to Flatbush, East Harlem to the Lower East Side. BlackBerry and flip-phone reveilles invaded sleep as shrill bells, beeps, mellow Usher ringtones, and the fierce challenge of a Lil Wayne cut, "Get a Life": *I'm just tryna get my own, I'm up early in the morning* . . .

It was classic slump time in the learning and development (L & D) phase. The initial excitement had settled into long days of classroom work that got increasingly difficult. Information technology was wires, pliers, and software. Business communications, with its exercises on proper e-mail etiquette—no shortcuts, no slang, no emoticons—was spinning off plenty of homework. There were news articles and essays to read, analyze, and comment upon that bristled with new words to look up and sentence structure to parse, plus reports and PowerPoint presentations to plan and prepare—individually and in well-functioning teams.

In its first weeks, Class Nine had faced and mastered a few hurdles that some students had thought impossible: shaking a stranger's hand while looking him directly in the eye and smiling. Confidently introducing oneself and the Year Up program in a short presentation known as the "elevator speech." Giving a guided tour of the facilities—at a moment's notice—to prospective applicants, donors, corporate partners, visiting city officials.

"Narcisco, you're on break, right? Would you kindly show these gentlemen our site?"

A smile, handshakes all around. No hesitation. With a trio of would-be applicants in tow, our student Narcisco headed off.

"So this is our tech classroom. This is where it all happens. You'll notice the Dell PCs, primarily what we work with. We'll be passing by the break room, where students can eat, hang out, and just chill between classes."

And so it went, as Narcisco's tour wove throughout the facility. Seeing the three smiling applicants off toward the elevator with good wishes and handshakes, their guide paused to address another visitor in the lounge before heading to class. "Can I tell you something? I just want you to understand that a month ago, I could not have looked them or you in the eye. I could not even be talking like this to someone I didn't know—somebody not from my neighborhood, if you know what I'm saying. It seems crazy to me now. To me, this is a really big gift—to finally be comfortable in my skin. Pro skills rocks."

Professional skills—known in Year Up vernacular as pro skills—gets far more personal than technical courses. I used to teach a version of it myself when we first began the program. As we have seen the importance of giving students the soft skills they'll need in the workplace, it has become a much more comprehensive class. Course objectives listed in the syllabus include mastering decision-making strategies, working out a personal schedule that ensures success, identifying and dealing with personality types and conflict behaviors, leadership skills, team dynamics, and team building. Business etiquette, a core topic in the course, covers everything from table manners for a business lunch to the finer points of handshakes, thank-you notes, and nonverbal communication—body language.

Slumped over a conference table, resting his head on his arms, Devon knew his posture was telegraphing a decided downturn in motivation. And sometimes in class, he was a bit too . . . um, expressive.

"I'm going to hold back more and fix my nonverbals," he vowed. Devon was feeling the slide on a chilly gray morning, down in his contract points and sometimes struggling a bit to maintain his generally upbeat demeanor. His site leader, Wil, had spoken to him a few times when he noticed the shadows creep over Devon's face. Devon said, "He told me, 'D, when you're up, the whole LC is up. And when you're down, we all feel it.' I take that to heart, I do."

He was trying to think of the good things that had already happened and the results he could already see: "When I go back to my old places now, like to my old church, they're all like, 'Wow, you've changed, your speech.' 'Cause I used to talk so much slang, like 'Yo yo yo, how you doin'?' Now I'm . . ." His voice dipped into a plummy baritone, well enunciated but . . . natural. "*How are you?* I love it. I'm going to take this wherever I go."

He said he was cool with "boom," an LCW code word for "Watch the slang." Should someone slip into street lingo, the "booms" sound from fellow students instantly, loud and clear.

"Yo . . ."

Boom! "You got a yo-yo or something? What're you saying?"

"So I axed her . . ."

Boom! "It's 'ask.' ASK. Ask, ask, *ask*."

"Just press control/alt/delete, dawg."

Boooooooom! Boom! We do not call our colleagues dawg, bro, dude. The corrections explode all around whoever slips up, with everybody piling on— and laughing. Devon gives as good as he gets, happy to be a well-intended word cop. "We correct each other. In Brooklyn, it seems like we all have each other's back. I believe every site is a family. We all want to see each other succeed."

Within the safety of a learning community, no "I axed" falls uncorrected by both staff and peers. And no offense is taken. Across all sites nationally, there are prescribed and gentle modes of language correction and growth. In New York, it's "boom." At our National Capital Region site, classrooms have a "stop wall"—a red stop sign surrounded by index cards bearing words that don't belong in the workplace. The subtext is firm but nonjudgmental: Slang is not a bad or inferior form of communication and has its place among friends. Proper usage is part of a necessary skill set to unpack in the workplace—and the wider world. Learn it, use it, keep it sharp.

For every outlawed bit of slang, there are scores of new choices. Weekly vocabulary assignments are woven in and out of written and oral assignments that help students use a new word, lest they lose it. "Vocab" had actually been fun for Malik, who was becoming a connoisseur of especially flavorful words. Already he had a string of new favorites and liked to practice using them. *Intuition. Colloquial.*

"And 'peruse.' Per-oooooze. I like the sound of it. I like the thought of it. Let us *peruse* life's possibilities."

Malik and his family had moved to Harlem two years earlier, to get away from the Bronx projects where his brother was murdered. Both of his parents had come to New York from Gambia, separately, just over two decades earlier, and they were no longer together. His father drove a taxicab. His mother had been out of work, disabled from an industrial injury at a biscuit factory; that business relocated to another state before her claim could be processed. Things were, to use a vocabulary word, *tentative* in the household. And the neighborhood wasn't too hospitable. It made Malik edgy sometimes, to have all that street life between him and the subway stop.

"In Harlem I try not to make too many friends because I don't want to surround myself with the wrong crowd. But I do have my cousins there. My cousin always tells me, 'Look at you now, nice and spiffy, like a working man. I see you in the morning with your briefcase. I'm proud of you.' My best friend tells me the same thing. They all make jokes, but in a good way—'Now you think you're too good for us, got a suit and tie on.' Most of them are congratulating me for doing something different. There's not much negativity."

He's not about to flash those ten-dollar vocab words too much at home. Every working man should be able to let his hair down outside the office: "I do revert back to my old slang outside of Year Up, but I also correct some of my friends. They complain but they accept it. They say, 'Oh, *excuse* me.' It's fun. It's good to have insight on both worlds. The new words, the correct grammar—they're tools, you have to know when to use them—and when not to."

Out on Broadway and 167th Street, dressed for success but running perilously late, Marisol had panicked at about 7:20 a.m.; the downtown trains were messed up again, and as usual, the station announcement was too garbled to offer any usable information. Police activity, a stalled train at Ninety-sixth Street—whatever, it was going to be a lateness infraction—a loss of points and up to twenty-five dollars of her week's stipend for not being in her seat when class began. She flagged a livery cab and off they sped to Brooklyn. She just couldn't afford to earn another infraction and lose more of her stipend. Worse, she was way down in points because of lateness. As they screeched up to the Flatbush Avenue construction site outside the Year Up building, Marisol handed over forty dollars and tore upstairs to the fifth floor.

The classroom door was closed.

Two minutes. Just two minutes. Stupid, stupid. Never again. Well, not often, anyhow.

Marisol was furious—with herself, with the transit system, with life. But later, as she took her place in Kenneth Wright's tech class for a hands-on session with computer hardware, the tension eased. She was surprised at the satisfying feeling that came from opening a PC's cover, taking its guts apart, and getting it back together again: power unit, hard drive, motherboard. All that once-mysterious stuff whirred back to life in a moment that startled and amazed her. *She did it!* The tiny screws and tools felt right in her small, well-manicured hands. "I feel capable doing that work. I didn't think it could be, you know, pleasurable. It's not at all scary. Just good."

She would have had a greater appreciation for what actually was going on inside when she booted up her own laptop too—that is, if she still had it. She did get her hands on it momentarily after her apartment was robbed. "Yeah, it's kind of a crazy story."

After the thieves had entered her apartment that terrifying day in May 2010 and Marisol had escaped out a side door, she had been outside on her cell phone to the police and to her aunt, who ran out to meet her. The police had told the two women to stand on the street and not confront anyone until the squad car arrived.

Marisol had obeyed—at first. "We waited for about a minute or two, but it felt like we were standing there forever. The guy was standing by a car, showing my laptop off to a group of people—maybe trying to sell it or something—and then I saw him close it and try to put it away in a bag. That's when I walked up to him, snatched it from him, and told him what a thief he was. I wasn't going to risk letting him get away because the cops were taking really long to get there. He told me that it wasn't him, that the laptop was sold to him by someone else, and if I wanted, he could take me to the person that sold it to him. Between all the yelling and confronting, the cops finally came and put the guy in handcuffs."

Marisol might weigh a hundred pounds—someday, and soaking wet. In hindsight, she realized she probably snapped for a moment, wrestling with a man bold enough to break into her home in broad daylight. But she had no margin in her life, no room at all for these lousy predators to snatch a single mom's *information,* her connection, her future—and so many memories. Her ex-husband gave her the laptop when she moved back to New York, newly single, with their son. Photos of Manuel's* infancy and their short time together as a family were all in that hard drive.

"I was furious, and I didn't really think about what danger I could have put myself in."

Once the alleged thief had been safely cuffed and put in a patrol car, there was no happy outcome. "The police took my laptop," Marisol said darkly. "They said they needed it for their investigation. I keep calling to get it back, and it keeps moving to different storage places, different precincts."

Nearly a year after the attempted theft, Marisol could troubleshoot and repair a series of ailing computers. She knew how—in theory—to face down a blinking screen full of help-desk queries and apply standard fixes to help thousands of potential clients. But in Washington Heights, she was powerless still: "You have to remind yourself, as much as you learn here, sometimes life outside is just stupid, stupid, stupid."

She struggled through her Year Up homework with an older, outdated computer in her mother's home; finding it incompatible with some assignments, she stayed after hours and worked in the tech room at Year Up. Marisol surprised herself with her own persistence. Growing up, it had always been so easy to slack off. Her mother did not force her to go to school when she didn't want to. She often found herself doing the bare minimum in classes. She could not remember having any sort of goal until now. She and

Manuel needed a better life, and they had to get out of that neighborhood. Year Up was their chance. "I'm still after that laptop," she vowed. "Though they probably just wish I'd shut up and go away."

In East Harlem that morning, Taleisha had begun her long day's journey at six, washing and getting into her professional clothes, which she tried to lay out for the week on Sunday nights. This left more time for getting her son up, fed, and ready for his day, making sure she had her homework, MetroCard, and cell phone, hoping that the balky elevators would carry her down the twenty floors. It was always a good idea to build in time for the frequent mechanical breakdowns that propelled her down the stairwells amid working neighbors huffing and cussing through the day's first, exhausting challenge.

At least mornings did not find Taleisha struggling with stroller, groceries, and young Jared, who was being cared for in the apartment for the time being. Since he was born on April Fools' Day 2007, he had been in seven different day-care centers.

After another morning's marathon, Taleisha sat in the break room, "just exhaling a little" between classes. The increasingly cold weather made her a bit tense, she admitted. Winters are always harder if Jared catches a cold or virus: "He has very bad asthma. He's had a lot of trips to the hospital for that since he was about three months. I have it too. I know how to take care of it, but his is more severe. He has the breathing machine, the backups. But it's very scary."

She had been alone and barely nineteen when she first knew the terror of hearing her boy struggle to draw breath. She had found that there are so many asthmatic children in Harlem, the emergency rooms have special respiratory triage. "They're pretty fast—if you can make it to the hospital fast enough." Though she had vowed never to live in public housing after her mother had moved them from a shelter to a city complex in Queens when she was a small child, she was trying to make the best of what had become her only option. And she had a goal: "We're going to be out of here by the time my son is five. I promise him."

In the housing complex, she talked to no one and invested little. There were a lot of troubled lives stacked up in those towers, and things flared up constantly: "There are always fires in the building, and I have to rush down with my son in the middle of the night. No one in my building knows who

I am. I didn't want anyone to know who I was. I just kept it me and my son all the time. It's a lonely journey."

But since September, things had changed, at least in the Year Up classrooms on Exchange Place. Though she still described herself as "a very private person," Taleisha said, "I actually made the most friends here that I have in my whole entire life. At my old job, they knew me because as a foster child, I grew up there in the agency. At school no one knew me. I kept it that way. I was always like that since I was a kid."

Foster care offers some hard lessons about making attachments, whether to foster parents and siblings, to schoolmates, or to neighborhood friends. Anything can change at any time. From age eleven, when she was taken from her family, Taleisha had practiced a shrewd risk assessment in deciding whom to speak with—and how much.

Even with the most loquacious, bubbly applicant to Year Up, there are conspicuous silences and gaps that admissions staffers look and listen for. After nearly a decade of working with urban youth and managing a crisis hotline, Charmaine has learned to be vigilant. Even though half of mental disorders begin by age fourteen, they may remain undiagnosed until young adulthood.

"Even though half of mental disorders begin by age fourteen," she explained, "diagnosis and treatment often come later. Diagnosis is harder at a younger age because of things that didn't show up earlier for developmental, biological, or environmental reasons. Transition, any kind of change, can be a trigger. For example, you see a lot of emotional and behavioral issues in college students who are newly away from home and pressured. The onset may seem sudden, but the root causes have probably been present for years.

"When we're interviewing students with gaps on their applications, we ask about it. They'll say, 'Oh, something happened and I had to come back home.' They're being cryptic, but you know there's something there. Sometimes, even though we might have had a hunch about some past trauma or instability, we still admitted the person, and we have to play it through. Other times you just can't see it coming. Even with this class we've had two young people who left because of major psychotic breaks."

Charmaine and her staff are well aware that there are limits to our intervention and help. We don't ever want or expect our staff to take on student challenges for which they are not equipped. We have social workers and clinical psychologists who are well trained in supporting our students through some of their most difficult times. The staff adviser assigned to each student is trained to know when to bring in the experts. One early incident in Boston showed us the consequences of trying to take on too much. Marcelle* was slipping back into heroin, and one of her instructors was doing all that she could to support her—including believing all of the lies that a heroin addict can tell. She was counseled not to engage with the student and to leave this to our clinical psychologist. Sadly, she didn't listen and got personally and emotionally involved to the extent that she burned out and had to leave our program.

Taleisha had risk factors. But she arrived with recommendations from coworkers at her social services agency. She was forthright about having run away from foster care to Georgia, where she was born, just before she "aged out" of the system at eighteen. "I always had a dream to go to Spellman College there," she explained. "Somehow, I thought I could make that happen." She came back when she learned she was pregnant, in the nick of time to have her baby in New York and qualify for medical care while still in the foster-care system. All this she explained in her admissions interviews and essay. But there was something else she did not speak of—not until this very moment, she said quietly.

"I kept a lot of things in, and that—mentally—was no good for me. At the agency we had therapists and I would just stare at them and not talk. I was nasty to a lot of staff, I admit it. I could be awful and put people off, just so they'd leave me be. So no one really knew why I wasn't with my mother—that I was being molested by her boyfriend—why I was alone all those years, in foster care. And how much I missed my brothers. But it builds up."

Taleisha's foster mother was still very much a presence in her life, a woman who seemed to have a special empathy for this silent, hurt, and angry girl. She kept warning her that her silence was dangerous. Taleisha recalled their constant clashes before everything fell apart: "My foster mother is a very tough woman. She just never gave up on me, she was like, 'I need to work with you more.' And I respected her for that. She always would tell me, 'It's just a matter of time. You're going to explode one day.' Because I would never speak to anyone. She said, 'I'll be here for you, but you need to talk to someone.' There are times I would come in and just look drained, fed up. She'd give me that lecture and I'd go upstairs and completely ignore her. And she was right, and she was the one that was there for me at that point."

Taleisha had just turned sixteen. And she found herself suddenly, finally, unable to cope—to go to school, to engage with the outside world, to "put one foot in front of the other."

"I just felt, I can't take it anymore. I ended up putting myself into a mental hospital. I volunteered to put myself there because I was very depressed. I had completely broken down. I was just angry. I broke a lot of things in my room and I was screaming at my foster mother, 'I just want to go. Just take me, please.' And she drove me to the hospital. I stayed there for about two months—long enough to make me realize I really didn't need to be there."

Taleisha laughed at the reverse logic; she had to check herself into the psychiatric ward to realize that she was okay. It was all relative: "It opened my eyes. Hearing other people's stories and how they got there, seeing a lot of kids that just completely lost it and couldn't take what was going on anymore.

"At first, I figured it would be like my safety net and someplace I could just be quiet and be myself. But I didn't want to stay there. I have so much more that I want to accomplish. I wouldn't talk to any therapists there either, and that was one of the reasons they kept me longer, because I wouldn't speak. But I talked to the patients there. And that's what helped me get through the whole process. It was an instant thing. As soon as I got there, everyone was telling me their stories. It just came out.

"From hearing their situations, I opened up more. It's kind of what happened here. I realized it could be a lot worse. I was like, 'This is not for me. I don't have to be here.' I think I just needed to speak to someone. Now I think that therapy—good, real therapy—is a good idea. I think that if I had spoken to someone all those years I wouldn't have thought about going to the hospital."

There was something about the "safe vibe" at Year Up that made Taleisha feel okay about being a bit less cautious and reserved there. But holding things closely is such a lifelong habit, she couldn't help but feel that sharing her story during orientation was some sort of out-of-body experience. "It was very weird, the milestone thing. I never would have thought that I would have stood up at any point and told my whole story. That day, as I started seeing people writing things on the chart I was, 'Okay, I think I could talk about why I'm here.' And that didn't exactly work out. Because as soon as I said something, tears just started coming down. I guess that was kind of my out-loud diary, and it was very invasive at that point. Yet I volunteered; that's what made it weird."

The craziest part, she thinks—*good* crazy—is how tight and supportive LCM became in just a few days as a result of the mutual revelations. "At first, everyone was sitting around in a big circle, nobody wanted to talk, and it was, 'Okay, I'm just going to do this program and get it over with.' Once that day happened, everybody was like best of friends. There was a really big transition."

She looked down at her fingernails, which were clean and well trimmed but unpainted, and gave a mock shudder.

"I haven't gotten them done since I've been here; that's more for financial reasons. I've gotten feedback on my hair. They said it was very strict and pushed back. I looked stern. I get feedback on my facial expressions as far as I'm always looking so serious. They said, 'You come off as stern. You want it done this way and that's it.' I can be like that, but I'm like, 'Wow, that's how you view me?' It was an eye opener. I don't want to put anybody off in the workplace—or scare them."

Taleisha smiled. "Better, right? It's not hard. I just have to think about it more."

Friday feedback is a fixture across all Year Up sites, a set time for students and staff to assess the week's performance, exchange comments, adjust attitudes, bestow compliments, and communicate frustrations. It has been a part of Year Up's DNA since the outset, another of the communication tools our start-up team learned from Boston nonprofit Teen Empowerment and customized over the years to best serve learning communities as they mesh and mature.

Friday feedback, delivered with staff and students seated in a circle, is a respectful transaction that emphasizes positives and frames negatives as "growth areas." It goes this way:

"I'm Tiffany, and I have some feedback for Brian."

Feedback donor and recipient must look directly at each other. Wording is crucial. Weaknesses or bad habits are presented as "growth areas." And whenever possible, they are preceded with a measure of legitimate praise: "On the plus side, I feel you are really doing well in IT, and the fact that you always have your hand up or you're yelling out answers says you really understand it. What I think is a growth area for you might be to tone it down just a bit and give others a chance to speak or ask questions. If the rest of us aren't catching on to a concept as fast as you are, it can be kind of intimidating, you know?"

Both rise and shake hands—with eye contact and a "thanks" from the recipient. Reaction or rebuttal is not permitted; feedback is not a debate but a well-intended, caring observation. The standards for interaction are the same, whether it is student to student, student to staff, or staff to staff. Trust is built on transparency and in the relative safety of a "family" circle.

Taleisha thought that feedback—formally on Fridays, but part of the warp and weave of most any day—worked well in LCM. "If you're honest and respectful, the feedback is taken the right way. Being brutally honest—that's just hurtful. It does no one any good."

Despite her solitary life, she had had some experience with group dynamics and the responses they can churn up—both rational and emotional. Before applying to Year Up, Taleisha worked as an administrative aide at the same social services agency that oversaw her as a foster child. She was assigned to a program for noncustodial fathers, a domestic issue she is well acquainted with.

"There's no relationship with my son and his father. I tried to have him go to that program because he wasn't ready to be a father. He was not willing to try. I feel the program made a lot of progress with a lot of young fathers. They came in very angry and not wanting to try. For a lot of them, participation was court ordered, so they were very resistant. At the end of the program there were a lot of 'thank yous' and 'You changed my life' kind of things. I saw a lot of success stories."

Andres Gomez was one of Taleisha's caseworkers—it was a tough go as both recall it—and once he left the agency to work at Year Up, he tried to persuade her to try the program. Taleisha was reluctant because she and Jared needed more than the Year Up stipend to get by. But soon her agency wages were in jeopardy.

"I felt my job was going to let me go because they had a budget cut. They let a lot of people go. They put me down as a temp, which took away my benefits, so it was time to move on. Just as I was going to give two weeks' notice, they ended up laying me off."

She fell down a bureaucratic rabbit hole—months of dead ends and endless subway rides with a squirmy toddler, trying to keep them both afloat: "I had to rush to apply for public assistance. That was a very terrible experience. I had food stamps before, but PA is way different. The process of applying is very hard. They set it up to make you feel defeated, as if you don't even want to apply anymore. There's a lot of nasty employees there, always losing my documents—so they claimed. It was hectic. And because I got laid off, I lost the voucher for my day care. So I had to take my son with me to those offices. He would get cranky. We were there one time from eight to four."

Then it was up twenty flights shouldering Jared, stroller, and a long day's humiliations—and up the next morning to do it again. The process of applying for public assistance took from July to September. During that time, and even after Taleisha got her Year Up acceptance, she had to make daily visits—on time, every weekday—at a job search center on 135th Street that turned up . . . nothing. The command appearances got more and more expensive and stressful with Jared in tow. He was finally done with diapers, which had been a huge expense on their tight budget, but he was still not fully trained, and the facilities in welfare offices were often not clean, functional, or available.

"Because of lack of income for transportation, it was hard to move around and make sure that he was fed. And clean. He had the training pants—those cost fifteen dollars for just a few, and it was a lot. I finally got public assistance a couple of weeks before I came here. They pay for my rent and give me money and food stamps. That helped me balance coming here—that and having my son cared for at home."

It took time, concentration, and perseverance to get through the Year Up application process as well. In as many as three face-to-face interviews and in a personal essay, applicants must show us that they are truly interested in the subject matter we teach. We need to see that they are motivated to make a change in their lives. If the applicant comes in with a challenge—be it single parenthood or homelessness—he or she must have a viable plan for getting to class and the internship in a timely and consistent way.

Taleisha met all of those criteria. She explained her situation fully in her essay, which telegraphed the sort of determination admissions interviewers look for: "Currently my son and I reside in New York City Housing. This is a place I feel no child should be raised. My community is flooded with drugs, addicts, alcoholics and teenagers that carry guns. When I lived in the projects with my mother I vowed that I would never return even though this was a financially smart idea, I cannot and will not stay here forever. Being that my son is only 3 years old he doesn't see the things that I see once we leave the comfort of our apartment and I refuse to wait around until he does."

Though Year Up is an educational program recognized by the City and State of New York and with college course accreditation from Pace University, it was problematic for Taleisha to convince her bureaucratic inquisitors that she should not still be looking for a job every day. "They still wanted to send me for interviews, and I kept telling them, 'I'm in school now.' It took about a week with the documentation to get approved—and then I was here. It's stressful and a lot of work—which I expected. But I believe it will be worth my while at the end."

During break time before professional skills class, Cassandra was remembering her own exhausting paper trail. To be able to work, and later to apply to Year Up, she needed to replace the documentation lost in her separation from her parents. She had been supporting herself with low-wage, off-the-books jobs, but that green card was the key to any kind of real career. She didn't know where to start, but at an age when many girls were plotting logistics for the junior prom, Cassandra took on the tedious and confusing documentation process: "I called immigration and just asked questions. They told me I could send to Jamaica for my birth papers, so I called my cousin in Jamaica. She got copies and sent them to me. I got a passport and paid the replacement fee for a green card. It's supposed to be three months, but it took me a year. I kept calling immigration. I booked appointments at the Federal Plaza. I went and asked about the holdup. They told me that I needed my court documents since I had got citizenship through my mother. I made another appointment, brought them, and within a week I got the green card. Finally I could work on the books to support myself. Altogether it took four years to become me on paper."

The "me" within, she said, "that very bruised creature," found a cathartic outlet during these difficult, nomadic years. "I had stopped going to church for a couple of years because of the experience with my family. But I found another place—not a Jamaican church, a Pentecostal church in Brooklyn. That's my other place where I can release everything. I pray. I sing—I used to be in a choir. Now I mime."

YouTube has a lively roster of performances by energetic "mime teams," young adults, chiefly in Pentecostal churches nationwide, who act out sermons, scriptures, and spiritual music, sometimes in the traditional mime whiteface and white gloves. Cassandra was part of a groundswell of young churchgoers joining these interactive worship modes: mime teams, praise dance groups, drama ministries. Both Devon and Damien had enjoyed miming performances within the East Coast network of Haitian churches their grandfather helped found. The brothers knew the best dance groups; they played music, danced, and sang in a shifting set of groups themselves.

Many miming and dance groups have team names: Insatiable Praise.

Vessels of Honor. Whispers of Praise. Some troupes have steps tighter than the Motown dance moves of yore; others use the balletic movements and waving flags of a gymnastics floor routine. A well-choreographed, expressive performance can bring a congregation, hollering, to its feet. Cassandra never paid much mind to the audience; she just went somewhere else, she said—somewhere very pleasant and nonjudgmental.

"It's something that comes naturally. I love miming because it's expressing yourself without words. And whenever I can, I dance. With music I release my mind; I don't think about my situations. What I try to do is get into so much activity to get away from reality and my problems. I did modeling, theater arts, everything. I do community service with the churches. Your problems don't necessarily go away, but if you keep a life outside them, they won't eat you alive."

She laughed and said there was an added, if unexpected benefit to her time spent at church: "There is a nice older woman who worships there. She has a washing machine in her house. She lets me come over and wash my clothes. I'm sure I would be crazy if I could not keep clean."

The long, gray day was working on a few people in Randy Moore's business communications class. Called gently back to the proceedings twice, a brooding student named George* snapped back: "I'm just not into it today. Please don't ask me to explain."

Class went on, but as the students settled down to a writing exercise, Randy summoned George out into the hall; neither was smiling when they returned. A midclass intervention with an inattentive or disruptive student is rare and never involves a reprimand so much as an "Are you okay?" As we define it, "strong support" means that someone is looking into the eyes of each student every day. If an instructor feels there is a serious problem, he or she will alert the student's site leader and adviser.

More common complaints are quietly tended to. An exhausted student working a night job might be directed to a lounge for a rest; an IT instructor will quietly hand off a sandwich to someone who has not eaten since the day before. Noticing one normally outgoing student sitting hunched and silent, Charmaine found that he had been suffering for days with a roaring toothache and no access to dental care. At a young age, Sharif had become the "man" of his household, with heavy family responsibilities. But he just looked young and scared as the pain grew intolerable. Charmaine took him straight to a clinic, where she was able to get the torment eased, the tooth treated, and Medicaid coverage reinstated for his entire family. His mother had been baffled by the forms.

Sometimes a bad day is simply that. George spent the remainder of class turned away from the discussion, staring into a blank computer screen. Immediately after dismissal, as students filed into the corridor, Damien swooped behind George and draped an arm around his shoulder. "Sup, man? Wherever you are today, I bet I've been there." He drew him into an alcove for a quiet talk. As he did so, the hint of a smile played at George's mouth.

"Damien, my brother," shot another friend walking past, "you are *infectious.*"

It was an apt use of a new vocabulary word. Plenty of times, Damien has earned gentle reprimands—from his instructors, from his site leader, Linzey Jones—for his tendency to burst into song at less than appropriate moments. Damien counters that it's not enough to just sing on Sundays in church. "Tough to keep back the joy within, you know?"

In general, Damien was a study in contrasts; his soft, bright V-neck sweaters, mainly in pastels and light browns, were always accompanied by a precisely knotted tie. A friend with fashion flair had sewed smart leather buttons onto Damien's inexpensive tweed vest for a tony, professional accent. But the shoes were worn and thin soled. Keeping the total look could be problematic. His smile was wide and frequent, but his low moments tended to creep in quietly and catch him by surprise.

One morning, Damien said that he was ready to talk about the issues that had driven his brother so low, the same buried stuff that occasionally blinded him with tears when he least expected it six years after their mother's death. He was glad for the focus required by Year Up and the program's insistence on feedback and constant self-assessment. Left to himself, he tended to let the tougher issues slide.

Sometimes he thought this up and down was a very Haitian thing. In his community, mortality often came too early, health care was always a struggle, and all the "big sicknesses," Damien thought, just wouldn't let them be. In his family: cancer, all kinds. Kidney disease. Diabetes. AIDS. His two cousins, taken in when both of their parents died so young, were "my brother and sister, period. No difference in how we love them." So when they lost their "second mother," Odette, Damien saw that it was a huge blow. "I almost think they were as broken up as we were." So many dead so early on. The Haitian way, he said, is "Just get on with it."

Premature mortality was a striking aspect of all milestones charts for Class Nine's three LCs: parents dying young, lost newborns, childhood asthma deaths, random shootings, relatives and neighbors lost to the wars in Iraq and Afghanistan. Damien was not surprised that he and his brother had both chosen the same dark moment in 2001 to talk about when explaining their chart entries.

"That's when my uncle died. He was one of the pillars of the family, my mom's brother Francois. That's who everybody looked up to, you know, the person that everybody runs to. He was on dialysis. He and my uncle Henri had the same blood type and he was all set to give him a kidney. Francois died on the eve before surgery—he was all prepped and everything. My mother got a phone call. They told us he died and that hit me hard. Soon my uncle Francois's doctor was at the door in tears. It put a setback on the family. It was the very first close death."

His recitation of their mother's diagnosis and decline is much the same as his brother's, but with an added dimension of survivor's guilt. Recalling the point where she had finished chemotherapy and doctors pronounced her scans cancer free, Damien remembered the happy day she shepherded them all to her barbershop. They all stood looking in the mirror together, Odette and her handsome sons seeming more alike than ever because she had just a few short patches of hair remaining.

"She said, 'Boys, we're all gonna get a haircut. I got the same shape head as you all, so we're going to look nice.' I looked at us all in the mirror and that's a time where I felt such a connection. I always had a connection with my mom. We were just laughing together, and that was cool.

"Then after a while she just started getting sick again. She had a cancer recurrence. It roared up at stage three to stage four, boom. That year was terrible. Just me and Devon, messing up. I didn't have many high school credits. I was always running off. Just cutting class, didn't care, ran with the wrong crowd, tried to negate the issues going on at home. I'd leave early, come home late. That's still my motto today. I don't deal with situations. Leave early, come home late.

"When she was in the hospital, I didn't want to deal with that reality. It was really sad—me and my brothers played rock-paper-scissors to see who was gonna go. That was selfish on our parts. It hurts still. When it was my day, I went to the hospital. I was in the room, then I'd leave and walk around. She knew that I didn't want to stay in there. I was just screaming at the sky, 'Take somebody else!' I was so mad. I went into the bathroom, and I cried. I whispered, 'How are we gonna live? Who's gonna talk to me?' Only my mom understands me, like nobody else. Only my mom, I can honestly say that. She's a listener. I'm really holding back, but . . ."

Damien had been looking up at the ceiling for some time, chin tilted upward. When he lowered his face, it was wet with tears that had pooled on his lower eyelids and spilled over. He took a moment to mop up and continued, "We had everything with her. I felt so bad. I beat up myself a lot. I'm recovering now."

By the end of her life, Odette was on a ventilator in intensive care and unable to speak. She and Damien had their own semaphore: "I'd be, 'Mommy, blink twice if you're saying hi back.' She kept on crying, and I said, 'Mom, why are you crying? Blink twice if you're sad.' Or I'd say, 'Mom, I got to go. Blink twice if it's okay,' and she blinked only once 'cause she didn't want me to go. I didn't like staying in that room, but every chance I got I stood by my mom and spoke in her ear, 'I love you.' I said, 'Blink three times if you love me back, 'cause it's three words.' She did it."

The twins weren't the only lost boys after she died. One night their father told them that their youngest brother, by then fourteen, had something to tell them. He had confessed to their father that he was in a gang and smoking reefer. It was, Damien noted, "a little, a baby gang," and the boy soon quit both activities. Typically, his brother Devon had blamed himself for ignoring the little guy, explaining: "I felt it was my fault 'cause my brother got no love from us and he felt like there's no love in the family. He'd reach out and we'd be, 'Nah, you're young.' I never took the initiative to spend time with my brother. I realize that caused him to go somewhere else. Now he's left it, he's on the right path. Now I'm beginning to show him the love. I never used to pray with my brothers. Now I do. Now I'll say, 'Come on, let's hold hands.'"

Though the twins had compared notes after their milestones experiences, Damien was surprised to be told just how far his brother had taken it: "He spoke about the time he wanted to kill himself? Hmmm. I got so mad at him when he did that. He thought I was going to support him, soothe him, and say it's all right. I cursed him out. It hurt me; that hit me hard. You're gonna leave me alone? Who am I going to talk to? I can't vibe with nobody else. If I were to do that, he would have got mad at me too."

Physically they were very identical, but they were so different in their response to crisis and loss. One nearly killed himself from pain; the other held the hurt at arm's length and, when the darkness rose at home, ran like hell and came home late. Since they had been at Year Up together, albeit in separate LCs, Damien said that he felt their fierce connection more than ever. And he was determined that they would both make it to graduation this time. Devon hadn't had enough credits to walk the aisle with him at their high school and earned his diploma months later.

Damien concluded: "I feel like the way I toughen up Devon is if I don't baby him. With him, I'm always saying, 'Get it together. I'm not playing with you.' If we have to fistfight, I will. I don't want to see myself succeeding alone. 'Cause through our life I always felt Devon had the back end of things. So when I see him now, he's stepping up."

No one knew better how tough it can be. Damien was in the financial operations (FO) track, and by the time he was ready for his internship, he would have learned the basics: public versus private corporations, introduction to risk and return, ratio analysis, how to read a financial statement. He'd learn how to critically assess a business, parse the corporate structure of banks and brokerages, and analyze a business case study. The *Wall Street Journal* was not widely available in Damien's neighborhood, but copies were always on the table in the Year Up lounge. And to read it, there is a whole new language.

"Equity! IPO! I'm all over it. Accounts payable! SEC!"

Let no one say that finance can't be fun. Team exercises ponder the variables and cost analysis in sending "pizza by mail." News videos, documentaries, and articles investigate the bad and the beautiful in finance—from Enron to Ben & Jerry's and Tom's of Maine. Finopoly, an online game developed by Fin24.com, an Internet financial newsletter, draws the student/player into virtual engagements with the markets. Maintaining a healthy virtual credit balance through wise trades creates a lively rivalry for bragging rights as a Rookie, a Suit, or a Tycoon. Call it Farmville for the FO set.

Damien had been making connections. "It's cool to know how this big world really goes around."

A swelling noise and shuffle in the corridor signaled the beginning of another class. Damien melted into the traffic, but he could still be heard singing a venerable gospel hook:

How I got over . . . how'd I make it over?

CHAPTER FIVE
"You Don't Have a Chance in Hell"

Boston, in the Beginning—2000

In her senior year at Brighton High School, Janelle Clark* was working after school in the dietary department at a hospital, assembling and delivering patient meal trays. In her final semester she was sure of one thing: She did not feel ready to tackle college. Her guidance counselor, Kirsty Ludwig, agreed that a wait might be prudent, but Ms. Ludwig was resolute when she called this bright, if shy, young woman into her office: "I feel that you have a lot of potential—and you are *not* graduating from here without a concrete plan for your future." Together they began to search for alternatives.

Wilfredo Pena was getting restless in a basement at Harvard. He was happy to have his job in the mail room. But there were dead-end signs ahead. Wil had just been reassigned from a central, bustling workplace to the smaller, cramped mail room belowground. He was glad that he could take courses at Harvard, but with his limited finances and the restrictions on employee course loads, he figured it would take him about a decade to earn any sort of degree. Wil was excited but frankly terrified at the news that he was about to be a father at twenty-one. How would he support his new family?

Areva Wattana* was a twenty-two-year-old single mother working as an administrative assistant for a group of physicians. She was also filling in with extra hours as a gas station clerk to support herself and her toddler son. Areva was living in her parents' home, but things were getting crowded and tense.

She had managed to scrape up the two hundred dollars for a wheezy old Toyota to get between jobs, but for her family of two, the future was about as iffy as the Celica's tired transmission.

They made a pretty diverse group, surely, and they lived worlds apart within the Boston area. But they all had two things in common: limited opportunities for advancement and tremendous motivation to overcome those limits, whatever it took. Along with nineteen other adventurous young souls of Year Up's Class One, they would change my life—and theirs—forever.

The half year it took for us to find one another was a time of bridge building, brainstorming, and dignified begging. I had to raise funds and a local profile. I had to raise my own consciousness about the individuals we intended to serve. It was a learning curve steep enough to induce nosebleeds—and occasional hand-wringing. And it was the very best of times.

Kate and I had moved back to Boston in August of 2000 with Cameron and Casey, my Year Up business plan, plenty of energy, $500,000 of our own to invest as seed money, and a few names and numbers—mainly business and school connections. We agreed: I would work without a salary for ten years (though later, the Year Up board insisted I limit my unpaid period to six years). As a family, we were well taken care of. But launching Year Up would require a lot more fund-raising. I've never found it difficult to lift a phone handset and make a respectful "ask." So as we settled our family into a Cambridge rental, I began making calls. Lots of calls. After all, I had been away a long time and we needed to cultivate a flock of local angels.

Looking back, there was something miraculous about that early flutter of wings. Within a few months, we would be blessed with a pretty remarkable consortium of volunteers, experienced social entrepreneurs, community organizers, dedicated teachers, brave early donors, and one stupendous landlord—all of whom listened to the logic of our simple plan and said: "Of course. How can I help?"

After a decade of looking across the ocean at grim headlines from America—from the Gulf War agonies to the L.A. riots and the beating of Rodney King, the O.J. Simpson trial, the Columbine massacre—I was heartened to find out how deeply people really do care about fixing what is broken in this country and the amazing lengths they will go to in order to help. Over and over it would be my turn to gaze at the six-figure check from a Boston philanthropist, at the entrepreneur who risked his own credibility by walking me into corporate suites all over town, and wonder, "Why are they doing this?" Since those early days, I've learned countless new conjugations of the verb "to serve."

I had already reached out to Tim Dibble, a managing general partner at Alta Communications, a private equity firm. I knew of him through Scott Donohue, a close friend of mine in London (Scott is now chair of Year Up's board in San Francisco). I had first outlined my program idea for Tim over the phone from London. His initial assessment was one I'm glad he kept to himself at the time: "Gerald told me about this vision he had to serve ten thousand young adults and bridge the digital divide, and I thought to myself, 'You don't have a chance in hell. But I like your spirit and your gumption, so I'd like to see how I can help.'"

The first thing Tim did was to put all of Boston at our feet—literally. Alta Communications then occupied a magnificent corporate suite at the city's premiere business address, the sixty-story Hancock Tower. Tim said that the firm had some office space to spare; why not launch this thing from there? They were also generous enough to share the support skills of a kind and capable administrative assistant, Ann Marie Dangler.

The planning began in mid-August. On a clear day from the fifty-first floor, I could look past the lush lawns of Boston Common, beyond the tourist-filled streets around Faneuil Hall, toward the crumbling low-income neighborhoods we hoped to serve most: Dorchester, Roxbury, Mattapan—definitely the other side of the divide.

We would recruit our students there and train them in the technical skills currently in demand in our local market. We would give them the professional skills to be successful in the workplace, then place them in internships with the best Boston businesses—yet to be determined. Students would earn a stipend throughout the yearlong program. We would meet at least half of our cost per student with what businesses paid for the internships. I had done the spreadsheets and studied what worked—and what manifestly did not—in all manner of other workforce development programs. At its outset, Year Up was far more sophisticated than the version in my business school application essay, but still a long way from what we have evolved into over the last decade.

I knew that to get this new business off the ground, we needed to develop liaisons with potential donors, with corporate sponsors to buy our internships, and with community and educational leaders who could channel students to us. As an experienced businessman, I could tend to that. Kate, who is good at entirely too many things, could pull on a rackful of hats, from fund-raiser to interior designer to student mentor. But who was going to manage the day-to-day operations, from scouting and hiring instructors to buying office chairs and wastebaskets?

From London I had spoken to a young man who was working at a marketing firm in Boston and looking to make a career change; a Bowdoin connection had suggested I reach out to him. Tom Berté explains how he became my first official hire—despite the daunting list of "musts" I charged him with: "My initial reaction was that the idea sounded awesome. I had founded a Big Brother program in my high school, so Gerald and I connected on that front. It was a little hard to understand why this successful millionaire in London wanted to do this. But at that point in my life I was keen to roll up my sleeves and get involved in something. I was all for it. I could tell how serious he was—not just somebody who had a big pile of money and wanted to play with it. He was fully focused, which was important to me. After all, this was going to be my livelihood. I thought he could pull it off—with some help.

"I first met him at Alta. I remember this beautiful setting and out comes Gerald in his cords and flannel shirt. And I'm thinking, 'Gee, he's so young.' We had several meetings. I said yes in August and started in early October. My biggest responsibility was project managing the launch. Gerald said, 'I need to be out meeting people, raising money and building relationships. You need to help me find subject matter experts to bring on board, build out the curriculum, find space, figure out the admissions process, fine-tune the team we needed to get this thing started—and oh yeah, find our students.' So I started as director of operations, and once we were up and running, I would also be director of internships."

Alta Communications was a busy, high-functioning hive, but Tim Dibble always made time to stop by and check in on our progress. Before long, we were having weekly lunches. I was aware that Tim had long experience as a dedicated Big Brother; he knew Boston and the disadvantages that beset so many of its young people. Tim had already served on a few philanthropic boards, including Big Brothers Big Sisters of Massachusetts Bay. But his most thorough education in the Opportunity Divide was via his Little Brother Curtis Blyden, the tall young man of color smiling in the family photos Tim kept in his office.

Curtis was raised in Dorchester and Roxbury by his grandmother. When she died, Curtis was just sixteen and alone. He went to live with Tim and his family in Concord and finished high school there, graduated from Curry College in Milton, Massachusetts, then spent two years in the Peace Corps in rural Mongolia. Most recently his commitment to service has led him to Suffolk University, where he is pursuing a master's degree in public policy and public administration.

With great pride and some worrisome moments, Tim had watched Curtis navigate both sides of the divide, as I had with David. He had come to understand the big issues as well as the small but stressful nuances in that sort of a journey. As Tim explains, "When he was living with us, Curtis could be of neither world—or both. In high school, he was not the white kid who's lived in town all his life. And he wasn't the kid who's being bused in, either. But going back to visit Dorchester, he was not the street kid anymore."

Tim totally got it. Our students were going to have to make similar transitions, over and over. There was no road map, no etiquette guide or safe-passage visa. Quietly, steadily, Tim and his wife, Maureen, gave Curtis the kind of support we hoped to extend to thousands more young adults. The more we talked, the more I began to suspect that Year Up had found a devoted champion.

And so it proved. To date, Tim and Maureen have spent more on donations to Year Up than on anything else in their lives; Tim acted as chairman of our national board for a decade and has always been there to support our mission and our students. Despite how busy he was at work or how many sports teams he was coaching for his children, Tim would always find the time to make a call on our behalf or to stop by the site to help cultivate a prospective internship partner. He has also been an active mentor for many of our students. In every one of those relationships, Tim's mentees have enjoyed a depth of concern and engagement normally reserved for one's own flesh and blood.

Tim is a Vermonter by birth, and a staunch New England loyalist. Having returned from some years working for Alta in San Francisco, he had a serious aversion to the clichéd view of Bostonians as "skinflint Yankees who threw around nickels like manhole covers." He knew it wasn't so, and he was happy to share the good news with a fledgling social entrepreneur like me. In fact, something pretty exciting was happening in Boston. As a young, successful player in that financial community, Tim had an insider's view of how newer forms of social entrepreneurship came to flourish in that old Brahmin bulwark by the bay. His observations confirmed what my research had been turning up.

Across the country, American philanthropy was in the throes of a sea change. The first big wave had formed just before 1900—the Boys and Girls clubs, Big Brothers Big Sisters, YMCA. That had been led by Mellons and Rockefellers and has been perpetuated over the decades by stalwart family, community, and corporate foundations. That model had dominated the philanthropic landscape for most of the twentieth century. But by the late 1980s, there was a second, nontraditional swell growing in Boston and elsewhere. It was a kind of giving that went beyond classic endowments and donations for building wings. Tim sees the Boston development this way: "There is a new generation of philanthropists here who are staggeringly generous. Most of them do it very quietly. But they're not hesitant to get really involved—this generation of donors is an active one. They are generous with their money *and* their time. From the eighties until now you had this incredible wealth creation at a very narrow end of the market—wealth of such a scale that people can't spend it in a lifetime. They want to do something different. These progressive philanthropists said, 'I'm not just going to give money for Harvard. I want to *do* something. Surely there are different ways to look at this.'"

Many of these newly minted fortunes far outstripped my good luck with Conduit. These donors were partnering with new agents of change, social entrepreneurs using business strategies to solve stubborn societal and economic problems. It's a dynamic, catalytic philanthropy with a mind-set focusing on growth capital, maximizing impact, and getting more personally involved in a cause with one's time and money. They were talking about scaling, retention, success metrics, and "venture philanthropy." Asking for spreadsheets and financials, they were vetting a program's potential for growth and sustainability the way they might when kicking the tires of a for-profit investment.

As they began investing in entrepreneurs and ideas, these individuals began to change the face of philanthropy by showing what's possible with all this wisely invested new money. Think about it: Forty-one trillion dollars in wealth will be transferred to the next generation between 1998 and 2052 through trust funds and other forms of inheritance. There are going to be a lot of young people saying, "Where do I get my philanthropic cues from?"

Many of us have looked to the Ashoka Foundation for some of those answers. It's certainly considered the beginning of this new wave. Founded in 1980 by Bill Drayton, Ashoka is a global association of the world's leading social entrepreneurs. Bill is a lifelong social activist, as well as a talented lawyer and management consultant—clearly a deft practitioner of integrated skills. Way ahead of the curve, he understood that many solutions to the world's deepest problems could be found in an activist citizen sector, and he set out to build it. Over thirty years, Ashoka has become a mighty engine for change, supporting social entrepreneurs and connecting them with forward-thinking funders. I'm now honored to be one of two thousand Ashoka Fellows in sixty countries. But I wouldn't have dreamed it possible during those start-up months in our borrowed office at Alta.

Boston had its share of innovators in social entrepreneurship, and I quickly made it my business to look up some of the boldest innovators in the field. The work of Alan Khazei and Michael Brown, roommates and 1987 graduates of Harvard Law School, had made a deep impression on me when I was doing my research. Both had passed up lucrative enticements from white-shoe law firms to cofound a nonprofit known as City Year in 1988. And I certainly agree with Tim's assessment of their contribution: "Alan Khazei started to break the mold. City Year's biggest contribution is that it started to change the dialogue in this community and others about how people viewed social entrepreneurship."

Tim was pleased and proud when Curtis became an employee of City Year. It is a youth service group dedicated to training and organizing young adults seventeen to twenty-four to give a year of service to their communities. Its bold premise—that young adults should commit a year's domestic service to their country—caught the eye of President Bill Clinton in the early nineties. Soon City Year became an inspiration for the federally sponsored AmeriCorps, the community service program that has deployed nearly half a million volunteers nationwide since 1994. They have employed their talents on everything from building affordable housing to teaching computer skills, improving early childhood education, cleaning parks—whatever local need was most pressing. They now focus much of their energy on keeping teenagers from dropping out of high school.

I made a cold call to Alan early that fall, and I couldn't have gotten a warmer response: "Sure, come over to City Year, I'd be pleased to meet you!" It's a testament to Alan's initial kindness that I now spend a few hours each week speaking or e-mailing with budding social entrepreneurs in need of advice. I realized later that I was one of scores of cockeyed idealists who showed up at City Year for advice. But Alan's focus and his enthusiasm made it feel as though I were the only one.

I loved the feel of the place the moment I walked in. The space that City Year shared with the Red Cross at 285 Columbus Avenue had the air of a campaign office, buzzing with earnest, purpose-driven young staff. They wore their red City Year jackets and their commitment with evident pride. I'll admit I was initially taken aback when Alan sat me in a room with a television, snapped on a video about his program, and walked out. But in the few minutes it took to play, I was captivated. I got a sense of the organization's journey to this point, its core culture, and its mission. When we sat down to talk, I had a long list of questions, more practical than philosophical. I was after some viable how-tos. I had a toolbox to fill.

Alan didn't disappoint; he spoke about the necessity of building a strong, deeply involved board and the importance of developing and maintaining a culture within your organization. He asked me, "Are you willing to try and learn everything that there is to learn about your field?" I'm not sure I realized at the moment that answering in the affirmative meant making a lifetime commitment. And I guess I made my case for our mission. Soon after, Alan wrote a strong recommendation letter for a much-needed grant we were seeking from the Boston Foundation.

By then, the "we" included me, Kate, and Tom. One of Tom's first assignments was to find a home for Year Up. From up in the glass tower, I wondered what kind of office and classroom space we might find in the catchment area for huge urban secondary schools like Brighton, Chelsea, East Boston, and Dorchester High Schools. We had already looked at some possibilities. But the notion of where to lease our bricks and mortar changed radically with the arrival of our second hire, a tiny and talented MSW with outsized energy and a ferocious passion for service: Linda Swardlick Smith.

How can I do her justice? Linda is a magnificent, radiant soul. She is always "on duty" caring for others—nights, weekends, holidays—no problem, Linda will deal, calmly and compassionately. Her support for our students is unconditional. And because she has such deep respect for them, she holds them to correspondingly high standards. Students know they can call Linda when they need her—and they understand and accept that she will also call them out when necessary. Tiny as she is, I have seen her face down a huge ex–high school linebacker, crane her neck to meet his eyes, and demand the truth: "I smell pot. Have you been smoking?"

She'll fight until her last breath for a struggling student but she is never a soft touch or an enabler. Drug and alcohol abuse is not tolerated, but everyone will be offered access to counseling and treatment resources in Linda's calm, nonjudgmental voice: "I'm here to help you solve this problem."

From our first meeting, Linda was pretty clear about what she considered to be meaningful work. I'll let her tell you what she was thinking when she agreed to come and talk: "I had been leading a nonprofit job training program for thirteen years, but then went into the for-profit sector. I knew my heart was in the nonprofit world, so I needed to go back. I wanted to be working with people who could get opportunities to give them good, livable wages."

One thing I realized straightaway: Linda had no middle or low gears when it came to social and economic justice. And if she was going to channel her crackling energy into a program, it had to be something that could really make a substantial change in young people's lives. I described the mission, and she really did seem to brighten as I spooled it out. I think I had her with "high expectations, high support." Luckily for me, Linda could see way past the modest beginnings I was proposing. We discovered that we were both big dreamers: "What Gerald described was very simple, straightforward, and an idea that could blossom into something that would be fulfilling to work on. And we could see that ten thousand people could be impacted. I didn't see it in the business plan, but in the dream—as something that could be reached with the right amount of work, team building, and the appropriate players. It was very exciting to think about that."

I knew Linda was the right person for us in terms of skill and soul. Although she started as a contractor, she came on as a permanent employee in February. At that point in her career, Linda had seen and done enough to formulate her ideal job description. She's since fulfilled it—and then some—at Year Up. Over a thousand of our Boston graduates have gone into the world carrying a piece of her mighty heart; as director of student services for Year Up Boston, Linda is still the first smiling face at the top of the stairs that greets arriving students every morning.

The love and respect students have for her goes beyond her obvious warmth and caring. She helps them get places. Linda's brand of advising became the template for our student support system. I learned from her that truly good, effective advising is about helping people learn how to solve problems for themselves. I've watched Linda many times as a panicked student comes into her office and says, "I got kicked out of my house last night. What do I do?" My early instinct would have been "Ohmygosh, let me start calling the housing authority." Linda begins with a saner, safer square one: "Do you feel okay?"

She'll assess how the person is, then tell them, "I want you to go to the Internet. Look up these three sources that might help with a place to stay. Call them and have a conversation and report to me what happened." She'll sit there with them as they make the calls and sometimes puts the conversation on speakerphone so that she can give them feedback about how to handle the next call.

Looking back, I cannot overemphasize her contributions. A few years into the program, I designed a survey that asked students to rate all the main elements of Year Up (from classroom work to feedback, internships, professional skills) in terms of how important each element was to their success. I also left a blank space in case students wanted to mention something that was not on the list. Forty percent of the respondents wrote in Linda as the number one reason for their success in the program—and said that the encouragement, coping skills, and reinforcement that she offered made the biggest difference.

Linda's requisites for taking the job should have tipped me off to the quality of support services she would offer our students, many of whom had little or no family or professional guidance: "I told Gerald that I would come on board if I could be the director of heart and soul. I meant that very seriously. I wanted a promise that I would never be put in a box. Which means that I could always be very creative in my thinking. There's so much to create for the program, we can put our heads together and think about unfulfilled potential."

Linda had another firm imperative we didn't quite agree on at first. I was determined to locate Year Up right in the middle of a low-income community. At that time it made sense to me to serve students in their own neighborhoods—it would be fitting professional training and accessible to all. I didn't question my logic here; Tom and I were still looking at rental possibilities in those areas when Linda walked into my office and sat down with a composed, determined face I've come to know very well. She began: "I think we may want to consider the value of locating Year Up right downtown, in the financial district, where the businesses are located and the environment is professional. Businesspeople will be much more likely to come visit if we are closer to them, and these are the folks we need to give our students internships. From day one, our students will get used to coming to a professional part of town, and they will have their heads held high as they walk into a professional building. It's all part of the transition they are making."

Just weeks on the job and Linda was asking me to reverse engines. I had already envisioned myself taking the T to Dudley Square every day and serving young adults in one of the tougher parts of town. It was the mental model I had held since my decision to start Year Up—probably born of my understanding of the insular life in David Heredia's public housing complex. If that population was conditioned and constrained to staying put, of course I'd go to them—and give them the skills passport to venture into the wider world. Also, like our prospective students, we hardly had downtown rent money. Tom and I had looked into possibilities near the financial district; the costs were just prohibitive for a start-up nonprofit.

I was prepared to argue with Linda, but her logic was tough to fault. For over a decade, she had run a training program for low-income women located in an office building right downtown. She had a damn sight more experience in this business than I did. And she pointed out another important aspect of the population we hoped to serve that I had completely overlooked. As Tom remembers: "Linda helped us understand that it wasn't going to be just one type of student. We had to accommodate a pretty diverse population. Latino students from Eastie and Chelsea may not want to go to a program in Dorchester, and vice versa. By suggesting the area known as Downtown Crossing, where all the metro lines come through, Linda saw that we could be accessible to all groups and avoid both inconvenience and territorial issues."

Tom and I were sold; since that day we have also made sure to locate all Year Up sites in viable downtown districts that put our students at the very center of the job market they hope to enter. I learned so much more from that early adjustment than just where to best locate our program. I've said it over and over during this long, unpredictable journey: I didn't know what I didn't know. At least I was getting better at recognizing that fact.

The search for downtown space turned up another real estate angel named Danny Levin. A Boston real estate broker, Chuck O'Connor, put me in touch with Danny, who owned several buildings downtown and was willing to let us take a look at Ninety-three Summer Street. It is just two blocks from the Downtown Crossing metro station, in an area with a lot of older commercial buildings and close to the heart of the financial district. It could be a perfect triangulation, assuming I could sell some internships with the big financial institutions anchoring Congress and Federal Streets.

Many of the Summer Street buildings had been converted into artists' lofts above existing ground-floor businesses. The fifth floor of number ninety-three was then occupied by an artist, a high school friend of Danny's, and her husband. Danny so believed in the project that he moved his friends out and offered us the space at a reduced rent—at considerable personal cost. He is without question the best landlord I have ever had, and we developed a great relationship over the years as we expanded in Ninety-three Summer Street to take the entire building.

That fall, we agreed to lease the top floor beginning in early March, expecting three months of renovation to convert it into classrooms and offices and get it ready for our first class in early July. Tom was responsible for getting the space ready, with a large assist from Kate, the world's best project manager. The help we had from Danny every step of the way was an unexpected but welcome blessing. As Tom says, "He is beyond—way beyond—landlord." Like so many other people around town, Danny had become a friend and advocate. Small acts—"let me call a few people for you"—led to great and lasting partnerships.

Case in point: a nonprofit power lunch that yielded amazing dividends. Soon after our return to Boston, I was at the offices of WilmerHale law firm talking to one of the partners, my estate attorney, Jennifer Snyder. We had just wrapped up that oh-so-uplifting conversation about who gets what when you kick the bucket when Jennifer said, "You ought to meet with my partner Marty Kaplan. He'll like what you are trying to do."

Marty agreed to meet with me, listened to my hopes and aspirations, flipped through my forty-page business plan, and said, "How about I hold a lunch for you? There are a few people I think you ought to meet." Two weeks later I was at the table with Marty and Pam Trefler, head of the Trefler Foundation, Deborah Jackson, a senior executive at the Boston Foundation, and Stanley Pollack, executive director of Teen Empowerment, a local nonprofit.

I don't remember what we ate, but in the end I pushed away from that generous table with more phone numbers and a huge takeout portion of goodwill. Pam Trefler and her husband, Alan, became our first six-figure donors—$100,000 a year for three years—and Pam served as a valuable and generous board member for the next six years. Deb Jackson helped introduce me to the Boston Foundation, which gave us a significant start-up grant with added benefits. The foundation's support was a seal of approval in Boston that would encourage others to work with us. Stanley Pollack would challenge and educate us in ways I'd never imagined. At the outset, I had the feeling that Stanley might have had his reservations about our chances of success. Maybe I struck him as pretty wet behind the ears. But that didn't stop him from taking our start-up team under his wing. Over the next three months, he schooled us in the youth-development techniques that he had honed over more than three decades' work with the young people of Boston.

All of these relationships proved invaluable. We owe it to one man who met with me for less than an hour, then decided to act. And Marty Kaplan kept on giving: WilmerHale became Year Up's attorneys and over the past ten years has donated countless hours' worth of pro bono legal services, and one of their insightful senior partners, Peter Handrinos, joined our board.

Richard Dubuisson and I have laughed many times at his audacity in applying for our first instructor's position. I'm so grateful that he took the chance. It's hard to imagine our first decade without him. He is a tall, Duke-educated Haitian who showed up magnificently mismatched with our job description—at least on paper. But Richard is warm, deeply talented, and persuasive. Through several interviews, it was a single sentence that resonated. Richard made an intriguing promise that I was convinced he'd make good on: "Gerald, I am going to end up being the best teacher you ever had because *I've been your student.*"

His story is indeed our students'.

"I was born in Port-au-Prince in 1972, grew up in Haiti, and moved to Miami in 1985, when I was thirteen. I went to a public school in Miami. I always got great grades, but because I didn't speak English I was put back a year into seventh grade. So in eighth grade I got into some trouble adjusting with my peers. My mom said, 'You're going to take a test at the Catholic school in the Haitian community.' I aced it and I got a scholarship. That school, Archbishop Curley Notre Dame High School—right in little Haiti—changed the course of my life. They were college prep. I was a top-ten student and ended up going to Duke.

"But I saw the difference between my life and my brother's life. He stayed in public school and saw his guidance counselor once in the three years he went there. My guidance counselor was my best friend at Curley. I was in her office all the time. That experience stayed in my mind about support and guidance for a young person and what that can lead to.

"So went back to Miami and started teaching. I tutored first, for fifteen dollars an hour. The teachers at my old high school noticed that all the students I tutored, their grades were significantly improving. So that summer, 1996, I was offered a job as a summer-school math teacher. And I caught the bug. I loved it; I was good at it; I related well to the students. The next year I taught algebra, trigonometry, and geometry.

"My fiancée, who is also Haitian, had family in Boston and wanted to come back here, so we did. I worked at Head Start, where I taught a computer course for parents of the children enrolled—Word, PowerPoint, and all. Then I found work as a corporate trainer at Gateway Computer. I wasn't happy there. I saw a posting for the position at Year Up.

"I had the job description on my computer at Gateway for over a month, thinking I'd never get it. They specified that they wanted an experienced teacher/facilitator to work with urban young adults and lead the education program. It required five to ten years' experience. The salary was advertised at $55,000 to $75,000 a year, more money than I'd ever seen in my life. A master's degree was required. I thought, 'There's no way I'm qualified for this.' But when it said, 'working with urban young adults,' I said, 'That's me. I can do that.' So I applied."

I read Richard's résumé and noticed the corporate training position at Gateway, which registered positively. We were going to be teaching young adults computer skills as a means to change their lives. Richard had not yet received his degree from Duke, in large part owing to some student debt that he needed to clear. As we got to know each other better, he told me about growing up Haitian in Miami and the searing prejudice he endured from African Americans. It was so painful that he changed the way he walked and totally rid himself of his accent—chiefly by watching a lot of TV and practicing "American" enunciation. Once I knew his story, Richard drove home his pitch: "There are some key people in my life—my mom with the kick in the butt and my guidance counselor—who saw my potential. Without those things I would never be here. So I know exactly what it will take for us to be successful."

I liked him, and I respected his honesty. We hired him in January 2001.

A month after meeting Stanley Pollack at Marty Kaplan's lunch, I visited him at his office at the Center for Teen Empowerment (TE) in the South End, where he shared his field guide to that mercurial and often misunderstood being, the urban teenager. He had a simple question for me: "What are you going to do if your students show up late for class?"

I looked at Stanley, not sure what the right answer might be. "Well, I'd ask them politely not to do it again, and please be on time from then on."

"And if they aren't?"

Hmmm.

Clearly, we had a lot to learn from Stanley. TE's stated mission is "to empower youth and adults as agents of individual, institutional, and social change." They help young people, and the adults who work with them, identify the most difficult social problems in their communities and give them the tools they need to work positive changes from within.

This takes in everything from delicate gang détente to learning how to talk—really talk—to your mother. TE helps mold dedicated young community organizers, who learn how to negotiate, mediate, and inspire. And Stanley is the first to tell you it's often not pretty. He understands youth development as well as anyone I have ever met, and through his hard work and dedication he has made a real impact on Boston's young people. He loves them with all his heart; he interprets their language and nonverbal signals with accuracy and compassion. He is also unsparing in his zeal to reeducate any adults in need—like me.

"I'm telling you, Gerald, lateness is a huge issue. You have to come to terms with it right away."

Not until we fielded our first class did I truly understand the very real difficulties young adults can have with time management and being punctual. Lateness infractions have always been a Year Up challenge nationwide. Often the problem is compounded by the fact that many of our self-supporting students still hold jobs while they are in the program, on after-school, night, and weekend shifts. And then there's simple biology. Nationwide, school districts have debated and changed high school start times based on research showing that biologically, teenagers are less able to fall asleep early. Puberty and its hormonal changes reset teens' circadian rhythms or internal clocks, pushing the onset of sleepiness as much as two hours past the 8:00 to 9:00 p.m. bedtimes of childhood. They stay up later and find it difficult to focus in the early morning. Unfortunately, starting later just isn't an option for a program preparing students to enter the workplace.

Beyond biology, there are psychological and emotional factors involved as well. On this issue and so many others, it was Stanley who explained to me that at their stage of life, young adults need to feel powerful. We need to provide them with functional ways to feel their strengths. Otherwise, he rightly told me, they will seek dysfunctional ways to feel powerful. Lateness, truancy—case in point.

Clearly, we had a lot to learn just to speak to our prospective students in a respectful way that got them in their seats on time. A formal contract, Stanley suggested, was a fair, noncombative arrangement that could be acceptable to both sides. Sign a contract that you can remain in the program only if you show up on time every day, and understand that if you pile up enough infractions—clearly stated in that contract—you effectively fire yourself. Your decision, no scolding, no judgment.

I was struck by the simplicity and mutual respect in such an exchange. We decided at that meeting that I would bring my team over every Friday from 9:00 a.m. to noon to be trained by Stanley in the art of using his system of feedback and contract, which became an essential element of Year Up's cultural DNA. I used to call Stanley all the time for informal advice as well, and he was always generous with his time. He also introduced us to his number two, Doug Ackley, who conducted some of the training sessions as well, and continued to train Year Up staff in years to come. Much of what we do today to help our students build mutual trust, communication skills, and support comes from Stanley's original techniques.

Beyond TE's well-honed communication tools, we all agreed that we needed to learn as much as we could about the population we intended to serve. How did they view themselves? What did they want from life? What were they willing to do in order to make a desired change? We had to start meeting prospective students and asking questions. Our listening tour took us all over town; it had its awkward moments and helpful revelations. Linda got the ball rolling: "We started talking to what I called the ambassadors, people that young people trusted—teachers, social workers, counselors, school principals, church people. Our ambassadors helped us identify and reach these young people. Then we had friends who would lend us the site to meet with them. We'd invite them for pizza and ask them lots of questions.

"We started to see people from El Salvador and Cambodia, Vietnam, students from new immigrant families that really understood the work ethic. And we also saw people who grew up in the city who said to themselves, 'I can do better than this. I don't have to work at dead-end jobs. I don't have to be selling shoes or working at Dunkin' Donuts my whole life. But I don't have the skills that I need.'"

When we asked them what they wanted from life, what kind of future they envisioned, their answers were as basic as the Bill of Rights.

They wanted to be part of everybody else's mainstream.

They wanted to be making good salaries at good jobs.

They wanted to be the kinds of parents that their own children could be proud of.

They wanted a good life.

How reasonable, and for so many of them, how very far out of reach. We were encouraged by their hopefulness; if we built the bridge, they just might come. We may have had to lure them in with pizza, but once the conversation was rolling, it was clear that we had a tremendous talent pool with the kind of motivation that would help them—and Year Up—succeed. Linda recalls: "I saw resilience and perseverance. It was very clear that they wanted something better for themselves. They wanted a different kind of life; they could see themselves dressed up, going to work; they saw themselves as responsible adults—they didn't see themselves as people that were just going to be a statistic. They knew that there was hope and opportunity, and they came to us with a foundation of goodness and of kindness, caring, and sensitivity.

"We knew that we could work with them. They had a real sense of solid sensitivity that not everyone else in the streets had. There was a sense of 'I can work hard toward something. I understand that you're going to put me through a very rigorous admissions process, to prove to you that I really want this.' We had made it clear that there was a limited number of seats in the first class. They clearly understood—'We have to prove to you that we will be resilient about obstacles.'"

I had a few things to learn about resiliency myself. By early 2001, I had landed some internships with the dot-com concerns we would train our students to serve: Razorfish, Sapient, Viant, Scient. I pitched my heart out for a product that was untried, untested, and not even occupying the chairs on Summer Street yet. Some days, it was like swimming in the Charles River wearing lead trunks. But we made some sales. As the deflation of the dot-com bubble continued to take its toll. I was as close to discouraged as I ever get. Then another lunch yielded a new champion in the astonishing, passionate person of Craig Underwood.

Wiry, scarily energetic, clean shaven from skull to chin, Craig was just the driving wheel to get me out of the very tough spot I found myself in early on. He was—and is—intense, in the best of ways. Here was a former partner at Bain and Company, an international consulting firm; he was then a successful entrepreneur who had left his business briefly to head south and take over the final political campaign of his father, Cecil H. Underwood. That gentleman was distinguished by having been the youngest man (in 1956) and oldest man (in 1996) elected governor of West Virginia. By virtue of his precocity, young Governor Underwood was the first-ever guest on the classic TV quiz show *To Tell the Truth*. This lion in winter lost his last election in a squeaker at age seventy-eight. Clearly, this was not a tribe of quitters.

Back in Boston after the campaign and pursuing a new business start-up, Craig wanted to explore other ventures. One issue that he had focused on with his dad's campaign was closing the digital divide in the poor Coal Belt state of West Virginia. He had proposed taking rebuilt computers from government and businesses and providing them to low-income students, along with free Internet access. Craig's own children were then three and four, and he saw what they were learning with easy access to computers; it just wasn't fair that poor children were being left so far behind. His previous nonprofit experience was with a preschool for homeless children. With that work, Craig had spent plenty of time with families in Boston shelters. He still had some sort of digital divide issue in mind when we crossed paths. Here is how he remembers that day and the whirlwind sales campaign that followed: "I came back really wanting to get into the nonprofit world, and I met Vanessa Kirsch, who was just starting New Profit, a venture capitalist foundation to invest in nonprofits. She invited me to one of these brown-bag lunches with Gerald, two other social entrepreneurs—and twenty people like me. I have ADD, and those meetings are hard for me to sit through. So I blurted at one point, 'Look, you're all great, we want to help you, but we don't know how. Let's imagine if you had a magic wand, what's the one thing we can do for you?'

"I forget what the other two answered. Gerald said, 'I have this model. I know it will work. I know I can get a great staff. What I don't know is whether I can place my students because I built my business plan when the dot-com boom was happening, and it was all built around teaching students

HTML coding and placing them with Internet companies. But those companies in Boston have just laid off half their staff, and they can't take the interns they committed to. To place my students I need contacts outside the Internet world.'

"So I think, 'Well, maybe that's something I can do.' I called Gerald and we had breakfast. He took me through the model. He said that the four pillars to bridge the Opportunity Divide were education, experience, guidance, and support. Everything about the model—paying students to go to school—made perfect sense. I loved the fact that there was a revenue stream [from the internships], and the students would actually earn the stipend Year Up paid them. As a businessman, that was very attractive to me. I had no idea whether you could teach urban young adults with only a high school degree or a GED technology skills in six months—but I believed in this guy and I wanted to get involved in that space.

"So I helped him write a sales deck. I'm an ex-Bain guy, so I'm pretty good at PowerPoint. Anybody I knew or met, I bugged them until they gave us a meeting. I combed the Bain network, my daughters' school network—the parents. Anybody we met. If I met you at a party and I thought there was a chance you could take an intern, before I went to sleep you'd get an e-mail from me.

"On the sales calls we made, Gerald would say, 'We'll guarantee you that the students will be trained to do HTML coding.' I had no idea what that meant. I eventually took a course to understand what it all was because I don't like to sell things that I don't understand."

Craig would also end up on our board. I look back on our road-warrior sales calls together as challenging but tremendous fun. After one long day I told him, "This better work, Craig, or we'll be shagging code together." He looked at me blankly and said, "I have no idea what that means." But shoulder to shoulder, we got those first twenty-two internships sold. Some of the very senior Boston executives Craig walked me in to see: Phyllis Yale, head of Bain & Company in Boston; Brett Browchuk, senior executive at Putnam Investments; David Kenny, CEO of Digitas. Based on Craig's introduction and boundless support for both our program and me personally, each of those organizations became founding corporate partners of Year Up.

Our first goals were modest: a single site in Boston and a first class of twenty-five or so with a faculty of five or six; we would think about scaling once we were satisfied that our basic model worked. As we developed the curriculum with Web design and HTML capability, plus business and professional skills, we also heeded Alan Khazei's advice about creating a strong, recognizable culture with a clearly articulated mission and ethics. We would come to call them core values. They hang on posters nationwide, printed and standardized in signature Year Up blue (Pantone color 661) and gold (color 131), in corridors and classrooms at all of our sites. Holding to these values is also part of our student contract. We asked ourselves what should be important to us as a community. There in our borrowed space at Alta, a handful of people were trying to lay a foundation that dozens—then thousands, we hoped—were going to have to live by.

Everyone made a list of ten things, and the value that turned up on all of them was respect. We should all, staff and students, be working in an environment where everyone respected one another, themselves, and the work we did together. The other most frequent thought on everyone's list was fun. That element would prove essential for a student body conditioned to just the opposite. The majority of our applicants would be coming off four stultifying years at overcrowded and underfunded, understaffed city high schools. Many of those who had managed to enter community colleges would be languishing in the uninspired remedial courses required by their lack of readiness.

Essentially, this widespread systemic failure was forcing them to pay—and pay dearly—for a fifth year of high school. We found that 83 percent of our Boston students tested as needing remedial mathematics. Nationally, 42 percent of high school graduates who go to community colleges are stuck in at least one remedial course. Generally, the broad-spectrum, generic aspects of remedial courses make them even more tedious than the substandard high school versions. Going into debt to buy an even dustier version of what public education denied you can be dispiriting and humiliating, and it's fundamentally unjust. Needless to say, fun is not on the syllabus for remedial English and math.

That doesn't have to be the case. We would find great success teaching English and even algebra in some of our learning and development modules by employing terrific teachers who understand and communicate *applicability*. It's easier—even fun—to master the fundamentals once you're convinced of their relevance to your aspirations in life. Even in those early months, we understood that preparing students to learn with a receptive attitude would be critical. We knew we could generate fun with a fabulous set of instructors and the right set of behavioral "musts." After much debate, we came up with five core values that have served us well throughout our growth:

RESPECT AND VALUE OTHERS

BE ACCOUNTABLE

BUILD TRUST AND BE HONEST

STRIVE TO LEARN

WORK HARD, HAVE FUN

Anyone walking by our classrooms and hearing peals of laughter coming from a highly technical session on quality assurance testing will see that the last value listed here is truly not a contradiction in terms. Six years into the program, we would go through some difficult yet essential soul-searching to add a sixth and essential core value: Engage and Embrace Diversity. We'll get to that interesting process in due time.

By late April, renovations had begun on the Summer Street space and Tom and Kate were combing auctions and closeout sales for desks, chairs, and other office equipment. Later Tom would rue his skill at collecting the bargain inventory as he loaded it all, piece by piece, out of rental trucks, into the building's back elevator, and up to the fifth floor. I had impressed upon Tom the golden rule of start-ups: If you can possibly do something yourself instead of hiring someone, do it. I realized this might well find me with a paintbrush in my hand, but I'd stand up to that core imperative—accountability—if and when the need arose.

By midspring it was also time to get serious about recruiting students to fill those chairs. We had to introduce ourselves to greater Boston. We had set a late May due date for applications. Linda was reaching out to community leaders and guidance counselors whom she knew to help get the word out, and we were able to put a PSA on a local radio station.

It was at one of our early dog and pony shows—Linda dispatched us in relays to make presentations at churches, schools, and community groups—that Richard and Tom met Nikki Patti, who would be our fourth hire. She was a bright and earnest twenty-two, just out of Boston University and teaching writing in a youth to work initiative that she and a friend had started. It was under the aegis of the Daniel Marr Boys and Girls Club, a forward-thinking nonprofit in Dorchester. Tom, who would have the good sense to marry Nikki six years later, recalls: "Richard and I were going to present in one of her classes. We saw Nikki teaching, and I was thinking, 'Wow, we could start her as an office manager,' which we needed, 'then move her to faculty since she's got so much more potential.'"

Nikki liked what she heard when Richard and Tom did their presentation: "It was the first I'd heard of the program, and it was so needed. It was addressing the problems I was seeing in my classroom at the time. The Daniel Marr program was a mini version of a Year Up, four weeks of classes and six weeks of an internship with the most basic skills. None of my students applied to Year Up, but I was enthralled. I went in and spoke to the whole staff at the time."

That included me, Linda, Richard, Tom, and Lauren Dunlay, a gifted volunteer instructor who kindly spent a year teaching IT courses for our first two classes. We hired Nikki in May, the same month we asked the leaders at City Year if we could use their large open space to hold our first major open house. Their answer was an unequivocal yes. City Year had a large, tiered seating structure in a spacious room that was perfect for speeches and presentations. It reminded me of "speakers corner" in Hyde Park, the crowds milling by, some stopping to listen, as citizens from all over could stand on a wooden soapbox and make whatever point they so chose.

We waited nervously at the appointed hour, hoping to draw a sizable crowd of young people curious about this new opportunity. Soda and chips stood ready on a side table, and each of us had our role to play. Linda, ever hands on, was literally canvassing the area beforehand, darting in and out of places like the nearby Starbucks, prepared to haul likely looking candidates in one by one if need be. About twenty young adults came that evening. And once the conversation began, it all felt so alive. It was really happening. Hard to tell, looking out at our audience. One young woman, Janelle Clark, looked as though she'd rather be anywhere else. She sat in the corner reading a book, barely looking up during the entire time that she was there. "I was just watching the clock, waiting for it to be over," she confessed a decade later. "They really had nothing to show us that this thing would work, though they clearly seemed to believe it would."

What we couldn't know was that Janelle also had a deep-seated fear of speaking in public. "That's what had me in a panic mode about college," she'd explain. "I thought, 'I can't be in a lecture hall with a hundred students trying to learn. It's going to freeze me up. I'm not going to ask questions in front of a hundred people.'" That day at City Year, as others participated in a discussion, it was easy to categorize Janelle's closed expression as disinterested or aloof. But this was not the assessment of the guidance counselor who had sent her to us. Not so either for Linda and Nikki, who later made a case in an admissions meeting for the promise and potential they both saw in her.

Slowly, and with great deliberation, we filled our first class roster of twenty-two places. While the renovation was still going on, a few students came up to Alta for their initial interviews. The Hancock Tower was a symbol of opportunity. But walking into the building through its revolving glass doors, presenting one's identification to the security guards—that did not happen all too often for the young men and women we serve. Years later—and three thousand miles away at our site in San Francisco—a young woman named Racquel, a twenty-two-year-old single mother now working at Wells Fargo, explained the feeling common to so many of our students: "Before my internship, I had never even set foot in an office building like this. Never even came to this part of town my whole life. That San Francisco was, like they say, shining on the faraway hill. I didn't feel it was open to someone like me. And suddenly I was right here, Miss I-can-handle-it Tech, serving 1,500 help-desk clients."

The lobby security at the Hancock Tower hadn't seen the likes of our applicants either. On one occasion I remember one young businessman in Alta's reception area looking quizzically as I came to greet one of our applicants at the front desk. His expression read: Am I at one of Boston's most well-respected venture capital companies . . . or is this the local Boys and Girls Club?

Our admissions process was not about high school or community college transcripts, SATs, résumés, or even proper grammar. They needed a high school diploma or GED, yes. But for an organization that would thrive on keeping and displaying excellent metrics, the selection criteria were astonishingly intuitive. In that first class, we actually called it a kind of magic.

"We could just feel that," Linda recalled. "We could sense that they had an inner strength that we could work with in the right structure. But we had to provide that structure, that very safe environment, a trusting place where there was lots of support—what we called overlapping circles of support. Lots of people were around them in terms of mentors, teachers, counselors. And all of us would work toward helping that person."

Linda had drawn those circles on a whiteboard in the planning phases, with an overlapping system of advisers and mentors to provide extra layers of support. Call it a blueprint for No Student Left Uncared For. They needed to feel that we all noticed and cared deeply that they showed up every day, that we were willing to go and capable of going way, way beyond a syllabus and an engaging instructor to make sure they were able to learn.

"Want to get paid to learn?" The announcer on Areva Wattana's favorite radio station, Jammin' 94.5, was delivering the PSA that Linda and I had written. The voice went on about free technical instruction with a stipend and a six-month paid internship at a top local firm. Areva was on her way home from work at a doctor's office, stuck in traffic on Columbus Avenue. She pulled over as quickly as she could to write down the Web site, Yearup.org.

Wil Pena wrestled with the decision to apply for some time. He had struggled to get his early childhood education in his native El Salvador; there was no one left willing to take the places of all the teachers who had been killed on the job during that nation's bitter civil war that began in 1980 and raged for more than a decade. Schools were bullet pocked and shuttered. As a small child, Wil knew that even to walk upright in his village was to risk being cut in half by automatic weapon fire. Despite language difficulties after his family immigrated to the Boston area, Wil had made it through high school and found the job in a mail room at Harvard University. He explained how he decided to take a chance on us: "I was still miles from earning any sort of degree. And at work things were getting worse and worse. My son had just been born, so I said, 'I've got to get out of here.' I heard about Year Up, looked at the flyer, and applied. It was a pretty rigorous process and there were all these promises—go through the program and doors are going to open. I was very suspicious. It definitely looked too good to be true.

"By that time, I was making enough to live on at Harvard. That was okay; I was doing better than other people that I know. But if I left, the Year Up stipend was like half of what I was making. I really took a flyer. I combed through their Web site, saw what they would be teaching. In the interviews I asked as many questions as I could, trying to get a sense if it was something legitimate or not. It was a huge risk to leave something I was complacent with."

———

I'm not sure any of us got a decent night's sleep on July 8, 2001, despite the fact that all five of us, plus Kate and a stalwart crew of other friends and family, worked down to the wire to get the place ready for opening at eight thirty the following morning. We had scrambled to get a city inspector to sign off on our certificate of occupancy. The fire department suddenly wanted carpet samples. Long after dark, Kate was still scraping gum off the floor. And as others seem to remember, I was seen making desultory swipes with a paintbrush at one windowsill for hours.

We were all lined up to meet Class One the following morning. Just a month out of high school and so nervous that she passed the entrance of Ninety-three Summer Street three times before finding it, Janelle Clark came breathlessly up the stairs. Curtis Blyden, on hand to help us out, leaned in and whispered to her: "Get into the classroom—now! You can't be late your first day."

They were all on time. Nikki, who recalls having the blithe "no problem, I've got this one" confidence of youth, had long been designated to deliver opening remarks. She remembers: "When the students came in, they were wonderful. And nervous. They knew they were the first class too—so we were all starting this new strange trip together. I was the first person to speak, since I'd been teaching for a bit. Thirty seconds in, I realized I had no idea what was coming out of my mouth."

Our calm, capable Nikki was blathering a bit; but within a minute she lost that deer-in-the-headlights look and managed a warm, cogent, encouraging welcome. Everybody relaxed. Sort of. And for twenty-two brave, motivated young adults, the year up had begun.

CHAPTER SIX
Don't Lose It Now!

Class Nine, Early January 2011

The skirt was short, the legs long, and the temperature in lower Manhattan struggling to reach freezing, but there came Cassandra, huffing into the lounge area a split second before 8:30 a.m.—without proper stockings and wincing at what she knew was to come. Bare legged! And it wasn't the first time. The lapse in professional dress would earn an infraction and some help. Charmaine looked at her watch and wondered when she could find ten minutes to run out and pick up a pair of L'eggs.

It was deep into a vicious, record-breaking Northeastern winter; January also brought the challenges of "third mod," the final learning and development module before students would be assigned their internships. Students were bearing down in their various tracks: financial operations (FO), information technology (IT), and, new with Class Nine, quality assurance (QA). Work was more demanding, the stakes were raised, and outside the Year Up offices on Exchange Place, the snow mounds were shoulder high and filthy. As on most of the downtown side streets, uncollected trash bags reached nearly to the building's second floor. Dress shoes would have been perilous; everyone was clomping around in professional dress and snow boots.

Cassandra had no decent snow wear. She was repentant about the stockings but clearly too stressed to have remembered everything in a hasty packing job. Unexpectedly, she had had to stay somewhere else the night before. Housing was still iffy; safety concerns had led her to move to another relative's home in Connecticut. She had been commuting to lower Manhattan from a tired old industrial city on a railway that ran on a balky, century-old overhead wire system. At sunrise she wedged herself between grumpy stockbrokers and Madison Avenue ad men. And she was having to pay nearly thirty-five dollars a day for the torment: late trains, cold cars, few available seats, a stink like a stock pen.

What with constant train breakdowns and a stipend dwindling from infractions and commutation costs—even with some extra transit funds from Year Up—getting to class on time was a daily rat race, and her contract points were dwindling. Buying lunch was often out of the question. "There are pressures," Cassandra explained. "Always more and different, but pressures. I'm holding on. But it stresses me out."

Classes were going well when she got to them. Her grades in business communication and in her technical classes were excellent. She was well liked and attentive to her colleagues. Somehow, she was getting her homework done, but she often looked tired. Crystal Fields-Sam, our New York office's director of corporate engagement and internships, had taken an unprecedented step and approached a corporate partner about the possibility of a small grant for housing, and the company had enthusiastically agreed. Arrangements were in progress, but it was still too soon to mention the possibility to Cassandra. In the meantime, Charmaine and Andres kept checking the youth shelters for openings. Given the bad winter in New York— economic indicators seemed to slide with the mercury—the supply was short and the wait lists long.

Across the river in Brooklyn, Devon sat with a printed essay in front of him on the table, thinking about his recent ups and downs. The essay was part of his required "recommitment," the exercise in self-assessment that happens when a student's point total falls below one hundred. Devon was dangling precariously at around fifty with four weeks to go.

"I fell below a hundred due to lateness," he explained. "So I'm supposed to do my recommitment now, in front of my QA class. I'm not ashamed. I'm not scared. 'Cause it was a given, me falling there. I was to the point where I started not caring again—just like in high school. But I was like, 'No, I'm not going to do that again. I'm not going to give up.'"

Devon wasn't the only one teetering. A concerned classmate had said to him yesterday, "Call Steven." Devon reached him very early this morning, and he could hear the downturn in his friend's voice right away: "Steven told me, 'I don't feel like coming no more.' I said, 'Come on, you came too far. It's like four weeks left. Don't quit now. Even though you've gone below a hundred points, you're going to quit *now*, allow yourself to fail *now? Push. Push.* Be on top of your classes.' He's like, 'Thank you for calling me, and I'll see you today.' I said, 'See you early?' 'Yeah.'"

Devon took on a lot of other people's burdens—too much, his brother thought, always trying to fix things for everyone, making it his business to make other people feel better. About a month into L & D, Devon had explained this tendency himself: "I always want to please somebody. Make sure somebody feels happy. I'd rather feel sad to make the person happy. But it doesn't have to be either/or. I realize that now."

That became clear once he found his place here amid his fellow strivers. Here was a time and a place to work on himself. Working on his own motivation and happiness was something his adviser from church had been suggesting since Devon's depression nearly killed him. "I get it. That's what it means, my year up. I've decided now: Let me get happy first. It's good to make myself happy. I'm always stretching my neck out for people. My spiritual mentor told me too: 'Learn to love yourself. 'Cause if you don't know how to love yourself, where's the gain? You're giving out love, love, love—but you have no love for yourself.' I never looked at it that way. So we decided— 2010 was the year to get myself in order."

Still, there was always time to make those motivational calls—just a little more neck stretching. Steven had made it in, on time, as promised, and Devon was there waiting. They hugged in the cloakroom. Steven was informed that today's wake-up and motivational call was courtesy of a triple ping around the horn: Malik to Devon to Steven.

"Whatever it takes, man," said Devon. "Whatever."

A few moments later, when Devon stood at the front of the room at the start of quality assurance class, some LCW tough love came at him like the downtown express. His recommitment statement was well delivered and full of generic vows to step up ("I realize I have to focus"). His site leader, Wil Velazquez, who had come to support him and hear the essay, asked Devon's classmates whether they had some more constructive and specific suggestions. Silence. Wil shook his head.

"Really? Nobody? I know you have some ideas to help Devon. This is not about hurting anyone's feelings—it's about keeping him here with us and making it to the finish line together. Anybody?"

Hands began to flutter upward.

"Get more sleep, Dev. Just turn off the Internet and go to bed."

"How about you plan your bathroom trips better so you don't have to miss things in class all the time and come back in saying you don't get it?"

Shante hesitated, then raised her chin, locked eyes with Devon, and let fly: "Just don't do this! Don't lose it now! We've heard all this before from you, but now there are four weeks left. We're here for you, all of us. So use it! We've got your back, Dev. You know we do."

She had hit home and she knew it. Wil thanked the students for their honesty and willingness to help. Class began and Devon tuned in to the day's plan as outlined by Raphael Crawford-Marks, a smiling, red-haired Californian much admired for his accessible teaching style and his refreshing perspective on this excessively cruel winter. He had recently transferred to Brooklyn from the Bay Area Year Up site.

"It's so great—I love this. I actually made snowballs yesterday." A demonstration of snow angel technique followed, and students still thawing their feet were smiling.

Born and raised in the San Francisco Bay Area, Raphael had not seen snow since his college years in Massachusetts. He was used to more temperate zones, having worked as a health educator for the Peace Corps in Honduras, developing AIDS information and support groups throughout that nation. A peek into his résumé sketched an accomplished thirty-year-old who met the Year Up standard of committed heart and mind—a talented teacher and technician with a strong instinct to serve.

Before he came to Year Up, Raphael had developed a sophisticated database for the San Francisco Department of Public Health—and found the time and inclination to provide Spanish translation for patients at a tuberculosis clinic there as well. Going out with clinicians on patient visits changed his perspective, and with it his career trajectory. He explains: "Clinical workers go out and observe patients taking their medications, because it's a long course of antibiotics—six months—and it has to be adhered to properly or it won't work. It just opened my eyes. I was seeing parts of the city I grew up in, places I had never seen, with levels of poverty and health crises that I had never imagined."

After that experience, Raphael had gone back to work in the private

sector at another Bay Area tech firm and found himself missing the direct human contact from his years as a Peace Corps educator: "I had fallen in love with teaching, but I still really loved technology and being a geek. I just didn't know what to do with these two very divergent things. I didn't know how to reconcile them. Then I saw posted on craigslist a job at Year Up Bay Area, which merged tech and education in this nonprofit that was empowering people economically—in a very effective way. It just seemed kind of perfect."

Get the right people in the right chairs. . . .

Raphael could easily have been pulling down six figures in a hard-charging Silicon Valley start-up. But it's worth noting that he strayed off the conventional path at age sixteen, when frustration with high school led him to take and pass his GED exam, leave school, and work at some entry-level tech jobs before enrolling in college in Massachusetts. His first instructor's experience was as a teaching assistant at Hampshire College's School of Cognitive Science. Raphael's thesis: "Computational Evolution of Teamwork and Strategy in a Dynamic, Heterogeneous and Noisy 3D Environment."

That mouthful might aptly describe LCW here as they team up to learn the basics of QA—running an array of tests on new software before it is implemented in a corporate framework, sorting out bugs, glitches, and clunky interfaces. This is essential for any corporation rolling out new software programs for internal use or for clients. Undetected, one coding hiccup can literally cost a financial institution millions. And new applications are being implemented constantly.

At present, QA is taught only at the Bay Area and New York sites; the curriculum expansion was a result of listening to the needs of corporate partners in both cities, JPMorgan Chase, Deutsche Bank, and UBS in New York and Mozilla, Wells Fargo, Alibris, and Salesforce.com in San Francisco. Bill Lehman heard their wish lists and "pain points." He is Year Up's national site director, a silver-haired sixty-three-year-old who has "tried to retire" twice before, after thirty years as a management and technology consultant—twenty-seven of those years at Price Waterhouse. He had been serving on Year Up's New York board and lending his deep Rolodex to help enlist more corporate partners. Asked to help recruit candidates for a new national position, he applied for the job himself and promised to stay "at least five years."

"My problem now," he says, "is how am I going to stop in five years? This place just gets to you." Bill generally "hits" two Year Up sites a week, with a lot of corporate visits in between. Since he is based in New York, he is a familiar sight dashing into the Brooklyn and Exchange Place sites or accompanying Crystal and her internship team to meetings with corporate partners.

"My job," Bill said, "is to do whatever I can to support the executive directors in each site, to counsel, advise, and coach them, from operations to staff to corporate engagement. I continue to use my Rolodex—and those of my friends—to work on the large accounts that could have multiple site commitments, like JPMorgan Chase and UBS."

As chief cross-pollinator, Bill brought his information on QA needs to the attention of Michael Brownstein, national director of academics and programs. And once the decision was made to create a new QA curriculum, it made sense for experts in the field to develop and teach it. We looked to our academic leaders Sid Ross in New York and Jessica Cogan in San Francisco to block out a curriculum. The instructors who led the development were Juan Carlos Vazquez in San Francisco and in New York, Raphael Crawford-Marks. Raphael had been teaching only IT in Brooklyn when we asked him to handle the expansion to QA. For a seven-week course, he needed lesson plans, software, syllabus, quizzes. Corporate partners' wish lists had helped tweak a list of core skills to be taught. But it was up to Raphael to put it all together—and quickly—in time for Class Nine's third learning module. He recalls a feverish few weeks that summoned that techie adrenalin he knew so well: "The fun thing was that I got to go back into that mode when I was working in start-ups in the Bay Area, getting all these technological solutions up and running as quickly as possible. Because I'd worked in QA I knew what was available. I went for open-source software that was industry standard that we could get up and running that wouldn't cost us anything. So our students are using free and open-sourced tools that are also standards for some big companies. It was a whirlwind, but it was also really challenging and engaging. And fun. I'm pretty proud of what came out of it, and I'm looking forward to revising and improving it."

Both Malik and Devon were under Raphael's tutelage in a class of sixteen, learning to track defects and to plan, develop, and execute both manual and automated tests. "Raphael is a pretty great teacher," Malik opined, "of some pretty deep and complicated stuff. It always seemed like a conversation, though—not a lecture. I felt we were all in it together, so it was fun. Not many days when we didn't find something to laugh about." The curriculum sections fell into neat if challenging sections on test plans, bug reports, test

metrics, and a welter of acronyms such as "FSD" (functional specification document).

There were some tough slogs uphill as Class Nine compared black-box versus white-box testing and peered into the thicket of the "traceability matrix." Raphael is not above bribery. He offered his QA students a modest but enticing proposal: If the class could keep its quiz average above ninety, he would risk the last shred of his pedagogic dignity by doing the dougie, a dance popularized twenty years ago by rapper Doug E. Fresh, recently revived and gone viral with a retread hit that beseeches: "Teach Me How to Dougie." Basic dougie requirements: rubber joints, snake hips, and a liberal dash of funk. Let's put it this way: Rapper Chris Brown looks great doing it. When teen heartthrob Justin Bieber tried to teach Barbara Walters to dougie? Have mercy.

So far, Raphael did not seem worried.

Notice: January 14 in Brooklyn, All LCs Present for Internship Announcements

The buzz was loud and growing as all of Class Nine filed into the largest meeting space in Brooklyn. The big day had arrived. Crystal Fields-Sam, whose team sells the internships, then matches corporate needs to students, had worked for two months to compile the first list of internship placements; a second set of announcements would come a week later. In this cycle, thirty companies were participating, taking in 103 interns. "Our placement process is really robust," Crystal explained. "We do everything we can to place the right student with the right manager at the right location."

For Class Nine, the process began in November, toward the end of the second learning module. Crystal involves most of the staff having direct contact with the students: "We have the site leaders and my team, and student services. And we have each student's adviser, who's been with them for twenty-one weeks, fill out a scorecard on their tech ability, people skills, and any additional comments that might help. The adviser gets that information from the instructors. We talk about this every week in our LC meetings."

With over a hundred students to place in the most appropriate spots, Crystal said, "It's essential to have the assessment filled out by folks who have touched our young adults and really know them well—we're very particular about that. And my team goes out and surveys the managers."

To that end, corporate managers are asked about those pain points. What are they short on? Which department needs more depth to cover its help-desk queries, trade captures, software testing? At every company managers are also asked what they are looking for in an intern in terms of skill and personality—someone who will mesh well with their employees and the corporate culture. Which traits might work best? Bubbly? A social butterfly? Or a quiet type who just loves "wires and pliers"?

The most workable matches, Bill and Crystal agree, are based on client needs more than any charitable impulse. Bill has collected plenty of feedback from workplace managers and CIOs on his national travels.

"The most successful clients are going to find ways for Year Up students to help them solve a business problem," he says. "One of the most common is high turnover rate in a department. At entry level, they try and hire four-year-college grads who will consider it busywork. They get promoted and leave. That issue was the starting point for our very large commitment from State Street in Boston. Our students are much more loyal; they're so grateful for the opportunity. Instead of leaving in a year, they'll last three or more.

"Another business problem is accuracy rates, probably for the same reason. If it's detailed work that requires a lot of concentration, the college graduate might say, 'Why'd I go to a four-year school to do this?' and error rates tend to be higher. Our students will have very good attention to detail. We know those students who are strongest in that area, and we match them to those jobs in their internships. There are fun stories about our students sitting next to a recent college grad and just shining."

Bill recalled a beautiful "aha" moment in a conversation with Steve Weinstein, the managing director of quality and test management at JPMorgan Chase in New York. Steve has worked closely with Year Up interns and suggested implementing a QA track. "Steve maintained that QA could be done more cost effectively by our students here than by his overseas outsourcer because the overseas operators' error rates were so high. That's pretty cool."

Keeping jobs in America and doing them better with qualified, home-grown talent hungry for the opportunity—what a sensible, workable fix for a challenged labor market.

Bill heard more encouraging testimony from Diane Schueneman, former head of global infrastructures for Merrill Lynch, who also served on

Year Up's national board. "When she was CIO, Diane ran a staff survey in IT at Merrill Lynch, and she noticed that in the functional areas where our interns worked, she got a lot of positive comments from the employees and a big spike in employee morale. It was based on their sense of contributing something beyond just their day-to-day job. It's energizing."

Beyond accurate performance, good job retention and loyalty, and the boost to employee morale, managers have also told Bill that Year Up interns have helped streamline their recruitment process. "If a company can see it as a hiring pipeline, they realize that it's a great way to look at somebody closely for six months. There's no hiring fee; they're already trained and integrated into the company."

In that tense Brooklyn meeting room, another phase of the students' Year Up was beginning. The end process of all the sifting, assessing, and corporate conferencing—internship announcements—is always one of Crystal's favorite days, a Friday afternoon choreographed to generate maximum suspense and excitement as students are called up to take their places on corporate rosters. The reward for five months' hard work is the opportunity to strive even harder in a top-flight professional environment. Announcement day can have the excitement of a game show with a gleaming opportunity waiting behind door number one: *Come on down!*

The room was packed, with interns-to-be arrayed in neat rows of chairs and staff standing alongside with the internship lists in their hands. Bill Lehman had popped in as well, smiling from a back row at a scenario he never gets tired of. A few students were visibly shaking with anticipation. Brief descriptions of the corporate partners and their history with the program preceded each list of names.

"American Express has partnered with Year Up New York since Class Two. To date they have hired five of our graduates, and most recently this partnership has expanded from seven to nine internship seats. American Express is a global payments company. . . ."

A series of rosters were announced: Bloomberg, Citi, Fidelity, GE, and Google. And then Vilma Schonwetter, associate director of career services, stepped up to introduce one of the biggest groups.

"JPMorgan Chase is one of our founding New York corporate partners, a national partner, and our largest partner in New York City. JPMC is one of the oldest financial firms in the world and is the leader in financial services."

She began calling names.

"Marisol Velez!" Flustered but beaming, Marisol made her way up the aisle to huge applause and whistles, especially from LCW.

"Cassandra Jenkins!"

Threading through rows to the front, Cassandra had the slightly dazed exuberance of a pageant contestant who has just won the crown, shaking her long curls, smiling and half crying, and mouthing, "I can't believe it." JPMorgan, $2.3 trillion in assets in sixty countries—with 240,000 employees. Joining Marisol and Cassandra in the lineup were thirteen others; site leader Linzey Jones had taken over the reading of names. Outside Year Up, Linzey is a musician and an accomplished performer. He was having a little fun—and ratcheting up the suspense—by giving hints.

"You always hear him singing before you see him. . . ."

Damien!

As classmates yelled his name, Damien extricated himself from a series of bear hugs, springing toward the front with a huge smile and both palms tingling from all the high fives on his way up. The announcements continued for the day's final corporate partner, UBS. No one was whooping louder than Devon when the UBS roster included his mainstay Malik, who leaped from his chair in surprise and joy.

When it was over, Damien, very visible in a jellybean pink V-neck sweater, tie slightly askew from the excitement, wove through the happy, noisy crowd with a slightly worried look. There were a few more internship commitments to finalize, and Devon had not been placed in this round. Damien knew how things stood with his points. Soon he had his brother in a gentle headlock, whispering encouragements. He'd be in the next round for sure; he was going to nail a solid spot, no problem, no doubt.

Outside on DeKalb Avenue, Malik was at the center of a happy knot of well-wishers; his grin had not dimmed since his announcement. Asked whom he would tell first, he put his hand to his ear in a telephone gesture.

"Oh, you *know* I'm going to call my mother. I can't wait."

By mid-January, all of Class Nine's interns had been placed. Taleisha was assigned to the Department of Youth and Community Development, the New York City agency from which both Executive Director Lisette Nieves and Charmaine had been hired. It seemed a good fit; Taleisha had been talking about combining her new professional skills with her past experience

at the foster-care agency. She surely knew about the issues facing urban youth. Marisol had been switched to Bank of America on a program that would rotate her through a few BOA sites in Manhattan. Devon was headed for a UBS operation just across the Hudson River in Weehawken, New Jersey.

There had been more family worries for the twins; they had been staying with their grandparents, whose home made for a better morning commute. But their grandfather, the bishop, had been in and out of the hospital with a serious illness, and the household was in some turmoil. Amid the worry, though, Devon had battled back—raised his averages and avoided infractions—with LCM cheering him on. Malik was happy for him and relieved.

"This time, you saw the motivation that he wanted to pick it up. Dev told me, 'Malik, I'm gonna get this done. Look at my grades now; I'm not fooling around anymore. I'm gonna walk the walk, not just talk it.' His grades improved a lot. I saw a lot of people, as Linzey would say, step up their game throughout the third mod. They knew internship was right around the corner. You didn't want to fire yourself."

There would still be final exams, essays, team projects, and hard work on the requirements to secure the college credits from Pace University. With all of that ahead, Malik had kept his head down and his eyes on the prize. He had also found time to do some Year Up community outreach work with Mariah Peebles, who was doing a two-year rotation at Year Up as an FAO Schwarz Family Foundation Fellow. The fellowship program is designed to train future leaders in the education and youth development field and to strengthen high-quality, high-functioning nonprofits that serve youth. Its goal: to provide recent graduates with the experiences, training, and mentorship needed to launch successful careers in youth development and education.

Part of Mariah's mandate was to spread the word about Year Up in urban communities. She needed to reach out in a way that could provide an enticing answer to a question born of past failures and disappointments: "What, another *program?*"

Mariah's best fishing companion in these languid pools? A personable, motivated student who had voiced the same doubts just a short while ago. At the first outreach program he helped with in lower Manhattan, Malik was nervous but pushed himself to get past it. "I spoke about why I chose Year Up, how it changed me—I just tried to connect with people that were in the same position as I was previously. I felt that I connected. They asked me about the work, how hard was it. The second one I did was rough."

This was in early December at a GED and college information event in downtown Brooklyn. "I was with Mariah and it was like a panel—other organizations were trying to recruit as well. They would come to our booth and ask questions. Mariah would start it off and I'd talk as well. Then Mariah left me to go to a meeting. I'm like, 'Oh, man.' She left me there for like two hours, thrown into the jungle. At one point I had like six students surrounding me, filling out interest forms. That really convinced me I could just talk to people without needing anyone. That was the first time I ever did something like that—it really brought me out of my shell."

The third outreach session was a homecoming of sorts. Malik volunteered to speak at the very place he had learned about Year Up, Harlem Commonwealth Council. That entrenched nonprofit enterprise was headed by its president and CEO, Dr. Joseph Tait, a respected veterinarian and long-time community activist. His is one of the many grassroots organizations nationwide that guide neighborhood youth to programs like Year Up.

Dr. Tait is a very busy man. Malik's father, a taxi driver, was a good friend who often ferried Dr. Tait between appointments. Shortly after Malik had graduated high school, his father, having already lost one son to the streets, voiced concern about keeping his youngest boy on the right track. Dr. Tait said he was sure he had a worthy endeavor to keep him off the streets for the summer. Soon Malik was acquainting himself with the business end of a rake.

"I was working with the horticultural society, restoring abandoned gardens. Dr. Tait said, 'I'm going to send you to this meeting. It's for Year Up. I'm only going to send four of you guys—make sure you dress professional.'" Everyone did but Malik, who showed up in shorts and a polo shirt. Dr. Tait was not pleased but let him go to the outreach meeting with a terse "Just tuck in your shirt." Mariah Peebles was there with a smile, some printed material, and two students then enrolled in Year Up, Maria Cucuta and Sophia Smith.

"Mariah is great, but listening to the students already in the program and talking to them really put it over for me," Malik recalled. And just half a year later, he and Dr. Tait were photographed together on a day when Malik was the student talking to prospective Year Up applicants. In the photo he is wearing a crisp dress shirt and tie.

"Before, I had no professional clothes. My father is a cab driver and he dresses well for the job, so he said he'd take me shopping. We went the day before orientation. Where did we go? A discount place he knows. He's cheap—I mean, what's the . . . *euphemism*? I just learned that word. He's *careful*. Right. He's budget conscious. So we got some shirts and ties. At first I was getting shirts with the snap-on ties, and I found out you can't wear snap-on ties."

Malik shook his head and grimaced at that bit of naïveté. "I had to get right with the ties. I learned to tie a real one from Ken (Year Up instructor Kenneth Wright) two weeks ago, but I still ask for help because there are different styles. I also tried YouTube."

Full Windsor, half Windsor—knotty problems, both. There are over six million hits on a couple of tie-centric YouTube videos. In this open-necked era of "business casual," Malik found that he was part of a vast brotherhood looking to step up their game in a tight job market. He practiced in the mirror at home and practiced some more. "I suit up and I just *feel* . . . serious. I like it."

Putting together a professional wardrobe is an economic hardship for many Year Up students. We hold regular clothing drives to collect new and gently used business attire—suits, dresses, sport coats. Designer clothing firms (such as Burberry) have outfitted entire classes with new coats and jackets.

Individuals, corporations, and other nonprofits help our students in many other ways. Donated services include tutoring, help with college research and financial aid applications, tax filing, and résumé reviews. All of our Boston students have the option to have their eyesight screened by Vision Coalition and over half of them take advantage of this. We found that 20 percent of those tested couldn't clearly see a blackboard. Necessary follow-up exams and eyeglasses are provided by Massachusetts Eye and Ear Hospital. An airline has given some of our West Coast students free tickets to meet their colleagues across the country. Tickets are donated for sporting events, concerts, opera, and live theater. Professional appearance consultations—for fashion, hair, accessories—are welcome confidence boosters.

Two dozen women in Class Nine, including Taleisha and Cassandra, got a huge boost midway through their L & D phase. They were the stars of a feature story in *Allure* magazine. All received total workplace makeovers, from hair to makeup, nails, clothing, accessories. Jarrod Lacks, an assistant fashion editor, helped coordinate styling and photo shoots over two days. As they were taken, gently, through hair, makeup, and wardrobe, the students shared their stories with a writer. Listening as they worked, stylists accustomed to demanding models and celebrities found themselves in tears.

"It was probably the most amazing experience I've had working," Jarrod recalled. "It was great to see—we had tears, laughs, smiles. You saw it all. The students were so incredibly honest about everything. It's just such a difference when you work with real people."

The magazine staff worked hard beforehand to give the women more to take away than confidence and styling tips. "We got all of the clothing companies to donate the items. We gave them bags and accessories, shoes. They'd go and get shot and when they came off set we would surprise them by telling them that they got to keep everything they were shot in. That was just a joy. We got some great stuff—Tory Burch, Donna Karan."

Jarrod said that shyness was tough to conquer in some cases, but it was not an issue for Cassandra.

"She didn't need any coaching. She put her clothes on and was modeling all up and down. Some were a little more timid. Especially in the dressing process, trying to find the right undergarments. It's hard when you're around a bunch of strangers and your confidence level is not that high. We definitely had to coach a lot of the young women to become more confident with themselves, help them see another side of themselves. A lot of them had never had special treatment. Not ever."

Beyond the excitement of the magazine story, which ran in January 2011, there were unexpected dividends. "We all just fell in love with the entire program and the women," Jarrod said. "Everybody fell in love with it. Even our market editors came to the shoot and they never do. Then we got invited to a Year Up banquet. We had a great time. Everybody just embraced the entire idea."

Siobhan Bonnouvrier, the magazine's style editor, became a Class Nine mentor. So did Jarrod, who was paired with Damien. Cassandra said she took away "the memory of an amazing, a fantastic day—such kindness." She also loved the vibrant tangerine dress chosen for her. "They saw who I was right away, I know it," Cassandra said. "Not just the girl with her clothes always in trash bags."

A week after the final set of internship announcements on January 14, students reported to their "on boards," workplace meetings with corporate supervisors and managers. These sessions included introductions, instructions, office tours, drug tests, fingerprinting, sitting for ID photos. When the supervisor at JPMorgan Chase called, "Cassandra Jenkins," no one answered. And when she finally showed up, late, for that very first corporate engagement, she knew what it meant. She had lost her place. The following Friday, Cassandra fired herself.

> The best way to predict the future is to create it.
>
> —Divine B

> Calamity is the test of integrity.
>
> —Samuel Richardson

All around the Brooklyn classroom, students had posted inspirational quotes they had churned up and found helpful. Refreshing to find advice from a hip-hop philosopher abiding on Facebook beside the wisdom of an eighteenth-century English novelist. But such are the eclectic results of Internet mining.

The staff internship team was trying out a series of preparatory exercises and discussions in the Brooklyn site's largest meeting room. Class Nine interns-to-be were spending a final week in a new orientation program designed to help ease their transition from the classroom to the workplace. In one session, review took the form of a *Jeopardy*-like quiz game. Divided into teams, students were brushing up on effective workplace demeanor.

"Team Four, choose a category."

"Professional skills for two hundred."

"Okay. Two nonverbals you should avoid at the workplace."

"What is fidgeting and yawning?"

"Yes! Choose again."

"Pro skills for four hundred."

"Correct nonverbal behavior includes . . ."

"What is nodding and taking notes?"

"Absolutely."

"We'll stay with pro skills for five hundred."

"Things always to be included in a professional e-mail."

"What is subject, friendly greetings, signature?"

"Bonus question. Anybody, any team—just tell me this: If you see something that needs to be done, what should you do?"

Group chorus: "JUST DO IT!"

And they do. Glance through the surveys of management comments rating every class of interns, and the chorus appears over and over:

"Very professional manner."

"Conducts herself in a polished, professional way."

"Fits easily into our team, with great willingness to help."

It's all beautiful music to Bill Lehman, who maintains that while many job-development programs can teach technical courses, success in the arena has a lot to do with finesse: "Pro skills is where the secret sauce is. Gerald has always said that the ABCs of Year Up are attitude, behavior, and communication. That's pro skills—and that's where the biggest difference is. That simply does not exist in many alternative programs."

On January 28, the final day of L & D, all learning communities reported to Brooklyn for their last full day together. After some general announcements, the three LCs gathered in separate rooms. Marisol, trim, tiny, and dressed all in black, headed down the corridor with a promise to herself: "I am not, not, *not* going to cry."

Malik confessed to mixed feelings as well: "It reminds me of high school graduation with all of my friends. I'm leaving this comfortable place where if you do something wrong you won't get penalized, you'll have more leeway. We're about to start this internship, and suddenly it's game time. Part of me is like, 'Oh, man, I'm leaving this comfort zone.' Leave my friends, people I built relationships with for the past twenty-one weeks, wow. Now we're all leaving this bird's nest. I feel kind of sad, but this is different from high school. This time, I feel that we have the necessary tools to not be nervous; we're just anxious for the opportunity. We have the social skills, better grammar, IT and QA skills. We feel ready."

Having gathered LCM in a circle, with the Milestones chart from orientation week hung on one wall, site leader Massomeh turned off the overhead lights and asked for quiet as she walked slowly around the circle. "Consider for a moment where you've been. What you've accomplished." She asked everyone to close their eyes and remember silently; her voice was low and almost hypnotic as she took them back to those first shaky days in September. Remember those Milestones too. Put yourself back in that room, that day, and think about how far you've come.

After some quiet reflection, students began to volunteer observations and experiences; the emotional level was high but happy. Taleisha didn't speak this time. Nor did she look stern—just comfortable. She had friends in the room now, people who lived not far from her uptown and met her for a movie or just to hang out. One student's nephew was the same age as Jared, and they loved to play together while the adults visited and talked—really talked.

A stocky young man strode to the front and began to speak about how his anger issues had subsided over the months—and the relief he was feeling. His lifelong struggle with a short fuse had gotten him into plenty of difficulty in the past. And he had had some challenging moments here as well.

"I was getting infractions for things, mostly lateness, and I blew up once on my adviser, which wasn't cool. Then I axed him . . ."

"ASKED him!" bellowed a full-throated LCM chorus.

"Okay, okay. I *asked* him why it was so important. And we was talking about . . ."

"WERE talking about."

Hector* was clearly struggling to hold on to himself and his train of thought under the well-intended corrections. He threw out his arms and blurted, "Okay! I'm trying to talk here—and it's still not easy for me. So lemme *ask* you all something. Just let me get it out, okay? Let me tell my story. Then afterwards, you can correct everything I did wrong. And I will thank you for it. But this is now and from my heart, so let it be. . . ."

And he finished his recitation, without interruption, about taming those anger issues, about learning to pause and think, to be less impulsive, to think instead of yell his way through a problem. Hector threw his arms wide and leaned back like an exhausted tenor at the end of a lung-busting aria. He heaved a theatrical sigh to great applause. As the noise died down, he sang out: "I AM HECTOR RODRIGUEZ! COMIN' ATCHU, WORLD!"

Once LCM had concluded its sharing, all gathered into a huddle at the center of the room, hands to the middle like a stoked-up football team on fourth and goal. They began a chant that grew faster and louder: "LCM, LCM, LCMMMMMMMMMMMMM!"

In the doorway, Bao Zhu, a Columbia University social work intern from mainland China, stood riveted. As the tumult died down, she ventured quietly: "I think I have arrived at a unique and important place."

Down the hall, LCW was having its final huddle as well. Wil Velazquez had finished delivering a fond, firm, and congratulatory send-off. Soon Class Ten would be in these seats. Seeing a couple of trembling chins—Marisol was holding up, but barely—Wil called for the LCW motivational chant best befitting the new interns' release into the wilds of corporate America. Hector volunteered and bellowed cheerfully: "Be as aggressive as a lion ... BUT DON'T BE A JERK!"

Winston,* who recently had to make the tough decision to leave the program for family reasons, had asked to come in and say a final few words. This he did briefly and with clear affection for the group. He asked Wil whether he could make a last request.

"Everybody worked so hard to keep our average up in QA. So I would like Raphael to stand up here with me—and do the dougie."

When the whooping died down, Winston and Raphael stood side by side as LCW did its best to slap, snap, and stomp a suitable beat. Winston had it all—the bowed legs, the shoulder pop and sway, the double-helix hair-smoothing arm maneuver. And Raphael?

Definitely better than Justin Bieber.

"Aw, give him his props. The man's soul is *deep*."

Two weeks after firing herself, Cassandra reappeared. She came in to see Charmaine, bringing a friend along who thought she might apply. Could Cassandra try again? Maybe right away in Class Ten—in March? Charmaine was welcoming and encouraging, but she urged Cassandra to give it some serious thought. When students are given a second chance owing to "outside" issues such as homelessness, family crisis, or pregnancy, the wisdom is generally to leave more time—at least six months—between terms. "It makes sense," Charmaine explained, "to be sure that any issues that might prevent their success are resolved and that they feel ready to resume the challenge."

Cassandra pressed her case, then disappeared for a couple of weeks. And when she was back in touch, her plans and her living situation were still uncertain. Could she try again in September?

"Stay tuned," Charmaine said.

The following week, Class Nine was on the job—except for the thirteen interns destined for three sites at UBS, which would be ready to receive them a week later. In the interim, they reported to Year Up every weekday and pitched in getting classrooms ready for incoming Class Ten. One of the two Manhattan LCs would be moving to Brooklyn with its extra space. Devon and Malik had made themselves useful by reconfiguring PCs, setting up tech classrooms, and testing equipment.

Malik was glad to dissipate some of his excess energy. He was feeling a bit jumpy about getting started, checking and rechecking the Metro-North timetables that would get him from 125th Street in Harlem to the mammoth UBS campus just a block from the train station in Stamford, Connecticut. The Swiss bank's presence sprawls across twelve acres there. Its three buildings and 1.5 million square feet include a trading floor the size of a football field. On the orientation tour, Malik thought the company café looked pretty good too. Great prices. A pizza and pasta station!

He had reason to be a bit anxious; though his track was QA, the company's needs had changed a bit and he would start out with more IT-related work before he moved into QA testing chores. *Don't worry,* he'd been reassured. *You'll learn on the job.* He considered the vast, unknown territory where he was about to land.

"Fixed Income Trade Capture? Wow."

Malik squared his shoulders and grinned. "I'll just have to defenestrate my weaknesses."

CHAPTER SEVEN
Oh, Pioneers!

"I DID MY INTERNSHIP AT FIDELITY INVESTMENTS. THEY HAD INTERNS there from Northeastern University, so they were used to college interns. This was different. We were different. There were a lot of questions, like 'What is Year Up? What skills do you have? How could they teach you to work in this kind of environment in just six months?' I really felt I had to prove myself. Every day."

JANELLE CLARK, CLASS ONE, BOSTON

How very scary those first weeks must have seemed to the twenty-two young hopefuls who took a chance on us. You can probably see why, for reasons of self-confidence and expediency, we insist each new student prepare and deliver his or her version of what's known as the elevator speech. It's about thirty seconds long, intended to answer that persistent FAQ: "What's Year Up?"

It was tough at first for Janelle and her classmates. We've gotten a lot better at helping students through the transition out of their safe, supportive LCs and into the business world. Today we have workplace tours in advance of those anxious migrations, an intensive internship orientation, and weekly interns' PDWs (professional development workshops) once they have been placed. "We knew we were guinea pigs," Janelle said. "And that was okay. We had everything to gain. And for most of us, there was nothing to lose."

Our first task was to help this excited, anxious, and very diverse group of young people get to know, trust, and rely on one another as a community.

The Milestones exercise that helped meld Class Nine in New York had its forerunners in some of the activities developed by Stanley Pollack and the experts at Teen Empowerment. They helped us learn and facilitate our earliest interactive exercises—we called some of them "icebreakers" in those days. It's as true now as it was then: We can't move forward until we help new students to get past their inhibitions, personal and cultural. Some of them *hate* it at first. I'll let Janelle tell you just how much—and why.

"Orientation is so intense; your head is spinning that week with so much information, so much interaction. You're trying to put your game face on. I think that was the first time the staff was doing some of the activities. After the first couple, I would say, 'Not this again.' There were a lot of activities that were touchy and feely, and I'm like, 'Oh my God, I don't know these people.' I can laugh about it now, we all do.

"I remember the activity that made me feel so awkward. Everyone in the group had to do a movement, then everyone else had to mirror it. Some were so nervous they did something simple like wave. Some did things that were so risky and drastic—like an extravagant dance move. I don't feel comfortable doing that. That was the one that had me saying, 'Oh my goodness, I don't know if I'm coming back tomorrow.'"

Janelle's classmate Areva was three when she came to Boston from Malaysia with her family. She liked to joke that she was probably the only native Malay with a serious Boston accent. But despite her linguistic assimilations, Areva's intimate world—everything from at-home language to food to child-rearing practices—was totally Malaysian. It was an insular circling of wagons common to big-city immigrant populations. And it can be very disconcerting for a young person like Areva to strike out alone and join a class full of otherness. Apprehensive and quiet by nature, she found orientation a huge challenge. Areva recalls: "I felt shy and uncomfortable because I'm always the one in the back of the class. Icebreakers—getting to know people—that was totally new for me. It was all the staff leading these things—Gerald, Linda, Tom, Richard, Nikki. We'd go, 'Seriously? We have to do this?' We'd get it over with, and in the end it helped us get to know each other and bring us out of our comfort zone. And out of our shells. Did it work? To this day myself, Wilfredo, Janelle—the majority of us are still in contact ten years later. We have our own little Year Up get-together."

Seeing these relationships endure is an absolute joy. Watching their beginnings can be even more exciting, especially when you check out the body language in the first couple of days. New students stare at their shoes a lot. Some can't make eye contact with one another or our staff. Some have been living on their own for some time before they join us; years spent in foster care or in homeless shelters can build up necessary defenses. If we have to nudge them out of a protective crouch until they can look one another in the eye, so be it. These exercises work. And as a very results-driven organization, we'll do whatever it takes to help our students succeed.

We had agonized over choosing the students for our first class. We wrote finalists' names on a whiteboard and asked ourselves, one more time, the questions we had asked our applicants: Were they truly interested in information technology? How motivated were they? How had they done on some basic language assessment? We looked hard at risk factors, not in an effort to "cream" the most likely to succeed but just to make sure they could make it to class every day. All of us had interviewed each applicant, and frankly, we didn't have a huge pool to choose from. Once we had narrowed our field, we considered how they looked as a group. Were they likely to get along and support one another? Was the class well balanced in terms of gender and diversity? Stanley had made it clear that we had to ensure they all felt secure in their surroundings. "From day one, you're building a safe, supportive community." Stanley had a thick manual of suggestions and exercises for getting to that safe place. He also had faith in our young adults.

His confidence was well founded. Once students start to really talk to one another, their own biases and misunderstandings fall as well. And the dynamic has persisted since Class One. Here's a scene from a latter-day lunch table in our Providence site. Billy, who is Ecuadoran, talks about how he wakes his mother up at 5:00 a.m. for her very long days in a factory.

"I kiss her awake, every single day. *Mama, it's five.* Kiss on the forehead. Another. *Wake up, wake up.*"

Unwrapping his sandwich, Kwan, who is Korean, looks shocked. "You people really *do* that? I see some of you all hugging in the hallway here. My parents never touch me, and vice versa."

"So what's up with that?"

"I know they love me, but in their culture you don't say that; you don't touch much. I know they're proud that I'm here, but they don't say anything about it."

Takwan, African American: "That's messed up. I mean, not really, no disrespect. We might be overcommunicators sometimes. My house has the volume cranked up, if you know what I'm saying. But nobody goes a day without getting hugged on some."

Kwan grins. "How about one of you adopt me for a day and I get some of that good stuff? When can I come over?"

Boardrooms are hardly exempt from similar gaps in cultural competency. An anecdote from Year Up's national board chairman speaks to how ingrained—and how wrong—some assumptions about our students can be. Paul Salem tells the story fairly often, and bravely. A Brown and Harvard Business School graduate, Paul is a heavyweight in the private equity industry as senior managing director of Providence Equity Partners. He has also been one of our deepest donors and supporters—but more on that later.

His engagement started with a typical misperception. Paul came to us through an "old boys' network" of financiers and friends. One day in 2004, he and his wife, Navyn, came to Boston to have a look at our program. I'm sure he hadn't a clue how the encounter with some students from Class One would affect the next decade of his life. "One of my friends, Ramez Sousou, who manages a private equity firm now, was also a classmate of Gerald's at HBS," Paul recalls. "He says, 'You've got to meet Gerald.' So my wife and I went to Summer Street to visit the Year Up site. It was in the afternoon, and I saw two young African American men come running by me, running so hard and fast that I looked behind them to see if there was someone chasing them. And I said to my wife, 'I wonder what they're running from?'

"Think about it—that's my first thought. And I go up the elevator at Year Up and there's the two young men still huffing and puffing. I said, 'What were you guys running from?' And they said, 'We were running to class. If we're late we get fined.' I said, 'You're running to learn?' Gerald happened to walk in, and I said, 'I don't know what you're selling, but I'm buying.' I've told this story to every Year Up class I speak to, especially in Providence, where we live. There's my discriminating mind saying two kids must be running from something. And the fact that they were running to learn has always stuck with me."

Within the next few years, Paul would donate more than a million dollars toward Year Up's operations and growth. And in our classrooms we continued to address the assumptions that pulled Paul up short that day. One young woman in Class One arrived at our regular Wednesday afternoon intern meeting at Year Up and announced, "I'm never going back there."

She explained that a coworker had asked her in the elevator where she was from. On hearing she was from Brazil, he had wondered aloud, "Don't we hire any Americans?" Her conclusion: "They must not want me there." A male student of color interning at a prestigious law firm was approached in the company cafeteria by a security guard who glanced at his proffered ID card and still uttered a terse "Come with me." The slights were not just confined to students. Richard Dubuisson was looking over magazines at a downtown newsstand when the vendor asked, "What do you want—*Ebony*?"

We can't stop these things from happening. But we've found that with carefully run discussions and interactives, we can explore and defuse some of the cultural and racial stereotyping that our students may encounter on any given day as they commute to classes downtown. They've told us they can feel the disapproving or anxious eyes looking at them. They see the reflexively clutched purses and nervous wallet patting. Those hurtful behaviors are as perplexing as the most insidious forms of cancer; their effects are pervasive, diffuse, and very difficult to extract cleanly. Unconventional tools are required.

Brendan Halpin, an instructor in Boston, devised an exercise. They took to it immediately. It's known throughout our sites as "Turn Your Back." Linda describes it this way: "We ask a group of students, 'What are the stereotypes that people have of you as a young person riding the subway?' They write their answers on some flip charts or poster boards we've tacked up. Their typical answers:

I'm violent.
I'm a nobody.
I'm somebody's baby mama.
I don't have any money.

"Then we ask, 'What do you think are the impressions people should have of you as a hardworking, motivated young adult?' Some answers I've seen:

That I can do what anybody else can do.
I can go to college and be part of the mainstream.
I can save money.
I'm intelligent, I'm fair and clear thinking.

"We tell them, 'Now turn your chairs around and only look at this last set of impressions. Put your backs to the first set. We're going to get rid of what's behind you. In fact, we're going to rip it up and throw it in the trash. Those are stereotypes that we're going to be done with. What we want you to focus on is your future. That's everything in front of you.'

"The physical part is reinforcing. They're feeling that they're part of something. *They* wrote it on the wall, *they* ripped it up themselves, *they* threw it in the trash. They realize they don't have to deal with what other people are thinking. They may have to cope a bit, in terms of reality—what's still out there. But not in terms of their own goals. And from right there where they're sitting, the attitude is visible: My back is toward that now."

It was so critical—and very fortunate—that we had a gifted staff member who had made that turn himself. Richard Dubuisson knew all about low expectations, dead ends, and stereotypes as a young immigrant of color in Miami. He had been particularly baffled that many of his humiliations were inflicted by young people with the same color skin; they mocked his walk and his Creole-inflected talk. As a teenager, Richard worked out his own ad hoc interactives, parroting "American-ness" from dialogue on sitcoms and cop shows.

What'chu talkin' about, Willis?

He'd study Gary Coleman's catchphrases in the sitcom *Diff'rent Strokes* and mimic Jimmie "Dyn-o-mite" Walker's skinny braggart J.J. in *Good Times*—whatever worked. Alone and determined, talking back to the idiot box, Richard knew instinctively what we would teach our students—that honing mainstream communication skills doesn't have to disrespect or diminish the essential You. Never lose the Creole, but do expand the tool kit.

When Richard, then twenty-nine, made his case for being hired at Year Up, he reminded us—as Stanley Pollack had—that "classic" pedagogy was hardly appropriate for a population that had been so relentlessly marginalized. He told us, "Good teachers can teach anything. The skills are good to have, but the *attitudes* are also hugely important. Anybody can be a techie, but they need somebody who's also going to be a role model and who's going to teach the intangibles—like how to survive in a corporate environment when you're the only person of color there."

He was right, of course. From the outset Richard was a critical anchor on a faculty that was deeply motivated, well meaning—and quite white. And true to his promise, he was the kind of teacher few of our students had ever encountered. We got our first taste of his style before we hired him, when we "rented" a bunch of students and asked Richard to show us how he'd teach a basic IT class. He recalls it this way: "We paid these students twenty dollars and I did a teaching session for thirty minutes. I covered very basic stuff like how to take a picture from the Internet and put it in your computer, some keyboard shortcuts. It was tech, but half of it was me talking to them about being professional, infusing tech with some motivational language. It was a hybrid of what I do now in any class I teach.

"It all derives from a personal philosophy—I know Gerald shares it— where we're not only content experts. Our students need us to be more than that. We need to be in the moment, when a student says 'Lemme ax you,' and I say, 'It's not "ax," it's "ask."' The lessons have to be real; they have to be immediate. Not just the lessons but the praise. Things like 'That was really good the way you explained what a server does—so let's keep it going.' It becomes part of what we do anywhere."

Sitting in on one of Richard's classes, you realize that he's multitasking as intensely as one of those guys on old TV variety shows who kept a lot of plates spinning on thin rods. But Richard doesn't dash about between his wobbling charges. He's cool, calm, and in total command. His moving gaze tracks everyone, steady and unblinking as a bank camera. It's a stringent, tiring vigilance to maintain, but it looks smooth and natural.

He says he learned how to read and manage our classrooms from a very "hard-core" facilitator in one of the work-development programs we observed during our start-up phase. Many of the students had just been released from prisons. Richard was impressed by the way the instructor seemed to know what was going on in all corners of a room at all times. Richard fine-tuned his own observational skills until he was certain he could do the same.

"When I'm in a classroom, I have a sense of where all my students are," he says. "There are times when I see somebody drifting, and I know why they're drifting, and I'll leave it alone and deal after class. Those are rare occasions. With students who are falling asleep—even if I know that you spent the night in a park, you need to stay awake for class. I will discreetly ask the student to step out, say, 'Put some water on your face. Go downstairs and get some coffee and come back.'

"I'll tell them, 'You look like you're struggling. But once you walk in, you engage. If you walk into the classroom, then you are saying, "I'm ready to learn, ready to participate and be engaged." Anything less and I would not be respecting how smart you are if I allowed you to sit here and not participate. And I can't do that; I respect you too much.'"

We have since deployed Richard's talents to classrooms beyond Boston. We have sent him to our sites in Providence and Washington, D.C., to help advise and orient new instructors. And his methods have infused our program as we've grown. Since our good fortune in finding him, we've become even more obsessive about hiring the best staff and keeping them well cared for and motivated. We constantly strive to create a supportive environment for our instructors, administrators, MSWs, and support staff. It's critical for all of our staff to administer the right ratio of caring and correction.

Those have never been opposing concepts to Richard. This is a man who can close the classroom door as a student six months pregnant comes huffing up the stairs, then record a lateness infraction. He'll also move heaven and earth—on his own time—to help her excel.

He also knows when and how to pass the baton to student services. During one morning's current-events session, the class discussed a horrific, headline-grabbing shooting in Dorchester that had killed a mother and her babe in arms. A female student quickly fled the classroom. She knew someone involved in the tragedy and had been struggling just to get herself to class in the wake of her loss. Richard alerted Linda, who took the student for a calming walk and talk and bought her flowers to acknowledge her grief. She carried the bouquet with her and made it through the rest of the day, in large part with the kindness of other students who asked about the flowers, then offered support.

Most days—actually, every day—there is also a lightness of being in Richard's classroom. Despite the man's seriousness of purpose, you hear a lot of laughter through the door as you pass by. *Work Hard, Have Fun.* Students may have memorized that core value during orientation, but they're continually surprised that you can get a lot of smiles out of installing a motherboard or resurrecting an ailing hard drive. We're all about *applied* theory, as Janelle was pleased to discover: "We had some computer stuff in high school, but it was all theory, no practice. Not related to anything in life. Once I got in the classes and started actually working with Excel and PowerPoint, I couldn't believe what those tools could do. We did presentations with business plans, formulas in Excel, all this creative stuff. It made the activities fun. They made it very interactive. I think that's what attracted me to the program from the very beginning. I'm a very visual and hands-on learner."

Wilfredo Pena was a self-taught computer user of above-average competency, and he appreciated Richard's telling him the limits of our early curriculum: "When I came to the interview," Wil said, "I knew most everything that they were going to cover in the intensive Web design track. Richard was very candid with me. He said, 'If you do the Web design track, you'll probably know ninety percent of it already.' I thanked him for being so honest and did the IT track instead. It wasn't something I was good at before, so I learned a lot."

Most students who come to us from poor or mediocre high schools would never say they view a classroom as a sacred space, inviolate once that door is closed. They may have been accustomed to sauntering in and out as they please. They may have been habitual truants. An implicit stasis develops in some large urban schools. In return for not disrupting the class, a teacher will tacitly agree to let a student (or group of students) get through the class without being pushed to learn. At Year Up, we don't play that game; it's counter to our core value of mutual respect. Richard had seen it all, and beginning with Class One, he declared a total change.

"The first day of class, there are a couple of things that I do. At eight twenty-nine I'm standing outside the door. At eight thirty exactly I walk in the classroom, close the door, and I start. Class ends at nine fifty. So at nine fifty exactly, I stop. If I go over, I apologize and tell them I owe them two minutes, and the next class I give it back. I have respect for their lunch and break time. So what I'm asking them to do is respect my time."

He doesn't raise his voice; rather, he wills you into giving your best. Two incidents come to mind. Early on, I believe it was with Class Two, the students were going through a bit of a lull—lots of "lates," absences, and a general slump in motivation. Richard stood in front of the group during the start of Friday feedback and with a strong, commanding voice announced, "Folks, *this* is Year Up. Those two words mean something. They mean quality, professionalism, and high standards. I expect all of you to adhere to the standards that these two words stand for and to build our reputation across this city." In that moment, you could feel a stir and a change beginning. The slump was soon past.

Great teachers know the most challenging questions to ask of their students and when to pose them. When Richard collected assignments, he would move along the rows and ask students, "Is this your best work? Did you put one hundred percent of your effort into producing the best work that you can? If not, I am going to ask you to take it back and show me what your best work looks like." He said this in a way that made students want to take that paper back, redo it, and show him their maximum effort.

His is a far more interactive form of learning than the old didactic model and its one-way conversation. Richard's is a more holistic approach that seeks to teach character along with regular curriculum. The role of character in learning is now the subject of some exciting new research and practice in both private and public schools. Richard's moral compass found the right coordinates long ago. He believes that building character is very much a teacher's responsibility, and that rote learning can never be as functional as meaningful dialogue. Richard made it clear that the classroom relationships were a two-way street; they depended on feedback in both directions. He developed his own form of contract. He says it was part of "setting the tone, early on." It goes down this way.

Picture a tall, loose-limbed, mellow-voiced gentleman with good posture, but relaxed. And yes, he's looking at you. And you. The gaze moves and settles gently. It locks eyes with a student, releases, moves on. After the silent scan, a question: "So. What do you expect of me as an instructor?"

He sees puzzled looks, some discomfort. No hands up.

"I work for you, so you're essentially my boss. What is it that you expect me to do in this role to teach you and train you?"

A brave soul pipes up: "Patience." Richard writes it down. Then another speaks up: "Don't be *mean.*"

"Tell me what you mean by that."

They do. It trickles out, then gushes, a torrent of pedagogical sins, slights, and humiliations they do not wish to endure again. Ever. Richard writes it down, types it all up that night, and brings it in the following morning in document form. A contract with this heading: "The following are the expectations this class has for Richard."

He has listed their terms, which he reads aloud.

"Everyone okay with that?"

He signs it.

"Hold me accountable for *all* of it. I'm expecting that."

He will also assume they will participate actively in his performance review. And he has a few added requests of his students. One of them: "English is not my first language, so if I make a mistake, please correct me. I expect all of us to correct one another's English."

I learned so much from Richard, beyond how to teach. Kate and I were agreed that we also wanted respectful, two-way relationships with our graduates. To that end, we hunted for an adaptable, good-sized, welcoming house where we could raise both our family and Year Up. In July 2001, as Class One was taking its first tentative steps, Kate and I found our perfect house within walking distance of Harvard Yard. It was solid, venerable—built in 1876—and recently, perfectly renovated. A big selling point was the grounds, quite generous by Cambridge standards and well suited to family sprawl and larger group events.

The house suited us perfectly, and we were delighted to find that it came with a bit of Boston history. We have hosted fund-raisers, poetry slams, student dinners, staff barbecues, and the biggest kids' Halloween bash in Cambridge in the same gardens and study where philosopher and psychologist William James lived and wrote more than a century ago. Better still, we learned that Julia Child lived a few doors down. My mom spent many happy hours watching Julia hold forth in three TV series shot in that Cambridge kitchen, which has since been reinstalled at the Smithsonian.

It's fair to say that at times our kitchen and dining room have more in common with the great hall at Harry Potter's fictional academy, Hogwarts, with Kate doing the wizarding. Somehow the head count and the table just expand. How many husbands dare ask, with alarming frequency, "Can we have fifteen people to dinner, my love? Tomorrow?"

Whether it's fifty or fifteen, Kate has never flinched, especially when I invite Year Up graduates unexpectedly. Extra plates materialize in a flash. Amazing dishes—in impressive quantities for ravenous young adults—are conjured and served up from "just what I found in the fridge." Kate knows how much I need the nourishment of these movable feasts. I travel constantly and work almost every weeknight after dinner. These dinners are a welcome form of decompression and reconnection. I take my place in our kitchen for what I call "sanity and a dinner plate."

There's a relentlessness to the workweek of a growing nonprofit, however voluntary. Other duties required of a "founder"—travel, fund-raising, serving on other boards—began to keep me from what I love best: being in the classroom, shooting the breeze in the break room, heading out to lunch with a few students. In the interest of self-preservation I issued an open invitation soon after we moved into the house: Any night I am in town and don't have an evening obligation, there is an extra plate at our table for any graduate who wants to stop by. (That invitation still stands. We inform current students that they're absolutely welcome once they have completed the program.)

I don't take for granted that the real effort to make this happen lands on Kate's shoulders. I'm just really fortunate that she was born with the graciousness gene. I watch her in mute amazement and thank her too many times afterward (she says), but I do believe her when she explains that sacrifice really isn't in her domestic vocabulary: "I enjoy the role of caretaker. I love food; I love family. Gerald doesn't care if he eats cardboard for a month. I really do. I feel that's one of the things I can do for him. You have to be at peace with it. I was educated at Wellesley with women who spent a lot of time avoiding it. But I'm a very traditional English girl who grew up in a pretty formal society. You do care for your husband. But it's not why I do what I do now. What's going on in this house is far beyond what you'd consider 'traditional.'"

It's certainly part therapy. Kate understands that these dinners ensure I don't get too far away from the mission that's most meaningful to us. Our kids don't mind "sharing Daddy" with so many very cool dinner guests. What grand times we've had. Mingling in the house and yard you'll find Year Up graduates and politicians, teenage mothers, Harvard MBAs, historians, hedge fund managers, former gangbangers, and American heroes. One memorable evening I was honored and thrilled to see our children sitting at the feet of civil rights giant John Lewis. They learned American history from a heroic participant as John told the story of his brave march across the Edmund Pettus Bridge in Selma, Alabama.

Some nights it feels idyllic and incredibly hopeful. But there are always moments that remind me just how far we have to go—witness another stereotyping incident with David Heredia. David was a young man by the time we settled in Cambridge. Things were going well for him; with a few strings tugged here and there and his own talent, he had landed a job in Los Angeles as a production assistant in the Disney animation department. Cornelia fairly bounced off the walls when he called to give her the news. He was enjoying his new West Coast lifestyle and he had an unexpected jolt when he came east to see family. He recalls: "I was visiting Gerald and Kate and they took me out to dinner in downtown Boston. It was great, and when we were leaving I was standing out front. A guy comes up to me and hands me his car keys and says, 'It's the '98 Lexus.' I said, 'What? I don't work here.' He said he was sorry, and I just couldn't be polite about it. I said, 'You *should* be sorry. That's ignorance.' I wanted to say so much more, but he was shocked and he just kind of left. Gerald came out and I was visibly upset. I didn't even want to explain it to him right then because I hadn't really processed it. I told Gerald later, 'It just shocks me that people still have that mentality.' "

Despite that unfortunate lapse, Cambridge was welcoming to us and our extended, ad hoc family. As ever, the neighborhood was full of restless brains and intriguing ideas. Kate and I reconnected with old college friends and set about tossing the widest net we could to draw attention and positive debate to the Opportunity Divide. A new friend then, Shawn Bohen had been at Harvard in a series of leadership roles that studied and tackled some of the toughest social, political, and economic dilemmas. Among the start-ups she oversaw were the Harvard Initiative for Global Health, the Hauser Center for Nonprofit Organizations at the John F. Kennedy School, and the Harvard Medical School Division on Addictions. She was totally wired in to the nonprofit sector and a valued sounding board.

In full intellectual cry, Shawn can be fiercely strategic, challenging, and funny. What I hadn't counted on was her persuasiveness as an ally in Kate's latest domestic campaign, a third Chertavian child. It was a landmark debate; a few months after Class One's graduation, Kate was pregnant with our third child, Callum, who was born in June 2003.

Adding to the family didn't mean Kate had any intention of cutting back on her Year Up involvement. In fact, she was ready to do much, much more. She'll tell you that she needed the work as much as I do: "I think the basis of our relationship is a really intimate communication and a belief in each other's abilities to do things. And a desire to help. I like to help. I feel most valued when I can assist at something. Gerald always, in a charming, sincere way, managed to get me to help a lot. Once I met the students and the staff and felt secure with the organization, I felt I was of value. And I did a ton for them."

As the program found its legs, I watched Kate deploy several talents I did not realize she had. How could I? Neither of us had ever done this before.

"I can raise money, definitely," she acknowledges. "I have no problems asking for money. Working at it together, I think we're a really good team, because Gerald can raise the big money and I can support him in doing it. We run events; we talk a lot about how we're going to do it, who's going to sit where. I can lend a pretty gracious aspect to it. I think there's a confidence and care when we entertain people. I hope no one ever feels like they are being asked for too much."

Kate knows and understands our donors and treats them with great respect. Yet she gets as excited as I when she meets someone interested in supporting our students amid a crowd of potential supporters churning through our kitchen. She absolutely knows how to make our case—and to whom.

"We're financially secure ourselves, so to ask other financially secure people to do something that you think is of value can sometimes be a gift to them. Our donors need to know the best possible things they can do with their money. No one loves fund-raising but it's part of the job."

Over the years, Kate and I have developed an understanding of the charitable mind-set. Most often, giving is by affiliation. If you know someone who has had cancer, you tend to give to cancer charities—that sort of thing. We go for the familiar as well when we ask potential donors, "What was your Year Up?" There is no truly self-made individual. Nearly every person we approach has had a significant boost from someone, and they rarely forget it. We also know how to reassure a donor on the safety of his or her investment. We take pains to develop personal relationships with them. We are careful and committed donors as well. Once they recognize that, they trust us as good stewards of their money. It's easy to show them exactly how it is spent. Kate and I both realize that the strongest persuaders were and are the students and graduates also at the table. We rarely hold an event without them.

Linda was continually refining and expanding her idea of "circles of support" for our students, and when she was casting about for Class One mentors it was a no-brainer that she looked to Kate. My wife was compassionate, intuitive, and patient—even when a panicked student's phone call might sound as we were about to doze off.

"I bet it's Areva."

I could hear the crackle of distress through the receiver and Kate's calm, patient responses on our end. It was indeed Areva. It had become clear early on that this stressed single mother needed a sounding board for some non-academic issues. As Areva recalls, she was determined to avoid the severe corporal punishments of her own upbringing. But she had a toddler son in his terrible twos, a tense, crowded living situation, and, with her Year Up work, very limited patience. In her harried home life, she felt increasingly isolated. She told Linda that she had no one to really talk to. Until Kate.

Areva was very anxious in the beginning, and she and Kate advanced toward each other cautiously. But she was determined to make a change. "My parents disciplined us the way they were disciplined," Areva said. "I wanted to break that cycle because it was harsh, getting spanked and stuff. Linda decided to pair Kate and me because she's a mom and I am. Having a mentor was new to me. I didn't understand the concept. It was kind of awkward at first, but I felt we got along very well. Her background in art opened up my eyes. She was wonderful. I kid you not, she was *there*. And she has a really busy schedule. It didn't matter."

They found time together over lunch, after class, and on the phone. And Kate did her best to help Areva navigate the turbulence. Kate recalls, "Areva was in a relationship with a man who became extremely violent. She finally extricated herself from that. But there would be other issues. She'd be on the phone going, 'I'm going to hit my child.' And we'd be saying, 'You can't hit your child, you must not.' It was so hard for her to struggle against that. She was afraid of feeling violent. I asked what would help. She said, 'I have no one to talk to when it gets bad,' and I told her, 'I don't care when you call me, night or day. I'm just going to say, "Don't do it."' "

The emergency calls didn't come too often. And Kate was able to acquaint Areva with a Western disciplinary technique that was less stressful for all involved. "I remember one evening," Areva said, "I was afraid of my own frustrations and emotions. When I called Kate, really upset because of something my son had done and my reaction to it, she said, 'From now on, take a time-out.' Time-out? I'd never heard of it. She explained what it was and said, 'Put him in a time-out for two to three minutes—calculate a minute per year of age. It's not for him, it's for you to calm down so that you don't do something that you will regret. From that point on, I implemented that, and I do it now with my daughter who is seven. Kate brought that different perspective on discipline that got me through a tough time."

Multiply what Kate did with Areva by twenty-two. Since Class One, all of our students have been matched with mentors in addition to their staff advisers. In the beginning, we drew on family, staff, and friends as mentors. As we grew, the pool widened to include staff from our corporate partners, graduate students, and volunteers from Boston's business community. Mentoring is a variable activity by nature when you bring strangers together. For many of our students, it's a new concept, and I understand why some of them can be skeptical at first. It doesn't always gel. And sometimes the connection reverberates way beyond that long, hard year.

I love being a mentor, and to this day I continue to be matched with a student from each class in Boston. Staying connected in that way is a link to the early days of Year Up and my deepest immersion with students. In the beginning, I taught a series of classes that were the prototype for professional skills. Like everyone else on staff, I was a student adviser. And I sold internships, courted donors, and continued my unabashed brain picking all over town.

So much changed after Pam Trefler, one of our earliest and most important funders, suggested I speak to Eileen Brown. At that time, in 2001, Eileen was the founder and president of Cambridge College. Cambridge is a special, visionary institution that caters to adults for whom access to a traditional college education had been either limited or denied. Billing itself as a private, nonprofit four-year college "for working adults," it was conceived and built on a simple plan: It saw diversity as an asset to a college community. It also aspired to a responsive style of learning—that is, tailored to working adults' lives in a way that is time and cost efficient. In the beginning, it was focused more on master's programs for working adults, such as teachers, to advance their careers. It has since expanded to include doctoral and undergraduate programs. The average age of a student is thirty-eight, more than 75 percent are women, and 43 percent are members of minority groups. Most of the classes are at night and on weekends, when working adults have the time to attend. Nearly 70 percent of the student body receives financial aid. The school's academic ethos runs to phrases like "Each one teach one" and "No one knows what all of us know." And here is perhaps its greatest achievement: The average undergraduate class size is eleven.

It works. Under Eileen's guidance and perseverance the college has grown to serve more than five thousand students a year, with satellite learning communities in Georgia, Virginia, California, Tennessee, and Puerto Rico. Step into an elevator at Cambridge College at its 5:30 p.m. start time and you are surrounded by students of all ages, religions, and races, each one determined to earn a bachelor's or master's degree. To this day, the graduation ceremonies there rate as some of the most moving experiences I've had.

Graduates are featured speakers; their testimonials are riveting and inspirational and routinely draw tears and cheers.

Eileen herself is quietly spectacular as an educator and an adviser. I first went to see her at her home office on Mount Auburn Street. Five minutes into our visit, it was clear that we were both passionate about closing the Opportunity Divide. To that end, Eileen shared her prodigious fund-raising skills. She was an invaluable mentor to me as I worked to raise more capital.

After our second or third meeting, sitting out on her porch in a pair of comfortable garden chairs, we agreed to join each other's boards. Not long after, at a Year Up board meeting, Eileen leaned to me and suggested a perfectly genius notion. "You know what? Your students ought to be earning college credit for what they are learning, and I think Cambridge College can help."

That began a long, careful process of working through how Year Up's students could become dual enrolled at Cambridge College and in so doing earn up to eighteen college credits through their participation in Year Up. This would lead us to seek and secure college partnership at all of our sites nationwide. Our program was changed forever as a result of Eileen's visionary leadership and the fundamental assumption upon which she founded Cambridge. Eileen absolutely believed that our students could prosper in college and *deserved* the opportunity to do so.

For Year Up's Class One, Eileen went even further. Four students received scholarships to Cambridge; two of them, Janelle Clark and Wilfredo Pena, completed degrees there while they worked—computer science for Wil and for Janelle, a bachelor of science in human service—that have since helped them advance their careers.

I wish I could tell you that I took our first student firing in stride. I suppose I saw it coming. Harry Duprey's* total points had been declining seriously for some time. He knew from the contract he had signed that by getting down to zero points, he would be firing himself. I had spoken to Harry about his persistent infractions many times, as had the rest of the staff. He was chronically late right from the start. Harry was a bright, extremely personable young man who always came ready with an answer to "And why are you late *this* time?" It was always something: The train was stalled; his alarm clock was broken.

We worked with him on strategies to get himself up, out of the house, and to Summer Street on time. His infractions grew, his stipend got smaller and smaller, and still no improvement. I spent half an hour talking with him about the importance of being on time and how he was in danger of firing himself from the program if his behavior did not change. A couple of days afterward, late again, he was just about out of points and out of Year Up.

In a feedback session, in front of Harry's peers and staff, I really blew it. My disappointment—and perhaps a touch of anger—were evident in the way I spoke to him. That is, it was clear to everyone but me. And a staff member was quick to point it out.

"Can I suggest that in the future you don't show that you are upset with a student? At the end of the day, it's really not about you."

Stunned, I looked around. I could see that the whole group felt that I had let them and the process down. Nikki Patti was there, and she can attest that it was a rare lapse but a critical one: "Gerald was emotional because he just wanted it so badly for the student. In that feedback session, he expressed a certain amount of discouragement. He got angry at the student. Not in a hurtful way. You would never see that kind of emotion from him today. Or even six months later. I think he learned very quickly why that didn't work."

Nice one, Gerald—mangling feedback to Harry just when it mattered most. Year Up's earnest founder tried to sort it out: Was I angry that he had let me down? Was I being hard on him for squandering the opportunity we had all worked to make available? I don't really think that was it. I already understood that if you make the mistake of relying on gratitude to nourish you in this work, you're in the wrong business.

No. I was guilty of something more dangerous. Nikki was right—I really wanted Harry to succeed. But I made the mistake of thinking that it was in some way my success and not his. That can lead you to take things personally, as I did in this situation. It may not sound like much, but that was an incredibly important day for me in beginning to understand what it really means to support someone and how to do that respectfully.

I realize that this is very basic stuff for those with a degree in the art form known as social work. But they'll also tell you that such understanding is learned from experience—and often the hard way. The most effective public service requires maximum humility and zero hubris. To really understand and practice this form of support takes a lot of practice and self-knowledge, and as I learned with Harry, it requires absolute self-control.

Teachable moment for Gerald here: The art of being good in this business is dependent on your ability to get outside of yourself. Sometimes you have to care so much that it may seem as though you don't care. An impassive look and an even tone are harder to master in fraught situations than I'd imagined. But since that day, if I am ever upset or emotional at a critical moment with a student, I will always wait until I have my emotions in check before beginning the conversation. There would be so many, many more moments to practice restraint.

The fact remained: Harry was down to zero points. By contract, we had to inform him that he had fired himself. Linda and I sat down with him to explain that he was no longer able to participate in the program. Since Harry's case, I have personally delivered this news to many students over the years, and it is always a tense, stomach-churning moment, no matter how many times I've done it. The meeting is difficult for all parties, and it's often sad, since our students really want to be here and do well.

Most times their reactions are much more muted and resigned than I anticipate. It's rarely a shock, since contract point tallies are read aloud weekly at Friday feedback and advisers are always in close contact with students who seem to be slipping. I suppose that some might be surprised that we actually stick to the contract terms and consequences. To be honest, I have worried at times about a student reacting violently, although this has never happened. When we deliver this news, we always emphasize that we are in no way judging an individual and that we will continue to support a fired student to help him or her find the next appropriate step to take.

It is always distressing for staff to lose a student this way, but it is best to keep a departure in perspective from the student's point of view. Far worse things have happened to many of them. They have coping mechanisms and a resilience most of us can't imagine. I was reminded of this only recently when Bekele,* a former mentee of mine, came to a late-summer barbecue at our home looking thinner but smiling. We hadn't been in touch for a couple of months. "Oh, I was stabbed on the Fourth of July," he told me. After the fireworks on the Esplanade, a group of young men had randomly attacked him. Bekele had been critically injured, but he assured me, "Honest, I'm okay." I'd likely be in therapy for months after an assault like that. Our young adults must deal with the threat of really bad things happening at any time. Just stepping out for a slice of pizza can be fatal; one evening Tim Dibble and I looked at each other in astonishment as the students we were with at a pizza joint matter-of-factly compared possible routes home that offered the best chance of getting there intact.

When we gave Harry the news, he was clearly unhappy, but he did understand the situation and accepted responsibility for it. We suggested that he might want to take some time at home to process the situation. He agreed to come back the next day to allow us to help him plan his next move.

Class One had some mighty long days. We began Year Up with workplace hours, nine to five. The decision to do the full day anticipated students' upcoming transition as interns. We would soon find that given the intensity of the L & D phase, school hours, eight thirty to three thirty, were a better fit. As the first year went on, more outside issues began to assert themselves. Complications with students' night and weekend jobs, family obligations, tangles with the immigration and justice systems, and some behavioral issues sent a steady stream of anxious students to Linda, who counseled them in a conference room that had a door she could close. We had decided from the start that no one—not even I—would have a separate office. It's open, egalitarian seating at all sites. The only exception today is student services, where privacy is essential. Once we expanded our space on Summer Street, we saw to it that they got an office, albeit a tiny one. Its door is open to all, and it has closed to contain so very many difficult discussions. It was a small, tight community by those first few years and news of students' troubles got around as we scrambled to connect their needs with the proper resources.

"They probably weren't prepared to offer that type of support, but they did it," Janelle recalls. "You would be shocked at what they did to help people make it through that first class. There were students who didn't have places to stay, so a few ended up becoming roommates. I think Year Up worked something out with the stipends where they made advances to manage their first and last month payments on the lease. There was another student with court involvement to clear up. They supported him with legal stuff, some immigration issues. They were really there to help."

Roosevelt Lisita's problems blew up just as he was on the brink of his greatest achievements. He was a terrific, dedicated learner. Roos did so well in his internship at Fidelity Investments that it extended him a permanent job offer. But since his twenty-first birthday was imminent, he would be aging out of the more protective children's system within immigration; as an adult, obtaining permission to stay in this country would be a nightmarish five- to ten-year process that very likely would end with Roos's deportation.

It was a sad story: Having been estranged from his stepfather, Roos decided that it made more sense to live on his own and take care of himself at the tender age of seventeen. After he graduated from Madison Park High School, a guidance counselor helped him find Year Up, and he was on his way to a good job and independence. Then he got wind of what had happened when his stepfather had appeared in immigration court to secure papers for the family. The questioning of his stepfather didn't go well:

"Where does your son go to school?"

"I don't know."

"Where does he live?"

"Don't know."

"You're obviously not his parent."

The officials concluded that it was all a sham and Roosevelt would not be eligible for residency. He would soon be relegated to the long and dismal process for adult applicants. It looked like the birthday gift for all of his diligence and hard work would be a one-way ticket back to hopelessness. It would take a full decade to correct this kind of unfair penalty; in August 2011 the Obama administration did an end run around stalled legislation and announced that it would not deport or expel illegal immigrants who had come to this country as children and graduated from high school or served in the armed forces.

But in 2001, with time running out, we were all frantic. I hired an immigration lawyer for him, but the decision seemed irrevocable. I ended up writing to Senator Kennedy's office and explained the case and its deep injustice to a hardworking young man.

The clock was ticking right down to the final day. Roos turned twenty-one on a Saturday. And it was the Friday before at 4:52 p.m. when we got a call from the senator's office saying, "Everything's done; he's approved." Roos and I just cried on the phone together when I called with the news. He was so happy. He's still doing a great job at Fidelity as a support systems analyst. Since then he has been promoted twice, paid taxes, bought a condominium, and graduated from college with a bachelor of science degree in business administration. He has also mentored Year Up students and become a United States citizen. Somehow, I think justice was done and America was the better for it.

If I had to come up with a signature characteristic of Class One, it would be their constancy; some of them are still with the companies that hired them after their internships. Most are still mutually supportive friends. But the most satisfying valedictory lies in the details of their pioneering journey. Here, from a few of them, is how their Year Up shaped their next decade.

WILFREDO PENA

"During the training phase, Year Up went for a tour to Fidelity Investments, which was right down the street. I'm always trying to absorb as much as I can; it's just how I am. During the tour, the guide in the tech area was wearing a doctor's gown, he was showing how these things work, and I'm writing things down like crazy. Apparently, my manager tells me, they called Year Up and said, 'We want the kid that was taking all the notes.' So that's how I ended up there.

"I went in as a PC technician to install software, troubleshoot, handle network problems. Fidelity had an intern protocol before Year Up. I was in a section with students from Northeastern and some college students from Ireland there in an outsourcing program. My immediate supervisor had just begun working there. He was very broad minded, didn't micromanage. I was lucky in that sense. He would give me a project, like 'Here's five computers that don't work. Can you do something with these?' Okay, fine. I ended up getting three of the five to work by using parts. There was a webmaster there. Because I did Web pages on my own, I wanted to learn more of how things worked. So every day when I had free time, I would go and ask him a lot of questions. And there were things I knew that he didn't. He gave me access to the whole Web environment so I could help him. Within three months I knew exactly how things worked. There was some business I developed for him. I was not shy about it.

"So I ended up getting hired, and I'm still here. The place I'm working in now is called Fidelity Center for Applied Technology. Essentially the mission of the department is to look at future technologies, maybe software or hardware, explore how something new can be brought in to help customers or employees improve their experience. When I started it was mostly gadgets like smart phones—like, 'Oh look, I can do e-mail!' Nothing like today."

Wil bought his second house not long ago, and he started his own non-profit for children with special needs from his native El Salvador. His Web pages are awesome.

AREVA WATTANA

"My second half of Year Up, I interned at an online backup company. It was a good learning experience. After I graduated, I was looking for a full-time job and Linda found out that a local nonprofit foundation here in Boston was hiring. I applied and got the job.

"I also found I was going to have another child. I couldn't live with my parents any longer; it was a packed house. My son and I went into a homeless shelter. It was for a very short time, just two and a half months. My caseworkers were amazed at how fast I got us out of there. I said, 'Another baby is about to come out of me. We cannot live in one little room.' I worked hard at my job, found us a place to live, and got on with it.

"In my work here at the foundation, I do some IT, updating software and handling computer problems, and other technical stuff. But I also do the Web site. It's ironic—I've done a 180 from my Year Up training, which was IT, always taking things apart. You learn hard skills there, of course. But I'm most thankful for coming out with a flexible attitude."

Areva's journey has come full circle with us in a nice way. When she was a student, her younger brother Bapit* came with her one day to a Year Up event. "He was just a little kid," she recalls, "but I was thinking about how he deserved a good future."

Bapit became a Year Up student in 2010, interned as a fund accountant at an investment bank, and graduated in July 2011. He was a terrific intern, and the bank offered him a permanent job, which he politely declined. He is now enrolled in college and using his tech skills to work full time in telecommunications and earn his way toward a four-year degree.

JANELLE CLARK

"Remember, I was one of the youngest, quietest students in that class. And starting my internship at Fidelity was like the first day of Year Up all over again. I'm eighteen, going into a federal building. The manager comes to greet me and says, 'Okay, we're going to get you a badge, then we're taking your picture and you're getting fingerprinted.' *What?* At that point I realized this is the real world. They're doing an intensive federal background check on me.

"I had my badge and I was feeling really good. I landed in an area of a lot of cubicles where it seemed everyone knew what they were doing. I was working to fit in, paying attention to the environment and studying the culture. In the beginning, I was feeling so homesick I was ready to go back to Year Up every Wednesday morning.

"At home, my closest friend saw the difference in me. I had changed my attitude. I took things a bit more seriously. She could see me pushing her after a while. I said, 'Okay now, I feel like I'm on the path toward the next step in life. What are you going to do? There's so much more to life than this little piece of the puzzle that we've been exposed to. I'm going to jump outside the box. Are you going to come with me?'"

Her best friend never did apply. But we were all impressed by Janelle's growing communication skills, her warmth, and the willingness of this once painfully shy young woman to "put myself out there a bit." A few months after graduation, we hired her at Year Up. The irony of her first position wasn't lost on the young woman who had sat reading her book during our outreach presentation at City Year. As outreach and recruitment coordinator, Janelle helped plan recruitment events, spoke at career and college fairs, interviewed applicants, and helped create new ways to let young adults know about us: digital presentations, TV, and more radio.

She then spent three years at an aerospace company before she felt a pull to return to the nonprofit area. With the expertise and certification of her Cambridge College degree, she is now a case manager in a multiservice agency that works to move families out of homelessness and poverty. And she wears another hat: As assistant director of workforce development there, Janelle recruits participants at open-house sessions. She meets with every person enrolled to help support them throughout the programs. In her way, Janelle is "student services."

"I enjoy the one on one and the more public outreach," she says. "I think I'm good at it. Who knew?"

Twenty of our twenty-two students from Class One graduated. Harry Duprey entered the military, where punctuality is requested in the most uncompromising ways. Another student had to leave the program for family reasons, although she still calls me from time to time. Of those twenty graduates, more than 80 percent are working today, and their salaries average almost twenty dollars an hour.

CHAPTER EIGHT
"Reach and Strive for 2005!"

I first shied away from being that intelligent student,
Now I am a positive black man that's all about MOVEMENT,
I claim my victory and will never concede,
Failure not an option, I will succeed.

—Rashawn Facey-Castillo,
from a slam poetry performance by Year Up
students, Boston

HOW DID YEAR UP GROW UP?
Quickly, deliberately, and with a continuous goal of upgrading the business practices that would make our results clear and attractive to investors, both corporate and philanthropic. As a businessman I could anticipate the tough queries we would get if we wanted to serve more young adults in more locations.

How can you do this in *six months?*
What's your retention rate?
You must be cherry-picking the best students if they're doing
so well.
Show me.
By late 2002 it was time for another contemplative porch session with Eileen Brown. Year Up's enrollment had grown from a manageable twenty-two to sixty per class, and we were bumping into one another in the hallways

on Summer Street. Once again Eileen and I settled into those comfortable chairs and talked about the future of both our organizations. We agreed that the college accreditation for Year Up course work was proving to be a good partnership. But we needed more room. And Cambridge College could use some additional income to help serve its students.

Solution: We would use its classrooms, normally empty during the day when Cambridge students were working. We would pay rent to use the space from 8:00 a.m. to 3:30, teaching the same curriculum we used downtown. So in early 2003 we started a full Year Up learning community of thirty students in Cambridge College's facility at 1000 Massachusetts Avenue. We used a section of the second floor—one small office and we had access to three classrooms "branded" with our signature blue-printed logo. It had a full-time staff of six.

Within a year, word of mouth would become our best and most common method of drawing potential applicants. Across all of our sites nationwide, positive buzz in a city's neediest neighborhoods is a mighty communicator. After all, seeing the changes in family members, neighbors, and schoolmates is believing. But in the beginning we were still experimenting with all sorts of outreach: radio, open houses, and continued visits to high schools, community centers, and churches.

It was pretty basic "social media," lots of shoe leather, and talk. Facebook was still being hatched by Mark Zuckerberg in Harvard Yard, a couple of blocks from our home. YouTube was about a year away. Print was still a viable option, so we decided to advertise in one of Boston's free newspapers handed out on street corners and transit stops. The *Metro* was passed off to rushing commuters by a corps of mostly young people who could be our students. In the fall of 2004, our ad caught the attention of a very hardworking and dissatisfied underachiever who reached out and grabbed a paper.

Rashawn Facey-Castillo was a nineteen-year-old with a GED, a magnificent cascade of braids, 110 reasons to be angry at the world, and a poet's powers of observation. To channel the frustrations that life dealt him, Rashawn had been pouring his thoughts into journals since he was eleven; he still has all those composition notebooks. He recalls the fateful moment: "One day I was getting on a bus and picked up a *Metro*. And the ad said, 'Earn while you learn.' It caught my eye and stuck with me. You always hear about racking up so much debt going to school. At the time, it didn't seem to me that there was much value to that. So I went to Year Up, and the first person who greeted me was Linda. She was so genuine. She kind of radiated. I felt moved, but I didn't know how. I felt she could see deep inside. When I sat down and spoke with her she was extremely candid about what she felt my potential was, that there was purpose and meaning in my coming there that day."

Rashawn took an application and went back to the crowded home he shared with his mother, a licensed practical nurse, and six other children. Tuning out the domestic din, he sat down and started his application essay.

"I wrote about why I feel I'm worth an opportunity. It was about counting myself out, feeling like the world had already had something against me. I had a chip on my shoulder because of all the anger issues that I felt, for so long.

"I lived in a single-parent home. Seven kids, not all my mom's children. I am my mom's oldest son. We moved around because of trouble between my mother and my father, who would come into the household, stay for a little while, leave, come back, they'd reconcile, then he'd be gone again. From an early age I was left to my own actions because my mom worked nights. As long as I can remember my mom has worked long hours, and she left it up to the older siblings to maintain the household when she went to work."

When he was about fourteen, problems erupted between his parents again, and Rashawn could no longer watch his mother endure what he felt was an abusive situation. He made a decision that I hope I'd make as well, although it came with significant consequences. Stepping in to protect his mother, Rashawn—a young man with no history of violence before or since—pushed his father down a flight of stairs, causing him to break both legs.

"So I got taken out of the house because of anger management and whatnot. I found myself running in the streets at a very early age. I would come home on the weekends and touch base with my mom. I had all types of jobs. I was going to school. There was never really a problem with me scholastically. My problem was how do I make money *now*? My mom has a lot of children; my father's not around; I've been taken out of the house because of my father. I felt there was a lot of responsibility on my shoulders."

He took any job he could find, stocking retail stores like Marshalls, Bradlees, and Strawberry, working as a health center custodian. For one endless summer he worked, underpaid and "under the table," at a barbecue restaurant. "I would portion four ounces of coleslaw, eight hours a day. Thousands and thousands. I would bring the money home and help with groceries, just trying to maintain the household."

Along the way he dropped out of high school, then got his GED at his mother's insistence. The incident with his father had left him with a mix of guilt and resentment—and an unwelcome brush with the juvenile justice system. "That perpetuated a lot of the negativity. I felt like my reputation was already established for me and I wasn't doing anything but fulfilling what people already saw in me. I was standoffish with people I felt had a negative perception of me. I didn't trust anyone outside of my inner circle, my mom and siblings."

He was touchy, aloof, and convinced that nobody really knew or cared about the injustices in his short life. Then Rashawn went through orientation with his new classmates at Year Up: "A lot of people had worse scenarios than mine. I was like, 'Wow, and you survived *that*?" At the end of orientation week, business communications instructor Melanee Grondahl was conducting a slam poetry exercise. Each student contributed a line that addressed the question "How did you find yourself here today?" As they wrote out their lines, Rashawn offered his services as maestro of catharsis.

"After we got all the students' lines together, I helped Melanee arrange it in a way that had a flow to it. We performed it and it was a very uplifting moment. A lot of people got really emotional; it was something that meant a lot to them. The poem was all about self-renewal. It was a very eureka moment for me. I realized that everything that was written in my journals actually played itself out in other people's lives around me."

One by one, Melanee's newly minted poets stood and rapped, half whispered, or shouted it all out: gripes, cheers, trials, and aspirations. Someone even channeled a plaintive voice calling from back in the neighborhood, bereft:

What happened! You left me broken and tired?
You were my best friends! You left me for Year Up.
Will I see you again?

For the new circle of friends in Class Five, the voices were still wary after a tough orientation week, but overwhelmingly upbeat:

Early in the morning, late in the game . . . I know I have to make it before 8:30 or I'll feel the pain.

Though Monday I was nervous, today I am not.
I was able to interact with my peers. It went better than I thought.

Exciting, exhilarating, can't wait to get up.
To experience change and never give up.

Who has made it through orientation? We have.
Who has strived? We have.
Who will continue to persevere through Year Up? We will.
We will make it through it all.

I feel lucky.
I feel happy.
I feel good that I got to know all of you.
Reach and strive for 2005!

Despite all this encouraging school spirit, Rashawn still wasn't quite sure what to make of us. Over the course of his L & D months, we had a number of long talks. He admitted that at first he was industrious for very practical reasons: "I wanted my full stipend check, no infractions, at the end of the week. I was never late, always tried to dress as dapper as I could. As far as language, it took me a little bit of time to realize there's a different way you should communicate, depending on where you're at. That came with the advisers and mentors going, 'Hey hey hey.' Checking it before we got to our internships."

Rashawn was referring to our practice of mining "teachable moments" that might come up on any given day. All of the staff learned to be hyper-vigilant for an opportunity. It might be a gentle language correction or a discussion on respecting one's colleagues that stems from trash left in the student eating area. Richard liked to begin some classes with current affairs discussions that might offer an ethics lesson. Sometimes students needed to tone down certain character traits that might not play well in the workplace. Rashawn, never shy to speak up, said he was glad to learn the wisdom of restraint. "I was grateful to have the corrections while we were still at Year Up. The classroom situation was protected and like family, but when we went to our internships we were on our own again. No one wanted to make mistakes."

Linda made a genius match when she found a mentor for Rashawn. He certainly needed a savvy, compassionate older male in his life. A year earlier, an investment professional named Brian Spector had called me on the recommendation from a friend. He was successful and prosperous as a partner of the Baupost Group, a Boston-based investment partnership, and he was ready to look for a meaningful philanthropic outlet. Brian is now the chair of our Boston board and has made a huge impact on our organization. Brian and his wife, Stephanie, have also become close friends. He and Year Up found each other at exactly the right moment.

"It had to be about 2003," Brian recalls. "After years of working very long days, I was at a point in my career where I had more time. I was looking to figure out how to spend my time and money on the best organizations in the city, doing things that I personally want to focus on. And that's helping people help themselves. I asked a friend who worked for a local philanthropic foundation, 'Who are the people in this city who do it well? I want young organizations with a different mentality.' I didn't want to find the next traditional United Way type thing. She said, 'You've got to meet Gerald Chertavian.'"

Brian called and suggested we meet for lunch. I told him the best way to understand what we do was to come on over to Year Up. He did so and liked what he saw. As we fielded our next class, he became a mentor to get deeper into the process. Rashawn became Brian's second mentee. "Rashawn and I have similar characters," Brian said. "We're both outgoing; he has a will to succeed, a drive. We just clicked."

By then Brian was sure that he had found what he had been searching for in our program. It's important to understand the appeal Year Up had for him. We've been able to build these relationships with new, results-oriented philanthropists like Brian in city after city because we use organizational process and a business vocabulary that speaks to them directly and with complete transparency. Just what did Brian need to hear?

"Gerald's got a good story to tell. He also speaks the language of business. So the ability to have a conversation with someone who thinks about numbers made sense to someone like me. I'm a numerical guy; he could speak numbers. You want to back people who have drive and passion and intelligence. He had those things.

"The organization was very results focused: Here's a young adult, and we can teach him tech skills and soft skills, take him from eight dollars an hour at Best Buy to a job where he's getting health benefits and fifteen dollars an hour. With a skill. It's like a lightbulb went on: This makes sense to me. I asked a lot about process: How do you make sure they're a valuable employee? I think Gerald understood that the process had to be set before expanding the program. He can't expand unless the process is good. He can take that platform and expand to other cities now because he has the process down. At Year Up they're learning *how* to learn, and it's wonderful to watch. The students have different goals and motivations at the end than they did at the beginning. That's what's kept me so consistently interested and engaged."

In his many talks with Rashawn, Brian also sensed the deep pull that a program like ours could create over time for inner-city youth struggling to get out—and stay out—of dangerous circumstances. "Many students have to face going back to an environment that others are trying to pull them back into. That's hard. You see how many referrals come from current students where they're pulling people up with them."

By the time he was finished with the L & D phase, Rashawn was definitely not looking back. He told us that he planned to mentor young people in his old neighborhood, a pledge he's more than made good on. But first he needed to find his own place in the work world. For his internship we placed him at 3i, an international venture capital firm headquartered in the United Kingdom. He was the first intern in its small Waltham, Massachusetts, office. Close work with his manager led to a surprising opportunity to broaden his vistas.

"I would work on managing their servers, building out their computers, making sure the CEO's laptop was functioning. Everything was so interesting back then—dot-coms were popping up—and I'm the only intern with a manager supporting an entire venture capital firm. I felt I had established myself, like *wow*.

"I worked as hard as I could, so much so that the company paid for me to travel to England and San Francisco with my manager to work on their servers. I get there and they're giving me projects: 'Here's what we need by week's end. It's on you to manage your time.' The hotel was paid for. It was a warm reception, and my manager took great care of me. He brought his wife; we went to dinner every night. It was a great experience altogether."

The first time Rashawn called me from England, he unfortunately forgot the time difference. It was 4:00 a.m. in Boston. I can still hear his voice crackling with excitement. He was out on the street, gazing at two iconic London sights, Westminster Abbey and Big Ben. And me? I was grinning from ear to ear, bolt upright and hyperconscious of how important this moment was for him. He had earned his way there, and it was so far from anything he had imagined for himself. I remembered how David's first trips to London had blasted open his perceptions of the larger world and his place in it. Rashawn had a similar reinvigoration: "I came back with a completely new sense of myself. I was reassured, I was motivated. I was no longer living in the shadow of my past. I felt very confident in my capability."

Not surprisingly, the company offered him a job after graduation. It had terrific potential and required him to work in England for his first two years. But Rashawn's mother had just had another baby. He didn't feel he could leave his family, so he turned down the job. His strength of character in making that tough decision was no surprise. How much I had wanted the opportunity for him, though.

But let's leave the new graduate pondering his next move for a moment and fast-forward to a phone call that would greatly change Year Up's future— and Rashawn's as well.

"Gerald, are you around on Thursday at noon? I'd like to bring somebody by to see the program."

Joe Smialowski was on Year Up's board of directors and a major champion of our program. He would not have called unless it was something important. Joe was just a little busy as vice chairman of Bank of America, where he managed all of the bank's technology and operations. In the few years that he had been a board member, he had always provided us with valuable advice as well as some priceless introductions. When Joe called, I cleared my decks.

"Of course, come on over."

On Thursday, Joe was standing in our bustling fifth-floor lobby with Joe Antonellis, the vice chairman of State Street Corporation, a leading financial services firm that was founded here in Boston in 1792. I was *very* happy to see him. Program builders like me can spend years just trying to get in the room with a top-level executive like him. State Street was locally venerable and, after two centuries, it was a global powerhouse in the financial services industry. This was the sort of dream corporate partner with complex and growing IT requirements that could potentially have a huge need for a substantial pipeline of qualified talent. Even when I was blue-skying my initial business plan, I couldn't have come up with a more perfect partner to help provide our students with opportunities.

Joe Antonellis was on the firm's executive committee and responsible for its massive technology operations. He had brought along State Street's executive vice president for global infrastructure services, Madge Meyer. I welcomed them with a huge smile, but I hardly let myself hope. Of course, it was Year Up students who sealed the deal. Madge Meyer recalls that day: "I asked Joe [Antonellis] on the way over, 'Why do we have to see these folks? What's Year Up?' He told me, 'Just wait and see.'"

They took our standard tour given by a student, and they asked plenty of questions. Madge found herself instantly engaged. "The students knew a bit of computer technology," she said. "But what impressed me most was that they could also speak really well in front of strangers, which is very unusual for any young person. They presented themselves very well. I remember thinking, '*How* does this happen?'"

We gave Joe and Madge a crash course in Year Up's "ABCs"—attitude, behavior, and communication. I knew from running a business myself that I'd rather have an employee with the right attitude; I can always teach him or her what he or she needs to know to do the job. Our visitors had the same perspective from their long years in business. Employers look for behavior before skills: the motivation and willingness to learn, the ability to communicate and perform as a team member, reliability. It also came back to the notion of developing character as well as skills in our classrooms.

We explained the parts of the program, including business communications, professional skills, and tech that helped us turn out well-rounded, workplace-ready graduates. I made it clear: We strive for alums equally comfortable engaging a corporate executive in the elevator and reassembling a server.

Madge locked on to our logic right away. "Most organizations only focused on technical knowledge, and not on the whole package," she said. "If you think about it, those ABCs are the fundamentals of being successful. I learned that students earned money at Year Up, and that they could lose money if they were a minute late. I was impressed with that too. It is the discipline people need."

As they walked out onto Summer Street, Joe Antonellis asked Madge, "How many interns do you want to take?"

She stopped, stared at him a moment, and answered, "I think twenty!"

"What? Twenty! Where did that come from?"

Madge explained that gorgeous round number: "That's all the slots I have. I want to give those young men and women a chance."

Joe Antonellis had a similar reaction: "What impressed me most was the professional environment that had been created and what Year Up did to train its students. I thought this could be really powerful. We are one of the largest employers in Boston, and we could work with young adults from the inner city to help them break out of that environment."

That January afternoon in 2005 was day one of a remarkable alliance. State Street Corporation became and remains our largest internship partner. Over the next several years, we grew the relationship from twenty interns to around eighty per year. Stemming from Joe Smialowski's initial introductions, over the next six years State Street has committed to more than 350 internship opportunities for our young adults. At Year Up, we have worked hard to match State Street's commitment. With Joe Antonellis's support, we expanded placement and our curriculum beyond technology to financial operations and worked closely with State Street managers to understand their needs. Joe recalls the shift: "I said to them, 'The relationship is going great, but we really don't hire a lot of desktop support folks. We need several hundred people each year in fund accounting and would love for you to prepare students for those roles.'"

We had always intended to have a curriculum flexible enough to trend with the labor market. Whether it is fund accounting, desktop support, retail banking, or, in the near future, opportunities in the health-care sector, we will always look to train our students for the jobs that are both here today and growing tomorrow. We recognize that almost all of these jobs require complex communications as well. A full course of ABCs raises them to a level suited to a wide range of applications.

We put our heads together with State Street to make the adjustments. But it hasn't been all business with that company. We have also been amazed at the basic kindness, commitment, and community spirit of the State Street people. Time and time again, we met employees at all levels of State Street who believed in our students and were willing to give them an opportunity to demonstrate their potential. That full engagement started at the top. Madge was totally invested with the very first group. She explained, "We used to have a scorecard, and we rated all of the interns—where they should improve, where they were doing well. I reviewed these scorecards with all of the managers. Our managers were very positive about the program and reported that all of the interns tried hard and really want to learn. We had a couple that didn't work out, but very few. Most of them all worked out really well."

Joe said he was pleased to diverge from the firm's long-standing hiring practices when it made good sense. "Our profile had always been to hire people who graduated from college. And sometimes those folks didn't have the same level of preparation as the Year Up students." We have had countless State Street volunteers over the years—mentors, guest speakers, tutors, guest teachers—and State Street's foundation has very generously supported our expansion in Boston with a significant grant. It is one of those rare organizations where the folks responsible for corporate social responsibility have a real seat at the table. They don't just get the fact that they need to build a diverse workforce. They live it each day and create the culture and the context that promote diversity across all tiers of their organization.

George Russell is the head of State Street's philanthropic foundation. Before he took the helm he was a banking executive with a respected national reputation as an ethical corporate citizen. George has spoken at our graduations, marched alongside our students during our Walk for Opportunity, and always been there to support and champion our efforts. State Street's global head of human resources, Alison Quirk, accompanied us to our first-ever Capitol Hill Day, speaking with members of Congress about why it is important to both support and expand programs like Year Up. They walk their talk in a way that gives me faith that together we can change this country and close the Opportunity Divide.

Which brings us back to Rashawn, a new graduate who was eager, capable, and in need of a job. Though he had not interned there and was not a known quantity, State Street agreed to extend him a chance. Following his graduation, it hired him as a contract worker—not permanent and as yet without benefits. For a year and a half he did great work for the company in IT. Madge recalls one of their conversations during that time: "Rashawn came to me and said, 'I love your organization, Madge. Although I got a very good offer to become a full-time employee in the fund accounting area, I would hate to leave IT. What do you think?' I said, 'Rashawn, it is a great thing if you have a broader background. You're young, you are going to be an executive one day, and I think this is a fantastic opportunity for you to move from IT. Why don't you go to fund accounting, learn a different part of the

business? That would be fantastic.' So Rashawn went there and got a permanent job, which is great because we do pay college tuition if you are a permanent employee. Rashawn finished college, and he did very well in the fund
accounting area."

It all worked; Rashawn finished at Cambridge College while he worked,
and he maintained an A average. I know because he sent me his grades every
semester. But it's not a fairy-tale ending for every intern, and not all has gone
smoothly as we have built our partnership with State Street. We have had to
course correct, tweak our curriculum, and manage the small percentage of
interns who do not meet our internship partners' expectations.

Timely intervention by our staff is critical in adjusting relationships and
solving intern problems. Sometimes the issues on the job stem from personal
difficulties that the interns' managers could not possibly be aware of. I remember getting a manager's call about one young woman who did not show up
for work one day during a grim winter because the heat was off in her apartment building and she was afraid that her baby, even in a sitter's care, might
become ill from the bitter cold. She had nowhere to go to warm up. When we
spoke to her, she was freezing, frantic with worry, and too embarrassed to
call her supervisor to explain the situation. When we contacted him, his
reaction was quick and compassionate: "What can I do to help?"

Perhaps the biggest test would come in late 2008, as our Boston team was
placing the largest class of interns in Year Up history in the midst of the global
economic downturn. The collapsing Lehman Brothers was Year Up's largest
client in New York. We also temporarily lost traction with Merrill Lynch, our
second-largest client during the merger with Bank of America. As the companies sorted through changes, this affected our partnerships. At a time
when many other employers were scaling back their commitments, State
Street rose to the challenge by hosting more interns than ever before. For
Madge and the rest of her team at State Street, she explained, it was simply
the right thing to do: "Our company always fosters a community-service
culture. And with Year Up it goes down all the way to first-line managers.
This is an opportunity to do something good for the community and for
State Street. I have attended every single Year Up graduation, twice a year.
Seeing the students get their certificates, hearing their moving stories, how
Year Up changed their lives—it really helped me to understand how fortunate we are to be able to do this for others. My mother always said, 'When
you have a chance to do a good deed, you do it right then and there, because

you may not always be so lucky to have a chance to do a good thing.' We grew up knowing that giving is a privilege. You are lucky to be able to give. And I was very lucky to be in the position at the right time to work with Year Up."

Joe Antonellis will be the first to tell you that it has also proven to be a sound investment. The young adults who are ultimately hired by State Street are less prone to job hopping than their peers with bachelor's degrees, saving the firm significant dollars in recruitment and training costs. "The Year Up interns have a desire to work hard," Joe has observed, "and they are staying with us." Just over six years after launching the partnership, it has become impossible to enter the State Street cafeteria in Quincy without bumping into a Year Up graduate. Joe summed it up nicely: "Ultimately, we're doing our job of being a good corporate citizen. And in this case, it also helps us to create a new source of talent."

With about 120 alumni working as full-time State Street employees, we see the possibilities for real, life-changing workforce development in our nation. Year Up graduates participate in a formal alumni network—just like graduates of Boston College, Harvard, and MIT. Alumni from the first round of hiring have now passed their five-year anniversary, moving up the corporate ladder to management positions. More recent hires work at mastering their first position while making progress toward a college degree. Essentially, State Street represents a corporate "ecosystem" for Year Up interns and hirees. Comparing notes and sharing information at different points on the job ladder, our graduates are finding the means to cross the Opportunity Divide—and stay there!

Today, Rashawn's title at State Street is an impressive mouthful: senior portfolio administrator/fund account manager. He is also the founder and CEO of a Boston nonprofit working to combat violence in the urban community. Above all, I count him as a good friend to our family. Our children leap into his arms and call him Uncle Rashawn. He is one of those graduates whose success has moved me deeply. A couple of times, after a long work-and-travel day that invariably ends late in our home office, I've clicked on a YouTube video of one of Rashawn's spoken-word performances and—to my surprise—found my face wet. How proud and honored Kate and I were to be invited to Rashawn's wedding in Saint Maarten in June 2011. Rashawn had been at Brian Spector's wedding, and Brian and his wife, Stephanie, traveled with us to witness this happy milestone. Our children were there, and the day was sparkling, the guests emotional, and Rashawn's bride, Nadjya, beyond radiant. It was another of those rare, crystal-clear moments that tells you, *Okay, yes, this is working. Push it forward.*

In January 2005—the same time Rashawn graduated and State Street signed on—we took another huge step and opened a second site in Providence, Rhode Island. It was the result of a year's cautious planning and fact-finding. When we decided to expand the organization, we drew a circle that extended no more than a ninety-minute drive from Boston in order to keep the process manageable and within easy reach of our most experienced staff and support. That circle also included Hartford, Connecticut, and the Massachusetts cities of Lowell, Lawrence, Springfield, and Worcester. We did all the research on each location and asked some basic questions:

How many disconnected young people live there?

How many entry-level jobs in tech are we looking at?

How much money is there? What's the giving capacity?

What does the public transportation system look like?

Where do the poor people live in relation to the jobs? Can they get there on public transportation?

What's the political climate? Is there someone in charge who would be supportive of this sort of program?

We worked all of the data for the cities into a comparison chart, and Providence came out with the highest grade, a solid B-plus. I had someone in mind to launch and run it as executive director. Twenty-six-year-old Sara Strammiello, who was then in her second year of Harvard Business School, was tremendously capable and wanted a career in nonprofit work. I also had an idea who might fund the expansion. Paul Salem of Providence Equity had been a donor and supporter since that amazing race to learn he had seen out on Summer Street. I thought he might help underwrite a start-up in his hometown. He could also walk us around to the city's civic leaders and to the businesses we would want to sell internships to.

Sara was just in her first year at HBS when we were introduced by a Bowdoin colleague named Peter Sims, who has always been a greatly intuitive matchmaker of talents. "You really ought to talk to her," he told me. After a long conversation over lunch, I decided that Sara had to work for us in some capacity. She had done volunteer work with Year Up, then worked for us full time during the summer with great aptitude and dedication. Clearly, she was a good fit for our organization and our students. So we offered her the Providence job in the fall of her second year. She accepted, with the understanding that when she graduated in June 2004 she would start full-time preparation to open Year Up Providence in January 2005. I'll admit that once she had accepted our offer, I did my unwitting best to torpedo her academic career. Typical phone call:

"Sara, we have to go down and meet the mayor of Providence today."

"But I have class."

"Forget class, I'll pick you up at eight a.m."

We traipsed down to Rhode Island constantly to meet people there and huddle with Paul Salem. Thanks to him, we built a solid local board and a strong roster of corporate partners, among them CVS and Citizens Bank. Despite a challenged local job market, which has only grown tighter, Paul believed that his city was the place for us.

"Providence was the logical choice," he said. "Rhode Island is small, so to be able to go see the governor, the mayor, is not that hard. This is an easy political sell. We're working with young men and women who have limited opportunities and job prospects and putting them to work. How can you argue with that? So we had the political buy-in very early. Mayor Cicilline just believed in the program—he knew it was well funded and he needed it for his city."

Determined to lead his fellow corporate partners by example, Paul took an intern from that first class in Providence. This was a bit problematic, as he explains. "Providence Equity doesn't do interns. We're a small shop and we don't even have an IT department. It's just one guy. I went to him and said, 'Take this intern.' So from Year Up Providence's first class we got Obasi Osborne. He was working at the Hot Club, a very popular waterfront place, washing dishes. He's got dreadlocks; he's a pretty laid-back type of guy."

Nonetheless, Obasi was fast out of the starting gate, professionally dressed, dreads neatly tied back and tech skills honed.

"Within a month, our IT guy told me, 'Obasi is the go-to person to fix any technical problem.' After his internship he was hired as a full-time IT

worker. He was doing a great job and gained the trust of everyone around here. Obasi was also one of the first people of color in our whole staff of about a hundred. That's obviously changing."

After a couple of years on the job, Obasi showed up in Paul's office for a talk about his future.

"I'm thinking about going to college," Obasi said.

"Great. Where do you want to go?"

"URI [University of Rhode Island], I guess."

"What about Brown?"

"You think I can get in?"

"Why not? You're smart enough."

Obasi did some research and found that he could work and go to school part time with Brown's continuing education program. He began that way, then was accepted into Brown's four-year degree program. "Whatever he decides to do when he finishes," Paul said, "he's got a job waiting for him here. He's a brilliant guy. And he's just that good."

Then there was the day the phone rang with the call you never want to get. "One of your interns just stole a computer, and he lied about it, and we have him on surveillance camera!"

Things work until they don't, right? I got an instant pit in my stomach as the chief information officer of a large financial services corporation screamed at me through the phone. He was livid and minced no words. I could scarcely believe what was happening.

"You told me you had students who were going to be good. These people always steal if you let them."

His words almost knocked me over. I knew his anger at the situation was no excuse to use racist language. That was a serious foul. But he was in no mood to have such offensive stereotyping corrected. I tried to cool him down.

"All right, you're really upset right now. What would you like me to do? I'm sorry. Obviously, I'm upset too. All I can tell you is this is not common. Would you like to press charges because he's committed a crime?"

He didn't want to go that far, but he felt the need to holler at me some minutes more. As I absorbed his fury, I started feeling my own emotions rise. I had worked so long and hard to build a relationship with this company. Given the number of meetings, the number of times I had pitched it, we're

talking months and years. And now I've got the head guy screaming at me? Oh Lord, why was this happening?

Once we hung up, I called the intern and asked him to come to our office. I also brought in the Year Up director who managed that corporate relationship to talk things over before the young man arrived. Kevin Barry is a wonderful man who handles our largest intern partnerships. Seeing years of his efforts potentially up in smoke, he was not happy. I let him vent, then thought long and hard about the lessons I'd learned from that first student firing with Harry Duprey, when I had let my emotions get in the way of the best service to our young adults. This was not a time to be angry, and I focused my energy on maintaining control. I was then able to ask the right question of the intern when he walked in.

"Are you okay?"

When he said he was, I pressed on. "I ask that because you're a smart young man. And I know something must be seriously wrong for you to do something that has such serious consequences for you, for Year Up, for our relationship with that company—and for the company itself. Everyone just lost. I'd like to understand what was going on in your life that led you to make a decision that has resulted in such bad consequences for everyone. I'm guessing something was really, really wrong for you to have made that bad a decision."

He looked confused and asked, "You're not angry with me?"

I told him what I had long ago come to realize in these difficult situations: Anger is not going to help anyone. The intern automatically fired himself from our program, and it was a sad departure. After he left, Kevin said, "Aren't you upset, aren't you *furious?* He just destroyed years of our effort."

Even I was surprised by the even tone of my answer. "That's what we do. When this happens, you can't be angry about it."

Intellectually, I knew this to be necessary and true. But if I felt anger at the lost effort, the damaged relationship, at least I knew by then to process it privately. Part of learning how to do this work is not to pass moral judgment, not to convey a message that implies, "You're a bad person." I can say instead, "What you did is not what I would do and not the code I live by. And what you did caused you to fire yourself, caused you to lose your chance to graduate. You can't get a reference from me anymore; I'm not going to lie for you." And that should suffice. He had already suffered a lot. So me trying to inflict more pain emotionally isn't going to help anyone.

If we really were going to be able to attract the sponsors and capital to grow, I needed a serious operations person, someone who could streamline and standardize our process, clarify our metrics, and keep the trains running come hell or high recession. Enter one of my most brilliant hires—if I do say so—Sue Meehan. She agreed to take on the multiple responsibilities of director of finance, operations, and student services. She would later become our first chief operating officer. I hired Sue to come in and really start to build the business. She does all that and ten times more as our resident process expert and unwavering conscience.

I think we were a good fit for Sue. She is a lifelong campaigner for social justice, a former political activist and respected corporate executive. As chief operating officer of Share Group, Inc., Sue helped build the premier telefund-raising firm for progressive nonprofits, growing the company from a start-up of three staffers to five hundred employees and twenty million dollars in revenue in ten years. She's worked on a range of local and national political and issue campaigns and spent her early career years working in higher education.

When Sue joined us in 2005, we started to professionalize in a serious, forward-thinking way. I had pretty much been running the organization myself. I can manage effectively and lead well, but when it comes down to process and structure systems, I yield the floor. Sue now understands much of the business end better than I do. I was lucky to find a partner who could complement my skills so well.

"I came in as the director of finance, operations, and student services," Sue remembers. "And over time my position morphed to COO. When I started, we had a Boston site and our Providence office was about six months old. My job was split between program responsibilities, the finance role, and trying to make sure we were building the infrastructure to support multiple sites. I looked first to urgent 'must haves' for multiple sites and initially spent time ensuring we had tight financial controls, strong cash-management systems, and structures for measuring financial performance by site. Gerald was executive director of Boston at the time, and I played a program role, overseeing admissions, career services, and operations. Being entrenched in program for the first three years was invaluable as my role evolved."

The growth we envisioned was not an issue for Sue, given where she had come from. "I was coming from a $20 million organization to a $5 million and was prepared to ensure smooth growth for Year Up. As we added new sites, I started focusing less on program and more on national functions, building systems that were essential for scaling—strong data-tracking tools, HR processes, program tools. I started working with Gerald on building a cross-site leadership team to run the whole company. Right now we have a collaborative national leadership team of fourteen people. Shared leadership has helped build a strong companywide culture and unified focus."

When I run the numbers, I see so much value in what Sue has helped to build. We've gone from a budget of $100,000 to $40 million. Our last staff retreat was for 180 employees. We have top-flight health insurance; we have increased our benefits but our per capita costs have remained constant. Our partnership has worked better than I'd ever envisioned, and I'm sure part of it is our mutual understanding of the job description "social entrepreneur."

"I've worked with other entrepreneurs where I've felt like I played the 'Whoa, put on the brakes!' role," Sue says. "I don't feel that here. Gerald is incredibly entrepreneurial, but he's not taking risks in the same way I've seen other entrepreneurs do. He feels very responsible for donors' money and to all our stakeholders in a different way than I've seen in for-profit entrepreneurs. It's very levelheaded. He's very on board with a conservative approach to keeping cash in the bank, not running things on a line of credit or living on a financial edge."

When I look at our entire infrastructure, from HR practices up to the astounding flexibility of our database, I think of Sue as a master builder. Given all of our unpredictable human factors, the order she has conferred is even more impressive. Just don't make the mistake of thinking she's all process and no passion. Sue drove our companywide effort to improve our organization's cultural competency—something we'll get to later. But like any good general, she also understands that the prize—social and economic justice—can't be won with an undisciplined corps. Getting the process under control helps ensure quality, and we insist on full participation at all levels. Any employee not using our main database as required will be called out for the lapse. Continued noncompliance risks a pink slip.

"In order to move this forward we have to have these structures in place, a system so that it runs really smoothly," she says. "I'm the one who does need to focus on the risks to keep ensuring that we're thoughtful in our planning, saying that we need to go slow. But Gerald's really supportive of that. He's never said to me, as other entrepreneurs have, 'You're worrying too much.'"

It's no stretch to say that I sleep better with Sue at the helm of our operations, helping chart a steady growth that's sustainable—especially in today's fiscally turbulent environment. I wish a lot of things in this business were as well considered and orderly as Sue's thought process. But that's just not in the cards.

"You don't fucking care about me!" Marcelle screamed. Tears and melted mascara coursed down her face and she was rocking from side to side as though in pain. Oh God. What was this?

No matter how solid and shiny our metrics were, things hardly run by the numbers in our students' lives. Four years in, I was still learning my own blind spots from the mental health professionals we'd brought on board.

"You think I'm lying," Marcelle went on, "and I swear to you I am not. I trusted you and this is how you treat me. I am fucking exhausted, and I am hungry. The reason I am losing weight is because I am pregnant and have been throwing up all the time."

In the fall of 2005, I found myself sitting opposite a shaking, hysterical young woman who had been called in to meet with Rob Fladger, a talented master level clinical psychologist whom we had hired earlier that year. He is a practicing clinician with several mental health agencies in Massachusetts and has taught in the psychology and human services departments at Cambridge College. I was certainly glad to have him controlling the situation that day—even if I wasn't exactly sure where he was going with it.

There had been rumors of drug use in the women's room, and Marcelle's behavior had become erratic and irritable. She was missing days and not calling in. Marcelle certainly looked terrible sitting there. Her voice was cracked, hoarse, and intermittently profane. She swore on her mother's grave that she was telling the truth. It was painful to witness and I was frozen in my chair. I had no idea what to do. Left to my inexperienced devices, I would have believed Marcelle. She was so convincing, and I already felt terrible that we were confronting an expectant mother with morning sickness in such an aggressive way. It seemed cruel and unnecessary.

Rob held his ground and pressed on. "Look, Marcelle, I know you're using. Your eyes are all dilated, you are rocking back and forth, and you are currently high. Let's all tell the truth here. Now, if you want to come back to this program, I need you to leave now, get a drug test, and bring us the result tomorrow. That's it; nothing else works."

I couldn't believe how sure Rob was of himself and how clear he was in both his delivery and his control of the situation. I realized at that moment that such incredible highs and lows would always be part and parcel of this work. Drug addiction is one of the most difficult situations to manage, and I am glad to say that not many of our students have had to cope with this devastating disease. When it comes up, you have to face it head on, without compromise. Required drug testing for all students would come later in our program. But we have never tolerated the use of hard drugs. We will help a student find treatment, but no one with an addiction is permitted to stay in the program.

The hysterics went on for twenty minutes longer, with more screaming and tears, until finally Marcelle agreed to get a drug test to prove to us that we were "full of shit." We gave her some food and called a taxi to take her to the testing center. She walked out of the building, traded her food for some money, and presumably found someone to sell her another bag of heroin. We never heard from Marcelle again, although her mother did call to curse me out for mistreating her daughter. As Linda says, "It's all in a daze work."

There was another confrontation from that time that has stayed with me—vividly. A young man named Jamal* had sent an abusive e-mail to a female student, and we quickly decided that our zero-tolerance policy for threatening behavior meant just that. Jamal would be asked to leave immediately. I was nervous about delivering this news, in part because Jamal was a big, strong guy and had a long-standing problem with controlling his anger. I resigned myself to getting hit. I'm not small, but I'm not a fighter by any means. I remember thinking that I would just have to take whatever happened.

Linda and I were the ones to deliver this news to Jamal, and for safety reasons we asked two other staff members to wait outside the meeting room in case things got out of hand. We have not had serious issues with violence among our students, but we do employ security guards in some cities now to protect students from dangers outside. Sometimes trouble can follow them from their neighborhoods, so we are careful to ensure that only students are admitted to our classroom areas.

When we approached Jamal and asked to see him privately, he immediately started saying, "No, no, no, please no," and began to hyperventilate. We walked him into a small meeting room and began to explain that he had fired himself from the program.

After a few seconds he got up from his chair, went over to the corner of the room, and sat in another chair with his sweatshirt pulled over his head. He was crying, yelling a bit, angry—just generally frustrated. I braced myself for the worst. Linda let this go on for a few minutes and then began a process of calming Jamal down.

She began by telling him that we cared for him and that we did not want to hurt him. With his hood still pulled over his head, he would scream back, "No you don't, you don't care about me!" Calmly, slowly, Linda would reinforce and repeat her words. Her voice was soothing yet strong. After about ten more minutes, much of it spent in silence, Linda began explaining to Jamal that she was going to move her chair closer to him. Little by little she did this.

What should I do? A five-foot woman of not much more than a hundred pounds was edging closer and closer to a nearly hysterical young man twice her weight. I was speechless and immobile. Nothing on Wall Street or at Harvard prepares you for this. I had to trust Linda's deep experience and instincts. After fifteen agonizing minutes of moving closer and closer, Linda let Jamal know that she was going to reach out and put her hand on his shoulder. He did not say no, and his crying was beginning to subside. Once she touched him, the tension seemed to abate. Linda again explained that we were here to help and not hurt this young man.

Suddenly he turned back toward us, pulled his hood back from his face, and said through tear-stained eyes, "Okay, what can you do to help me?" We talked for another ten minutes, and then Linda walked Jamal down to the street level, where he left, knowing we would still be there to support him even though he had just fired himself from the program. The whole affair lasted about forty-five minutes, and afterward I was exhausted from the tension and emotion. Linda seemed fine, as always. I don't know where she puts the psychic fallout, but she always has plenty of strength left for the next time.

By its nature, social entrepreneurship has to meld the compassionate with the corporate. But as you can imagine, it's not easy to find staffers who can interact with global financial institutions and talk a stressed student down from a scary ledge in his or her internship—all in a morning's work. All Year Up employees must have direct relationships with students as advisers or mentors in addition to their other duties. It's what keeps us true to our mission and ensures that we always remember who we serve. But finding that combination of heart and head makes for a serious HR challenge.

There are plenty of ways to find and vet talented employees who will be a great fit for your organization. You can hire a headhunter or put the word out with your own network, as I often have with my social entrepreneur/ Bowdoin/Harvard nexus. Whatever the initial connection, I also try to put prospective employees through a foolproof exercise I've been using for years. I ask them initially why they want to serve urban young adults. I tell them up front that I don't care how much they know until I know how much they care. I listen closely to their answers, and whenever possible I like to see how they interact with our students with a very casual but critical litmus test.

When Casey Recupero showed up at our offices for an informational interview in late 2004, I knew that he was persistent. He had endured two weeks of phone tag during a particularly busy time. I had no particular job opening, but I had promised a friend that I'd speak with him. When we finally talked, I found that Casey had an intriguing backstory. And he seemed hard-wired into a life of social service. I asked him to come up and see what we do. It was a typically hectic day on the fifth floor at Summer Street when I caught a glimpse of him in the doorway as classes were changing—a perfect opportunity to toss him into the swim. This is how Casey remembers it: "I stood in the hallway right before class, and the place had great energy. I felt a blur go by me. And a voice said, 'Oh, *you're* the guy. I'm Gerald. Just talk to these guys.' He left me with a group of students and walked away. It's a great test of if you want to work here. If you're not comfortable interacting with urban young adults for ten minutes, you're probably not one of us. Whatever Gerald's test was, I passed."

Casey, who is now the executive director of our Boston site, hailed from what he calls "the whitest state in the nation," Vermont. He came to us by way of deep social service in Africa, a Harvard education, and a challenging upbringing that had him negotiating very adult situations in the second grade.

"I tell our students I've lived on both sides of the Opportunity Divide," Casey said. "I didn't have the racial issues, which are huge. But because of some of the things my mother and I went through, I was a social worker at heart by age eight. It was never a question for me careerwise—whether you want to call this social work, social justice, education, service."

He was the son of a hard-pressed single mother. And though he was much loved, their domestic life was turbulent.

"After my dad, who is a really decent human being, my mother chose men in her life that weren't nice to her and weren't nice to us. There were hectic moments where we were pretty poor and getting public support. There were a lot of alcoholism issues with some of the guys that were in our life. I was never in the kind of dire straits as many of our students at Year Up. But we certainly experienced some of those things that put you on thin ice."

Like our students, Casey persevered. In his small town, he was the first person in twenty-five years to go to Harvard. "My grandmother convinced me to apply. She said, 'Here's the fifty bucks. Write the application.' I came down for admitted students weekend, and it brought me in contact with a lot of really smart folks. The first course I took was African history, which really quickly steered me down a path. I majored in anthropology and African studies. As I was reaching the end of college, I knew I didn't want to be an investment banker, doctor, lawyer. I knew I wanted to work in sub-Saharan Africa."

Casey went to work for a Boston nonprofit called World Education, funded by the State Department and active in thirty-one countries, primarily in sub-Saharan Africa and Southeast Asia. "I managed a chunk of our African portfolio for five years," he says. "It required shuttling back and forth from here to the field, working on community development projects. I loved that. I saw amazing things happening with pretty low resources. But ultimately I hit a wall."

Casey explained why he was back in Boston looking for a change. The travel schedule had been killing. But more important, the bureaucratic requirements had left him feeling too removed from direct contact with the people being served. He was missing that connection. I could believe that. As I watched him that morning, he was completely at ease and engaged with the students I left him with.

It was the kind of gut hire I couldn't make now, with all the established HR procedure we've since set up. But I knew within a few minutes of sitting down with Casey that he had to work at Year Up. I told him that I wanted him to come on board, as soon as possible. The position would be one he created for himself, tackling a long list of special projects I had in mind. So much was going on as we grew; he could try on plenty of hats and we'd see what fit. I'll let him describe just a few of his duties: "I was the point person with our board. I documented process for new sites, developed our first government-relations strategy. I built a model of the way to manage corporate partnerships. As one of our first site leaders, I worked at developing learning communities."

We had a lot of questions on that front. We wanted the tight, caring community visible in the group photo of Class One. But we needed to serve so many more students. What numbers worked best? How much could class size grow and stay effective? Casey settled in to build an effective model that we could use at any future sites.

With all of Casey's intense and effective multitasking, it became clear that I had found someone to step in and run all of Boston, to free more of my time for development and expansion. Within a year, Casey took over the day-to-day operation of Year Up Boston and the significant new space becoming available at Ninety-three Summer Street. At that point, although our mini site in the rented space at Cambridge College had been very cost effective, we decided that it made more sense to consolidate all of our operations into one building downtown. Our accreditation partnership with Cambridge continued, and many of our students continue to use the college credits earned at Year Up toward degrees there.

Casey, Sue, and I had countless meetings about building an organization that could take Year Up national. "I just wish someone had taken photos of the whiteboards from those sessions," Casey jokes. "There were lots of circles and arrows."

On a day that we sat and looked back over those early strategy meetings, Casey had phone and e-mail messages stacked up from legislators, corporate managers, civic leaders, and more. But he had put it all on hold for one of his advisees, who was in deep crisis. "I spent at least seven hours over the last two days working on a pretty tough issue with Alonzo," he explained. "I have fifty people reporting to me, and that amount of time is a pretty big hit. But people help out. And you don't sleep very much. It's easier when you know everyone else is doing it too."

Two weeks into his internship, Alonzo wanted to quit. He had already missed some work. He was a new father, very poor, and very stressed. He wondered: Maybe a mindless nine-dollar-an-hour job made more sense than our stipend. Casey had been consulting with "Team Alonzo" to talk him out of leaving and help him see the long-term benefits of staying. He outlined a plan to spread a wide net beneath our shaky intern.

"I needed to speak with the Year Up staffer who manages that corporate relationship. I also want to talk to my site leader. And social services. Alonzo and his fiancée have a nine-month-old son. He missed a day of work for her to go to the dentist, since they don't have backup child care. That's totally understandable, but you're going to get fired if, as he has, you miss three days out of your first eleven. You need to get to work. Student services has referrals for child-care help. I think we can put that circle of support together."

Casey would make more calls—to Alonzo's manager on the job, to his city caseworker, to his fiancée. Rightly, he would stop for a moment to question his own motivation in resolving the situation: "Am I doing this because I think it's the right thing for him or because I don't want to burn our relationship with that employer? I don't personally want to fail as Casey. So am I talking somebody out of something just because I want to win?"

Team Alonzo's collective agreement with Casey's course of action eased his mind on that score. "I'm comfortable with my own response because I'm convinced that there's a success to be had here for him. I believe the right thing for Alonzo is to finish the program."

With a half dozen capable professionals at work for this intern and things still very much up in the air, I could walk away from Casey's desk knowing one thing for sure: He was absolutely the right guy to help us move forward because he'd never leave a single student behind.

For a while, it looked like a win for Team Alonzo. He went back to work. Casey recounts the rest:

"There were more hiccups—some serious, some hilarious—as we worked through the practical issues that Alonzo would need to address in order to successfully complete his internship. One memorable session focused on his household budget. We were sitting around a table totaling up everything he could think of. This much support from food stamps. This much from Alonzo's stipend at Year Up. This much outlay for diapers and baby formula. Is food in there? Yep. How about the cab fare that his girlfriend needs to get to the grocery store once a week since they don't have a car? Got it.

"Finally we felt like we had the final picture loaded into an Excel spreadsheet and patted each other on the back. Alonzo and his family would have

$142 left over every month! Something made me ask Alonzo one last time if there was anything we might have missed. 'Well, I don't want to put anyone's business out there, but . . .' Alonzo said. Blushing, he shared that the prescription for the medication for his girlfriend's mental health condition had run out and that she had found marijuana acted as a good substitute. Alonzo hurriedly explained that he had long since stopped using himself, mindful of Year Up's zero-tolerance drug policy, and was encouraging his girlfriend to find a new doctor. But in the meantime he wanted to ensure his budget was complete. Suppressing a smile, I watched as he jotted down the expense and reran the calculations. I still think it's the only household budget I've ever seen with 'weed' as a line item.

"After a few days of this type of collaborative problem solving, we worked with his manager to reset the internship with a 'clean slate.' The manager outlined some additional support they'd be providing (training, more frequent check-ins), and Alonzo thanked him earnestly for the second chance. Things were looking up. I went up to visit him on the job, met some of his colleagues, got a tour. Seeing him in action and sharing lunch in the corporate cafeteria, I felt that he was finally on the right track. This was particularly great news since we learned that he had been meeting the company's expectations, and there was a ninety-five percent probability of a full-time job offer if Alonzo completed his internship.

"Unfortunately, his girlfriend was putting tons of pressure on Alonzo to quit the program, since his commute/schedule was putting strain on the family. And eventually, he did quit—eight weeks after his return to work. The e-mail came out of the blue. Short and to the point, it was addressed to his supervisor and cc'd a member of Year Up's internship team. With a subject line reading, 'Apologies on My Behalf,' the message started with 'I'm deeply sorry for how my internship ended. An unfortunate emergency came up at the wrong time and I could not continue.'

"I've learned not to take moments like this personally, but it's hard. Why didn't Alonzo communicate to me directly instead of via a secondhand e-mail? If he really wanted to continue with the program but was derailed by an emergency, why not ask for help?

"Over the next week, I left some voicemails for him on his girlfriend's cell phone, since he didn't have his own. But I stopped calling when his girlfriend left me pretty nasty voicemail. I'm not sure she ever believed in the possibility that Alonzo could succeed in a professional career. I don't think she realized what that success could have meant for her, Alonzo, and their son. The last we heard through another Year Up student, Alonzo was okay but still living at the margins. It's very disappointing, but this is part of what the Opportunity Divide is all about."

CHAPTER NINE
Guilty by Association

"I WAS A CRACK BABY," ONE VIBRANT, SMILING YOUNG WOMAN TOLD me when we met at the ribbon cutting for our newest site, in Seattle. She was entering our first class there, and I had asked her to tell me a bit about herself. The starkness of her self-definition was startling. Born desperately ill, in unspeakable pain, racked with seizures—where do you go from there? And at what point, if ever, does that grim beginning stop defining who you are? She told me that her mother was still struggling with her drug problem almost two decades later. There had been a second daughter, also born addicted, who did not survive.

There is not a day when our staff and students don't wrestle with the consequences of such random unfairness. But it took me a few years of life at Year Up to realize that we couldn't serve our student population properly without a deeper understanding of another critical divide: the absence of any *expectation* for a positive future. Complete hopelessness is ground zero for many of our students. Given my own fortunate upbringing, that outlook was foreign to me—and almost incomprehensible at first. But I was fortunate enough to connect with some willing and patient guides familiar with that dark, lonely place. You'll hear from some of them shortly.

I had done some of my own research on the psychological issues we might expect to encounter. As I dove into the literature, I discovered that social scientists had been studying hardships faced by urban youth for decades. And as they collected and analyzed the metrics of misery, they began to see chronic, uncontrollable stressors result in hopelessness. The pathology remains very difficult to treat as long as the sufferer remains in the same environment. The prevailing ethnographic wisdom suggests that adolescents react to uncertain futures by losing all hope, which can lead them to engage in high-risk behavior.

That's hardly a news flash. But a 2003 study by John M. Bolland sought to finally measure the depth of the problem. It was titled "Hopelessness and Risk Behaviour Among Adolescents Living in High-Poverty Inner-City Neighbourhoods." Questionnaires given to nearly 2,500 low-income urban young adults in Alabama asked respondents about engaging in unsafe or risky activities. It had long lists of indicators to check off: "carried a knife," "cut or shot by someone else," "trying to get pregnant," "suicide attempt," and so on. The findings: Nearly 50 percent of male respondents and over 25 percent of females displayed moderate or high feelings of hopelessness. And the numbers showed that hopelessness was indeed a reliable predictor of risky behavior. Bolland's conclusion: "These results suggest that effective prevention and intervention programmes aimed at inner-city adolescents should target hopelessness by promoting skills that allow them to overcome the limitations of hopelessness."

I suppose that's some validation—it's what we're all about at Year Up. But with or without such programs, nearly every study, including Bolland's, also mentions resilience as a key factor in a young person's quest for a decent future. Resilience is that "magic" that we were looking for in our first applicants. Inner strength, with strong support, is what helps our students pass through all that "outside noise" to complete the program. And they have to stay vigilant at all times. We used a catchphrase to caution students from the outset: You can get through the nine to five here; it's the five to nine when you're not here that we worry about most.

After a decade of this work, I can say that the damage done by hopelessness is as big a problem as ever. The good news: Time and time again I've seen it overcome with coping mechanisms that are as unique and inventive as our students. The young men you're about to meet all possessed the magic elixir—what Barack Obama famously called "the audacity of hope." But as the fine print says on so many "miracle" product labels, results may vary.

In 2006 I was paired with a new advisee named Warren Bramwell, better known as Dubs (for *W*). When I first met him in the fall of that year, I was taken aback by the words tattooed in cursive across his forearm: *Loyalty*

Is Limited. I remember thinking that it was a sad statement to have jabbed into your skin. Why did he choose to remind himself of this pessimistic conclusion—and in such an indelible way?

Yet again, I didn't know what I didn't know. That's been a persistent theme in my life as an adviser. The antidote to such cultural ignorance: Listen, ask questions, learn, and above all, don't assume anything. Loyalty to friends and family is deeply important to me and unlimited as far as I'm able to provide it. But I didn't challenge Dubs about his worldview. I summoned my own motto. *Never pass judgment; it's not your place.*

"'Sup?"

That was Warren's usual greeting when we first met. His voice is low, smooth, and inviting; I still find myself listening to his rap songs in my car. Dubs is calm and warm yet somewhat guarded, a bit like a cat that walks around you a few times before it decides to get closer.

So we did some circling at first. Though Dubs was my advisee, he also quickly became my teacher. The day he explained to me what it feels like to be truly hopeless changed my perspective and the way I do my work. The depth and complete acceptance of his despair took my breath away. Here was a good, kind, smart young man telling me in totally unemotional terms that before he came to Year Up he genuinely believed that only two options remained available to him: "death and jail."

He had felt this way for as long as he could remember. As a result, he felt there were no consequences to his actions. The script was written and the last act of the play already determined. Dubs explained how this core belief can leave a person numb and affectless: "If I wanted to rob you, I would just rob you. It didn't matter to me."

To hear him describe that feeling—or lack of feeling—was both chilling and depressing. He wasn't trying to show me how tough he was. He was just being honest. It might rain today; I might have robbed you. Simple fact, nothing personal. But things seemed a bit better as the weeks went on. Dubs had offered the robbery example as a comparison to the way he was feeling at the moment: "Now I can see that if I make good choices, good things can happen. I can move up; I can progress. I have some control over my future."

He performed really well during the learning and development phase of the program and earned his internship at a publishing house. There he also met expectations and had a strong supervisor who expected a lot and refused to cut Dubs any slack. I was so proud of him; I visited him on the job and watched him complete the IT tasks put before him with speed and self-assurance.

Throughout this time, I knew there was a court case against him from three years earlier, when he was sixteen, that loomed over our heads. Dubs had been accidentally shot in the knee; he was arrested at the hospital on a weapon possession charge. I kept hoping that it would just fade away, much like his grim adolescence. But it didn't. One day he told me that he had been summoned to appear in Massachusetts Supreme Court, Criminal Division.

It was close to the end of his internship and graduation, and he was doing very well. We were both resolved that this was not going to get in the way. In the three years since the gun incident, he had traveled so far and learned so much. Dubs's hope was fragile but holding as the court date arrived. I went to the courthouse with him. The security guards waved me around the metal detector at the front door: "You're a lawyer, right? No need to go through that thing."

They steered the young man of color behind me through the metal-detecting frame with a grunt and a gesture. Within five minutes' interaction in a closetlike consulting room, I was enraged by Dubs's court-appointed attorney, who was insulting, dismissive, and scolding him as though he were a stupid child. I don't get angry at work—almost never. But that day I could feel the blood rise to my temples and I was close to losing my temper.

I stepped outside and called a friend who is an attorney. I asked him, "Can I fire the court-appointed attorney? Now?" "Sure," he said, "as long as you are willing to hire someone to represent Warren." I went back into the windowless room and notified her that she was dismissed. "Please leave right now," I told her. "We'll take it from here." Over the next few weeks, we hired a good attorney. I met with the DA twice and tried with all my ability to keep Dubs from going to jail.

Finally the DA pulled me aside and said, "You know, I never see someone like you coming to the side of someone like Warren. That's a positive gesture. But Gerald, I have to be honest with you. Even my boss's boss can't do anything to help your friend." Then I learned what the words "mando minimum" mean. It didn't matter what the circumstances were or that the transgression had happened when Dubs was a boy. All his progress counted for zero. There was a mandatory minimum sentence for his act, and he was going to jail.

I pleaded with the DA's team to delay his sentencing until after graduation, and I was grateful when they agreed to that. Dubs's mom and sister came to the ceremony, along with his newborn nephew; later Dubs sent a family photo of that proud moment from prison. We all hugged and smiled for the cameras. But a sadness hung over our little group.

That evening, I was with the Year Up staff celebrating graduation at a local karaoke bar, and my cell phone rang. "Gerald, I don't want to go to prison tomorrow." Dubs sounded so forlorn and so damned young that I wanted to cry. I just kept telling him what my mother used to say to me during tough times: "This too shall pass." But it sounded hollow even as I said it. *Ten months, mando.*

Soon after, Dubs's tutorial taught me a few things about "life inside"— and its murderous effect on hope. I've kept his letters from jail, just as I keep the joyful ones from graduates thriving in new jobs. Dubs wrote in small, meticulous block printing on legal pads. Rereading them, I am always struck by the tremendous waste. As a new prisoner he was locked down twenty-two hours a day. Once he was allowed out of his cell a bit, Dubs played a lot of chess at Suffolk County House of Correction, tried to "stay out of trouble."

This was no simple thing. The minimum-security jail was not far from the streets where he had gotten into trouble. And he was transferred to a new unit full of old associations: "Two of my boys from the neighborhood are on this unit also, so we look out for each other. It's kind of weird because while I was out and going to Year Up, I kinda faded from kicking it with them and they bring that up and joke all the time."

Back on the block—the cellblock—and going nowhere.

Dubs penned some vivid scenarios. Cellblock enterprise was lively, from hair braiding to numbers running and sports betting. After a big Patriots game, bookies made their rounds at great risk, Dubs wrote. "It's always funny watching them collect on canteen day. That's usually the cause of most of the fights besides fighting over street names."

Dubs and his cellmate, or "celly," caught the entrepreneurial spirit as well, buying sixty-cent bags of Jolly Ranchers candies at the canteen and melting them into lollipops in a microwave. They were molded in the small paper cups collected from prisoners getting medications in them. Profits were modest but steady until someone began cutting into their trade: "We're starting to get some hefty comp from the kitchen crew in the 4 Building. They are making lollypops in different shapes and we can't figure out how they're doing it."

His tone was jovial, but the whole crazy enterprise zone was senseless and heartbreaking. This was a guy who could solve a computer problem with one hand tied behind his back and three more help-desk clients on hold. And jail was just a continuation of the conditions that landed him there: Young men with zero opportunities and too much dead time. Dubs noted that he had read five books, "which is 5 more than I read last year." But he complained that they were "all these urban books 'bout drugs, violence and some crazy stuff" lent by a new cellmate from "upstate" who was finishing up a ten-year sentence there. He had a request: "I was thinking, Gerald, rather than you putting money on my canteen, would you mind sending a book?"

As the weeks ticked away, he had mixed feelings about his impending release: "I've been trying my hardest to keep out of trouble and keep a positive head on. But Boston's been getting real hectic lately and I got a feeling it's gonna be worse come summer. For some reason I'm really starting to stress. I mean I can't wait to be free but I'm confused about what I'm going to do once I'm home. I know I want to get back in school and get a job. I still want to focus on the IT because I'm good at it. But I don't know how I would go about getting the ball rolling. Basically I'm asking what can I do?"

He came to our home soon after he was released from prison. We tossed a baseball in the backyard, had dinner with Kate and the kids, got him some clothes to wear, and then just talked for a few hours about what the past ten months had been like and the bizarre codes of behavior he had been forced to learn quickly—or else.

Dubs spoke about matters too dark to have included in his letters, which he had written to help keep himself connected and upbeat. I just listened. He explained how a series of insults must be countered with fights for a pecking order. Just to survive, he had fought eleven times and been in solitary confinement for nine and a half of the ten months.

Once when he had been released from solitary, he had been ushered in handcuffs to a cell that had a sign on the wall reading: DON'T PUT ANY NIGGERS IN HERE. He had looked at the prison guards in disbelief as his new cellmate was being brought in—a white guy whose greeting was "Get that fuckin' nigger out of here." Dubs inhaled and told the guards, "Take the cuffs off. We might as well just start fighting right here." He had been out of solitary confinement for twenty minutes before he had to defend himself. Again.

I asked him what else he had fought about.

"Well, I'm on the bottom bunk, and the dude gets down and takes a leak at night. It's splattering around and I'm sleeping next to that; that's a fight. That's disrespecting me. So now I have to fight."

His first night in, trouble had started over the simple act of sharing. "I had a box of pretzels. Someone asked me for a pretzel and I gave him one. And someone's like, 'Oh, dude, he just disrespected you.' Why? I just gave him a pretzel. His answer: 'You don't give anything away in prison. Someone just insulted you.'"

This, he explained, was called suffering a "short"—being disrespected. The pathology in that pretzel logic turned my stomach. Dubs wasn't buying it; he knew it was screwed up. But the fact that he had had to survive in that kind of environment made me fear for the hopes we had seen grow in him over the previous year.

Please don't read this and think I am soft on crime. I am not. If you break the law, you need to be accountable for your actions. In this case, though, I knew that justice was not being served by a mandatory minimum imposed on a boy who had hurt only himself. I knew that society was the loser and that we were all worse off.

Our children had a good time with Dubs during that visit. There are always students around, at dinner or just visiting, and Cameron, Casey, and Callum have become pretty fine hosts, greeting guests with a handshake, full eye contact, and an easy smile. They look after people as quietly, naturally, and completely as their mother does. I don't usually go off separately with a student for hours, but Dubs and I had a lot to talk about. After he left, I was putting our son Cameron to bed and he seemed a bit serious. He looked down from his top bunk.

"Dad, can I ask you a question? Are you going to adopt Dubs?"

"No, why do you ask?"

"Because you only play baseball with me."

"Unfortunately, he just got out of prison, and I wanted to make sure that he knew that I still cared about him. That I didn't judge him because he got out of prison."

Cam was quiet for a second, then picked up his head.

"Dad, I idol you."

I kissed him and attempted a dignified exit. His sweetness was a blessing. It took some of the edge off what I had felt seeing Dubs and his bag of clothes off into the night.

Dubs never tried going back into IT work; the jail time had dulled his confidence in the field. He felt he was forgetting those skills and might do better working with his hands. A few years later, as he was about to pass the test for his commercial driver's license, Dubs said to me, "I'm sorry I didn't turn out the way you wanted, you know, and that I don't count as one of your successes. But I am trying my best."

He was wrong to say that, and I told him so. We honor everyone's journey. His had been a rough one. And if Dubs didn't end up a tech star, so what? I see him as one of our most successful graduates, and I am proud to call him my friend. He may wear that depressing tattoo for life. But he is close to erasing the restrictions that belief once imposed on him. He is well and very much alive to the possibilities—and to aspiration. In early summer of 2011, Dubs called me with great news: He got a job as a long-haul trucker. A few more weeks' training and he would be heading out in his own rig, his own man. The road was wide open, and he was not about to look back.

By any professional standards, Jesuino Vicente is a success: He was in Boston's Class Six of 2005—one of the first IT-track graduates to be hired permanently by State Street, where he worked for over four years before moving to John Hancock and most recently to Brown Brothers Harriman. It's an impressive résumé, and his talents have made him well regarded—and well employed.

But as he worked at these downtown institutions, Jesuino was still living at his parents' house in Dorchester, in a neighborhood plagued by gangs and violence. Jesuino was never in a gang. He never picked up a gun or hurt another human being. Here are some standout events in his life that won't appear on any résumé:

2002, Shot in the abdomen. Case of mistaken identity. No arrests.

2009, Shot in the face. Random shooting. Perpetrator now in prison.

2010, Lost his hard-earned new BMW to a "random torching" when his car was parked on the street outside the house he grew up in.

The fire destroyed three cars and set a nearby house on fire; evidence of arson was provided by police and fire department reports. His insurance company is flatly denying Jesuino's claim for the total loss. The car dealership is expecting regular payments for a car that doesn't exist, and his solid credit may be in jeopardy. He has hired a lawyer to pursue his claim. He is weary of it all but philosophical.

"Every time I turned around, something else bit me in the butt. I tell myself every day: I've been through so much. I can't stop now. I have to keep going."

None of this "everyday" information would appear on Year Up's alumni database. We only knew the great stuff—the string of impressive hires. Jesuino offered the update when we asked him to come in to national headquarters in Boston and help us tell the story of his childhood friend Nicklan Rosa. Jesuino's success had inspired Nicklan to apply to the program in 2008.

Sitting in a quiet conference room, Jesuino turned his head and pointed to a dark spot on his right cheek. "This is where the second shot went in. The bullet was stuck in my ear canal. I still get vertigo, but I'm happy to be in one piece. I was with John Hancock at the time, and the people I worked with couldn't believe what happened." His manager knew Jesuino well, and they were friendly outside the office; Hancock paid him for the month it took to recover from surgery.

"They were great," Jesuino said. "But you always have to wonder what people are thinking when they see something like that. If you look at the 'hood from the outside, you don't see anything but a bad perception of the people who live there. Me, for example. It's hard to overlook the negative stuff. But we should talk about Nicklan now. I am here today because what's said about him is very important to me. I would like to be on the record—to do him justice, you know?"

On paper, Nicklan Rosa didn't look so good.

He applied to Year Up in the summer of 2008, and his admissions file was bristling with potential negatives: He was bumping right up against the age-twenty-four cutoff for the September class. He had been out of high school for seven years. During that time he had entered and dropped out of both Roxbury Community College (with an intended major in computer information systems) and a Florida for-profit college that had aggressively marketed a rosy future in electronic game design.

The catch in Florida: The course work required technical skill levels an inner-city high school graduate was unlikely to have. In this case it was competency and certification in C++, a programming language typically used in game design and requiring calculus. Nicklan explained the problem in his Year Up application essay: "After being introduced to the beast that is C++, I thought there was no possibility of me being able to grasp such a program." He failed the course twice, then passed it but ran out of money and options before he could earn any sort of certificate or degree. Like many low-income students unable to afford even state colleges, he had found a willing lender in the faraway university he chose—an institution whose credits are not recognized by or transferable to many nearby colleges, including Florida State. Yet according to a 2011 comparison done by *Time*, its tuitions for some majors are as expensive as those at Harvard.

Jesuino remembers his friend's distress at the time: "When Nicklan got back from Florida, he had no source of income. And he's like, 'J, you're doing pretty good, you're working, you got a nice car. What are you doing, man? I don't see you on the streets.' I explained, 'Remember that program, we got offered the opportunity by our guidance counselor after high school?' He said, 'Aw, that thing?' I told him State Street took me as one of the first interns. And hired me full time. He said, 'Wow, you actually made your way in the door?'

"I told him I couldn't put it into words, what the program did for me. Nicklan was really interested. When he got the application, he was worried about the essay. I said, 'I can help you. You can just tell them the truth—your past is your past there."

In his essay, Nicklan calculated the heavy impact of his last attempt at career training: "The next ten years I will age to 34 and at that age, I hope to be debt free. Attending school for Game Design surely didn't come cheap—as a matter of fact it was about $30,000, plus living expenses."

Nicklan wasn't lazy. There had been jobs as a driver, a janitor, a dietary aide, and a general worker at the Convenient Corner store. And he had tried other ways to generate income; our admissions staff had turned up two pages' worth of brushes with the justice system, from driving with a suspended license to "possession with intent to distribute," shoplifting, resisting arrest. Still, in his neighborhood, said Jesuino, Nicklan was regarded as a positive guy: "Nicklan was all around in high school, a mathematician, a lot of history knowledge, and very genuine. Everyone called him 'Professor' because he was like a teacher. He'd share his experiences. He had lost one of his closest cousins to gang violence. He was trying to stay away from revenge and stuff and telling the rest of his cousins, 'You guys need to focus on your life.'"

During the admissions process, Nicklan had been frank about his missteps. Approximately 19 percent of our student population has had some interaction with the justice system. We think it's all the more reason to support a young person clearly motivated to make a change. We don't believe that anyone should be characterized entirely by his last act. But we have zero tolerance for sex offenses and violent felonies; our first responsibility is to protect the students in our learning communities.

The misdemeanor arrests made Nicklan ineligible for the financial operations track, where background checks are much more intensive and far less forgiving. But there were indications that our IT curriculum might be a good fit: Nicklan was voted most tech savvy in the 2001 graduating class of Brighton High School. A recommendation from his employer at a convenience store stated that he was "smart, good with computers." He tested very well in our admissions learning assessment.

The most encouraging sign was the way he presented himself in person. Everyone who interviewed this young man felt he was genuinely, desperately ready to make a change. Even his e-mail address reflected a certain ambition: looking4work07@xxx.

Nicklan had a healthy sense of humor and held himself accountable. To our application question "How would your last English teacher describe you?" he wrote, "Had brains, no heart." His self-assessment: "I'm very disappointed with the way my life has turned out, but I still have faith in myself and my abilities. . . . After seeing the success a high school friend of mine is enjoying because of the opportunities Year Up provided, I believe that Year Up is another chance at life."

A staff evaluation concluded that while Nicklan's past associations had caused him to make decisions not in his best interests, "Presently he has experienced a conversion of thought and attitude. Recommended."

Into the second week of classes, signs were encouraging. Nicklan had already been helping three other students with their IT work. He was cheerful, engaged, and turning in good work on time. He stayed late on September 18 to finish an essay on the derivation of his name, which means "conqueror," according to his research. At about 5:00 p.m. he handed it to his instructor, Lovie Elam, and boarded the Red Line at South Street station, bound for his home in Dorchester.

At about seven that evening, Year Up Boston's executive director, Casey Recupero, was downtown at the State Street offices attending an event honoring Boston black professionals. He stepped out to take an emergency call from Chelsea Tanaka, a site leader on the fifth floor. She sounded distraught. There had been a shooting in Dorchester. The police weren't releasing a name, but word on the street—via some of our other students who lived in the neighborhood—was that the victim was a student from Year Up.

By the time he reached me at home, Casey was back in our office, where he had finally confirmed the awful truth: Nicklan had been shot several times just steps from his back door. He had been pronounced dead a short time later in the hospital. It took me a while to process the fact. Our student—murdered? While I sat in our kitchen debriefing my kids on their school day, someone had left Nicklan to bleed to death in his parents' driveway.

Jesuino heard it on the street. "The word spread pretty quickly and people were asking me, 'Hey, don't you know Nicklan?' I was confused, like, 'What are you talking about?' And there it was, my childhood friend and he's gone. One of his family members found him in the driveway. Everyone was like, 'Oh, Nicklan didn't deserve that. He never picked up a gun, never tried to hurt somebody.' Here he is trying to do good with his life and someone comes out of nowhere and takes it. I just kept thinking, 'Is this going to happen to me as well?'"

I didn't know Nicklan well; his class, scheduled to graduate in July 2009, was just a week and a half into the new term. But after getting the news, I kept seeing his big grin when we were partners in an orientation exercise in his fourth-floor LC:

"My name is Gerald and I like pizza."

"My name is Nicklan and I like lobster."

After the shock came the worry: What to do? One member of a tight community had been murdered, and we had classes the next morning. That's where Casey shines as a leader. He can cut through it all and figure out what needs to happen—quickly. So he called an emergency meeting for 6:00 a.m. and pulled the essential people together. Staff and students who would be arriving in four LCs had to be told and the day reconfigured to meet their needs. But how?

Casey cautioned that we should account for all sorts of reactions: "We want to share this news and provide a lot of support to help them process whatever they're going through. But we have to recognize that people are going to take it really differently.

"Someone who didn't know Nicklan may be very upset. And someone who did know him might say, 'Hey, this happens in our community; people get killed. I want to go to class and I don't want to talk about this right now— that's what's making me really uncomfortable.' So you want to allow for some normalcy for folks coming to Year Up as a safe place away from this stuff. To bring the violence inside isn't something we want to do."

No society has precedents or standard coping mechanisms for so many dying so young. Though we had trained professionals on staff, we were feeling our way cautiously. The next morning, in each LC, we told the students what had happened. We had grief counseling sessions for those who felt a need for it. Naturally, feelings ran highest in Nicklan's fourth-floor LC. We announced that we weren't going to go into a normal class schedule until afternoon—and then only for those who wished to attend.

Harry Lindor, one of our tech instructors, has a warm, comforting spirit, so we asked him to preside over this difficult convocation. We sat in circles and went around the room, each student and staff member sharing how he or she felt. And as Casey had predicted, we had a wide range of reactions. So many of the students said it just brought up all of the fear and all the past death they'd dealt with—that it was as though they'd been shot again themselves. Or they flashed back to scenes of violence they had witnessed. Many referred to it as a sort of posttraumatic stress, having one of your classmates murdered—again. Just like in high school. Some didn't speak at all.

Notably, despite the general shock and melancholy, there was no visible anger. We heard no calls for revenge. Instead it was mentioned that Nicklan had a younger brother and that hopefully, in the interests of his future and safety, no one in his community would "do anything stupid." Students' main concerns were more practical, soulful, and piercingly sad: Could this family afford to bury their son? What could they do to help? At such a tender age they seemed to have a well-developed grasp of funeral expenses.

Casey had prepared a statement for any press queries, but no calls came. We should have known. Nicklan's murder didn't rate much ink. I kept thinking that this would have been front-page news if his skin were a different color and his address in a different zip code. The *Boston Globe* account devoted six lines to both the deaths of Eduardo Escobar, twenty-seven, and Nicklan Rosa, twenty-five, under the headline BOSTON POLICE SEEK HELP SOLVING TWO RECENT SLAYINGS—both shot to death, one in Mattapan, one in Dorchester, no suspects—followed by the number for the Crime Stoppers tip line.

The *Dorchester Reporter* offered this terse account: "Nicklan Rosa, 25, was shot to death in the driveway of a home he lived in at 26 King Street on the afternoon of September 18. Police say that an unidentified lone gunman targeted Rosa in what they say was likely a gang-related dispute."

"Likely gang-related"—it's accepted shorthand for "that's all you need to know" about this young life lost. Nicklan's family was from Cape Verde, an archipelago republic about the size of Rhode Island three hundred miles off the west coast of Africa. And at that time in Boston, there was a lot of drug activity and violence involving Cape Verdean gangs. Nicklan acknowledged that he had kept some questionable company. He wrote in his admissions essay that he dropped out of community college because he "didn't associate with like-minded individuals" and missed too many classes. Occasionally, he had a few beers with neighborhood guys at the Dublin House, a known hangout for one of two rival Cape Verdean gangs.

Jesuino, who was born in Cape Verde, can describe the origins of the conflict that began with a small dustup between friends in the midnineties and escalated into a monstrous neighborhood terror. Original sins may have been forgotten; for current gangbangers and their scorched-earth policy, Nicklan was guilty by association. And, notes Jesuino, by his address.

"You never chose a gang, but it's all about where you live. That's where me and Nick stood at that time. We would have to live, go to school, in all that havoc, and we were trying to be really positive about our future. Nicklan was never a gang member or anything, never tried to hurt anybody. Ten people who knew him would tell you the same.

"I don't care what the newspapers said. That's what I'm here to qualify. Just look at what happened to me. I walked to the store to grab some milk for my parents. On my way back, someone saw me with this coat that looked like some gang member's coat. And with the hood on it, I kind of fit the description of that gang member these guys were hunting. It's hard to know how to dress to go out of the house. These guys just saw my friend and me and shot like ten rounds. I can recall trying to go over and help my buddy and he was gone. My friend had a child and he's gone. Me, in critical condition at Boston Medical Center. Everybody knew the kind of person I was, not bothering anybody. I just went to the store to grab milk."

We don't categorically reject former gang members, nor do we ask about those associations. We're not looking for ways to disqualify potential students. Instead we look for clear motivation to make a change. We look for hope. We are not able to serve applicants while they're still in what we call a precontemplative stage. That's when a person hasn't even thought that there's another possibility for his or her life. He or she is sure that everything has been predetermined—and that it's going to end in one of the two grim scenarios Dubs had locked in on.

Nicklan had pushed past that sense of futility. He had moved on to the contemplative stage we listen for closely in a series of admissions interviews. We look for someone who has progressed to thinking, "Maybe there's another option for me out there. Maybe I don't have to go down the path that the statistics and the media and everyone else tell me I will follow." Nicklan had figured that out. He was positive and very bright technically. He was accepted into the program for his abilities and because he believed he could change his fate. We were all convinced that he could pull it off—and stunned when his past reached out and dragged him under.

On that long day following his death, the reality of that missed chance just grew darker as the hours passed. Once the students had left for home at three thirty, the staff gathered and I was surprised—and a bit embarrassed— to find myself crying as Casey began a discussion of the day's events. I couldn't help breaking down. People often ask me, "What's hard about Year Up?" and I tell them, honestly, that nothing is. It's not work for me; it's great. I love it. Having a student hurt in any way is the only thing that can unmoor me.

I pulled myself together as we gathered information about Nicklan's funeral. Instructor Lovie Elam put students' written memories of him together in a binder to present to the family. Our students had also collected money, which Year Up matched, to help with the education of Nicklan's brother and the family's expenses.

"Do you even know how to get to Mattapan?" one young man asked me. Some students were worried for our staff when they realized that we intended to pay our respects at Nicklan's funeral; the neighborhood was that bad. I drove to the service alone and parked as close as I could. As I entered the crowded church, an intense wailing hit me squarely in the solar plexus. I had never experienced anything like it. Cape Verdean grief has an almost physical presence, expressed in loud, continual sobs, piercing wails, and Creole laments. It's a cresting wave of sound that asks, fundamentally: *Phamodi?* Why?

Jesuino had a hard time getting himself to the church. "I went to the funeral, but I had bad past experiences seeing people in the coffin. I just couldn't look at his face because that would completely break me down. I was trying to hold back from crying. I don't think I cried until like two years after—when I counted how many of my childhood friends were dead. So I probably just looked stern or cold that day—because my heart is so accustomed to losing people, close friends. It's an intense funeral, lot of wailing, a lot of anger and tension."

I took my place in the long line leading to Nicklan's coffin. It was horrific, to kneel in front of a young man who had been shot. His lips were deflated and cracked. The mortician's makeup only underscored how unnatural a scenario this was: We had just wasted such a good young man.

Finding a spot to stand in the crowded church, I looked out at the assembly and I was struck by the contrast between the groups of Nicklan's old neighborhood friends and his new ones from Year Up. The difference went way beyond hair, clothes, and demeanor. Everyone was terribly sad—but you could pick out the faces bearing the protection of determination and hope: *That is not going to be me.*

To that end, classes resumed a normal schedule.

I offer the cases of Nicklan, Jesuino, and Dubs here to illustrate the tremendous odds some of our students are fighting—as well as their strength in the face of them. Their accountability—another Year Up core value—helped us decide to take the risk with them. None fell back on that knee-jerk excuse sung by Jets gang members in *West Side Story:* "I'm depraved on accounta I'm deprived." Jesuino was utterly blameless. And Dubs and Nicklan owned their poor choices. But the greater shame is ours. How can they find their way back—and a future—in environments so full of deadly traps?

While Dubs and Nicklan were just discovering our program, Gregory Walton was already making outreach and fund-raising appearances with me—as he still does. He remains one of our most convincing and effective representatives. "Former inmate" is not something that would flash into anyone's mind upon meeting Greg, a January 2007 graduate from Boston's Class Five. He's married to his high school sweetheart, Alicia, who has her own business. He's committed to giving back to the community he grew up in and is five years into a responsible and high-security job at one of the world's top universities, Massachusetts Institute of Technology. In late 2010, Greg was nominated and confirmed as the first alumnus to sit on Year Up's national board of trustees. With their first child, JR (Gregory James Walton Jr.), on the way, Greg and Alicia bought their first house in Brockton, a tidy, comfortable ranch.

Visit Greg on the job in Cambridge at MIT and you will be struck by the evident trust placed in his ability—and in his character. "You have any more like Greg? Bring 'em on," offered Chuck King, Greg's supervisor at the university's IT Deployment and Maintenance Services. Greg's workstation is the nerve center for the thousands of computers relied upon by MIT instructors, administrators, and staff.

"We're entering the matrix," Greg joked as he used a security pass key to enter a room beneath MIT's legendary "infinite corridor," which connects all its main buildings. PCs and Macs needing repair and reimaging are stacked along two walls. Atop a shelf is a quiet but mighty Baumgart server that allows Greg and his team to remotely access and repair computers almost anywhere on the globe—and all around this huge campus. Greg also holds the security code for storerooms full of new Macs and PCs delivered to grateful employees. "Boy, do I get smiles," he said. "It's like Santa has arrived. Or if they're in trouble, Superman." He also has the keys to a gray Ford Escape hybrid parked outside a vast loading dock for large and outlying deliveries.

"These rooms are all alarmed with key-card access. What I love about MIT is that they let me know they trusted me—I had access pretty much out of the gate. Same with the Ford, a real trust factor there. Macs, Dells, monitors, printers. It's part of my job to keep track of the stuff. I'll come down and take a census on my BlackBerry, what we have and what we need to order."

From August 2004 to 2005, when Year Up Boston was fielding its fourth class, Greg Walton was in prison on a weapons charge. He had passed over his guidance counselor's suggestion to look into our program when he graduated from high school two years earlier and headed instead to college—a disaster he'll describe himself. When Greg and I speak to potential donors, prospective students, educators, and legislators, he is the one who gets mobbed afterward with questions and congratulations. Needless to say, he's best at telling his own story in a quiet corner of his busy workplace: "Basically, I've been on my own since I was seventeen. I did a few bounces as a young kid, between my mother's residences in Boston and North Carolina. My mom battled drug addiction when I was younger. I have never met my father. My mom told me who he was, but he didn't believe I was his son. He's living up here, he's gotten my number, but he hasn't reached out and I don't think about it much.

"When I was six, I lived with my great-grandmother in Dorchester, and I went to Boston schools all the way through. Before I was at my grand-mother's I was in foster care with my older brother. After my great-grandfather died, things were too much for my great-grandmother, so I moved in with my uncle. In high school, I had a 3.75 GPA, was on the honor roll, quarterback of the football team, got tons of letters from colleges. I'm not sure I was learning much, though. Socially, I was cool with both sides of the fence, with the guys doing bad things and the nerds.

"I was seventeen when I graduated. Attending a summer program at Salem State University was my first time out on my own. I wasn't focused. I spent time on things that weren't important. I just got lost, no motivation, doing a lot of video game playing, focused on girls. The thing I really didn't understand was that it wasn't high school—and I was paying for it. I'm still paying for it now.

"Given my background—I was effectively parentless, a ward of the courts or whatever—I was supposed to get top funding for college, but I really didn't get that much. I had a lot of jobs on campus. I went into my freshman year and flunked. Badly. The following year I got my grades up to Cs, but I wasn't engaged at all. At college I met somebody I had no business being with. He dealt with drugs and guns. He was a commuter student, drove a big fancy car. It all looked pretty nice. Once I got involved with him and some bad stuff in 2004, I distanced myself from the people who had my best interests at heart and really went into a funk.

"I left Salem State in spring of 2004. The arrest was in August 2004. It was on a weapons possession charge. In Massachusetts that charge carries a mandatory one-year sentence. I had already been incarcerated in South Bay correctional facility in Roxbury—less than a mile from where I had been living—for six months when I was finally sentenced. I took a plea, which counted as six months served.

"I had a lot of family things happen while I was incarcerated. My older brother—who didn't want me to go down that path—was in the same prison with me on a parole violation. My uncle was the father figure I related to through my teen years. While I was incarcerated he died from cancer. I couldn't attend the funeral. These were things that really woke me up. At least this was the first time I had somewhat of a comforting relationship with my older brother—he knew what my uncle meant to me.

"I came back in August of 2005. I was twenty-one and not sure what I was going to do. I started getting in contact with people who knew my situation; they knew I was a smart kid, hardworking, wanted to do something. When I got back in contact with my guidance counselor, she suggested Year Up—again. I got in touch with Linda.

"I was happy to be accepted, to know that they would give me a chance and not hold my past against me. But I have to admit that in the beginning, I thought the program was bull. I'd been to college. They're going to pay you for getting credit? And I'm not paying a dime? I thought, 'This is bogus.' It turned around in the first week."

It was heartening to find out that Kirsty Ludwig, the same guidance counselor who had steered Janelle Clark to our Class One, had also sent Greg our way. We were glad to earn that sort of endorsement in one of the city's largest high schools. Early on with Greg—it may have been orientation week—I took him aside for a talk about leadership. I had been watching him. He was outspoken, easy in front of a group, but could veer into a potentially disruptive mode. Greg remembers: "Gerald was the first to give me feedback. He sat me down and said, 'Listen, I can see you're going to be a student that leads your fellow students into greatness, or you can lead them in the wrong direction.' I had that leader mentality but I didn't know how to control and use it yet."

Still on his own, Greg needed to work part time to make ends meet, as many of our students do. He kept his job at Stop & Shop, a supermarket, heading off to work four to five nights a week once class let out at three thirty. He worked until the store's closing time—midnight—did his homework, and got up and did it all again. Greg did a good job in his internship at cMarket, Inc., an online auction service for charities. The company was not able to hire him after graduation; as he conducted a job search, he stayed at the supermarket, kept networking, and volunteered at a youth organization in Roxbury on weekends. After six months' persistence and networking, he landed at MIT.

On Greg's laptop there is a PowerPoint presentation that he takes back to his alma mater, Brighton High School, once or twice a year. It's the same huge school that graduated many of our students, including Nicklan and Jesuino. Greg takes a vacation day from work to be available to students during school hours. His former coaches and teachers send students to Greg's assigned classroom throughout the day.

He calls the presentation "Looking Back, Looking Ahead." The opening photo is of a prison cell, which features a steel sink built atop the lidless toilet. The most popular part of the program: a list of the top ten strategies for "How Not to Fail—and End Up in Jail." Greg covers all the things he wishes someone had told him when he was in school there, from personal money management to creating a network ("85% of jobs are through some-one you know!"). Some of the tips are pointed and specific: "You enjoy mess-ing around on Facebook? Maybe you have a kind of crazy page? Do you want a good job sometime in the near future? Well . . . *Keep it tidy!*"

Some students at his presentations wear that hooded, you-can't-tell-me-anything attitude. Others engage, which is why Greg keeps going. "It's not me just speaking; it's a conversation. I don't care if it's just one student there that listens and takes the information. I just like to have them think about what they do, why they dress the way they do, things they should take into account. When I was there, too many of the things I did were more perception driven—worrying about what everybody else thought rather than what I wanted."

Greg is more than halfway through his degree program at Cambridge College, thanks in part to the credits he earned at Year Up. He has a time-table and a plan. We gratefully deploy him whenever he has the time. He's at home both back at Brighton High and with CEOs, senators, economists. One evening we had done a presentation together for potential donors at New Profit's annual meeting. I looked across the sleek and modern meeting space at Microsoft's Cambridge campus and saw Greg still in deep conversa-tion after the dinner and discussion had broken up. His suit was sharp, his conversation direct and compelling enough to have a scrum of multi-millionaires leaning in to catch his words.

The room's dramatic lighting created a halo around him. He was holding a gorgeous flower arrangement; knowing that Greg's wife, Alicia, has a floral-design business, a New Profit staffer had given him a centerpiece for her. He stood there like an Olympic champion on the medalists' platform, with a pocketful of business cards that any up-and-comer would be thunderstruck to have. I knew he would drive home to a safe address, a loving wife, and a limitless future.

I faded off, content—thrilled, really—to leave him there holding forth. It's a joyful sight that left a guy like me walking into the soft night feeling content and peaceful as the Charles River rolled by. And of course, Metrics Man was doing the math: I know how many young people—in his commu-nity, and at Year Up—can look at Greg and think, *That's going to be me.*

CHAPTER TEN
"I'm Having an Intern Moment"

Spring/Summer 2011,
Class Nine in the Workplace

"Any 'aha' moments for anyone this week?"

Several weeks into the internship phase, Year Up staff members were fishing for student epiphanies, large and small. Of the 103 interns who were placed, 99 were still on the job by early spring and doing fine. All of Class Nine was gathered in the Brooklyn site for PDW—professional development workshop—held each Wednesday morning. Students meet with their advisers to discuss how the internship is going and talk about feedback collected from their workplace managers on a regular basis. Group sessions cover everything from résumé sharpening to conflict management and a popular special PDW: separate men's and women's retreats that address gender roles in the workplace. After Wednesday PDW, interns head to work by 1:00 p.m. to finish the day.

Together again, if just for a few hours a week, the three LCs caught up with one another and swapped tales of the working life in banks, brokerages, hospitals, law firms, private equity firms—and the NFL. Hands went up to volunteer the week's highs, lows, and lessons.

"The financial acronyms are killing me. So I made flashcards to study on the subway."

"My manager says I should stop shaking people's hands so much. They don't do that there."

"Right. I got some feedback too, on 'over-communicating.' Too many e-mails."

"Nobody wears a jacket and tie on my team, but I still feel better in my full professional rig."

"Never—ever—send an e-mail without checking that you unclicked 'Reply to all.' My new rule: check all e-mails three times before you hit 'Send.'"

"I'm always trying to avoid what we call 'having an intern moment'— like standing in front of the elevator with the senior managers and being so nervous I forget to push the button. Oh, man."

Next came the welcome sweetness of "morning praise," the segment of PDW when the internship staff reads aloud comments from corporate managers. Their observations are part of regular surveys rating interns' performance on the job. Any less positive issues—attitude adjustments, skill sharpening, dress and decorum—are discussed privately with Crystal's internship team.

Richard,* the sole intern placed at Google, was clearly a good match for that high-energy workplace: "Richard might just be the most eager person I've ever met. He drives himself to greatness and is always willing to jump in and help. Richard has awesome customer service skills and is growing his technical tool box every day. I've been very impressed, no complaints."

The bankers were pleased as well:

"Malik is doing wonderfully in my area. He just finished QA tools presentation, started learning QA tasks, and is helping test in QA for one of my apps."

"Marisol has been doing such a super job supporting our clients in various locations that we gave her a support responsibility at a site that is currently in the process of moving out of a building."

"Damien has hit the ground running. Seems like an energetic and enthusiastic and well-mannered young man."

At the end of PDW, the interns chatted for a while, then headed off for quick lunches and work. In thirty offices across Manhattan, Connecticut, and New Jersey, corporate managers were waiting for them, testing interns' skill sets, monitoring their phone manner and client interface, observing them in team meetings—and tossing the occasional curveball. The work-days were longer than during L & D and the expectations greater. Class Nine leaned into this demanding new harness and pulled.

TALEISHA, AT YOUR SERVICE

"Thank you for calling DYCD's Youth Connect. Taleisha speaking. How may I help you?"

Just a few blocks from Year Up's Exchange Place site, Taleisha had set-tled well into her internship at the Department of Youth and Community Development. Marta* and Sophia,* two other Class Nine interns, had also been placed there.

Taleisha reported to Anthony Ramirez, an energetic young man with a decade's service to young people's programs in the South Bronx and now, at DYCD, across all boroughs. As director of the agency's hotline, Youth Con-nect, his cell and desk phones are rarely still; he runs on "black coffee, two Splendas." Agencies like his must step up their games as statistics for New York City youth continue to spike on the wrong side of acceptable. Here are just a few markers.

In the summer of 2011, when Class Nine would graduate, over seventeen thousand children and teenagers were in city homeless shelters—the overall shelter population had peaked during the past brutal winter at over forty thousand and was still close to that record.

Class Nine's peers, the city's eighteen- to twenty-four-year-olds, were at greater risk than ever: 23 percent were living in poverty, nearly 20 percent had not earned a high school diploma or GED, and birth rates for women in that age group were rising.

Urban young adults were still being killed or hurt at an alarming rate. Nationally, 26 percent of homicide victims are eighteen to twenty-four years old.

In the face of these growing challenges, Anthony Ramirez said that he was grateful for the can-do, professional services of this trio of Year Up interns. "All hands on deck, you know? Service agencies are slammed." He explained his agency's mission: "The DYCD funds nonprofit community-based organizations in the five boroughs to provide a host of services for young people and their families. They include after-school programs, run-away/homeless youth services, immigrant issues, family support, literacy services. We're really more of a contracting agency." As it happens, DYCD funded the noncustodial fatherhood program that Taleisha had worked with. Youth Connect functions as the DYCD's public face. It provides information and referral services for youth and families, Monday to Friday, nine to seven, as well as online and on social media.

The DYCD is on the sixth floor of a no-frills office building on William Street. Its doors are decaled with City of New York seals and the office suite is furnished with standard-issue cubicles. These quarters are far more modest than the sleek, chrome-and-glass corporate environments that many of Taleisha's classmates have settled into. But the space has an upbeat energy and a very human scale. The business of betterment gets done there, one referral at a time.

Bolted to the ceilings above the main work area are two electronic signs similar to the news tickers in Times Square. Numerals in red lights, always in motion, are glowing reminders of the agency's service mission. They flash critical information for Youth Connect: the number of calls handled so far and the number of callers waiting.

Taleisha and Marta answer calls all day, every day, in addition to their tech and administrative duties. The line averages over four hundred calls daily. As spring deepened, the volume grew heavier with inquiries about summer job programs. The interns were trained to assist callers and make referrals from a database of over six thousand source providers. Their first week on the job, they were paired with a resource specialist, who helped them learn to use the referral books, directories, and Web sites and save key sources to their desktops. And they learned to answer and route calls.

"So far, I really am happy with this placement," Taleisha said. She was pleased to be a part of a city agency that is functional and courteous toward the people it is intended to serve. Years of being barked at and otherwise disrespected by some of the city's less simpatico public servants had sensitized her to the most effective phoneside manner. "It's very much in line with what I think my strengths are. I'm fine with handling the calls. A lot of them are routine, asking about summer programs, ESL classes, GED testing and all."

Other calls have an urgency that she recognized all too well.

"I'm getting kicked out of my house tonight."

"I'm aging out of foster care next week."

"Immigration just took my father."

The tougher calls required patience, a firm grasp of available resources, and an empathetic ear. Taleisha listened. "Yesterday I had one from a mother who just wanted her son out of the house. He had been in juvie three times already. He wasn't listening to her, his probation officer, or the police—things had gotten very hectic. She sounded pretty desperate and she wanted to know how to get him into one of those boot camps. I was able to refer her to a place that could give her information and tell her about those types of programs and the cost. They're expensive, but I explained to her that in certain cases the court might support that for a young person really in need of that sort of supervision. She just didn't know where to turn anymore. I really felt for her."

Another distraught mother called about her daughter, who had a long-standing drug problem.

"She's just *twelve*. And her mother was so frightened for her and tired of fighting the pushers for her child, you know? You have to take your time and let them tell you about the extent of the problem so you're sure to give the proper referral. You hear a lot of pain in people's voices. But sometimes you hear gratitude and just a little relief at just having been pointed in the right direction. It doesn't sound like a huge thing or a final solution, but just knowing where to turn and what services are available can be a help—if you feel you're alone and drowning with a problem." Taleisha sighed. "I just hope they get what they need. There are so many cutbacks."

Already, Anthony said, e-mails had arrived thanking the agency for the interns' help and kind manner. "That's unusual, that people take the time to do that," he said. "And it's great to see."

Like the rest of the Class Nine interns, Taleisha, Marta, and Sophia teamed up to prepare PowerPoint presentations about their workplace—a "cultural anthropology" assignment that would also be part of a portfolio of assignments, presentations, exams, and essays submitted to—and assessed by—professors at Pace University in order to earn their college credits. Everyone stood up and presented their workplace projects on successive Wednesday mornings during PDW; some of their corporate managers attended.

Homework during internships is considerably lighter than during L & D, but time management—that pro skills fundamental—is more crucial than ever as students juggle longer hours, some outside jobs, and parenthood or caring for other relatives. Taleisha was also learning to prioritize a wide range of duties. "They're really multitasking," explained Meka Nurse, DYCD's resource coordinator, who helped train Taleisha. "They need to be good at PowerPoint—we have her designing cover pages for directories. And while they're updating databases, they're still on the phones. No one comes off the phone lines just to work on a project.

"Taleisha is also verifying information within our directories for juvenile justice. She's tasked with going through each listing, making sure the contact information is correct, the services are provided. She's also helping with e-mail correspondence. She writes a good, professional, informative e-mail. So I'd say she uses her skills fully here."

Stepping out on her lunch hour, Taleisha merged into the flow of downtown office workers. She was looking chic and professional in a blue suit, black pumps, and the short, neat hairstyle that suits her taste—and her time pressures. Work is followed by a brisk trot to the subway; it's always a race for timely pickup at the day-care center. And she has long been occupied with finding a place in a good school for Jared, who just turned four. To celebrate his birthday, she splurged and took him to "the soul circus" in Queens—the traveling UniverSoul one-ring circus that barnstorms inner cities—and they had a great time.

Jared was in another day-care facility—his eighth. She has struggled with finding affordable early-childhood education. "I applied for Head Start for him when he was two," she said, "but the waiting lists are huge and we've never come close. There are so many people wanting places, and they just keep cutting the funding and the facilities. The situation is pitiful and getting worse."

A month earlier, a Republican bill in the U.S. Senate had called for cutting Head Start funding even further, by an additional two billion dollars. The bill failed but the battled raged on. Amid testy congressional debate, New York senator Charles Schumer remarked in a speech, "We don't face the current deficit because of Head Start."

Taleisha was not holding her breath for any positive resolution. She had no expectations of securing the good- or even mediocre-quality public schooling that thousands of other families are already in line for. Kindergarten waiting lists were at record highs. She planned on doing what she had long been used to—finding a solution herself. "I've been looking around for a private school for him, but I haven't found anything yet. By the time he's ready, I hope I'll have it figured out. But for now, the day-care situation is okay. My brother, who's nineteen, can pick him up for me if I get held up. He works for a cousin who owns her own hair salon, and she understands the child-care situation."

This is one of the brothers Taleisha had missed so much. He had recently moved back north. After a decade's separation, they had a lot of catching up to do. Over a chicken sandwich, Taleisha ticked off what she felt she has gained since the previous September: "I think I interview really well. I come across as serious about my career—but I do remember to smile. I have a good, tight résumé. I have computer and business and professional skills, and I had no difficulty using them as soon as I got to the job. Right now I'm doing something I think I'm well equipped for, that has some meaning for me. Though sometimes at the end of the day when I'm getting my son ready for bed I'm so tired I could cry."

She massaged his legs, as she had since he was tiny. "He'll only let me do it when he's tired now," she said. Then he dropped off quickly and she could do any homework and household chores and lay their clothes out for the following morning. "I guess it's a good tired. When you're depressed and unemployed with nothing going on, you're tired all the time for no reason. Positive fatigue I really don't mind."

DAMIEN, SHARP-DRESSED MAN

Both of the twins were performing well in their internships; they had also found that the communication skills learned at Year Up had additional benefits. For some months they had been dating identical twins. This can get complicated on a number of levels.

"Year Up to the rescue!" Damien said, only half kidding. He admitted that he had employed the caring diplomacy learned in Friday feedback sessions to great advantage in matters of the hearth—"our big noisy Haitian family"—and the heart. "My family just yells over it, but it's helped on the relationship front. I just have to be careful not to use the Year Up language—stuff like 'growth area' and 'feedback'—that makes her suspicious. But I'll talk softly, calmly. *Positive* suggestions for ... uh ... meaningful change."

He waggled his index finger as she did and slid into a higher octave that telegraphed feminine misgivings: "Don't think I don't know you're pulling some of that Year Up stuff here. But I can't be mad at you. 'Cause it just sounds *gooood*."

Damien landed at the JPMorgan Chase facility downtown at Four New York Plaza, where Cassandra would likely have interned had she stayed in the program. His area was known as private equity fund services. Damien was there to serve clients' requests for reports and information, and when he arrived each morning, he opened his company e-mail to scan and prioritize the day's requests. Stephan,* another intern, sat just a few cubicles away. Sometimes, in iffy moments, he and Damien found it reassuring to pop their heads above the partitions and get a smile or a raised eyebrow that telegraphed, "Oh, yeah. I hear you."

Damien navigated the vast, well-appointed maze of cubicles there with confidence and a smile, stylish as ever in dress shirt, vest, and tie. He had modeled a bit and concluded that it wasn't really for him. "But maybe something on the business end in fashion," he said. "You know, Ralph Lauren has some killer financial guys behind the runways." He was delighted when Year Up paired him with a mentor, Jarrod Lacks, who is an assistant fashion editor for *Allure* magazine.

"He is so cool and so accomplished," Damien says. "And he's full of good advice. I've been up there to see the fashion department and see where he works. He's made me realize there are things I can do in that sector where I can put the skills I've learned to use. But I can talk to him about a lot more than career things. He grew up very different than I did, and he has really good perspective. Sometimes I meet him at his office and we just walk around Times Square. And talk, and talk."

It was instant chemistry, Jarrod says, despite a bit of initial shyness on Damien's part. Raised in Virginia, Jarrod came to New York after graduating from the art program at Virginia Commonwealth University, got himself an internship at Yves Saint Laurent's New York office, made sure he did a noticeably spectacular job of it, and networked his way to the magazine hire. After Jarrod helped supervise the *Allure* photo shoot for the makeovers of Class Nine students, he signed up to become a mentor. The first time he and Damien met, they talked for three hours, about everything.

"From the start, he was hilarious and we just connected," Jarrod says. "It was like we were meant for one another. I understand the way he talks, the way he thinks, his interests. I can give him a lot of ideas and positive criticism. It's just been a great partnership."

Career advice is only part of it. Jarrod soon realized that Damien needed a sounding board for other life issues, including the changes that were still happening at home. With their father remarried and beginning a second family, Damien and Devon were shifting between homes. Moving in to help with their critically ill grandfather was stressful. Through all of the upheaval and emotion in this large family, Jarrod was there—exclusively for Damien.

Jarrod also had to help his mentee through some serious slumps during L & D and his internship. "I've had to tell him, 'Damien, you need to be more positive. Okay, today your job is not giving you the motivation you need. You feel like you want to quit. Just focus.' I knew there was a lot of outside stuff. He was concerned with his father moving off with his new family, them moving out, that he was going to have to take care of himself. That's scary."

Jarrod knew something about leveraging that first internship. And he tried to convince Damien that it was best to take a longer view of things.

"I just said, 'This is the right path for you right now, Damien. You're going into this corporate world, and it may not be your number one choice, but if you can get this right, it can be a great step for you to build up some sort of financial stability. You can always go into something a bit more creative. You keep your connections and you can move around.' I tried to get him to realize that it was a great step for him, to try to connect and stay there. Make the best of it, save up for the future."

Occasionally Jarrod also had to be a bit stern regarding one of his mentee's chronic lapses. "I had to stay on top of him about being on time. He's always late for everything. I wanted him to realize the value of time, especially when you're on somebody else's time. You have a responsibility. He would just always have an excuse—had a really late night, his laundry hadn't finished. Time management is just so important. It's one of the big things that I tried to get Damien to see."

They had plenty of fun as well. Damien was thrilled when Jarrod invited him up to the *Allure* offices to watch him prep for a photo shoot. He dove into the accessories closets, chatted with editors and stylists, and generally had a ball. "He walked around and spoke to everybody. He has such a great way with people. We're complete opposites. He's a bit more creative with his clothes than I am; I'm so plain and so not into fashion for myself. He's just such a fashionable little guy."

Looking good on this job is his pleasure, Damien said. And even during his down periods, he takes a certain pride in getting his work stitched up and properly starched. A stack of finished reports, some of them half an inch thick, sat on Damien's desk waiting for distribution. He explained, in newly acquired financespeak, how he put them together: "I look to see if I get any new request for my department, then action the request on a unique server and database. And I keep a record of whatever I do. This means creating evidence packets to assure auditors that every request sent in has been executed accurately."

It is exacting, detail-oriented work. And no singing allowed.

"No problem. *Look where I am.* And when you think about it, I am performing. Appearing here daily, and doing my best."

DEVON, IN CONTROL

Outside the UBS facility in Weehawken, New Jersey, directly across the Hudson River from midtown Manhattan, Devon was facing a tough challenge for a young man struggling to keep his eyes on the prize. The day was warm, stunningly bright, and breezy outside on the waterfront office park. The river and the city rising above it shone intensely; young office workers lingered at an outdoor café. Devon conceded it had been difficult to leave such a day and head into the yawning atrium leading to the UBS offices. But there he was, in a long roomful of cubicles, bent over a painstaking assignment that would take him as long as two weeks. A photocopied document thick with charts and diagrams lay open in front of him.

"That's right, it's in German," he said glumly. And then he laughed. Slowly—knowing little German besides "Volkswagen"—Devon had been translating the document into English using an Internet translator and his own best instincts. "The grammar is reversed sometimes; you have to read the translation carefully to see that it makes sense." Hour after hour, page after page, he had plowed along. Never mind those tough QA assignments of Raphael's—there could be no greater test of focus and commitment than a solid week or two of this. Given his slumps and slides in the L & D phase, was he worried?

"I've got it. I'm all over it. I already did some in French, German, and Spanish. I did them fast and I did them well—ahead of the deadline. And I am bearing *down.*"

He was even way up in his contract points—over three hundred, he said. Like all interns, Devon's performance was monitored by regular performance surveys from his manager, which were sent to Crystal Fields-Sam's internship team at Year Up. He had minimal infractions and not too many intern moments, either—unless you count dozing off for a few seconds one late afternoon while deleting all those umlauts. Or the 180 double-sided pages photocopied on one side only when he hit the wrong button.

"Don't sweat it," soothed his UBS manager, John Knierim. "Nobody can tame that machine; it's a beast." John explained that management for this area of bank operations was based in London, and Devon had arrived during a period of considerable change. "This group is tasked with production support for the Americas, in records management. We maintain legal and compliance systems."

As nonpermanent employees, interns have limited access to all company databases, John said, "so we've given him important tasks for documentation. The thing he's working on arrived in only a paper version. And in German. It's documentation of some vital information. With the reorganization, we need it to get up to speed with applications. We can't obtain an electronic copy, so we asked him to put it in the Google translator, make sure it's accurate, then copy and paste the translation into an electronic document, including all charts. And he's been in all of our team meetings. He's worked some of our run books, which are step-by-step listings of tasks on installations. He's handled everything we've thrown at him."

Okay, they'd had a little fun with the intern. "I told Devon we have casual Fridays. We don't. I don't think he fell for it, though, when I also said we had a spandex day."

Besides some changes to the team's structure, there were rolling tsunamis of platform and application changes. "We work seven or eight platforms, with changes each week," John said. "We make sure they all get approved, and he's helping. We also make sure we QA our work, and Devon has been key in organizing those changes so I can pass them up the chain. QA is tough. And we're in the midst of a big platform change—that's a two- or three-year project."

Such long-term perspective does not come naturally to the very young, but Devon had begun to see and appreciate the ever-expanding picture of global commerce. More notable was that he had maintained focus after weathering another family crisis—the death of his grandfather, the bishop.

Both twins had moved back in with their grandparents over the final weeks to help. The morning after his grandfather's death, Devon reported to work. John Knierim was very surprised to see him. "I said, 'What are you doing here?' But that's the initiative and the ambition that he has. I told him, 'It's appreciated. Go home.' I was impressed but a little bit saddened for him to think he had to come here. You need to take care of your family."

This Devon had, as always. But this recent set of filial duties had required some serious logistics and problem solving. His first step prior to his grandfather's funeral was to contact the local police about traffic issues; over two thousand mourners were expected, and that many did indeed show up. "Just like for our mother, his daughter," Devon noted. "There was a lot to do. Our grandfather had founded this church in the sixties and started up a whole network of Haitian churches since then. He was very well known and respected."

It was another difficult and very close loss. This time Devon faced it as a capable young adult rather than a frightened adolescent. He focused on details for the service, the accommodation of the many speakers, the crowds. Immediately afterward, he was concerned about their grandmother. He and Damien were still staying with her. "Some days she's okay; other days she forgets to do basic things like eat. It's a really deep grief thing. But I figure I—we—can help with that."

Back at his desk, Devon summoned his powers of concentration and consulted his notes on "crazy" foreign grammar constructions and document management; words spewed out of the on-screen translator and got neatly tapped into the holes in his charts.

Handeln . . . trade.

Einkommen . . . income.

Verlust . . . loss.

Sometimes he clicked the option for voice pronunciation.

Eeesh. All those gutturals made him wince. "No music to that talk. No music at all."

MARISOL, DESKSIDE AND REMOTE

Marisol's three-year-old son, Manuel, had been very shy and apprehensive walking into the noisy Brooklyn space filled with Year Up students and guests, who were mostly family. It was the much-anticipated potluck supper.

The little boy clung to Marisol's mom and asked to leave—until suddenly he saw a familiar face on-screen in a slide show and yelled out.

"Look, Mommy—that's you!"

It got a big laugh from his mother's classmates, who had been hearing about him all those months. Marisol had been part of the decorating committee for the evening. Her mother arrived with Manuel and some potato salad she had made. Scheduling had not left Taleisha enough time to get all the way uptown and fetch Jared, but she did arrive with several boxes of doughnuts. Malik, an enthusiastic cook, had improvised a macaroni and cheese dish studded with juicy bits of chicken. Devon was impressed: "People just jumped on your stuff, Mal. They drilled right through it."

A committee of students and staff had worked long and hard on the evening. The long row of steaming chafing dishes reflected Class Nine's wide-ranging culinary heritage: lo mein, noodles with hoisin sauce, southern fried chicken, *pastelitos* (small meat and chicken pastries), *du riz djon djon* (Haitian black rice with mushrooms), skewered chicken satay, enchiladas with green salsa, Trinidadian curry, lasagna, Venezuelan *pernil* (pork shoulder). No one was shy about diving in. LCW brought in so much food, they had to stow the leftovers in the break-room refrigerator. "We didn't have to spend money on lunch for a few days," noted an appreciative Malik.

"It felt like family," Marisol said. "I feel the same about coming back on Wednesday mornings for PDW, just coming back home and being with everyone, even for a couple of hours. I need to see my *people*. It settles you somehow and you can get back out and do what you have to do. Have I made friends for life here? Absolutely."

For Marisol, who was soft-spoken and somewhat retiring in a group situation, the internship at Bank of America presented an unexpected set of challenges. It was decided that she would rotate through three of the bank's offices in midtown Manhattan, which meant three sets of coworkers and help-desk clients to meet and interact with.

"I was nervous, but I feel it's worked out really well," she said during a meeting with her supervisor, Mark Bronnberg, at her primary location near Times Square. He is a genial, understanding family man himself who had been supportive on the few days that Marisol had to stay home when her son was ill. He said that he had gotten good reports from the other locations and was pleased with the way his experiment was going. "Previous interns didn't rotate," he said. "Here we felt because the user base is so different in various sites it would benefit Marisol to see what's going on in a few of them."

He had supervised Year Up interns before and saw to it that Marisol had a standard orientation at his office. "I introduced her to the team, asked her to shadow the techs, got her involved in team meetings. We have group chat online every morning. She asks questions—she learns the culture basically through that chat. That's the easiest way to get someone acclimated to this environment, seeing what goes on with the whole team throughout the day."

Once Mark had seen Marisol handle "break/fix" issues, basic repairs, computer reimaging, and equipment replacements by phone and deskside, he deployed her to the other two sites. She was relieved that her first solo task was something she had learned to do at Year Up. She installed a set of dual monitors, and the employee was pleased. "We had been prepared in L & D that we'd bump into some really nasty people as clients, but I haven't yet," she said. "Everyone is nice. They understand that I'm learning and I may not know everything. They're always really impressed when I do fix their problem." Her only hardware repair went well: "It was fun. I had to change a video card on a desktop because the old one wouldn't take the new monitor that the user had. So I had to switch them out."

When a frustrated user saw results, Marisol loved to see the sun come out. "Big smiles. And lots of thanks." An average day—nothing was "typical" in this rotation—went like this: "I'd go in, check voice- and e-mail, see what's going on in the queue. If there's any open tickets, I go visit the user or call them first to see what problems they're having. I go and troubleshoot. We pushed applications, helped users set up their desktops if they ordered any new equipment."

For a group of employees that was moving to a New Jersey office, she was given sole responsibility for the two groups of users remaining; their permanent tech had already moved. "I really liked the users over there, they treated me very well, and on the last day it was like, 'Please come with us to the new building. We need you.' It was nice to see that I could help them and how happy that made them. It always felt good." Better still, she had just found out that other users were now asking for her.

That kind of feedback buoyed Marisol's confidence week by week. All that behavioral coaching she had gotten in pro skills "really paid off" in practice. Corporate anthropology seemed a bit abstract in PDW, but she soon saw the value in learning corporate pecking orders once she began traveling among the bank's different offices. Workplace tribes have differing needs and behaviors. "The pace and the attitude depends on the kinds of clients you support, like traders. Moneymakers versus back-office people. If you're working on trading with that fast pace, they won't be happy that I'm learning on the job. But in a slower back-office environment, they tend to be more patient. The key is following through—for everybody—the way you tell them you will."

Unexpectedly, she found that some of her toughest tech issues were piling up toward the back end of her internship, back on Forty-seventh Street with Mark Bronnberg. She explained: "A hard day is when there's tickets that I don't know how to fix. I'll see that there's a lot of tickets, and I want to help, but I don't want to take one, go to the user, and seem clueless about what I'm doing. I try to ask someone for help, or if everyone's super busy, I'll Google it. I've found many solutions that way. Sometimes when I see that no one has taken the ticket for a long time, I will—and just throw myself out there. I let the user know, 'This is the first time and I'll try my best.' I've had some victories with that."

Pushing herself, taking that sort of risk, was not something she could have imagined nine months earlier. And she felt she had made some progress on a lifelong timeliness issue. It was no easier to get up and out of the apartment, but she had held the line on infractions and switched to the A train—"much, much faster"—to hit her start time in all locations. As a working mother, she appreciated both the Year Up parenting program that she, Taleisha, and ten others attended during L & D and the women's retreat that was part of PDW.

"The women's retreat was the best—it was empowering. There were workshops, like Know Your Worth, and something about emotional intelligence. They were cool. One of the speakers was pretty touching; she made us think. The girls were at the Manhattan site, boys in Brooklyn. They wanted us to speak freely and the same for the boys too. They had workplace tips specifically for women. It was mostly learning how to watch the way we speak—and knowing that we don't have the upper hand in the corporate world."

Her spirits had been "pretty high" most of the way through. She felt she was far more optimistic than when she entered the program. But given her life's disappointments, she tried to keep her expectations realistic.

"I still think one day at a time. I still have space to grow and I still have space to mess up. At first I used to think about getting hired all the time. Now I hear people in the company discuss not having any plans to hire anyone soon. So I backed up on that one. Either way it's a good experience. On Tuesday my manager and I went together to troubleshoot an issue. I told him I feel like such a newbie again. He said, 'That's good. That means that you're learning more.' He couldn't fix the problem either, and we got help elsewhere. He said, 'It's always going to be like that in this area, but you've learned a lot since you started here and you can work at any company now. You know the basics and you're pretty good at it.'"

Once in L & D when she was "way down in points due to lateness," she took the subway downtown and had a visit with the guy who had gotten her into all this. He warned her strongly to "get it together, Mari." She heard him. She bore down. So there she was, working help desks at three locations at one of the largest banks on the planet because that beautiful guy—Jonathan, Year Up Class Six, New York—had paid it forward.

Jonathan's work and extraordinary drive, says Crystal Fields-Sam, helped Year Up secure a bigger presence at American Express, where he is now a permanent employee. Marisol had loved and trusted him since "back in the day," when Pokémon and boy bands ruled and they ran together in a pack of elementary school friends. She felt for Jonathan when they were fourteen and his home life came apart; she missed him as he bounced around between his older siblings' homes in Rhode Island and Pennsylvania. When Marisol came back north after her marriage ended, Jonathan and the rest of their old friends welcomed her back with a joyful uptown get-together. Then he nagged her about Year Up until she applied.

Jonathan told her how hard it was, no lie. He said he loved everything about his internship at AmEx. He graduated from Year Up with awards, citations, and a chorus of corporate praise, but without a job offer. "What happened next," Marisol said, "is amazing."

Jonathan was happy to elaborate in a lounge at the massive American Express tower, the same spot where he had talked Marisol through her tough spell. Though he grew up just a few miles north, at twenty he had never been to this part of lower Manhattan, where the World Trade Center towers had stood. The first day he reported for his internship, he got woefully lost in the temporary walkways and footbridges that still circumscribe the construction site now known around the world as Ground Zero. Sited on the western lip of that lasting scar, the AmEx tower was badly damaged on 9/11. The tower was completely restored when Jonathan was searching for it. But he was too disoriented to see it.

"I had to ask a cop," he remembered.

He and Marisol always laughed when they talked about another thing that almost blinded him to the opportunities he has now: "my hair."

Jonathan realizes now that it was an emotional block of sorts. He had begun the program with some tough orientation milestones as well. And when he took up a marker to list them, one date loomed over all: July 24, 2003, "the day my mom passed from cancer." Jonathan was not sure why—a silent but in-your-face rage against fate maybe—but he had not cut his hair since his mother's death. Then Andres Gomez told Jonathan he was all but accepted to Year Up—but that corporate America would not take kindly to the nearly waist-length locks. "I almost didn't join the program," he admitted. His brother wanted to know if he had gone totally nuts. "Dude, you've been doing absolutely nothing for so long. Now you've made huge progress getting into the program. *Just do it.*" Jonathan waited until the last possible day before orientation, then cut his hair and donated it to Locks of Love. In the end, he reasoned that donating to a charity that provides human hair wigs for cancer patients was a better way to honor his mother.

At AmEx, Jonathan was the exceptional sort of intern who volunteered for anything, anticipated needs, and lunged for any task that would expand his skills. "I was just happy to have been there," he said. "I didn't expect to be hired. I knew I had the skills to go out and get something else." So just before graduation he had arranged to do part-time IT work at Fordham University until he could find something permanent. No one at AmEx had spoken to him about the possibility of a permanent job, so he was already looking elsewhere. He had been getting advice on his search from an AmEx employee who took an interest in helping him. "She was the assistant to Matthew Robinson, the chief technical officer of AmEx. She came to graduation with a couple of other people from AmEx, including Matthew. I was stunned that they came."

The CTO came over to Jonathan and his proud older brothers after the ceremony. They shook hands and Matthew asked, "What are you doing next week?"

"I'm working part time with Fordham."

"How would you like to come back?"

"Are you serious?"

"Come next week and we'll move from there."

Tossing aside professional decorum, Jonathan gave his corporate officer a huge hug.

It was the perfect graduation gift. "*Yes!* I'm in!"

In the months afterward, Jonathan saw his red security badge denoting temporary worker status morph to the desirable, permanent blue. Better still was the change from the Year Up stipend. "My starting salary was over $35,000—absolutely amazing, considering I started at zero. Finally, I'm moving forward. If it wasn't for Year Up teaching us how to manage money, I don't know if I'd have my apartment. There was such a lack of everything when I was growing up that when I first got the job, I wanted to buy everything. Then I said to myself, 'Let me save here. I'll buy only what I need.' And it got me the first and last month deposit on my apartment—which I'm so grateful for."

After all those years of couch surfing with relatives, he had found his first independent home—a one-bedroom apartment in the Briarwood section of Queens. Recently, Jonathan had moved up to "white glove service" at American Express—as a tech for the executive suite, on call to a high-ranking set of officers right up to CEO Kenneth Chenault. It took in some remote work, some deskside—and the occasional home service call to some stunning luxury high-rises and townhouses.

Jonathan told Marisol all about graduation. She had been thinking about that moment a lot. "Manuel has already tried on his little suit. He wore it on his birthday. Which almost wasn't such a happy day since his father got mugged right in front our building. It was a new twist too."

The robber had a gun—that was nothing new. But he held it to the head of her ex-husband's young nephew, who was with him. "He said he'd blow his head off if he didn't give him everything. They got his wallet, his phone, money, everything. He was pretty shaken up when he got upstairs. And his nephew too. I can't wait to get out of there. It's just insane all the time now."

Marisol enjoyed working in midtown Manhattan at three Bank of America sites. But she understood that the greatest success in the workplace wouldn't afford her a protective bubble when she got off the A train at 168th Street every night. On the day that all of Class Nine received new trench coats donated by an upscale designer, she and Mark Bronnberg searched the office for a shopping bag to camouflage it, lest she be relieved of that very desirable garment before reaching her apartment.

"I just heard that Jonathan moved to another apartment that's even better," she said. "We're going to get to a place like that, Manuel and me."

What of that laptop with his baby pictures stolen from her last apartment? Still in police custody?

"I've played phone tag for over a year. Guess it's time to move on."

Marisol laughed. "You can't believe what I've learned to let go. I guess if you want to move ahead, it's not a bad thing to lighten your load."

MALIK, ON FIRE

On March 22, Malik took an earlier train than usual from 125th Street in Harlem to his internship at UBS in Stamford, Connecticut, and walked the two long blocks from the station to the sprawling corporate campus. As he traded "good mornings" with lobby security, he concentrated on steadying his nerves.

I've got this. I know it cold. I won't mess up.

For nearly three weeks, at the request of his manager, Ajit Patel,* Malik had been doing research and interviewing members of his team in fixed-income trade capture, finding out what each of them did and learning the finer details of financial applications and products used globally by the giant Swiss bank. From his window office, Ajit watched his intern politely making the rounds, notebook in hand, asking for time, information, and, tacitly, patience. Malik asked about financial products with mysterious, somewhat fanciful names: Boomerang, SwapsWire, Laredo. Since his team included managers in Chicago, he had to call them as well. Making those cold calls was daunting, he said, "but people really seemed to want to help." He had to do hours of Internet research as well.

Ajit intended the exercise as solid if strenuous orientation for Malik and as a review and update on the products and apps for other managers. He explained, "Malik's first task was to understand the trade capture area and to learn, basically, what is fixed income? He talked to all these people to find out which apps they are working on and what each financial product does within the trade capture area. He got his information and presented that to me—he explained, 'These are the risk factors. These are the conformations and settlement systems'—he showed me the full front-to-back flow. He did very well."

Once gathered, the information would be put into a comprehensive, cogent PowerPoint presentation, which Malik was also to deliver verbally via conference call to managers as far away as Europe and Asia. *Global managers*—listening to him, judging his performance. He had just turned nineteen the previous week.

"Maybe it's good they all can't see me. Or me see them."

Malik was at his place in the conference room well before the appointed eight-thirty call. He had practiced his presentation with Ajit, taken some helpful feedback and pointers, then sent the PowerPoint in an e-mail to the managers, from Stamford to Singapore and beyond. A few local managers filed into the conference room as he waited by the phone. This is how he remembers it: "I had the feeling that I usually got right before I played big basketball games. I was anxious, because of the buildup. My phone rang and Ajit introduced me to the team. It reminded me of the tip-off; once the ball was in the air, it was time to perform, no turning back. I gave them a brief intro about myself and what I would be talking about. The whole time I was speaking I was in a zone, focused on remembering the terms and applications."

He plunged into a highly technical thicket of bond options, credit default swaps, futures. All were neatly diagrammed and defined in his PowerPoint. Malik held steady as he reeled it off to the team, conscious of pacing himself and not speaking too quickly. "I had about thirty slides, but before I knew it, I had finished presenting. Ajit asked if anyone had questions. There were a couple of queries I was able to answer."

Silence. Then, from across the oceans, there was applause on the line. A few congratulatory e-mails arrived soon after.

"I was in a state of disbelief."

Soon after, Denise Hebner, the regional programs lead for Group Technology Americas—and the point person for all Year Up interns at three tristate UBS sites and Chicago—got a text message from Peter Williams, managing director for fixed-income IT. It read: "Our Year Upper, Malik, is doing very well. He did a presentation on our applications that had information some of our GSD (Global Service Delivery) guys weren't aware of."

Peter Williams is the team's senior executive. Early on, when the fixed-income trade capture team went bowling—to get to know their new interns in a relaxed setting—Malik had his own intern moment, born of nerves when Peter showed up at the lanes: "I threw a gutter ball."

Malik's cubicle in the busy, high-security UBS facility at Four Hundred Atlantic Street in Stamford was bristling with pink and yellow Post-its. There was so much to ingest and remember, so little time. When he opened a drawer, there was trace evidence of a teenager: candy wrappers, more crumpled notes to himself. Most of his UBS coworkers were dressed in office casual. Malik was in a well-cut navy blue suit with a perfectly knotted red tie. "I'm down with the tie thing now. I like to look sharp." Per Denise's instructions, all interns held to the Year Up standard of professional dress despite the khaki office casual that surrounds them. "I have not dropped the bar with the dress code at all," she explained. "I tell the managers, 'Do not pressure these interns to down-dress like yourselves.' This is a safety net that always keeps them up and focused."

A few days after his first presentation, Malik was set to reprise it for his fellow interns in Stamford and, via teleconference, for those in Jersey City and Weehawken, New Jersey. From a wall-mounted monitor in the teleconference room, Devon grinned encouragement and waved. Also at the table in Stamford was Tiffany Cummings, a former intern from Year Up New York's Class Five who had proved so exceptional, said Denise, that the others around the table had claimed their opportunities here in her spectacular wake.

Tiffany was one of the first two Year Up interns whom Denise got approved on a trial basis in 2009. To her supervisors Denise presented her request as a strategy to help diversify the Swiss bank's workforce. Alas, Tiffany could not have arrived at a worse time. The financial crisis started and UBS was going through major restructuring. "It was very uncomfortable," Denise recalled. "I brought in two interns for an exploratory program when the firm was in a state of change. I had Tiffany and a young man named Christian."

He was capable, but not the best fit for UBS. "And then there was a super motivated Tiffany," Denise said, "who wanted her life to change and would do anything to never go back to working minimum-wage jobs. She wasn't going to let it happen." Nonetheless, at the end of Tiffany's stellar internship, Denise could not hire her permanently so Tiffany went off to work at another firm—but I retained contact with her."

As it is with some other corporate partners, all entry-level applicants need a college degree at UBS. This makes it highly competitive and highly unlikely that a Year Up intern will be recruited directly after an internship there. "To help set expectations, I make that clear from day one," Denise said.

So far, two large corporate partners with multisite commitments, Bank of America and State Street, have waived the degree requirement, given the performance of Year Up interns. At UBS, while research and discussion are under way for a pilot program in client services that could possibly circumvent that four-year-degree requirement, a fellowship program was created for outstanding candidates to attend college and continue working at the bank up to twenty hours per week post–Year Up graduation.

Denise emphasized that developing such alternative routes for retaining interns with the company was not a charitable impulse but a smart and mutually beneficial business transaction. "The expectation as an employer is whether we can identify highly motivated interns can blend into our culture," Denise said. "If all I'm doing is taking them and training them for six months and getting managers engaged, it's nice, but there's no end result for UBS—and it's not a success for us. Success for us is building a diverse pipeline and retaining talent. The fellowship provides the flexibility the intern needs to matriculate as well as the opportunity to build professional skills while contributing to the team. Tiffany is the absolute role model and the best example of why diversity in the workplace is a business decision. It's not a stretch to say that Tiffany and the interns who have followed in her footsteps motivate Group Technology to stick with Year Up and keep finding ways to make the program work for the firm."

By any standard, Denise is a true champion of the program, visiting classrooms during L & D, arranging tours of UBS for all of Class Nine, and developing materials—a project Tiffany is spearheading—to help interns select and apply to colleges. Denise and Tiffany were invited to Capitol Hill to present a series of panels about programs targeting the underemployed. Along with Year Up's executive directors, participating corporate executives, and graduates, they spoke to legislators and their staffs about Year Up's success in workforce development. Denise voiced the same long-term perspective that spurred her company's commitment: "The idea was that if we wanted to change the way our pipeline looked, we needed to make an investment in diversity. UBS group CIO Michele Trogni values the program and wanted to go deeper with Year Up and give it a chance—to see if there were more professionally savvy interns like Tiffany Cummings. We increased our interns to thirteen here, then we added three at the new Chicago site. So for the year we'll end up taking twenty-eight interns across all sites."

The expansion represents a nearly half-million-dollar investment in Year Up talent. Just how exceptional is Tiffany? "I waited over a year to be able to hire her," Denise said. Tiffany is a business analyst working on strategy, analytics, regional reporting, and shaping and supervising the Year Up internship program. Denise added, "We are cultivating, managing, and developing her into a leader."

For Tiffany, Year Up has also been a family affair. She was in New York's Class Five; her husband, Ojay Cummings, preceded her in Class Four. Couple and sibling enrollment in Year Up is not uncommon; transformations are most visible to those closest to a striving student. In this case, a struggling young couple well below the poverty line—and with a newborn—became a solid, two-income family.

"Ojay completed his first internship at Merrill Lynch during the height of the Bank of America/Merrill Lynch acquisition," Tiffany says. "Due to that redundancy, he was not hired, which led to an internship opportunity provided by Year Up at Montefiore Medical Center, in the Emerging Health IT division. He has worked there for almost two years now and is doing very well."

Ojay worked in desktop support at two locations for the huge hospital; he has received two promotions and several citations as employee of the month. Besides their two-year-old daughter, Deanna, Ojay has guardianship of his younger brother Shabri. Thanks to a flexible work arrangement provided by UBS, Tiffany is two years into her undergraduate degree program at New York University. She hopes to finish in June 2013. And she has a dream beyond that: graduate school in NYU's JD/MBA program. With a double law and business-school degree, she would like to specialize in employment law and do pro bono work "helping those in my former situation."

Which was?

"Poverty."

To that end, she worked for months developing materials to help this class of UBS interns make informed college choices and financial-aid decisions. That day, with the interns assembled for Malik's presentation, she handed out information packets. Malik and the other interns described her as a role model and group mentor. "Tiffany is just there for all of us. She's like a guidepost, an adviser," Malik said. "She'll remind you about networking around the company, letting people see you, keeping the brand up."

During his presentation, Malik was in his zone again, and the session went well. When the New Jersey crew had signed off and the monitors went black, Malik stood gathering up his extra printouts with a serene smile.

Here was the raging adolescent who, at age fourteen, roamed the Bronx projects mourning his brother with a gun in his hand and what he calls "a mind-set of revenge." Here was the boy who was declared irredeemable in elementary school, who, despite his clear intelligence, spent a few exasperating years in special education classes, stigmatized, he recalls, "as a slow SPED kid."

No one working with him at UBS would ever have guessed that. And no one needed to know. Malik's years in special education did not escape notice in the Year Up admissions process. Nor did they rule him out. Charmaine explains: "We looked at him being in special ed. He passed our learning assessment. He's charismatic and he speaks well; those are the things that made him stand out. He described himself as being *bad*. So many young men of color here in New York were put into special ed because of behavior and it went with them through high school. Many of them dropped out. Luckily, Malik finished. He comes from a neighborhood where friends and siblings dance around the law. This is his opportunity to be in a whole different world, and he's embracing it. He's here, he's enjoying it."

In his desire to put distance between the streets that took his brother and his own future, Malik had been—yes—"perusing" colleges in the New York state university system far from the city for the fall after his Year Up graduation. His college application essay was about his journey through Year Up. He did not dwell on the hardships and tragedy but on the transformation. He wrapped it in a butterfly analogy: pupa, chrysalis, taking wing. After three drafts, he knocked it out of the park. He admitted to a few butterflies of his own as he slid the envelopes into the mail slots.

"I know I'm college material now. I hope I convinced them."

The biggest leap was convincing himself that he'd hold on out in the wide world—"out of that Year Up cocoon." He still owned his incorrigible years, and it was clear he still had some affection for the wild boy he had been. "As long as he stays just a memory."

Had he really been bad, as he said so often? "I was misbehaving in every way you could think of. Basically, in the area I grew up in you just get sucked into that. I'd throw eggs at cars or snatch and run from a store or harass the store owners. In school I used to be an outcast, curse at teachers, not listen, get in fights. My fourth-grade year I had, like, four fights; I got suspended three times in one month—and that's when they transferred me out of elementary school to a different one, which handles special-ed kids."

His mother had four other children to raise, including a daughter two years younger than Malik who had Down syndrome; she worked nights and often wasn't there to take the calls from teachers and guidance counselors. When she punished him, the boy stoically accepted "those butt whuppings" and just grew hidebound. For Malik, as for so many children at great risk, the difference was one tenacious, caring person who grabbed his shirtsleeve as he teetered at the abyss.

"My fifth-grade teacher kept saying, 'You're a smart kid, Malik. Why are you behaving like this?' She was right too, because when I wasn't making jokes or starting trouble, I would do my work and I would do it very well. She'd seen the potential in me. So that was my first Year Up moment, I guess you could call it.

"At first I was kind of disrespectful, but she would man up with me. We'd go back and forth with each other and we finally found middle ground. That's when I really started to focus. She earned my respect for doing that. She was really pushing me, giving me new outlets for how I could get out of special ed and get into programs with the regular students."

On the cusp of adolescence, he wondered if being the wild child would still seem cool. "I started thinking of middle school. Kids will look at you and think that you're really slow. So it was 'I have to get out of this.'" The realization that he could make a change came far from New York. He spent seventh grade in public school in Kentucky, where his older brother lived. "I didn't go to SPED. The school system was better; it was more structured, more disciplined. I could focus in a regular-ed situation. I wouldn't even say I was bad. Academically I did well."

As he did at Year Up, in L & D. And with self-discipline, contract adherence, points. By late spring, Malik's college acceptances began to come in. And some workplace realities offered another sort of education. One day, his manager, Ajit, was let go. Malik was stunned at first; he had just said good morning, and forty-five minutes later his boss was gone.

"His computer screen was still on."

It was explained to the team as another case of redundancy. "In fact, I'd been reading about it and gave Ajit an article about how FIC (fixed-income capture) was shrinking in this economy," Malik says. "I don't know if he had time to read it. He was always working."

Malik was reassigned to another manager. He did another big presentation. Then one morning in late June, Denise called him in to discuss what he would describe as some "very excellent dilemmas." It seemed that he was about to have some choices. Take an acceptance to a college in the New York City system, live in Harlem, and stay on at UBS as a fellow, working twenty hours a week while he went to school. Or he could take that four-year college experience upstate—far from the streets that still worried him.

Of course it came down to money as well. Malik sat at a Mexican restaurant down Atlantic Street from the UBS complex and studied the copies of the grants and loans the SUNY system had declared him eligible for. "Debt. Never had it. Don't want it. I've never even tried for a credit card because I don't ever want to fall into that. It's scary." Notations from his advisory sessions with Year Up staff, Tiffany, and Denise filled the margins of the aid package statement. Sensing his heart's desire, having heard his reservations about staying in Harlem, Denise had a proposition. Well, the details were still in the works. But there just might be a way to help him earn and learn.

For a couple of weeks, like any nineteen-year-old excitedly weighing his college possibilities, Malik lay in his room at night beside the curling papers with inspirational quotations he had tacked up way back at the beginning of L & D. He hadn't read them in ages, and truth be told, some of them seemed a bit corny to him. He went back and forth on his big decision.

"Choices! I have choices. Both good. I fall asleep telling myself, 'Hold on. Do the right thing. Don't mess up now.'"

He couldn't really discuss it with his mother. She was back in Gambia, where a brother had recently died. And she was also having a bit of a vacation, since a program for special-needs children that had long been helpful to the family had found his sister a two-week camp in a program run by NYU. "Someplace green. She was really happy to go. And maybe my mother can get a little rest."

He grinned and folded up the well-creased paper. "She'll be back for graduation on August 2. I think she needs to see it to believe it."

CASSANDRA PAYS IT FORWARD

As Class Nine was nearing its homestretch, where in this wide, hectic world was Cassandra?

Charmaine had left the door wide open for her to return and cycle through another class, taking a different curriculum track—financial operations—to broaden her skill set. She had heard nothing but a few vague suppositions on her whereabouts from Cassandra's bright, striving legacy, a twenty-one-year-old Jamaican woman named Solange* who was doing beautifully as a student in New York's Class Ten. Like Cassandra, she had been left behind when her mother went to New York to work, mostly at live-in nurse/caregiver positions. When she was able to send for Solange, the child lived with a close friend of her mother's ("In Jamaica, everyone like that is your auntie").

Likewise, Cassandra had become family of a sort when they were both quite young. Solange explains, "Cassandra is my godsister. We grew up together in church, her church in New Jersey. We have different branches, and every year we have a big convention and all the churches come together. So that was how we saw each other. Then we got older. She just disappeared and I hadn't seen her in a while. All this time, she was living in New York, having had to leave her family. When I went to the convention in the Bronx, one night I was in church and she was sitting in the front. I didn't know who she was. She'd cut off all her hair. We made eye contact and I was, 'Oh my God, what are you doing here?' I automatically thought she was here with her parents. I didn't know the story.

"We talked. She told me the story, what had happened to her. She was living in the Bronx with her grandmother, but she told me she was in the process of looking for an apartment."

Cassandra also told Solange about Year Up and urged her to apply. Two false starts at college complicated by bureaucratic errors had made some of Solange's completed course credits nontransferable and jeopardized her loans. She had given up. She worked small jobs, babysitting and as a temporary salesperson at Kohl's. "After that I was left with nothing. During all of this, Cassandra kept nagging me, 'You should go to Year Up.' She kept saying, 'They pay you.' I'm saying, 'Fine, what's the application fee? Do you need financial aid?' And she kept saying, 'No, it's not like that.'"

This went on for months. Every time Solange saw Cassandra, she was mystified: "Why are you always dressed up?"

"It's the program. I'm telling you—come."

"You've got to wear slacks and skirts every day?"

"Yes, it's called being professional. Girl, they're *paying* for my school." Cassandra chose her moment and bore down. And finally Solange listened.

"Cassandra gave me the pitch, the whole rundown. And it motivated me because I realized, 'Okay, what's left? I have nothing else to do.' At that point Cassandra knew she was going to JPMorgan Chase as an intern. I said to myself, 'And *you're* going upstate.'"

"Upstate" is Sing Sing prison in Ossining, New York, where Solange's older brother was incarcerated. She worried about him constantly and visited him faithfully. But she admitted to Cassandra that it didn't amount to much as a life's calling.

"I need *something.*"

Cassandra insisted she attend an open house at Year Up. Sensing her friend's anxiety, she promised not to leave her side. Solange could sit with her in class and see if she liked it—with one condition: "You've got to dress professionally."

"Just to walk in? Okay, but that's strange," Solange remembers thinking. "I dressed up and I came in. I liked it. It wasn't too big. I thought you could get more attention and learn more. So I signed up, went through it all. Charmaine interviewed me and it went well. Then they called me for a second interview. Andres seemed like he was trying to scare me, saying, 'Are you sure you want to be in this program? Why? Do you know it's a lot of work? It's nothing like college.' I said, 'I'm ready, this is why I'm here.'"

Solange thinks that beyond just hauling her to the door, Cassandra's persistence kept her in the program. "All along, Cassandra has been boosting me, clueing me in to things that would happen. I needed that to be mentally prepared. If I came in any other way, like by myself, I don't think I would have made it this far. Because there are days you're going to feel, 'Oh my God, I can't do this.'"

Solange had long wondered about Cassandra's strength in spite of everything that had befallen her, wondered how she could push herself to do so much when she had so little support. Since she was ten, Solange had been back living with her own mother, "my total support and cheerleader. Cassandra's so alone. I asked her, 'How do you *do* this—to come off as if nothing happened?' We look at someone, they seem all together, but we don't know how someone feels."

Not long after that happy day of internship announcements, Cassandra had confided to Charmaine and Andres that since she was about to be homeless again, she didn't feel she would be able to do her best at an internship. To be on time, professionally dressed, fed, and energetic just seemed an impossible hurdle in the grip of the long, hard winter. "She was supposed to live with *me*," Solange said. Her mother, now a licensed practical nurse working at a hospital, had moved the family to a small house with three stories. "Cassandra could have the whole second floor to herself. Or a room. Everybody was prepared; we cleared out the rooms. My mom was, 'Where's Cassandra? What's going on?' We've been calling, talking to her. But she's been undecided so we left it alone."

Cassandra never moved in with the family and was not heard from for a month or so. Signals since then have been mixed and sporadic. There was a family death in Jamaica, then another. A possibility of a nursing program in Atlanta . . .

"She just crashed," Solange said. "And for some time now, even on Facebook, no signals."

Cassandra being Cassandra, her friend was sure she would turn up and have reinvented herself yet again.

"I admire her ambition, that she's so motivated. She's always on the go, very energetic. Sometimes you can't keep up with her. You just never know what her next move is going to be. She's always thinking ahead. I just wish her the best all the time. And please, please be careful. I'm still kind of mad at her for giving up this opportunity."

CHAPTER ELEVEN
Abdul, in a State of Grace

WHEN I FIRST REACHED OUT TO SHAKE THE HAND OF ANOTHER NEW Boston student named Abdul Tijani, I certainly noticed the network of ridged scars and discolorations across both hands. They continued past his wrists and up into the sleeves of the well-pressed suit he wore, with a perfectly knotted tie, a crisp dress shirt, and some rather unique African-made dress shoes, every day. I would never have asked about his hands—or about the fading scars on his neck. Clearly there had been some major trauma. Plenty of students arrive at Year Up with scars from knife wounds and gunshots and a host of less visible traumas. Unless they volunteer, we don't ask.

In fact, I didn't know the details of Abdul's past before Year Up until after he had graduated and another life-threatening crisis put us back in close touch and he explained his earlier life. I knew him as his classmates did, as a warm, hardworking, diligent young man determined to use his year up as a toehold toward a better life. The opportunities extended young adults by their time in the program—from professional training to a living wage and health care—are meant to reverberate through their lives, and those of their families, for years to come. Abdul is a great example of how that works; he made use of every resource available. His story also shows the extraordinary resilience our students bring to bear, and their stubborn resistance to any characterization that suggests "victim."

In his honor, graduates in three classes at Year Up Boston during 2007–2008 were chosen to receive the Abdul Tijani Award for Courage, recognizing students who have persevered over significant obstacles along their Year

Up journey. We would have proudly kept up the tradition, but Abdul—gently and politely—asked us to discontinue the award. Though he had spoken with humility and eloquence at the presentations, Abdul told us that he was not comfortable "on a pedestal." Down the road, he suggested, perhaps we could come up with another way for the students in our learning communities to share the often astonishing life stories they bring to our doorstep. After all, Abdul reasoned, his was just one of so many hard journeys.

I'll let you be the judge of that. Abdul's odyssey, while extraordinary, does illustrate the ways in which we hope to serve all students during their time with us—and long after graduation. With courage and grace, Abdul has leveraged his year up all the way—career training, solid employment, health care, a path to postsecondary education. This is the way Year Up is supposed to work—even when fate tosses its worst in your path. Abdul's odyssey also reminds us that a bright, motivated young man of color can face equally grim and senseless perils in a poor, war-ravaged third-world country and in one of America's great cities.

Abdul was born in Nigeria and raised in Sierra Leone in West Africa. He is one of many students across all Year Up sites who have come to us after a difficult beginning in a distant culture. They started life in El Salvador, Cambodia, Rwanda—places where very bad things have gone on. They arrive with unspeakable memories that surface without warning. Deep trauma rarely heals itself, so Year Up staff members stay vigilant for signals—subtle and overt—that a student's past is casting a shadow on his or her future.

Another young man from Africa told me at the end of a long classroom day, "I just *can't* study. I can't keep my head straight." When I asked him why, he explained, "I keep seeing the picture of the gardener shooting my father." His father and the other man were from different factions in Sierra Leone. They had worked side by side as gardeners for decades before the civil war there—the same upheaval that Abdul lived through—turned sane people murderous. The student told me, "I just keep seeing the bullet going into my father's chest." I asked whether he had ever talked to anyone who might help him grapple with that horrific image plaguing him. He had not. We got him some help immediately. How could we possibly expect him to concentrate on software interfaces until he could come to terms with such post-traumatic stress?

Meeting Abdul, there is a serenity and a ready laugh that draws people to him. For a quiet man, he's pretty unforgettable. On the morning he came to our Boston offices to help with this book, people popped out of doors left and right at the sound of his voice. He is a tall, lanky gentleman in his late twenties with a confident bearing, a killer smile, and a warm, expressive baritone. His very light accent is hard to place; he speaks excellent English, in addition to three languages from West Africa: Creole, Mende, and Yoruba.

What follows is a good-news story. I felt it was most appropriate to ask Abdul-Rahman Adeyemi Oladipo Ishola Tijani—who has the wisdom and manly grace of a genuine Yoruban prince—to tell it in his own words. He laughed easily and often as he took us back through his journey. You might not imagine it was possible to laugh at all during such a narrative. But then, you don't know Abdul.

"I was born in Abeokuta, Nigeria, in 1982. My father is Nigerian, my mother from Sierra Leone. They met while students at the University of North Texas in Dallas. They got married, gave birth to my older sister in Dallas, and decided to move back and settle in Nigeria. Two years after I was born, my father died, so I never knew him. It was a car accident, a head-on collision. My mother took us back to Sierra Leone. But then a civil war broke out in 1991. It continued, worse and worse, until 1999, when it really got bad. I was not going to school; it was just chaos. There were no teachers, no operational schools—it was pretty much about survival.

"You were constantly worried about if you're going to see tomorrow. Your basic necessity was food and continuing to live. My mother is a very strong, very resilient person. She's a lecturer in home economics for one of the universities. She's very religious, a Christian. She was always saying, 'God is going to see us through,' even when we were hearing gunshots left and right and bullets were flying around us. We had no glass windows left from all the shots and ricochets.

"We were living in Freetown, the capital of Sierra Leone. That was the most secure place, with the government offices. But even in Freetown we started seeing firsthand the awful things that we had heard about—the atrocities committed by the rebels. Senseless killing was happening around us. As children, we were all in that state of hyperawareness: Drop and lay on the floor. If you're walking, walk against a building.

"Just seeing how my mother operated—her fearlessness through it all—gave us the courage to hang on. For example, in the middle of all that chaos she would start looking for food and then cook. Everybody's on the floor with their hands over their head, thinking they're going to get hit by a stray bullet the next minute. She fed everybody that was home and all our neighbors that were seeking refuge at our house. We were in the dark, always. The only flashes of light were from gunfire.

"Now I can sit back and look at how my mother was during that time—just appreciate and wonder at that fearlessness. Indirectly, but affecting us deep within, it had so much to say to us about perseverance. Through her, everyone got through that stage. She was the reason others came to our house for refuge: Rosaline Tijani.

"After the rebel situation died down, I was already two or three years behind in school—all of us were. The city, the whole country was still in pain and chaos and essentially nonfunctional. And I was wanting to leave that awful scene. I wanted to know my dad's side of the family, see the place I was born. After the war died down, my mother said, 'Well, I think it's a good time to go to Nigeria. You're not going to school here. We're still just trying to survive here, so I think it would be best.' I was sixteen.

"So in 1999 I went to Nigeria and I got to meet my grandfather and my grandmother, the whole side of the family. My grandfather is sort of a head-man there, not exactly king or chief, but somewhere in between. In Nigeria they make a big deal of this position and the leader's family. So when I arrived, they had this whole ceremony of the prince coming—me. The whole tribal politics—to this day I really don't know how it works and I have very little interest in all of that.

"I ended up staying with my father's eldest sister in southwest Nigeria in Ibadan, the largest city in West Africa. We went to Lagos to see a relative, me and my aunt's daughter. This cousin had become so close, so welcoming to me. She was the one helping me with the language, with everything new and strange to me. On our way back from Lagos to Ibadan, we took public transportation, which was nine of us in a vehicle like a station wagon. I was in the backseat. My cousin was right in front of me.

"We were in the inside lane trying to go past a long diesel truck when it started veering into our lane. Somehow, the driver got off the road onto a grassy area. The exhaust pipe was dragging and fire just ignited right in front of me, behind my cousin's seat, just *whoosh*. Almost like an explosion, and it spread everywhere—and we were going like seventy or eighty miles an hour. The car veered down this deep valley, engulfed in fire. We were all trying to get out. I remember I had hold of the burning seat in front of me. Everyone is in commotion. I remember vividly realizing something—that my father had his accident on that same highway. That hit me and I was like, 'I don't want to die here. My father died here and I want no part of that.'

"I hit the back windshield, which shattered. Once I was out, I saw that my hair and eyebrows were all burnt, my clothes on fire. I started rolling back and forth on the ground. The accident happened about twenty minutes outside town. People were dying left and right on the way back to Lagos. My cousin died three days later. Long story short, of nine people, I am the only one who survived.

"They took us directly to a government hospital, where they don't have much care, no supplies. I was there for three days on just a drip. No antibiotics, just laying there while people were trying to get ahold of my family. They came and took me to a private hospital. About a week after the accident, I nearly died. The whole bed was vibrating, I was trying so hard to breathe. The doctors thought I was going to die, so they stopped what they were doing and covered my head up. And left me for dead. Slowly, I just started breathing again.

"I ended up spending seven months in the hospital. I couldn't walk or use my hands in any real way. My hands were stuck. It came to a point they got so infected I was this close to being amputated, both of them. Of the many times I went in for a surgical procedure, I think I was under anesthesia only once. The doctors would be making faces, they wouldn't even look while they were cleaning my hands. I was sixteen. There is no formula for dealing with that sort of pain. But I can say that the thought that death would be better never came to me. I reasoned that if I could survive the war, this was something I could survive as well. The only thing that was bothering me was not knowing how to deal with my new self. A boy with no workable hands? I lay there, day after day, reconciling my outlook on life. But my hands—so stiff and useless. The doctors told me this was how my hands were going to be; I have to get used to it. Those words kept me persevering too. I knew if I let my hands stay like this, they're going to be useless. There was no such thing as therapy. No exercise. I'd be lying in bed, trying to bend my hands and fingers through the gauze, crying the whole time from the pain of trying.

"I had seen many burn victims in Sierra Leone during the war. I saw that they had little mobility; they were just rigid. So I kept on my own program.

It would be bleeding, I'd be crying, screaming, asking for medication. But I always kept focus on that exercise. So I became my own therapist per se.

"But . . . I started gaining control of my hand. I could hold a spoon. People had been doing everything for me, and I was finding ways to do things by myself again—I was learning to feed myself, scribbling, trying to write again. Slowly the infections started healing and my hands were healing. But what was I going back to? I'm not going to school, because nothing is rebuilt or functional in Sierra Leone. I'm just tired of being here. My mother said, 'You had too much stuff going on with you in Africa. Move to America and start life afresh.'

"So in 2000, September 11, I came. My sister and brothers were in Dallas already. My mother's elder brother is a Lutheran pastor in Dallas, so he got me a student visa and a scholarship to come over and attend Lutheran High School. I graduated with honors, then there was not much I was doing. I had no money for college. My sister had just graduated from college and had a job offer in Boston. So in the summer of 2003 we both came to Boston. She worked as a residential counselor for the mentally disabled.

"The only reasonable outlet I saw for myself was to be in school. How and what I would study I did not know. Or how to pay for it. I felt like if I'm in school, I can't go wrong. School seemed a sort of normalcy I craved for so long. I found out about Year Up through a friend at a place I had been a volunteer mentor, African and American Friendship, Inc. The whole idea of being paid to go to school—it was too good to be true. I was skeptical, thinking this has got to be a joke. Who pays you to go to school? I came in to Year Up and spoke to Linda—and her being the electrifying person that she is, I decided to apply.

"I started in Boston's Class Seven in September of 2005. As soon as classes began, I started seeing where this was going. Everything that they had in place made sense—mentors, guest speakers from the business world and education, exposing us to things about the business world that I had no clue about. I made sure that I excelled in all my classes. I was on time; I followed all the guidelines and procedures. No infractions, no fooling around.

"When I started Year Up, they had Web design and IT—help-desk stuff. It was mainly troubleshooting PCs and networks. Computers and electronics have intrigued me since I was little. I'd take my toys apart. I took my mother's electronics apart. So I already knew a good deal of the technical things. What made the difference was polishing those skills and knowing how they related to business. And I was learning to present myself with professional skills, business communications, working on relationships with machines and with coworkers—the tools you need.

"The most challenging aspect for me was time management. And I'm really grateful for Gerald for emphasizing the importance of it, in the pro skills and in our conversations. The most critical thing Year Up taught me was to realize that in the classroom and the workplace, your sense of time and how you use it is not personal but communal. That was a huge wake-up. And once I understood that, I was always on time. I also benefited from Friday feedback. The feedback sessions were good and unbiased, and they grew as we grew as friends and started making connections.

"I was excited for my internship, which was at BBN Technologies in Cambridge. They actually started the ARPANET—an early military version of the Internet—the first person-to-person e-mail sent over a network and the first use of the 'at' sign in the address. It was a great place to be going, where the Internet was born. Transitioning from class, I was eager to know how things worked at that level—networking, systems, how calls get routed.

"I learned a lot at BBN. Where it was a lot of high-end stuff, like programming, I was more of a shadow at first. Then I'd troubleshoot a printer or some connectivity issue that a client was having. They gave me those little assignments that progressively led me to other fields of understanding the full range of what the company did. I was the second intern from Year Up. After six months I had attained an understanding of technical support, monitoring the usage, making sure everything was up and running to get Jane Doe through her job. It was both remote and deskside service. Swap out a part, run a script. Figure out what's wrong. At the end they were trying to hire me, but there was a hiring freeze."

Here I'm going to interrupt Abdul's narrative for a moment to explain a bit about our postgraduate relationship with students. Among the biggest complaints we still hear about other work-development programs is that there is not enough reliable connectivity to actual jobs, and little or no follow-up. This makes no sense to us. New hires are often most vulnerable to layoffs during market contractions. At Year Up, we're often able to help our students reconnect. In building close relationships with our corporate partners, we hear of other job openings or additional paid internship positions. We know who's hiring and for what, and who might be expanding their operations in a particular field. We hear which companies are moving toward hiring on contract. The position may not be permanent, but it can tide a graduate over until something long term is found.

Employers listen when we recommend a Year Up graduate. In companies that we have strong, long-term relationships with, it's understood that anyone we send to them comes in with proven success on the job and a verifiable set of references. Beyond the internships, companies also look to us as a pipeline to recent graduates who have been in the workplace—and performed well—for some time. When Abdul's internship company could not hire him, he did the wise thing—he stayed in touch with us.

"Kevin Barry [director of corporate partnerships] at Year Up Boston helped me get a contract position at Fidelity Investments. I had gotten to know Gerald and Kevin in the office over lunches—they taught me the value of networking and how to make it work. So I worked at Fidelity for another six months, doing backup of the transactions that they processed.

"I completed that and they tried to hire me too, but there was no room. I started over again—on yet another September 11—this time as a contract IT worker at Stop & Shop, a big supermarket chain. This was also through Year Up. They take a lot of Year Up interns in different locations. I was only supposed to be there for six months. Four months into it, in December, they decided to give me a full-time position. Their headquarters is in Quincy and their data center, where I work, is in Braintree.

"I started doing the help desk and support. We support twelve hundred or so stores, make sure all the computer equipment that runs the stores are up and going—cash registers, price checkers, self-serve checkouts—we monitor it all. I loved it. I had a good job, my girlfriend, great coworkers, an apartment, a car. A good life. I could hardly believe it. Everything was going smoothly.

"Until February of 2007. It was a Friday. I headed to Dorchester to pick up one of my friends. We got to another friend's house. I parked my car and we were walking to the back of the house. My friend got out ahead of me, so he was further down in the driveway. A car came up on the main road. My back was to the street. I was walking to the back of the house. 'Is T there?' That's what it sounded like someone said. Next thing I heard was *bam bam bam bam bam*. I felt like somebody kicked my right leg underneath me, and I fell. I saw flames against the dark and I realized—from back in the war—I was being shot at. I just covered my head—the old instincts just kicked in. *Assume the position.* I think I screamed for them to stop. You could hear the gun had no more bullets, I could hear *click click.* Then a screeching sound—and that was it.

"I tried getting up and I realized I couldn't even stand. I lay there. It was all snow and blood all over the place. I took my phone and threw it at my friend and said, 'Call the police.' I was conscious through the whole ordeal again. As I lay there in the snow, I was thinking: 'I just really need to lay here until the ambulance comes and not be in a state of panic. *I need to stay on top of this.*' When we were in the ambulance, that's when they started discovering how bad it really was. The gun was an automatic. I got shot five times, three times in the right leg, once in my left leg, and one time in the back that pierced my small and large intestines. The bullets in my leg and rib cage were there for a year because it was too critical to touch.

"I woke up Monday morning in another hell. More pain. My sister and brother were there, and I was trying to talk with all these tubes going down my throat. I came to understand that my leg was the critical issue. One of the bullets had severed a nerve. I couldn't feel anything from the knee below. So many things they tried. They took parts from this leg, veins, trying every-thing, and it just wasn't working. The kneecap was pretty much blown off.

"So it came to an amputation. I was twenty-five. I started thinking: 'What's a leg?' My mom had arrived from Africa. I had hold of her hand, my sister's hand as well. I had a prayer. And then I said, 'Okay, let's make it happen.'

"The leg was amputated three inches above my right knee. Oh man, that was another pain I couldn't describe, the nerve. I felt my leg was still there, and it felt like I was walking on hot coals. The doctors were saying, 'That's phantom pain. It's common.'

"They moved me from ICU to the rehab center in Boston Medical. I was still learning to get around and work on the muscles above the amputation. And there was another difference in me no one saw and I didn't speak of much. The bullet really tore up my intestines, so for a year I had to deal with a colostomy bag. That really hit me. The whole irony about moving away from all that madness and craziness back in Africa, to come here and start out fresh. Just to get hit again with all that. Yeah, I'm laughing now. Fate does you like that—you'd better laugh.

"And you'd better stop wondering *why* you survive it all and wonder *how* you will continue to do so. How to prepare for the future and the unknown? Because now I really know there's nowhere to run. I literally can't run—not from the next awful thing. Or the one after that. If there's a problem that comes at me, there's a different way I have to go about it. And I'll figure it out. I'm not the type that gets hung onto a victim identity. You can never victimize me. No way.

"I can say this: You never really know what you can deal with until you are in that situation. That's something that has always kept me going. Every situation I conquer, there's a barrage of other things that it brings into understanding, per se. It gives me a feeling of a concurrent wholeness or something. Because I'm gathering all of these things that I'm experiencing, turning them over, looking at them closely."

This time Abdul had the best of care. I cannot tell you how many students come to us never having had health insurance or the most rudimentary preventive care. Our student-services staffs in all cities are proficient in locating clinics, prenatal facilities for pregnant students, vision testing and correction programs, dental charities. The few students not smiling in a Year Up group photo may simply be embarrassed by their teeth since their families could not afford dentists. Others may have had to forgo other necessary treatments because their parents were unable to cope with Medicaid forms—another thing our staff is able to help them negotiate. Reaching Abdul's level of health services—full coverage through employment—can be a lifesaving advantage for graduates and their families. Since Year Up alums tend to be well liked and respected in their workplaces, they also have the advantage of support and understanding from employers when something bad does happen—as Jesuino Vincente had at John Hancock in the wake of his random shooting.

"All this time in the hospital and in rehab, I was on short-term disability. My employers at Stop & Shop and my coworkers have been really good to me throughout the whole thing. They have gone over and beyond to make sure they take care of their person. And I try to do my part. In the rehab center I was doing exercises and my nurse couldn't keep up with me. I went from the wheelchair to the crutches, and I was going all around the floor of the rehab place. I'm just not a bed person. I'll only be in bed if there's no way out. The whole time, after the shooting, I was on the phone a lot with Gerald and Kevin. When Gerald and his family came to see me in the rehab facility, I showed the children my new leg—I told them I thought it was really cool, how they got the color of the prosthesis to match my skin.

"During the time I was getting fitted with my first prosthesis, I found that my insurance only covered eighty percent. I had to come up with like four thousand dollars. Kevin Barry at Year Up always kept in touch—he's been a great friend all along—and he said, 'I've got some people who are willing to pay for the other portion to get you the leg.' So that happened. In the end, the orthopedics company waived that payment for me, so I returned the money.

"I got out of the hospital in April of 2007, and in June I returned to work. On crutches. I had the reversal of the colostomy a year later. Oh man, that was such freedom. That aspect of things was challenging. You have no control over anything. But you can observe. Observe how your body really works in a way you never would have. That's something that has become a dominant factor in my life—to learn to observe without bias or prejudice.

"I was doing okay with that first leg, though it was difficult to get a sense of control with it, and it was heavy and bulky. And Jason Rizzo,* the prosthesis technician, was not satisfied. He thought we could do better for me. There was a new computerized leg—they called it 'microprocessor controlled.' But it was so new that the insurance company had not even approved it. They didn't understand it and it was too much money, so they wouldn't support it. But Rogerson Orthopedics, the prosthetics company in Boston, kept pushing, and I guess they found a means to support it—maybe because of the overwhelming casualties coming back from the wars in Iraq and Afghanistan. They pushed for me because I'm a young able-bodied person, outgoing and agile. I would use it to its fullest capability.

"This technology was so cutting edge—a leg with microchips and Bluetooth connections—that I ended up flying to Orlando, Florida, with Jason Rizzo when he got his training and certification to work on it. I was sitting there talking to the manufacturers, and they said they needed somebody, a student or whatever, to use this new device. They said, 'Abdul, you're the perfect person to test this out.'

"So they decided that they would make me a candidate for this C-Leg [computerized leg], which cost about forty thousand dollars, and I didn't have to pay a cent. Rogerson, Jason's company, decided I was going to be their guinea pig per se, and they waived what would have been a serious copay on the leg. The people in Orlando were shocked to see the way I walk with the leg—making me what they call an 'accomplished user.' They had never seen somebody adjust so fast with the device.

"Here, check out this leg—amazing, huh? All shiny metal with blue ball joints at the knee and ankle. It has a microprocessor with two sensors, one down here in the ankle and in the knee. They talk to one another about fifty times a second, in real time. They pace my movement; if I'm moving fast, the computer knows it has to catch up with me. If I'm in an unstable position, it will stiffen the joint for me to give me support until I recover my balance.

"It's a pleasure to get around more easily at work. My position is a help desk analyst. We support all the machines over all those stores, close some stores, build new ones. My task there is more of a mediator. If I can't fix a problem, then I have to find a vendor to dispatch to the location to fix it and get that store up and running. Since it's a retail operation, it's very time critical, so we're all there on rotating ten-hour shifts, four days a week each. I love it. *Love* it.

"But yes, I am leaving the job soon—to be able to go to school in Texas, where I'll have my family's support. I'm going to study computer science, take classes at Brookhaven Community College in Dallas County. Classes are relatively inexpensive there. I just sent my transcript and they're evaluating it to see about which Year Up credits transfer. I'll be going full time. Once I'm settled with that, I'll start looking for a job around that. My primary reason for being there is school. That's why I'm leaving a job in this crazy economy. Because I see the value in education.

"I started evaluating my position at work as well. There is no room to grow because the next step requires a certain experience, an advanced degree, more technical classifications. Ten years from now I don't want to be saying, 'I wish I had done this.' So I have to be proactive and do something now while I'm young and have energy—and the zeal. I have no distractions with family, a kid. Now that I have this opportunity, I may as well take it now and run with it—and not look back. I'm taking a leap of faith. After all, you'll learn how to swim while you're in the water, not by sitting down.

"I think a lot about all that has happened. And I decided, I'm just going to start blogging, writing these things down. Not so much because I want people to see what I'm doing, but just for me. Thinking out loud. I also keep working on my strength and agility. Most of the time I'd rather take stairs just 'cause I need to exercise. Otherwise, the right leg is going to get weak. All of the muscles above and around where an injury occurred—thighs, hip, pelvis—need to be worked on constantly. They get tired real quick on you. So in a parking lot, I'd rather park far away as opposed to looking for an easy way out. That's why I never applied for a handicapped parking permit. There's a whole lot of people that need that more than I do."

As you can see, self-pity and resignation have never slowed Abdul's plans for himself. That's pretty much the attitude of Vanessa Nieves, recipient of the Abdul Tijani Award for Courage in 2008. Before applying to Year Up, Vanessa had endured eighteen-hour workdays at an egg factory in Maine, then lived in a homeless shelter with her husband and young son in Boston. But—as Abdul puts it—she persevered. She kept her family cared for and her course work on track. She did her internship at State Street and accepted a position there. She and her family are well housed and secure, and Vanessa is one of our more active and committed alumni volunteers. As I write this, there are hundreds of Year Up students enrolled who demonstrate the right stuff, and the tough circumstances, for a Tijani award. But we have to agree with its namesake: Survival and success are the most meaningful reward.

Abdul is busy with his next goal and relishing the opportunity to work toward a degree in computer science. Year Up is still with him. He went to Texas with transferable college credits earned with us, and he is now enrolled at Brookhaven Community College. He has also been able to capitalize on his technical skills and his solid work experience to find a job with AT&T as an information systems tech. Six years out, Abdul says, "I am still a Year Upper."

He stays in touch, mainly with Kevin Barry, who has been so solidly in his corner. He reports that he is getting around with his computerized prosthesis just fine, despite the occasional glitch he described in a typically wry Abdul e-mail: "My bionic leg has been very good to me. We've developed a very cozy relationship. A couple of weeks ago she was very defiant and rebellious though. It took some serious coaxing to get her to put her coat of manners back on. She was being a bit too sensitive but we made amends and resolved our dispute. So far I have no complaints."

CHAPTER TWELVE
The Soul of a New Machine

IF WE'RE GOING TO CONTINUE TO PUT MORE AMERICANS TO WORK, WE'D better be running a good business ourselves. Without that, no matter how much we care, we won't be able to close the Opportunity Divide. The better we run Year Up from a financial and business perspective, the more we can help our students achieve economic justice. I'm going to talk about business in this chapter, and money—how we raise it, how we invest it, and how we run our organization to keep attracting and earning more money. I believe in using every capitalist tool, from the most basic financing strategy to cloud computing. As you'll see, we created a financial prospectus (similar to a Wall Street IPO document) and provided financial transparency that substantiates our results. We have used these tools to connect with a receptive new breed of donors who see themselves as venture capitalists investing in America's future.

All of it, from our personnel policies to our infrastructure and reporting systems, is based on principles I learned in Harvard Business School, then used to grow a for-profit technology company. I drew on both of those experiences to write a hybrid business plan for my new nonprofit. I'm honored that Year Up is now being taught as a capstone case study in the social entrepreneurship course at Harvard Business School. I'm more than happy to answer the persistent question from donors and other stakeholders: *How do you make Year Up work?* I'd like to lift the hood and show you how it runs. I think we've gotten rid of the chewing gum and Band-Aids that held Year Up together during the start-up years. Our streamlined model began to take shape in 2004–2005.

First I need to acquaint you with the brain trust that makes it all happen. Beginning in 2004, as we sought to expand our services, I was also conscious of our growing need for human capital. If we wanted to expand the mission itself, to get more systematic about activating the grander plan that had begun to assert itself way back in the Rutgers Houses, we needed a bigger, stronger, deeper team. We would have to grow beyond our merry band— Linda, Richard, Casey, Sue, et al.—in order to build out more sites and spin off a national leadership team that could oversee it all.

I wanted the best. Yep, *the right people in the right chairs.* I know my strengths; I'm a very keen talent spotter. When hiring, character matters to me more than hard skills. I look for someone who understands and cares deeply about our mission—then I evaluate how much they know. A case in point: Meet California-born Tynesia Boyea, a highly skilled engineer with a challenging start in life.

"My parents had me really young," she says. "They were sixteen and seventeen. They never got married, split up, and my mother was in a series of abusive relationships afterwards. She was one of those people—I can look back and see it with my grandmother as well—who seem to have certain patterns and trajectories preordained. Where you're born predicates where you're going to be.

"For my mother, there was never a stable home. There was violence in the home. The way she took care of herself was to hop from man to man. The one she finally married beat her up—and beat me up. I was abused. Every single stereotype you can think of in terms of a broken home—we were right there.

"When I was eight, I moved in with my dad. It was a more stable environment because he was in the military. His side of the family was very supportive, but he was stationed in a lot of different places. He got married and had kids and they weren't great with their money. It's a different type of Opportunity Divide than my mom's. It wasn't the violence, but our life together had big limitations, the stuff that happens when people have kids young.

"I was doing well in school, but my parents didn't have money to send me to a four-year college. It was just assumed that I'd go to community college and stay close to help around the house. My stepmom did nails. A woman came in for a manicure one day. Her name was Deborah. I was fourteen then. And she said to me, 'What are your grades like? Where are you going to college?'

"I said it would be someplace where I can work, someplace my family can afford. And she said, 'Oh no, girlfriend. You're going to the best schools because you have the stuff to back it up.' For whatever reason, it became her personal mission that I would go to a really good school. She took me to visit schools, to social gatherings, she was teaching me how to dress professionally, how to interact in different social circles. She was the turning point in my life.

"She worked for a defense contractor and had some familiarity with the tech fields. So it was because of her I went to Duke University, where I double majored in computer science and electrical engineering. I got a job at General Electric and I was doing great. But I decided I wanted to go to business school and explore more options."

Though her story sounds like ones we'd heard often in our program, Tynesia wasn't one of our students. When I met her in the spring of 2004, she was twenty-six and completing her first year at Harvard Business School. We had interviewed about forty applicants selected for us by New Sector Alliance, a nonprofit that connects undergraduates, recent graduates, and MBA candidates with paid fellowships. We hadn't found anyone that suited; plenty were willing, but none had the number-crunching, quantitative skills we needed at the time. Ty's application came in after we had resigned ourselves to not filling the spot. I figured that looking at one more wouldn't hurt.

Looking at her professional qualifications and hearing her story, I invited her to tour our facility straightaway. This was a young woman who manifestly proved out our bedrock belief that no matter how difficult their upbringings, our students have as much talent as anyone, given the opportunity to develop it. I wasn't sure what Tynesia could do for us. I just knew I had to get her to come downtown and our students would do the rest. Year Up is just five stops on the Red Line from Harvard Square.

"I rode into Year Up," Ty recalls, "and just fell in love with it. I said, 'Oh my God, that's my sister, that's my brother. That's my uncle.' I know my family—it wasn't as though they were dumb people or bad people. They just had a different set of opportunities and role models."

Looking back on her mentorship with Deborah, that supportive manicure client, Ty says, "That was *my* year up." She understood what we do right away. In short order, she had a desk at Ninety-three Summer Street, where we had just admitted another new class. "I worked there for three months in the summer of 2004, and in that time I saw our young people go from speaking in a way that would not be helpful *at all* to getting the jobs that students at Harvard were fighting for. I'm an engineer and I knew what to do with the Year Up raw data I'd been given. Just run the numbers and it's evident— something is working here."

There was one aspect of our students' success that Ty couldn't find an algorithm for. "Mind-set. There's a certain freedom inherent in having nothing to lose. I think that's the nuance that I bring to the program from my background. Adversity ends up being the very strength that drives you. Once you learn the rules of the game, the worst that can happen is you lose a job. By the time our young people have gotten into these jobs, they've gone through a lot worse."

We kept Tynesia very busy, researching issues that were critical to our future. "I had several projects," she says. "One was to develop a dashboard for critical data that could be accessed at a glance by people throughout the organization. I took a lot of that from the analytical work that I had done at GE. Another project was to look at whether or not we should get out of Web design as a curriculum track. The softening local market for those skills showed that we should phase it out, and after that we focused strictly on IT."

Already she had helped us with infrastructure and curriculum. There was a third and very important assignment. We knew we wanted to add at least two new sites in major cities to the two we already had. Our original start-up in Boston was growing quickly, and we had proved that our first replication could be successful in Providence. We decided that for the staff's logistical ease, the next new site should be no more than an hour's plane trip from Boston. We looked at Washington, New York, and Philadelphia and decided that the first two were our best options.

Summer had ended and Tynesia went back to business school, but I knew we couldn't let her go. When you see talent like hers you have to grab it, by any means necessary. We needed help with feasibility studies of both potential sites to see if they would work for us in terms of student population, a viable donor base, public transportation, and potential internships. I knew that Ty's analytical mind could crunch the raw data we had gathered in a heartbeat. Would she? Could she take on the work and her studies? Ty's response was typically resourceful. "The board asked me to continue to prove out and refine the research during my second year in business school. I finagled some stuff with professors so I was getting credit for doing analysis."

I watched her professional, incisive presentations, and I saw the compassion and engagement she had with our students. "She's outstanding," I thought to myself. We had to have her to help us go forward. So we kept tossing more challenges her way.

"I worked straight through my whole second year at Harvard. I'd completed the feasibility studies for the New York market and the D.C. market. Assignment complete. I thought, 'Okay, now I'll go back to GE.' And the Year Up board said, 'Why don't you launch and run D.C.?' "

Like Sara Strammiello in Providence, Tynesia was pretty young at twenty-seven for the job of executive director but so very energetic and capable that our decision to offer her the ED job was unanimous. As with Sara, I was shameless in luring Ty away from class for Year Up business. After all, we were on a mission, and in my mind she was already a key piece of the team. "My last semester at HBS," she says, "I started laying the groundwork for launching the site. I was flying into D.C. with Gerald, meeting with foundation people, companies. In June of 2005 I graduated and was officially executive director. And our class was to start in March of 2006."

Tynesia is the first to admit that the nation's capital presented us with a daunting learning curve. D.C. is a sprawling, wholly unique, and complex city, deeply poor and urban in some sections, comfortably suburban in others—with a considerable international community as well. Yet for all its diversity, a clubby, inside-the-Beltway insularity could intimidate newcomers like us. Even the new site's title was an issue, since our intake area would reach as far as the notoriously mean streets of East Baltimore. To include and invite potential students in all areas, we decided to call it Year Up National Capital Region. It's a necessary mouthful, hereinafter referred to as NCR. We located as accessibly as we could in an Arlington office building two blocks from the busy Rosslyn Metro station.

"I think if Year Up had to do it over again, they probably wouldn't have picked my site to go first," Tynesia said four years into it. "It's probably still one of the most complex markets that we have—the District, the commonwealth of Virginia, Maryland. The students come from all over; everything is always three times harder. Then throw in the federal stuff on top of it, and you've got a bit of a mess. We were fortunate that I didn't know any better. I just knew the students are great, the model worked in Boston and Providence—and why wouldn't it work someplace else? Even now, people are like, 'You did *what?*' "

It helped that we had a mighty champion in D.C.—the same man who had made those vital internship connections for us with Fidelity and State Street in Boston. Who was that strong persuader in the conservative gray suit?

"Joe Smialowski." Tynesia generally smiles when invoking his name. "He happened to be moving to D.C. at the same time I was. He was taking over as CIO at Freddie Mac, so that was our first internship partner. Back then, Freddie Mac was the largest philanthropic contributor in the area. So Joe hosted this lunch for us and invited all these influential people. He told them, 'Year Up is coming, and if you accept this invitation, Ty gets to reach out to you.' So I met with hundreds of people that first year, just bouncing around. After time, the network started closing on itself."

Serious, self-contained, and constant, Joe seemed to pop up everywhere we needed a boost in the business community. I was introduced to him in Boston by our board member Gail Snowden. At the time, Joe was vice chairman and head of technology and operations for one of the most powerful institutions I could dream of in terms of a corporate partner: Bank of America. In short order, Joe made it happen: Bank of America agreed to pilot our internship program, and soon after, Joe joined our board.

From 2004 on, thanks to Joe's endorsement and our students' great work, Bank of America would widen its embrace to include internships in Atlanta, San Francisco, and New York. The bank's foundation has awarded us several significant grants to help expand to those cities and enable more students to get on a path toward economic stability. Bank of America's commitment continues to grow, from the many "foot soldiers" such a huge organization has sent our way as volunteers to the presence of Kerry Sullivan, president of Bank of America Charitable Foundation, who lends her expertise by serving on our national board.

Think about it: One man with a dazzling career in the nation's top financial institutions saw the justice and the good business in our program. Along his own professional path he has connected us to a level of funding and internship support that has effectively fired a set of booster rockets for Year Up. Try to pat him on the back for it and Joe will be out the door in a hurry, plotting the next step. He has thought of us with each high-profile career move. When he was at Freddie Mac, he served as the first chair of our NCR board. He then relocated for another top-level corporate position at Citi in New York and is now a trustee emeritus of Year Up.

While he was in Washington, Joe's networking kept Tynesia and her internship team hopping. All that "bouncing" on corporate calls had yielded a roster of internship partners that drew from the tech industry, government, finance, hospitality, media, and more. They would come to include AOL, the

Washington Post, the Carlyle Group, Perot Systems, GMAC, Johns Hopkins University, Lockheed Martin, Marriott, PricewaterhouseCoopers, the U.S. Department of Agriculture, and the Brookings Institution.

Of course, we got a leg up from Joe, but our young ED was dauntless in suiting up for hundreds of meetings with educators, officials, and corporate executives, calling it a victory when she got her foot in the door enough to secure just one internship. Her pitches wouldn't have been nearly as convincing if she hadn't believed in the talent she was selling. "It was the strength of the students that kept us in business," she insists. "They did a great job in their internships."

The proof is in the quality and depth of the relationships Ty and her team have built in the corporate and civic communities. Never mind the capital city's reputation for dismal schools, partisan bickering, and bureaucratic inefficiencies. I could swear I heard America singing—humming at least—when Ty and I paid all those calls explaining how we'd put the metro area's most disconnected young people to work. Seeing the creative ways that D.C. has risen to meet the challenge would touch the callused heart of any cynical Beltway pundit.

Some give money; others share their time and knowledge. A key factor that helps Year Up "imbed" in companies and urban communities is that there are so many levels of engagement possible. What has evolved in the NCR site is a good example. In October 2009, Venture Philanthropy Partners would announce a vital partnership with our NCR site, committing up to $4.5 million in funding and strategic assistance. On a more personal level, undergraduate students at Georgetown University's McDonough School of Business coached our students who were involved in a business plan competition hosted by the school. The volunteers included about thirty students from the Georgetown Aspiring Minority Business Leaders Entrepreneurs (GAMBLE) student club.

On all levels of engagement, it's a pretty lively dialogue. Dropping into the NCR facility one afternoon, I followed the sound of laughter and loud applause to a packed classroom. Students were hanging on every word from a panel of three high-level technology professionals who had volunteered their expertise. The topic was "Higher Education and Certifications in the IT World." The subtext: how to leverage what you've learned at Year Up to plot a career trajectory light-years past entry level. The message: no limits.

The lead-off speaker was a national expert in secure network solutions who had worked for the government. In addition to starting his own company, he has been a consultant to a number of federal agencies. He is an impressive African American role model for our students, a witty and dynamic speaker who can keep you on the edge of your seat talking about "the thrill of technology." That day he told his audience up front, "Half of you don't know how brilliant you are."

He advised investing time and money in pursuing advanced technology certifications beyond Year Up, such as a Microsoft Certified Systems Engineer: "In today's market, certs are the yardstick."

Some certifications are worth more on the open job market than others. He pointed out that his nephew was currently "earning $300K," having pursued a sought-after certification. There were audible gasps as this tech superstar drove home his point: "Research the cert!"

Notebooks flew open as he moved on to his next topic: "How to make sure your résumé doesn't get put in the junk pile."

One savvy tip for today's tough job market where employers scroll through huge data drifts of résumés: "Identify and use key words that will pop up in a search. If you don't have them, *it doesn't get read*." Students all but mobbed the panelists afterward, hungry for more.

The following day there were more enriching extras, thanks to an internship partner that has engaged Year Up on several levels. I climbed into Ty's SUV with a few other staff members and we followed two busloads of students—the entire class—out to AOL's sprawling campus near Dulles Airport. They were being hosted in the company's well-appointed meeting spaces for what was billed as an "individual entrepreneurship retreat."

Many businesses host informational days and tours for Year Up students to help them experience a live, functional workplace while they're still in the L & D phase. It's a great motivational tool for an aspiring job seeker and a terrific bridge for the many students who have never set foot in an office building. The day at AOL was meant to be a more personal retreat—a well-deserved "me" day for this hardworking group of students to explore their own motivations and aspirations. So many of them had been too short on expectations or too preoccupied with mere survival to really think about some pretty basic questions. As it was, Ty and another staffer would be driving several students back into town before the day was over, since they had to get to outside jobs every weekday after Year Up classes.

The program's facilitator set an introspective agenda shortly after we took seats in a large, comfortable auditorium.

Who are you?

Where are you going?

How are you going to get there?

As they broke into smaller discussion groups, I set off to visit Year Up interns and graduates on the job in the company of Todd Alston, a senior technical director who was a huge champion of our program. Todd, who has since left the company, was active in one of AOL's "business resource groups" (BRGs), the Black Employees' Group. He helped round up mentors and volunteers to work with Year Up interns from other BRGs, also known within some large corporations as "affinity groups." They included Amigos at AOL (Hispanic), the Women's Network, Out at AOL (gay and lesbian), Desi (employees from India), and AIG (the Asian Interest Group). It's such a reassuring and helpful coalition; within this big company our supporters are as diverse as our students.

I'll confess that I was excited when Todd led us through locked passages and into the NOC, or network operations center—the high-security command center for AOL's huge operation. And there, scanning two monitors, was a Year Up intern. After our introductions, Todd spoke gently but firmly to her.

"I see you haven't responded yet to a text from your supervisor. Don't you think it would be a good idea to take care of that right now?"

As she complied, we wound through warrens of cubicles and met a few tech teams that included Year Up interns and graduates who had become permanent employees. One young Latina woman was introduced as "our rock star." She had been on the job for almost a year, hired directly after her internship. She had tacked a sign up in her cubicle that read, M.I.T. OR BUST! She said that her team—four male employees sporting the exuberant "business casual" favored by young techies—made up the best advisory and cheering section she could wish for as she planned her application to that tech citadel in Cambridge.

"We don't want her to leave," one coworker explained. "But we all think she should go for it."

Not at her desk that day, and something of a local legend, was Canvas Richardson, a Year Up graduate who had been hired at AOL despite a stringent hiring freeze. "When they're that good," Todd explained, "you'd be crazy to let them get away." Canvas had no doubt heeded that pro-skills drumbeat: Make yourself indispensable.

Back in the auditorium, everyone was tucking into box lunches. They looked happy, energetic, and relaxed. The students leaving for their afternoon and evening jobs wedged themselves into Ty's car for the ride back to Arlington. Traffic was building, so we had a good, long talk. One young man made my day. "I feel like I'm cared for, you know? I've been on my own since the middle of high school, and I'm not really used to that. But it feels pretty good." That afternoon I left for the airport with more confidence than ever in Ty's carefully chosen local team. They've done an amazing job of navigating the crazy quilt of populations and work sectors in D.C. I also reaffirmed a longtime manager's assertion: One great hire does beget others.

Next up, Wall Street. We found affordable space for our Manhattan offices in a building housing several nonprofits, just steps away from the New York Stock Exchange. Every time we plan a new facility we get a little bit smarter. Now we sell the internships before we set up shop in a new city. We raise a lot more money before we open the doors and we do much more analysis. We make sure people want us. The process is now more consistent and documented. A lot of the work is already done before the ED starts. And we're even more careful— perhaps agonizingly so—about the person we choose for that position.

We had to get it absolutely right in New York City. That's a pretty public stage if you're going to fall on your face. The city had no shortage of managerial talent at hand to get the site up and running. But I wanted the perfect person. Tim Dibble and I had interviewed a lot of well-qualified candidates in our search for an executive director. As always, I could count on Tim to see people clearly. I've come to rely on his skill as an interviewer. Sometimes it was tough to listen to him dissect someone I thought might be able to do the job. He always seemed to find a weakness: "He hasn't proven he can raise money" or "She has never sold into a corporate channel" or "He has no profit-and-loss experience."

After months of searching, time was ticking away and I was getting anxious. One of my finalists had just walked away from our last meeting at a Starbucks—he was barely out the door—when Tim began a withering takedown of his qualifications. I knew Tim's people instincts were excellent, but after so much work on that hire, it was hard to hear—again. A couple of sentences in, I stopped him.

"Look Tim, I understand. We need to find an experienced, well-respected, well-connected professional—preferably of color—who has the right skills and is passionate about our mission."

We'd been holding out for the perfect fit. But was that realistic?

The very next day, our energetic headhunter, Kathleen Yazbak, led us to a woman named Lisette Nieves, then in her midthirties and well into an impressive career in public service. She had leaped the Opportunity Divide from central Brooklyn to Oxford University, where she was the first-ever Puerto Riqueña and Brooklyn College student to be chosen as a Rhodes Scholar. After graduation she became part of the start-up team for AmeriCorps in Washington, D.C. Lisette was very connected in city government and activist communities, knew the politics, and had deep experience working with urban young adults. When we approached her, she had just completed a stint as chief of staff at the New York City Department of Youth and Community Development.

Bingo! Maybe.

"I spoke with Gerald for two hours," Lisette says of our first meeting. "And all of his concern centered around 'Did I care about young people?' I found that fascinating. That's so *not* an issue for me—it's a given. But I realized he's really coming at it from a soulful place. It was the part of any applicant he cared about most. That's what made it really special, like, 'This is going to be unstoppable.'"

At this point we were way past making intuitive "gut" hires like Richard and Casey. There was now a set of established criteria for the job, and the hire would be subject to board approval. Tim smiled as I made the case for Lisette before the board. He and I knew that this Puerto Rican woman raised in the Bronx had an agenda as uncompromising and impeccable as her credentials. Everything in her résumé had a consistent subtext: social justice.

Once we cleared board approval, it was immediately clear that our collaboration wasn't going to be all "kumbaya." When I told Lisette that if she took the job she would first come and observe in Boston for a few months, her reaction was swift and blunt.

"No I'm *not*. Are you crazy? Just give me the check; we're going to start it."

She was impatient to get moving. With her experience in youth services, she was well aware of the city's urgent and growing need for our program. She also had keen radar for nonprofits that are more about rhetoric than real, measurable change. "I used to fund workforce programs. Many were able to account for how much they were spending, but not necessarily the longevity of their graduates' success. The accountability was spotty at best," Lisette says. "With Year Up, I saw this incredible business model that could be linked to the heart and soul of our work. In a sustainable way that can be grown. This operation was totally transparent, with their books wide open."

Lisette made it clear that she respected our methods. But on her turf, she wanted to do things her way based on her experience and what she believed worked within a strong youth development framework. She was direct about what she felt my role should be in her start-up: "I need you to open doors for me to your professional network. My network of Latinos rarely has the wealth that yours has—and we need a *lot* of money."

Her frankness was leavened with humor, and I was glad for it. Race had rarely been spoken of so openly and plainly in our program. It should have been. After all, I was the white guy at the helm of an organization serving mainly students of color. And our board and leadership team weren't anywhere near as diverse as our student body. Simply knowing that more racial issues should be discussed openly is very different from knowing how to do it in a respectful and productive way. Lisette set down her own guidelines in one of our earliest conversations.

"I told him, 'Gerald, we're always going to have an honest relationship. You come clean about what you need from me in a meeting with donors or corporate partners, and I'll come clean about what I need from you. If I need you to sit and smile in a meeting with donors or corporate partners to telegraph your confidence in me, you smile. If I need you to back me up, you talk. These are the rules; no big deal, right? There will be times when you need me to speak up because I give you credibility. I show that you have buy-in from the Latino community. My academic pedigree can put cautious donors and corporate partners at ease. I'm happy to do that. We're here for the same goal.'"

I couldn't take offense since Lisette was absolutely right. Sometimes I did need to be the white guy smiling. But I'm not going to lie—there were some moments of serious discomfort.

"I think that first year I was probably viewed as challenging and badass and didn't want to go by the rules," Lisette says. "And I didn't, because those rules weren't grounded in the principles that I held around youth development. You hired me; I can get to that goal; I don't have to use your process to get there; I have my own. I remember saying, 'This is the place I'm supposed to be because I *don't* want a scripted job.' I didn't realize how much I tested Gerald on this. But he let me do it."

As we took those many meetings together around the city, I began to see things a bit differently. It wasn't always a pretty sight. As a woman of color, Lisette heard racist and sexist innuendo in ways that I could not. One afternoon in New York, after she had been the model of diplomacy during a meeting with a donor we very much needed, Lisette shocked me by saying, matter-of-factly, "That went just fine. But you do know the man is completely inappropriate and has major issues with women?" Seeing me go ashen, she rewound a few of his remarks for me, including some gratuitous references to Latina women. And subsequent encounters proved that she was right about him.

This white guy from Lowell was reminded, once again, that I still had a lot of work and soul-searching to do in order to develop a bigger ear for the slights and hidden agendas of entrenched racism.

From the outset, she reminded me that her greatest work satisfaction in any job rested on a single core ethic: "It's living my values. In terms of self-knowledge, you have to be resilient in all these worlds outside the one I grew up in—the world many of our students grew up in. Every day with them reminds me: 'You could be taken back there at the drop of a hat.' You can sit there with a young person and they're living parts of your story you haven't even told yet. With some things, you're still not able to go that deep. But you remember. You squirm."

Lisette would put her bold, indelible stamp on Year Up New York and on the hearts and minds of our students. But before she would welcome any of them across the threshold, she wanted to add an application requirement that had not been mandatory in our process: "Drug testing. I insist."

I was startled and concerned, but I listened carefully to her argument. She said if we were to be in business in New York City, we had to do this because the top-tier corporations would test as a matter of course before taking on interns. At that time it wasn't the case so much in Boston and Providence, and therefore we did not drug test our students. However, employee drug testing was becoming more commonplace, and we realized that it was actually in our students' interest to do it from the start. How devastating would it be to work hard for six months in the L & D phase and have it all negated if you failed a standard drug test on your first day of work?

New York started the testing process off, and we had a significant and spirited discussion across the whole company about how to handle the matter companywide. Some argued privacy and civil-liberties issues. Ultimately, we decided that testing was the right thing for our students in all locations to better safeguard what they were working so hard for. The question was how to do it, exactly what to screen for, and what consequences a failed test would result in.

Let's face it: If an applicant tests positive for cocaine or heroin, he or she probably doesn't need Year Up, or at least not yet. He or she needs counseling. We don't have much tolerance for hard drugs—and besides, our students are poor. They don't tend to buy cocaine. If they test positive for marijuana, we say, "Okay, do you want to stop for the duration of this program and when you're at your job? Because it will prevent you from being successful." If the answer is yes, we don't judge or scold the student or turn him or her away. We say, "Please stop using. We'll test you again in six weeks. But understand you won't be successful in the program if you don't stop."

The logic is simple. We explain it in an honest, open conversation with an applicant: If you can't or don't want to stop, either you don't really want to do this program or you need drug counseling. We're not condemning you for using marijuana. It's for you to decide. To me that's an empowering approach to the challenge: Put it in the student's hands.

Now across all locations, the issue is first broached in a standard question during an application interview: *Could you pass a drug test today?* Regardless of their answer, they're apprised of the rules: If you test positive the first time, we test you again, and if you fail the second, you've fired yourself.

After months of more work and constant shuttle diplomacy from Boston to Manhattan's corporate towers, I was thrilled to take my place on the steps of Federal Hall on Wall Street for a group photo of our first New York class in September 2006. Within the five years she promised us, Lisette would more than fulfill her mandate, taking an operation that began with a $500,000 seed grant to a $6 million-per-year, dual-facility site with a deep and loyal bench of corporate partners.

As Year Up New York was just hitting its stride, a young man living with his parents and six siblings in David Heredia's old apartment complex, the Rutgers Houses, found himself in the minimum-wage doldrums. Roland Cody, a policeman's son, had been marooned there since his 2006 graduation from Boys and Girls High School in Brooklyn. The school's motto is "Failure is not an option." Roland was beginning to take issue with that.

"I tried college—City Tech—right after high school because my parents insisted, but I lasted just two weeks. I had been working at Starbucks but left. It was the wrong situation for me. Barista. Cashier. You see there's nowhere to go with that. Time started dragging along. I had to do something, so I started working at Pathmark, a supermarket in my neighborhood. My aunt, who works for a social-services organization, gets e-mails from different youth-oriented programs. She told me about Year Up. I wasn't super interested at first, but when I heard one track was investment operations—hey, that had something to do with money. Real money."

Roland gave up on our application process twice, finding it too demanding for "just another program." Then he finally decided to sit down and write the required essay simply because he had nothing else to do. To his surprise, he was accepted. He says he liked Year Up more than he had imagined, but its rigors made him think about quitting a few times during L & D. "I stuck with it because I felt a lot of people had a lot invested in me and I didn't want to let them down. And I sure didn't want to be back as I was after Starbucks."

After Roland finished his class work in investment operations, he was assigned an internship at JPMorgan Chase. He says now, "I have no idea *where* I'd be if that hadn't happened."

Within a few years, JPMC would widen its commitment further than any of us dared hope. The bank now takes our interns in six cities and has made outstanding Year Up students eligible to apply for its scholarships to Syracuse University, where the bank maintains a technical facility and employs students as interns.

JPMC also works closely with us on developing new curriculum tracks. Our job is to listen to our intern partners and to understand where we can help them. Roland's supervisor, Steve Weinstein, played a lead role in implementing the QA track that would be operational for Class Nine. Testing newly installed software was becoming a serious growth area in his department and throughout the industry. Steve recalls, "I told Year Up, 'I'll offer up my team to work with you guys to create a curriculum.' I had some meetings there; I had Bill Lehman over; we walked the floor and I showed him my tools and techniques and flows. I said, 'You've got to get a trainer. I'll give you a brain dump.' And they put together a curriculum. Our first experience with those interns was terrific. We had them testing at least two weeks sooner than anyone else we hire."

This is how it's supposed to work, anticipating needs in a changing job market and being flexible enough to train for them. JPMC is also working with us on a pilot program for banking's evolving retail sector. We have never considered placing our students in lower-wage, high-turnover teller positions where they would be likely to hit glass ceilings. But as banks expand and refine their retail force to include credit cards, fraud detection, customer service, and financial operations, there may be new positions more suited to our students' skill levels. In several meetings to explore these possibilities, JPMC managing director John Galante, who oversees technology for Chase Wealth Management division, made it clear that he sees retail financial as "a huge opportunity" for our graduates. And when John talks, a keen entrepreneur listens.

If anyone can be considered our godfather at JPMC, it's John, who has never forgotten the leg up that began his career path. He was a young aspiring teacher on Long Island with a wife and baby. While finishing school and student teaching, he made ends meet as a sanitation worker and with a second job with his father's flooring company. Installing carpet and tile at the home of an executive at Salomon Brothers, he got to know the home owner, who told him, "You're a hardworking guy; you've got a family. There's a lot about teaching you could apply to Wall Street." He encouraged John to apply at Salomon and helped him begin a career there. By the time he reached JPMC, John had become a volunteer sports coach and mentor in his community and was very active in his company's philanthropic programs.

John's introduction to Year Up was made over a business lunch by our busy matchmaker, Joe Smialowski. As John recalls, "Joe said they were opening a Manhattan office. Would I be interested in hearing more? One thing led to the other and I fell in love with the whole concept. The first year I think we took two or three interns and had a great experience. Since then we've expanded. We're up close to ninety interns. We have some interns in Boston. We sponsored the opening of the Chicago Year Up. We're also participating in their Seattle office. Sponsoring an opening means seeding—taking some interns, helping them with contacts, and doing everything we can to help them get started."

As a managing director of JPMC, John has plenty on his plate. But he always makes time to get to know interns in each class. Roland Cody reached out to John after weeks of hearing his name invoked. As in "I've got to get this Galante report ready" and "Has that testing plan passed Galante?"

Pro skills had given Roland an ear for what we call "corporate anthropology"—just who the players are in a company and how its hierarchy is structured. It had also taught him the value of networking. When John showed up in Roland's department one day, our intern introduced himself with a funny reference to the "Galante factor" he'd heard so much about. They stayed in touch.

Roland is a positive, personable young man whom anyone would want to know better. John also learned from his manager, Steve Weinstein, that Roland had distinguished himself on the job. "I was new to managing the interns," Steve recalls. "We had no playbook yet. So Roland found himself a natural place to fill. We said, 'Roland, could you load these documents into our repository?' He got a book on understanding what the repository was. He took it upon himself, he educated himself, and we realized we can give him more."

Roland did exactly as he had been coached, leveraging his existing skills with research and networking. The motivational issues that had becalmed him after high school would have surprised anyone at the bank. After three months, Roland was handling a newly arisen duty that otherwise might have cost the company dearly in search, hiring, and extra fees to an outside contractor. Steve explains, "Roland had an aptitude for this product the bank uses called SharePoint, which is a document management tool built by Microsoft. All our documents are stored on SharePoint. This program was just starting up, and we needed someone to go deep into it. Roland somehow gravitated and said, 'I can be the administrator of that; I can load all these documents.'"

And why not? Roland had already aced every task he had been assigned. He had worked closely with the man who had been in charge of the SharePoint introduction, and that employee had just left. Steve and John readily agreed to let Roland try. "So he became what's called the SharePoint administrator," Steve says. "He just moved to that and had the aptitude to manage it." As his internship came to a close, Roland was asked to please—*please*— stay on. It was a far more celebratory moment than the day he hung up his barista apron.

"They brought me on as a consultant for six months, then as a full-time employee. I sat down with John and Steve one day and they asked me what else I wanted to do with the company. I brought up Syracuse. I had worked with the interns from their tech program there. Working and studying—and getting subsidized—seemed to work well for them."

Steve's response was "Anything's possible." They looked into it. The bank's partial tuition for interns might be available, but despite his technical brilliance, Roland's grades weren't good enough for admission to Syracuse. When it looked like they were close to a solution and Roland might indeed be headed for the university after all, Steve was surprised at his initial reaction. "Roland was very apprehensive. He wasn't prepared for that life. He had all these ties to a band; he's a gospel singer. He couldn't cut the ties. I said, 'Dude, it's like winning a quarter-million-dollar lottery. You have to give it a try.'"

Roland agreed to some conditional terms set by the university and JPMC. "They needed a way to measure me. So they put me in classes for the summer and fall and said if I maintained a 3.0 average they'd bring me on as a full-time student. During that time, the company paid for everything. I kept my GPA up and I was able to get in."

Many weekends now find Roland on a Greyhound bus from Syracuse to Manhattan. His gospel/rap group has a record deal. There are studio sessions, some videos to shoot, marketing meetings. He works for JPMC at Syracuse and in the New York area during the summer. Seven Syracuse interns now manage the SharePoint duties he used to handle alone. Roland taught them. The man who almost passed on Year Up because of the application essay sounds excited about his next semester of course work. "Philosophy. Counseling. *Writing.*"

Roland chose them from a category he has come to savor: electives. That's exactly what we value in the evolving relationship between Year Up and JPMC—choices. We want our students to have even more curriculum options and more points of entry in an increasingly tight and changeable job market. We need to stay agile and connected. And we need a lot more students like Roland to keep those employers wanting more.

It was in New York one day—when everything seemed to be working perfectly, more internship partners were signing on, and I was as optimistic as I've ever been—that I gamely stepped up for another interactive exercise during a staff retreat.

"It was similar to Milestones, what's called a purpose statement, just with staff," Lisette recalls. "You had two minutes to talk about 'What is your purpose in life?' No one can interrupt you, and you have to dig deep. You can't imagine the things that you hear. It's always very emotional. And after the first ten seconds, Gerald just broke down and cried. He pulled out this poem that he carries in his wallet from his mother, along with her picture. And he started reading it. He made a very strong stand in terms of what his mom had been in his life, and about David. It was really powerful. There wasn't a dry eye in the house. Now everyone at my site thinks Gerald cries all the time." Here Lisette laughed. "But no, he doesn't. Not at all."

I was surprised and puzzled at my reaction that day, and it hasn't ever happened again. I didn't spend too much time trying to analyze it. I explain myself constantly to corporations and donors, but it's rarely in such personal terms, and in the presence of close peers. It could have been the stress of being asked for an instant answer to that very old question again: *Why is he doing this?* Maybe it was that ride in from the airport past David's apartment building fifteen minutes earlier. Maybe I was just missing my mom. Maybe I was feeling the strain of the big organizational changes we were trying to manage. As we approached serving three thousand students at that point, I might have been feeling the weight of the millions still without opportunities. That occasional lurch of the heart and mind happens—and not just to me.

What about my strong, Brooklyn-born ED? I'm here to tell you that when Malik stood up and spoke of his murdered brother, when Cassandra talked about sleeping on a frigid playground slide, and Taleisha wept for her lost brothers, Lisette, bumming tissues from Charmaine, was a magnificent mess. It happens every time. She also tears up when she speaks of her father, who died a few years back. He was a good man who wrote to local elected officials to find his children when they were in foster care. Despite his family's difficult beginnings, he and his two daughters grew into a close and loving relationship. "Life is so full and wonderful for me now," Lisette explains. "And that's precisely *because* I can never, will never forget."

You've probably noticed by now that we've been fortunate to have very extraordinary people work with us, from our EDs to the fresh-faced volunteers from Vista and AmeriCorps who come and go with the tides of fellowship grants. It stands to reason that we need to take very, very good care of them. When Sue Meehan took over daily operations, she found that our respect for staff was already hardwired. "The financial commitment for professional-development dollars was built right into the budget," Sue says. "Each staff person knows there is money—two thousand dollars—for you to invest in yourself. Instructors use it to go to conferences or to take a course in IT. Some people use it for professional coaching, some to help with their education. They take courses that relate to Year Up or courses helping them toward an education degree. People have taken Spanish classes, things that develop them professionally and tie them more to our students."

We are liberal with benefits for full-time employees, offering full health and dental coverage, including everything from prescription drugs and vision care to long- and short-term disability. Our benefits package is well above the average in the for-profit sector. People ask me, "How can you do that, given what it costs these days?" And I ask, how can we not? Our staff is doing an important and vital job serving young people, and we should treat them well. That's respectful. Our ethic of "high expectations and high support" applies to everyone. The way we treat students and staff is the same, and as long as we follow that guideline, we won't screw up.

Thanks in part to these policies—and despite the rigors of the work—Year Up has an employee attrition rate that is well below the industry norm for youth-serving organizations. And we were recently recognized by the *NonProfit Times,* which ranked Year Up fourth on its 2011 list of the fifty best nonprofits to work for. We're proud of that peer recognition because it derived from an anonymous survey of our staff members. You can't game that kind of response—but you can certainly appreciate it.

We also commit a good deal of time and money to training staff in a wide range of skills and sensitivities. For instance, given the level of violence in Boston—those horrific, escalating crimes that have hurt students like Jesuino, Abdul, and Nicklan—we had an expert on urban violence and related inner-city trauma speak to all Boston staff. Intercession—the four weeks between graduation and incoming classes—is a time of staff regeneration that we cannot do without. It's generally in February and August. And though we first intended it as down time for the staff to do planning and preparation, it's proven to be a necessary breather. Sometimes we do team building, professional development, and staff retreats—all designed to help equip and reinvigorate them for the next class.

During intercession, we take a solid few days to look critically and honestly over the past six months and explore what we have done well and what we can do better. It's a cathartic, nonjudgmental process, and it works. Many of our most significant improvements and innovations come from those sessions. The process has fostered a strong spirit of continuous improvement.

We've found that this kind of regular self-assessment can institutionalize innovation in a company.

Companywide retreats, held every eighteen to twenty-four months, are amazing affirmations and terrific fun. There were 180 of us at the last one in April 2010 at Mohonk Mountain House in rural New York State. "That piece is just so critical," Sue insists. "It's for people to feel part of the whole, to have some time together to share the joys of this work—and talk about the real challenges of it. It's also a time to dream big together. That's really important."

It's easy to dream. It's fantastic, and I'll never give it up. But moving a mission forward that could ideally serve millions of disadvantaged young adults has some daunting logistics. It's like flying a single-engine plane at ten thousand feet. If you want to get to thirty thousand, you need a new plane. After a lot of thought and many meetings with Tim, Sue, and Casey with all those whiteboard scrawlings, we set to building a stronger, streamlined, and more powerful organization with a national leadership team that could coordinate with local site staffs and boards.

First, we needed a better central brain—not unlike the companywide SharePoint that Roland Cody managed at JPMC. Ours would have to collect, calculate, and display our encouraging results with an added set of features: mapping and managing human relationships. Effective social entrepreneurs need spreadsheets. Dashboards. And yes, pie charts. How could I get enough people to invest if I couldn't assure them, in black and white, that their dollars would be well spent?

As a former technology consultant, I knew we had to find a better way to gather and use our data. I knew it would cost dearly to build—roughly 5 percent of our budget. This amounted to several hundred thousand dollars at a time when I would have walked over broken glass for a four-figure donation.

My business case for the major upgrade was a list of nonnegotiable requirements: We need a system that is a unified database able to capture all of the relationships we have between students, donors, internship partners, volunteers, and staff. We have to track how our students are doing and how our program is operating. We need to show how each individual internship is progressing, as well as how the main accounts with corporate partners are faring. It needs to handle fund-raising—efforts, targets, and results—all in one database. This would become the central brain; everyone would log what happened in a relationship there—with donors, internship partners, students, staff, volunteers.

Our business is predicated on relationships that must be articulated from all directions. The person who donates a dollar may also be the person who recommends a student. You can't lose track of all those relationships. They're vital. Sue went shopping for a brain that could process it all; it took her half a year, talking to many vendors. Finally she came to me with a decision. "We're going with Salesforce.com."

That San Francisco–based "enterprise cloud computing company" satisfied her that it would be able to help us manage all of our complex relationships. It engineered the platform, the underlying architecture we're using, and it's working beautifully. If someone has sold an internship, I get an e-mail. It's a great pick-me-up. That's twenty-two thousand dollars in our coffers right there. When all such information gets pushed to me, I can reorganize it and present it as needed. By pressing a key, we can create a set of up-to-the-minute reports. We can put them into pie charts and graphs for sales calls and donor meetings—each tailored to its target. Every Monday, we get a report pushed to us on the health of the business across a variety of metrics.

Don't think for a minute, though, that there's no soul in our shiny Salesforce.com machine. It's just as powerful a tool in tracking and supporting our students. Site leaders, advisers, instructors, and student-services staff can log in to check on how each student is doing in terms of contract points, support services needed, internship reports. Seeing such a full picture helps us identify someone in trouble so we can work with him or her sooner rather than later.

The minute a student fires himself, in any city, a staff member must go on our Salesforce.com site to change the student's status and document what happened and why. I've chosen to have the system automatically send me an e-mail when we lose any student, anywhere. I can see who the adviser and mentor were and the reason for the firing. When a student leaves, the graph of the site's retention rate changes automatically. That's the beauty of these systems. It's all done for you, and it's extremely powerful.

I love the way we can use the system. It has made our company run so much better that I tend to brag about it like a kid with a souped-up muscle car. I was in San Francisco presenting our case for funding to the leadership of Salesforce's charitable foundation when I got a bit carried away. "Can I just show you what we're doing with your stuff? It's so cool. We're running our whole bloody business with it."

I was projecting some of our reports and dashboards on a screen, saying, "Guys, watch what's happening." Suzanne DiBianca, the head of the foundation, stopped the meeting. "Oh my goodness," she said. And right there, she e-mailed the founder of the company, Marc Benioff: "These guys are incredible. Do you want to donate some money to help them?" Two minutes later he answered, and we were given a donation of ten thousand dollars.

Soon after, through its philanthropic arm, Salesforce.com donated a number of software licenses to us, which is a huge help. For instance, now I'm able to have our information—tens of thousands of records—accessible on my BlackBerry without cost to the program. Salesforce has also provided us with access to volunteers and helped us connect with other philanthropic partners. Its CIO was on our local board in San Francisco. Better yet, it takes Year Up interns.

Teaching technology with good equipment and cutting-edge software is very expensive. We could not have built our classroom infrastructure without a lot of help from other significant partners in the industry. For the first several years, IBM provided almost all of the PCs and servers that powered our tech lessons daily. Microsoft has been equally supportive in providing us with software licenses, donations, volunteers, and internships. Without this kind of support, just trying to pay for necessary software upgrades could all but put us out of business.

And now let's get back to money. Serious money. You can't afford the people, the infrastructure, the benefits—the mission itself—without a constant, renewable source of philanthropic investment. Type As like me can make good fund-raisers. In my case, it's partially due to a lifelong habit of setting ridiculous goals, announcing them to anyone who might care, and going full tilt until I get there. This could result in serious ego issues if I weren't reminded, over and over, that the mightiest fund-raisers for Year Up have been our students.

Case in point: Jim Pallotta.

Having made it my business to learn who made Boston's philanthropic community tick, I was well aware of Jim and his special interest in young people and their futures. He is one of the nation's most successful hedge fund managers, also known for his generous philanthropy. I was determined to meet him. When Tim Dibble let it slip that Jim would be at his house for their annual barn party, I got myself over there and was able to persuade Jim to stop by Year Up and see for himself what we do.

Jim grew up in the tough North End of Boston. He's frank and down to earth and can talk to anybody. We were sitting in an office on our fifth floor, discussing the program with a few students I had called in. They were professionally dressed, greeted Jim properly, and looked him in the eye as they spoke about their experiences. We took a tour of the facility, and as we walked along, we saw two young men in our reception area waiting to be interviewed for the first time. They were sprawled on the couch, wearing baggy jeans and backward baseball caps. I made the introduction.

"Jim, these are some folks who are applying to Year Up. Gentlemen, this is Mr. Jim Pallotta." Neither rose up from the couch. Looking down at his sneakers, one applicant mumbled, "'Sup?" Jim looked back at them, then at me. He pulled me back into the meeting room. His tone of voice was somewhat challenging.

"Did you just plant that? Because if you're telling me that those guys coming in to apply will end up like the other students we've been talking with in just a couple of months, we're done. I'm in."

I assured him it was all for real, took a deep breath, and aimed for the moon. "Jim, I'd love you to join our board. I need you to help us build this program and meet some of the right folks. And I'd be honored if you'd consider making a significant financial commitment to Year Up."

"Done. Done. And done."

Jim committed a seven-figure amount. He provided us with many key introductions and years of invaluable advice and board service. I don't know whether any of those guys in the reception area ever entered the program. I hope so. Regardless, I'd love to shake their hands.

Jim Pallotta made his multiyear pledge to Year Up in 2004, and it was a tremendous operational boost. A year earlier, the Smith Family Foundation had provided Year Up with its first million-dollar commitment to help us build capacity and scale the organization. Richard Smith, the patriarch, joined our board of directors and provided consistently astute business advice. It's hard to overestimate the transformative nature of these gifts, as they fundamentally shift an entrepreneur's focus from keeping alive today to building for tomorrow.

I've never been able to identify the X factor in securing donors. I would guess that it's some recombinant mix of serendipity, sincerity, commitment, and a lot of hustle. In this new age of results-oriented philanthropists, running our company with the rigors and systems of a for-profit business has also worked miracles with potential donors. Paul Reeder is one such vigilant investor. For two decades, he has headed up a highly successful Boston-based hedge fund, PAR Capital Management. He's methodical, disciplined, and a heck of a nice guy.

Paul has invested generously in Year Up, largely on the strength of our data presentation, financial transparency, and results. On a recent visit, when I called on Paul with our national director of development, Sandy Stark, I cut to the chase, since he's a busy man.

"Paul, I'd love for you to re-up for the next five years."

Paul had already taken all our annual reports and done all his own spreadsheets and analysis, much as he would do with an airline or an automotive business. He asked us an hour's worth of tough, penetrating questions, just as he does with a publicly traded company. At the end he said, "Excellent, thank you very much. I'll give you my answer in a week." Before Sandy and I left him, I asked, in true Year Up fashion, "Could I just get some feedback from you? You invest in companies based on analysis. You've obviously taken time to do that on us. How'd we do in terms of giving you what you needed?"

His reply underscored the case for building our central brain. "I would put you in the top twenty percent of all public companies I talk to in terms of the rigor and quality of the information and the clarity of thinking you have around your business." I resisted the urge to high-five Sandy as we waited for the elevator. Soon after, Paul re-upped for another significant gift.

Some investors might find it a bit over the top, but we raise growth capital with a document that takes the form, content, and language of a corporate IPO. It wasn't my brainstorm; I got the idea from one of the nation's most forward-thinking philanthropic families, the Jensens, led by the late Ronald Jensen, a successful entrepreneur and founder of United Insurance Companies, Inc. Sadly, he was killed in an automobile accident in 2005.

Soon thereafter, I met his son James at a New Profit dinner. James is the managing trustee of the Jensens' private family foundation, the Jenesis Group. Jenesis focuses its efforts on the education and development of underserved youth and young adults. Social entrepreneurs are its change agents of choice.

Ron Jensen was an experienced businessman who had raised money on Wall Street. He recognized that there will be certain junctures when a social entrepreneur has his or her organization poised for a quantum leap forward. He believed it essential to provide a social entrepreneur with timely growth capital to take those major leaps in functionality, structure, scale, and impact. I wanted to know more and traveled to meet with James in Dallas.

James showed me an initial partnership offering (IPO) document, a concept he and his father had created to raise money for the launch of Ashoka North America back in 1999. He explained that they had conceived of an IPO approach as an innovative way to raise capital in the nonprofit sector. Their inspiration had come from a desire to appeal to like-minded entrepreneurs. I paged through it and said, "You've given me a great idea. We're doing the exact same thing."

I flew home carrying a copy of that original IPO in my briefcase and James's promise to fund a consultant who could help us create a similar document for Year Up. We hired George Overholser, one of the nation's pioneers in raising growth capital, to help us think through the model. What new ways could we employ to raise growth capital to get to our next stage? How would we build sustainable revenue engines to keep the ship going?

George gave me an intense tutorial during a three-hour drive to the annual New Profit Gathering of Leaders at Mohonk Mountain House. We agreed that the old model of philanthropy was limited. The way it used to work, when you went out to raise a ton of money, it was to do two things: erect a building or fund an endowment. "We're not doing either," George pointed out. "We're taking chunks of donated money to grow a business."

Venture capitalists and private equity firms do exactly that. George was all for adopting the discipline of their model, insisting that it was wholly applicable to the nonprofit sector. As he explained it, "Let's think about that structure and put together deals where you can say, 'Well, I'm investing a chunk of money to take Year Up from three hundred students a year to a thousand.' That's a one-off cost on infrastructure and people to get there. Now, at the end of that time, Gerald, you're on the hook for making sure there are repeatable streams of revenue. For you that's largely around internships."

It made sound business sense to me. We pulled a team together to work on it: Casey, Sue, Ty, Craig Underwood, and Tim Dibble. George continued to educate us around the idea, and we used the Jensen document as a template. With Monitor Group's help we crunched the data for the next five-year plan and came up with a serious figure: We had to raise eighteen million bucks.

James Jensen was impressed with our program, revenue-generating model, leadership team, and results. Having spent forty thousand dollars to help us research and create our first "prospectus," the Jensen family made a six-million-dollar anchor investment to catalyze the campaign. I can't think of a better way to honor Ron Jensen's visionary approach to effective philanthropy. James Jensen is now a valued member of our extended think tank and someone I can always go to for advice and encouragement. Over the next nine months we raised another fourteen million dollars to surpass our goal. We then put our heads down to deliver what was in that plan.

In 2007 I was still team building. When Shawn Bohen, who had become a close friend to Kate and me, came over to talk about a career change, I was all ears as a friend—and as a hopeful employer. I'd been waiting patiently for the right moment for a few years. No one I knew had deeper experience helping nonprofits develop and flourish than Shawn in her work running the Hauser Center for Nonprofit Organizations at Harvard. As a research center and think tank, her university-wide program gathered many of the keenest minds in social entrepreneurship.

Within days of being offered the job, Shawn informed me, politely but firmly: "I know you think you need me as a director of development, and I am happy to help raise money. But that's not really what you want me to do nor what this organization needs me to do." Oh Lord. I could feel that warm feeling rising from my neck into my face, a sure sign that something is getting me upset or embarrassed. After all this time, and a long search for candidates, our front-runner was telling me it was the wrong job?

She went on: "I get what you're doing, but now you've got to lift your gaze beyond how you might just serve more students. You need to think about *systems* change, about how to use what you are learning to change the country. You need someone to help you think about influence. Growth does not equal impact."

Of course she was right, just as Vanessa Kirsch had been several years earlier when we began our relationship with New Profit, Inc. Vanessa founded New Profit to help social entrepreneurs gain access to serious venture capital. She is understandably demanding in vetting potential partners like me. "So what's your theory of change?" she asked in our first meeting. "If you don't have a plan to ultimately fix the problem you're addressing, then you may not be a candidate for our portfolio. We want to back social entrepreneurs who have a plan, a big plan, an *audacious* plan to tackle the root causes behind the social problems they are addressing."

I had bristled a bit at first. Wasn't it good enough that we were busting our butts on a daily basis, providing incredible opportunities to a group of young adults who truly deserved it, and getting great results? Thankfully, Vanessa didn't give up on me. She and her team got me thinking seriously about the bigger picture. Year Up exists because of systemic failure elsewhere. Instead of trying to scale the program forever, the ultimate goal should be to figure out how to reduce the need for programs like ours. Better still, we should ensure that they are well integrated into the existing educational and workforce-development systems so that they have a sustainable and repeatable source of funding. By becoming part of the system, we can change it from within.

Shawn is the consummate consigliere, a sound adviser and ideas person. She can look ahead and around corners very well. She saw what this organization needed to grow into, and she has played a big role in defining how we grow. She had some tough questions for me.

"Are you really going to build a McDonald's-like franchise and put one of these things on every corner and try to skin the cat that way? Is that really what a creative, serial-entrepreneur guy like you wants? You're not going to want to run the trains. That's not your gig at all."

She had me there. We agreed that what we had been calling indirect activities (influencing educators and workforce-development providers, doing legislative advocacy) were logical next steps toward systems change. "What I can really do," Shawn said, "is get us where we need to be three years from now so we can bust out. This is a problem we can solve."

We settled on her new title, director of strategic growth and impact, and started looking for our next director of development that same day. Eventually, after a lot of searching, we found the perfect fit in Sandy Stark, who had a deep background in growing both for-profit and nonprofit companies. Sandy had worked her way up from entry-level secretary to vice chairman at Key Bank, becoming the highest-ranking woman there. She found the time and energy to earn her BA and master's degrees as she advanced her career. Her long-range vision was just what we needed to solidify and expand our fund-raising capability.

With a solid leadership team in place, Year Up was flying along with a mighty retooled engine that had all the bells and whistles to carry us along to the next phase of growth. Our crew was larger and stronger, our staff and students well cared for, our civic and business profiles more visible. But we were not about to start congratulating ourselves. When I started Year Up in 2001, The Annie E. Casey Foundation estimated there were 3.7 million disconnected young adults in this country. By the time we turned toward widening our influence, there were almost a million more.

CHAPTER THIRTEEN
"We Are One Year Up"

Presently,
When you look in my direction,
What is it that you see?
It only takes but seconds to form your impression of me
So while I have your attention,
Let me dissolve your common misconception
Cuz regardless of what I'm wearing
I see success in this reflection.

—from "Common Misconception," by Rashawn
Facey-Castillo, Year Up graduate

KELVIN,* A BOSTON STUDENT, STOOD LISTENING INTENTLY AS BRUCE,* a Year Up staff member, spoke to him about an urgent matter. Kelvin was well dressed in suit, shirt, and tie. His hair was in long, neatly kept dreadlocks. *Inappropriate,* Bruce informed him. He needed to lop off the dreads, which are regarded negatively in business. They're just not professional looking.

It went on in that vein. When Kelvin walked away looking troubled, Lawrence,* another staff member, confronted Bruce.

"You could have handled that better."

"I'm just trying to help the guy."

Bruce is white and Lawrence is of color. They debated civilly, but there was a low tension in their voices. Lawrence had some questions. If Kelvin was properly dressed, was he unprofessional just because of his hair? Who defined what "professional" looks like? Did Bruce realize that it takes a very long time to grow dreads and that they may have a deeper resonance with someone's self-identity than a corporate manager's distaste? Might it have helped to suggest to Kelvin that while some businesses might disapprove, it could be possible to find a company that wouldn't judge his potential based on his looks?

Bruce was growing more uncomfortable, but Lawrence pressed on: There might be a less negative way to tell Kelvin that his hairstyle could impact his acceptance in conventional business. How about a bit of empowerment in this touchy situation? Why not help Kelvin understand that cutting the dreads was *his* decision to make? Bottom line: Was there a less judgmental way to give a student the 4-1-1 on life in the corporate fishbowl?

I had seen similar scenes play out many times with varied outcomes as applicants and admitted students came in wearing dreads, cornrows, and braided hair extensions that didn't fit the dominant (read: white) notion of workplace propriety. I've been drawn into those delicate conversations myself, and I've been called out for my own missteps.

Early in our work together, I genuinely believed I was paying Richard Dubuisson a compliment one day. "You're compassionate, articulate . . ." He took me aside and asked quietly, "When was the last time you told a white person they were articulate?" Richard explained what I did not see or feel: "For people of color that's heard as 'Gee, for a black person, you speak really well.'" Once again I didn't know what I didn't know.

There's no PC road map for negotiating these curves. We have always discussed race on an as-needed basis. More times than I'd care to remember, we have had to counsel distraught interns who have encountered insensitive or outright racist remarks at work. Given the diversity of our students, the multicultural minefields involve a good deal more than race. Sensitive issues keep arising:

Should you assign regular homework on the first night of Ramadan?

Are hijabs (Muslim women's head scarves) okay in an internship?

"Women, they're *women*." Over and over our staff keeps reminding young men whose habitual speech runs to "So I was talking with these two females." Sometimes, the correction is met with legitimate bafflement: "What female has a problem with that? Plenty of them say it too."

What do you do with that?

How do you talk about race, religion, and gender issues in a way that's mutually honest and respectful?

For that matter, why am I talking about race this deep into Year Up's story? Because it took us until 2008 to realize how deliberate we needed to be on the subject—and how essential it was to invest seriously in adopting a companywide diversity policy and a statement of identity. For an organization that pushes back constantly against common misperceptions of our students and their abilities, we were pretty low on in-house guidelines. We tended to deal with matters of race, religion, ethnicity, and gender on a case-by-case basis. With our eyes so much on the prize—closing the Opportunity Divide, one student at a time—we were rather shortsighted.

Early on, Richard had also cautioned me on the consequences for Year Up's future. "Right now I'm the only person of color on a staff of eight. So every time I open my mouth it's for all people of color. You have to think about that ratio if you want to have long-term viability and authenticity in this organization." I heard him, but we continued to be more reactive rather than proactive when it came to grappling with racial issues.

It was at a routine staff meeting in Providence in early 2007 that another plain speaker raised the question again, directly. I was sitting with Sara Strammiello, Richard Dubuisson, and Joe Gerena, our Providence site leader, who had also been the pastor of a multidenominational, multicultural church. We were talking through our new performance management system, which rated staff members' professional competencies in various areas, such as people skills, ability to set direction, leadership, etc. Suddenly Joe piped up, "What about cultural competency?"

Silence. None of us had a satisfactory answer. Cultural competency, as we define it now, is a lifelong process of developing the knowledge, values, skills, and will that help us interact with a diverse group of students and stakeholders. It takes in all aspects of diversity, from race to language, gender, religion. Achieving that competency requires that you educate yourself continually and confront biases and unconscious assumptions when they appear.

Why didn't we have a policy for our own behavior around this issue? Just having the question raised told me this was a turn in the road we had to make, and soon. Shortly after Joe's well-intentioned challenge, Sue Meehan proposed that we spend time and money exploring the ways in which Year Up could seriously improve its cultural competency and diversity on a number of levels.

We gave it a crisp corporate name: an initiative for diversity and cultural competency. Then we rolled up our sleeves. Sue launched the project with Tamika Mason, our director of organizational development, who readily agreed on the need for it. As Tamika conducted orientation sessions in Boston for new hires from all over the country, she fielded direct questions: "What exactly is Year Up's diversity policy?"

Tamika heard one attendee look around his future workplace and note, "I don't think there are many *leaders* of color."

That was initially true of our national board, which at its outset was mostly white and male. Our leadership positions in the cities we served were much more representative of our students' population, but there was room for improvement.

As work on the initiative progressed, there were some tense moments with existing staff and board members. "Sue and I were still in our planning phase," Tamika recalls. "We had hired a solid, experienced outside consultant to help, and we were talking about it to a meeting of all of our executive directors. They had just watched a three-part PBS series on racism, real estate, and redlining in America that our consultant had recommended."

We now use that 2003 series as an educational resource for everyone at Year Up, including students. It is a shocking, well-researched piece of history that reveals how our government and banking policies systematically denied property ownership to citizens of color after World War II while the rest of America was buying first homes under the GI Bill. The film notes that Levittown, that model postwar development on Long Island, New York, is still 96 percent white.

When the lights went up after the film, Kweku Forstall, an African American nonprofit executive we had recently hired to launch Year Up in Atlanta, spoke up. "We shouldn't talk about diversity unless we're really serious about it." The room was instantly on edge. What did he mean by that? Kweku pushed it further: If we're truly committed to diversity, shouldn't it be one of the program's core values?

There was a similar intake of breath at a national board meeting when Sue and Tamika were giving a briefing. Tim Dibble, then chairman, declared flatly, "I don't think I really need to watch a video on redlining." He explained that he had participated in diversity efforts at work and found them ineffective exercises that "ran around in circles."

"You're mistaken, my friend. You do need to watch that video."

The voice belonged to national board member Gail Snowden. She grew up in Roxbury, and as a scholarship student, she was the only African American in her New Hampshire boarding school. Gail is now CEO of Freedom House, a nonprofit dedicated to social innovation and alleviating poverty in Boston's most distressed neighborhoods. Prior to that, she distinguished herself in a thirty-year career at top financial institutions. In fact, Gail had been Tim's boss and mentor in his first financial job at BankBoston. They were longtime friends. Had they never discussed race?

Our fault lines were showing and would grow wider if we backed off. Uneasy moments like these reinforced our resolve. Since the initiative's start in March 2008, we have made some necessary changes.

Our hiring practices now ensure that we draw from diverse pools of candidates for positions at all levels.

All new employees and students are briefed on Year Up's clearly articulated diversity and cultural competency policies.

We have developed a set of companywide standards for discussing and defusing sensitive moments such as the one that began this chapter.

We continue to invest the time and funds for regular, companywide reviews and educational sessions on diversity issues.

The composition of our national and local boards increasingly reflects the population we serve in any given city.

Year Up graduates now serve on our national and local boards.

We are developing supplier policies with guidelines that must include women- and minority-owned businesses as vendors of everything from paper clips to expert consultancies.

Trust me, it's not an easy thing to convince a multimillionaire board member that he or she really must hold hands with a nineteen-year-old from the inner city in an exercise to illustrate the divide in privilege. We don't expect miracles from two-hour sessions held in hotel conference rooms, just more thoughtfulness. We realize that appointing Year Up alumni to our local and national boards won't magically make students and graduates feel more like full stakeholders in our organization. But it's a beginning, and it's the right thing to do.

We also felt a need to declare our day-to-day commitment right in the classrooms. Prompted by Kweku's observations, we held an organization-wide discussion about that glaring omission in our set of values. At the next company retreat in New Hampshire, Kweku was onstage as we unveiled a poster bearing our sixth core value: ENGAGE AND EMBRACE DIVERSITY. It is on the wall, printed in bright Year Up yellow and blue, in every one of our locations.

Big lessons can also spring from small moments that are made teachable with a communication tool known as an "ouch." It's another measured, non-judgmental form of feedback. Any board member, employee, or student feeling the sting of a racially or culturally insensitive remark—such as my faux pas with Richard—says "ouch" to the speaker. Or "Hey, that's an ouch for me." It's a civil but firm heads-up. Calmly and respectfully, the discomfort is explained and, we hope, defused. The intent is education without intimidation. It sounds like this:

Ouch! from a student to the blond tech instructor trying to explain a concept with a skiing metaphor: "Excuse me, but I'm lost here. Most poor folks don't ski."

Ouch! to the student who has returned with only sausage pizza to be paid for and shared by his classmates: "I appreciate your grabbing lunch for us all. But you know I'm Muslim—I can't eat pork."

How are we doing? Progress is incremental and steady. We can't use Salesforce dashboards to measure understanding and tolerance. I am encouraged by some small epiphanies and great acts of courage. The morning I addressed Class Nine's town hall meeting in Brooklyn, the convocation began with a reminder for compassion and forbearance. This was in the wake of a viciously homophobic crime that had just made headlines. A gay man, his brother, and two other teenagers were kidnapped and brutally tortured for days in the Bronx; seven young men were later arrested for the crime. Staff member Karen Fleshman lit a candle and asked for a moment of silent reflection.

"Can I say something here?"

Jason, an outstanding and well-liked student, stood up and faced about 140 classmates and staff.

"I would just like to remind my colleagues that—I know you don't mean to hurt anyone—but casual remarks I've heard in class have been painful to listen to for a gay man. I'd just ask you to think about that. Think about who might be sitting near you when you say those things. Just, please . . . *think*."

He was so brave in that moment. It was also clear that Jason felt quite safe in speaking his mind, as difficult as it might have been. If we've made our own house a bit more secure and tolerant, I do feel more confident about sending our students back out into the world. On all levels, they're our best ambassadors and agents for change.

Anyone who interacts with our students can tell you that. A couple of years into her tenure as ED in Washington, Tynesia told me that she had become aware of a grassroots effect as our students engaged with staff and internship employers. "At its best, Year Up is a transformational experience for everyone it touches. In order to do our model well, staff members have to undergo a transformation in the way they talk and think and address students. They have to lose whatever biases they have to make sure they're constantly investing in our students' assets—instead of focusing on liabilities. That ripples into the corporate partners. All of it stimulates learning and growth, which is very powerful."

Dreadlocks will continue to bounce through our corridors. New "ouches" will sting, be acknowledged, and get defused. We'll maintain the effort, in our budget and in practice. Without question, we're a more capable and viable institution for the long run having taken this on in a meaningful way. We'll always have lively internal debates, and not just along the lines of cultural difference. Should things get a bit heated, we reset the discussion with a reminder of our unity and purpose: "We are one Year Up."

In the fall of 2008, as we were finding our voice with a diversity policy, we were also expanding coast to coast. At the same time, the economy had begun suddenly, speedily contracting. As some of the most venerable financial institutions teetered on the verge of collapse, many nonprofits began circling their wagons. Sue and I were spreading our funds around twenty different banks in a panic. We looked hard for budget cuts but left the diversity funding intact. We had to. We needed to get even stronger in this area, considering our expansion plans that would diversify our student body even more.

Immigration issues have always been a significant aspect of our student body's challenges. As we planned sites in two more gateway cities on the West Coast—San Francisco in September 2008, followed by Seattle in March 2011—our student population was getting even more multicultural, and its risk factors more complex. Year Up Nation had never been more heterogeneous—and in more need of our services. Our students need to be authorized to work to be admitted to the program. Yet even if they have passed that hurdle, the children of immigrants may face many other road-blocks trying to enter the skilled labor force. Our first West Coast site was called Year Up Bay Area. The first student roster in San Francisco was beau-tifully, strikingly multieverything: racial, lingual, national. That came as no surprise in a state that categorizes 24 percent, or roughly 1.5 million, of its public-school students as "English learners" speaking over fifty-five lan-guages. The Year Up program is located in the business district near the Embarcadero in a brick building that was once the fragrant headquarters of Folgers Coffee.

Launching and leading it for us was Executive Director Jay Banfield, who had made his own traverse of the Opportunity Divide. Jay grew up on public assistance in Somerville, Massachusetts, and made his way to Stan-ford University in Palo Alto. His deep experience in business, nonprofit man-agement, and city government made him the right person to help us gain traction in the Bay Area.

The immigration issues that have impacted our students in a gateway city like San Francisco are part of a huge and increasingly contentious national debate. I have been party to it for a decade now, supporting our students in immigration hearings and attorneys' offices and in the difficult, private moments when it's my job to just listen. I wish that some of the harsher antiimmigrant factions could hear the real stories of our so-called illegal strivers.

Of the twenty-four students who made up that first class in San Fran-cisco, no one entered the program with more impressive computer skills—and less comfort with English—than eighteen-year-old Thom Moa.* He began life on his family's small duck farm in the province of Battambang, Cambodia, an agricultural area known as the "rice bowl" of that country until it was commandeered as a torture center during the years of Khmer Rouge genocide. Thom's rural childhood left him well acquainted with hard work, carrying river water to the ducks, feeding them, collecting eggs, all before a long trek to school.

He came to California with his mother, brother, and sister in 2002 at age thirteen to join his stepfather, a naturalized U.S. citizen working as a home care attendant in nearby Modesto. By high school, Thom was a self-taught tech wizard who had bought and built his first computer piecemeal. He worked an entire summer making muffins and Chinese pork buns at Happy Donuts until he could afford to buy the parts. "Always I knew, the computer is really the future for the world," he recalls. "My first was only an eighty-gig hard drive—pretty basic. I bought hardware, memory case, motherboard, a little bit at a time. I put them all together and it was working fine."

Thom unspooled his stressful odyssey to Year Up's doorstep one evening in the employee lounge at a multistory Wells Fargo office. He did his internship there and was hired as a help-desk technician immediately at a salary that helped lift his family out of poverty. The unedited version could make an epic film. A couple of times during his long recitation, Thom lost his composure as he tried to describe the frustrations and privations his family suffered. "As the oldest son, I felt responsible. I could never do enough, never fix it."

Thom's stepfather stayed at his live-in caregiver job when the rest of the family moved to San Francisco to escape the gangs, drugs, and poor schools they were faced with in Modesto. After a few years in this country, Thom spoke Khmer, Cantonese, and "pretty bad English." His family was quite poor despite a patchwork of minimum-wage jobs.

Of necessity, Thom has always been a resourceful self-starter. When a computer store quoted $375 to fix his girlfriend's broken PC, he decided to tackle it himself. "Sitting in front of that computer with two dictionaries, one Cambodian, one Chinese, I translated everything I saw on the screen, four hours a day for two weeks, trying to fix it. I got it back up. That encouraged me."

At Thurgood Marshall High School, he spent most lunch hours hanging with his IT instructor in an effort to learn more. In short order, Thom was the school's unofficial systems administrator, keeping its aging fleet of a hundred PCs in working order; there was no one available on staff to do it. He did so, unpaid, for all four years, worked a series of part-time jobs, and grew vegetables in his landlord's small yard to stretch the family budget. His high school transcript was impeccable ("except for English class"). His extracurricular activities were impressive; they included an internship at a dental practice and membership on a prize-winning environmental studies team. He wanted very much to go to college.

But the INS had come calling. Since Thom's mother and stepfather lived separately owing to the live-in job, the immigration agency contended theirs was a sham marriage and issued notice that all but Thom's stepfather would be deported should the alleged fraud be proven. As the case crept along in courts hopelessly clogged with immigration cases, the pressures on the family built.

"We had to fight for three years without status. That means they renew our green cards, but we are not allowed work. We can go to school but not get financial aid. We cannot apply for food stamps, anything. Only my step-father worked, since he is a citizen, and he made $1,600 a month to support five people. We survived because my mom sold the farm in Cambodia. They wired the money over here. It was hard."

Thom's parents were called in for the dreaded marriage interrogation. As the eldest and best English speaker, Thom had to witness his parents' humiliation as agents questioned them separately about their domestic life in an effort to prove fraud. The sessions were videotaped—ultimately a good thing, as Thom recalled. "They ask them, 'How many times do you have sex in a month? What color are the bedsheets?' It's really private and my mom is very traditional, so it's hard for her to answer. Plus she gets scared because the interviewer is threatening her. No interpreter really speaks our dialect. It seemed hopeless."

His mother cried out in the night and began having serious physical and mental health problems. By Thom's senior year in high school, there was still no resolution, but he went ahead and applied to UC Berkeley, the ultimate brass ring for high school overachievers nationwide. He got in, but there was no celebration. His family's legal limbo made him ineligible to apply for the needed financial aid. He had spun out various scenarios to try to afford school—working full time at McDonald's, bunking with a friend also headed for Berkeley. Nothing was workable, and he had to let the dream go. "It came to a point where I didn't care about my green card anymore because we were all dying in this life. I tried to comfort my mom, but sometimes the darkness inside you covers everything."

In June 2008, right before graduation, Thom went to his guidance counselor in despair. "She knew my family situation. I asked her, 'Do you have anything for me to do—or do I just continue McDonald's?' She showed me the Year Up flyer that said you got paid, they teach you computer skills, and you get college credit. I thought it's most likely lying. I have nothing to lose and it says 'free'—why not give it a try?"

You might be wondering what Year Up could do for a young man so computer savvy. Though Thom could build and repair almost any machine, he needed to boost his software literacy. His business communications instructors can attest that there was plenty of language work needed as well. "I rewrote homework so many, many times. My business e-mails—I hate to remember." Having worked only in places that issued paper hats and hairnets, Thom learned that he would have to acquire some new cultural competencies as well.

"Professional skills was the *most* important thing—I didn't realize how important it is in American society. Here, if you look professional people respect you. In my country, everybody's too busy trying to survive. They don't have time to care about professional dress. All that Year Up taught us about surviving in the business world proved to be true. The elevator speech was very hard for me. I hated that; I struggled. But I can talk to anybody now."

The family had finally gotten some help with their immigration crisis when a teacher, concerned with the growing stress she had seen in Thom and his siblings, referred them to the Asian Law Caucus. A grateful Thom now does volunteer and outreach work for that nonprofit, which represented his family pro bono. "It was proven that my parents are legally married, no fraud. The court decision was granted by a judge. Viewing that DVD of the interrogation, the judge said it was not professional, the answers we provided were reasonable, and we explained everything. We cooked a lot of food to celebrate and my dad is crying, all day. We're all so happy."

During his internship at Wells Fargo, Thom grew close with his manager. "He's just like a brother to me; he showed me everything he knows. He encouraged and inspired me every day. He's twenty-six and came from the same kind of background as me—he was by himself since sixteen, working since high school. We just help each other. When he's busy on a ticket, I can take care of the office and make sure customers are happy."

Thom was very worried about his job prospects in 2009. The *New York Times DealBook* column reported that Wells Fargo was expected to begin large layoffs tied to the recession and to redundancies from acquiring Wachovia. He knew he was good, but had he made himself indispensable? "As my internship was ending, everybody was sending e-mails to my managers. The supervisor said, 'Thom, I can't *not* hire you. Managers and executives say they want you to stay. The customers say that, and they're the ones paying the bills every month. It's my honor to have you as part of our team.' I was crying, I was so lucky to get an offer."

Thom's younger brother is now enrolled at UC Santa Cruz; he was issued his green card just before the admissions deadline. The whole family pitches in for tuition, room, and board. Thom is beginning evening classes to pursue a college degree. As the eldest son, he feels he should keep working full time—and then some. At Wells Fargo he has earned a promotion to PC/LAN analyst and two raises within eight months. His side business, selling used computer parts on eBay, has proven lively enough to distinguish him as a "PowerSeller." He and his sister have put offers on a few homes in the super competitive Bay Area market. They are not discouraged by being outbid so far. "We are happy," Thom says, "and will keep looking until we get one." And oh yes—he is also buying and reselling cars.

"I think I am at heart an entrepreneur. Thank you, pro skills."

In his darkest hours, when deportation seemed imminent, Thom spun plans to put those acquired skills to work in Southeast Asia. I'm sure he would have figured something out. But what a loss it would have been to the American workforce.

Three thousand miles east in Providence, similar barriers had been raised for a young Salvadoran single mother who had wanted very much to attend college. Oneyda Escobar grew up in this country, excelled in high school, and spent her entire senior year working on college applications with her guidance counselor. Though she was truthful about her nonresident status, she was admitted and completed her freshman year as a day student at a state institution.

"I had all the financial help I needed and I was really excited," she recalls. "I thought this was great. I'd reapply for FAFSA [Free Application for Federal Student Aid] for next year so I can get the help again. They sent me a letter saying I wasn't eligible anymore, that I was never eligible in the first place for financial aid because I'm not a U.S. permanent resident. I wouldn't be able to return to school unless I paid off my debt from the year before—they billed me for eleven thousand dollars."

If she ever managed to pay that debt, starting school again would be far more expensive. As a nonresident, she also would be ineligible for in-state tuition. Worse, she says, was losing credit for the course work she had completed successfully. "I can't get the credits I earned unless I pay the bill. There's no way I can go back and retake them, a whole year, two semesters. And there's no way I can get a loan to pay that bill. I have no credit history. My mother and I have tried every possible way to apply for a loan."

Oneyda worked at KFC, then at a department store for $7.20 an hour, and quit soon after a promised raise topped out at just twenty cents more an hour. The next job, as a hostess at Olive Garden, paid better, but it was a long commute away and workers were often sent home early when the restaurant wasn't busy. A cousin told Oneyda about Year Up. She was doubtful until she had completed all of our admissions interviews. "I thought, 'There's a *way* for me—there's actually a way to go to school.'"

Oneyda recounted her story on an afternoon in December 2010 when the U.S. Senate was scheduled to vote on the embattled DREAM Act (Development, Relief, and Education for Alien Minors), which would have allowed illegal immigrants with a high school diploma or a GED to apply for conditional U.S. status if they were under the age of thirty and arrived in the United States before the age of sixteen. It would have removed some barriers to postsecondary education for deserving longtime residents like Oneyda, allowing them to receive financial aid and in-state tuition.

Though the House had already passed a version of the bill, Oneyda was glum about its prospects in the Senate. "I highly doubt they'll vote in the DREAM Act today. I know there are a lot of people who are against it. I was just telling my sister we can't wait for it forever."

When the DREAM Act was defeated in the Senate on December 18, 2010, by a vote of 55–41, Oneyda was already well employed, with a clear pathway back to college. She did us proud as the first Year Up intern at an international medical supply company. "A month before graduation, my manager pulled me aside and said, 'We want to take you on right away in a contract position. Once we do a head count, you'll be hired full time with benefits.' I was so excited. I knew they had a lot of people applying for that position with college degrees. And they wanted *me* to stay. That meant a lot to me."

She celebrated with friends from Year Up, then went back to work. The company has found that Oneyda's Spanish is an added asset with help-desk clients in Puerto Rico and the Dominican Republic; employees in Ireland ask for her by name as well. Working a night shift, she has more time with her son. "When I look ahead, I see a lot of opportunities for me because of my employers. One of the managers had heard my speech about my college goals at a Year Up event. He came to me and said, 'I know how much you want to go, and to progress here you have to have a college degree. We can help you with tuition reimbursement.'"

She has put the first college disappointment behind her. "I'll just have to lose those credits." Now a part-time student at Community College of Rhode Island, Oneyda was able to transfer her Year Up college credits; she expects to earn her associate's degree by fall of 2012. She has moved into a two-bedroom apartment with her son. She credits her financial independence to her job and the practical math she learned at Year Up. "I wish high schools taught that stuff. They even taught us about credit cards and money management."

Oneyda is paying her success forward. We count on her help at outreach events all around the Providence area. There are still thousands of young adults in that city in need of opportunity, and she's a great motivational speaker. Sometimes, as she's getting him ready for his day, she talks to her son about their future. "Even when I was at Year Up, I'd say, 'Okay, Giovanni, I'm going to school, you're going to day care, but in the end it's going to pay off because I'm not just going to some part-time job anymore.' Just talking to him about it, though he doesn't understand yet, felt great."

If Giovanni can avoid most of the negative effects felt by the children of undocumented immigrants, it will be a victory with residuals for generations after him. A 2011 study published in *The Harvard Education Review* found that over five million children currently in this country are "at risk of lower educational performance, economic stagnation, blocked mobility and ambiguous belonging" because they are growing up in homes affected by their families' illegal status. Just some of the adverse and stressful factors: constant fear of discovery, parents' low-wage jobs, lack of health care, and a hard awakening at adolescence when they are denied the ability to work, obtain driver's licenses, or get financial aid for college. You have to appreciate what they're up against simply with the labels they must wear. Honestly, can any innocent child be called "illegal"?

In the fall of 2011, three years after Thom was unable to attend Berkeley, the state legislature passed the California Dream Act, which would allow undocumented immigrants who grew up in this country to get state-financed college scholarships and loans. Texas has had its own version since 2001, permitting foreign-born children of illegal immigrants to pay in-state college tuition. The California law was a more recent end run around the stalled national DREAM Act legislation. A partial version of the California bill allowing undocumented immigrants to accept private financial aid was signed into law. Only partial public financing for those undocumented students was allowed as some continued to deride it as a "waste" of government money. A *New York Times* editorial hailed the state's pioneering effort with some simple logic that resonates with Year Up's mission and our diversity policy: "Hopeful, striving, well-educated people are a resource any country needs. Consigning tens of thousands of bright minds to an illegal existence and dead-end jobs ... that's the flagrant waste.... "

We knew that there was a need for Year Up in the eastern Sun Belt, where urban populations had surged and the business boom of the 1990s had cooled. Nonetheless, when Monitor Group, our research consultant, delivered the numbers of young adults languishing without opportunity there, we were surprised. Atlanta, with its sprawling suburban adjuncts, is home to twenty-three thousand young adults classified as disconnected and who fit Year Up's target profile—the fourth highest in the nation behind New York, Los Angeles, and Chicago. There were plenty of robust businesses in Atlanta's sprawling metro area that could be potential internship partners, from Coca-Cola to SunTrust Bank, Georgia-Pacific, and the automotive supplier Genuine Parts.

Just how we were able to connect with this large population of potential students is one of the more encouraging experiences I've had since Year Up's inception. Four southern gentlemen of a certain age, success, and stature stood together and said, "Come on down." They continue to move heaven, earth, and checkbooks for us. Collectively they reinforced the bedrock faith that's been key to our success: *What is wrong in America can be fixed by what is right in America.*

I give you Year Up Atlanta's four tireless horsemen: Doug Ellis, Cecil Conlee, John McDonald, and Sam Allen. Together they provided all of the start-up capital, the space, the connections, and the advice that Kweku Forstall needed to bring Year Up Atlanta to full, robust, and striving capacity. They are all Harvard Business School graduates from its class of 1963, some retired and members of a national philanthropic endeavor known as Partners of '63, which focuses on supporting educational nonprofits. Mostly in their seventies, the partners asked themselves a pretty basic question: "What's the best thing we can do with the next phase of our lives?"

In Atlanta, that's Year Up. Cecil Conlee became our founding chairman there and cochaired our capital campaign. Sam Allen let us use space in his office before we secured our permanent location in a downtown office building. Doug Ellis and his wife, Florida, held gracious receptions in their home and helped us gain significant foundation support. Tireless at age seventy-nine, John McDonald would accompany me on every visit that I made in Atlanta trying to raise money and support. Often he'd pick me up at the airport. We'd start out at 7:00 a.m., driving at breakneck speed to Buckhead and downtown Atlanta, finishing late in the evening seven or eight meetings later. Exhausted, I'd watch John's taillights rocket into the distance and think, "How the heck does he do it?"

Like the others, Cecil Conlee spent loads of social and business currency, built up over decades in his city. He'll tell you he spent it freely but judiciously. The first introductions had to be the rainmakers. "It was hugely important here to get the endorsement of the most influential organizations in the city," Cecil says. "If you're in Atlanta, think Coca-Cola. Their Robert W. Woodruff Foundation—he was the founder of Coca-Cola—is one of the largest in the country. Getting their endorsement is the Good Housekeeping seal in Atlanta. So that was one of the first targets to legitimize our mission here. They gave us a very significant grant to get our capital campaign started. Then we went to SunTrust, the oldest and first of the big independent banks, as an early internship partner."

Cecil and our search committee went through fourteen hundred résumés before they came up with Kweku Forstall, a deeply thoughtful leader with more than twenty years of nonprofit experience in the Atlanta community. At about the same time I began planning Year Up, Kweku had led a nonprofit start-up in Atlanta called Project Grad, which worked within the school system there to get more students earning diplomas from high school and college. After nearly a decade, the program was still limited by a school system in deep turmoil. Kweku was persuaded to try an alternative.

"Project Grad tried to work within the system, in their classrooms, to try and change behaviors," he explains. "It was probably naive to think that we could do that. At Year Up, we work with students eight thirty to three thirty for twenty-one weeks and then afterwards during internships. We have their full attention and we have a lot of leverage. That's one big difference that made me more optimistic. We have incentives, stipends, earning the internship. The public school system should hold students more accountable. We don't have social promotion at Year Up. The value of accountability is lived out here."

So, of course, is our core value of diversity. When Jim Cruz got accepted into our first Atlanta class in March 2009, admissions director P. W. Reed sat him down for a serious talk on the subject. It took him a bit of time to lay things on the line, as Jim remembers.

"He was trying to get to the point of telling me, 'You're going to be the only white person.'"

In addition to managing admissions, P.W. oversaw outreach in Atlanta. He and Kweku had agreed on a mandate that was as inclusive as possible. P.W. explains, "I want to bring in students that are not just African American but also Asian, Latino, and white. That's the greatest challenge here. Out of 154 candidates for the next class, we may have interviewed seven people that are *not* African American."

None of that mattered to Jim, who lived in McDonough, an outlying section of the metro area. He just knew he needed our help. "I told Mr. Reed that it was fine. I was there for the opportunity, and if I could meet some people on the way and make some friends, that was good too. I kind of liked being the different person."

Jim wasn't beset with the severe risk factors many of our other students cope with. His parents were divorced, his mother and sisters had moved away, and many of Jim's friends were in post–high school limbo as well. College wasn't affordable; opportunities were few. Jim also faced an unpleasant deadline for coming up with a plan. "I was working a minimum-wage job close to my home. My dad was threatening to kick me out if I didn't do something better with my life. There was no way I could afford rent with that job. I was considering the military, but I didn't really want to go."

Jim's father, who works in the tech field in Atlanta, heard the equivalent of a Year Up elevator speech—in an actual elevator—delivered by someone he met in his workplace. Had he heard about this program for young adults who have hit dead ends? Jim's dad gave him our Web site information and after three interviews, he was in. Jim was allowed to remain at home while he was in the program. "I had to go to Year Up or he was going to kick me to the curb. I guess he wanted to see me make something for myself. He pretty much was kicked out young as well. Tough love, whatever. Money-wise, college was not an option. Anyhow, I struggled with math and anything technical, except computers. I excelled with computers."

Jim's biggest challenge in completing the program was not his "minority" status in that first class; he expects to have the friends he made there "for life." He had no trouble getting up at 5:00 a.m. to travel the thirty or so miles to Year Up or to his internship at Genuine Parts in Marietta. He did not incur infractions. "The biggest challenge was transportation," he says. "I had a car, but it would take an hour and a half or an hour and forty-five minutes to get there. When my car broke down, there was a bus—but the stop was six miles away."

Jim was one of the first two Year Up interns at Genuine Parts, which has become a strong corporate partner in large measure because of that first experience. "My Year Up colleague was in the telecom group," Jim explained. "And I was in PC support. Eventually they hired her in another department. She's very mechanically inclined. She was a mechanic while she was in the program. A lot of us had to work two jobs to try and keep up and come here. There were a lot of sacrifices made."

Jim was hired by Genuine Parts in February 2010 as a systems support analyst. "I was excited—I had a piece of paper that said they wanted me to come back. My dad looked at that paper and was definitely proud. That was a big step for me."

Our interns' success at Genuine Parts was a huge win for Year Up. When he is courting new internship partners, Cecil Conlee finds it useful to cite that company's positive experience with our interns. "I tell them what the vice president of HR at Genuine Parts has said: 'This is the best thing we've ever done. We're getting a pipeline of potential employees who are background checked, drug tested, trained, and we get to watch them for six months. So when we hire one of them, it's almost a slam dunk.'"

Once he had banked some savings, Jim was happy to be able to move out of his father's home on his own terms. He found roommates on craigslist to share a rental house closer to his work in Marietta. "Then as soon as I got my job, my car broke down—again. I couldn't afford to get it fixed yet. I was taking the bus, but my house was a mile from the bus stop." He timed it; skateboarding took fifteen minutes; walking took forty-five. For six months, just past dawn and in all kinds of weather, Jim was a regular if curious sight, skateboarding in jacket and tie, then walking into the office with his board tucked under his arm. "I'd get a few looks," he recalls. "But they saw a guy doing whatever he has to do to get to work." Finally he had saved enough to get his car fixed. He still drives the same 1995 Nissan Sentra. "I like saving money now. I like having a cushion in case something does happen. I'm going to drive it into the ground if I have to. I've had the clutch go out about three times." It helps to work for an automotive parts company. "I do get discounts."

Jim knows plenty of young adults back in McDonough still floating between dead-end jobs and nothing at all. We ask the question of our students all the time, in all of our locations: *Do you know someone who could use a Year Up?*

"A lot of my friends could, but they still like to party and hang out," Jim says. "They're not ready to grow up. There's someone in the program now I referred. I met another guy at Subway and I told him about it. He's been working with me to get him enrolled. I do feel obligated to give back. I'm on the alumni board. All of us graduates know what it's like out there. My role is chairman of benefits. I'm looking to see what type of discounts and benefits we can get for the students."

Strengthening our alumni network across the country is a top priority now. For an organization that preaches networking, building a long-term resource of mutually supportive graduates is a step toward security in an ever-changing job market. We make it clear: Our door is always open, as long as you need us. "Even if you didn't get a job right after graduation, Year Up is there for you," Jim says. "They follow you, pretty much through life. I feel I can talk to them anytime. I still see the friends I made there. If something happens, I'm sure we can get each other into jobs at different spots. You can be all those things to each other—good friends, colleagues, and business contacts."

Cecil Conlee sees a familiar parallel: "As HBS grads, if something happens midcareer, we pull out our yearbook and start networking. I told Gerald—the ideal outcome for Year Up is a point when a graduate says, 'Okay, I need to make a career change. Where do I go? Which Year Up alum can help?' Now our biggest source of new students is alums."

The morning after the 2008 presidential election found us gathering in New Hampshire for a staff retreat. Arrival time was extraordinary as staffers from all over the country greeted one another, some weeping with joy: A person of color was about to become leader of the free world. As it happened, *PBS NewsHour* reporter Paul Solman and his crew had arrived to film a segment about Year Up for a series on social entrepreneurs. A few times, interviewing our staff, Paul had to momentarily halt production. He kept tearing up as well.

Presenting ourselves at the White House security gate six months into the new administration's term, Shawn and I found ourselves in a similar, if much calmer, state of incredulity and hope. The Obama administration had just opened its Office of Social Innovation and Civic Participation. We were there to further the case for joint efforts between government and social entrepreneurs.

Year Up was just finding its advocacy voice in some national dialogue. Back in 2007 we had joined America Forward, an education coalition of social entrepreneurs that met with each presidential candidate during the campaign. The alliance included youth-oriented programs from Teach for America and Knowledge Is Power Program (KIPP) schools to iMentor and the "I Have a Dream" Foundation. To all of the candidates the coalition proposed creating an agency for social innovation in the White House, whatever the new administration. The most enthusiastic response had come from the Obama campaign.

Shawn and I were at the White House to speak with Michele Jolin, who, along with Sonal Shah, was designing and setting up the Social Innovation Fund and other policy tools to drive investment toward new and better solutions for our nation's most critical social problems. We explained more about Year Up and our work in the National Capital Region. A question was raised: What percentage of our student body is male? The White House was looking for a venue for a Father's Day appearance. Apparently our 63 percent male ratio appealed.

Over the next few weeks, security and administrative personnel visited our site, saying only that we might be receiving a visit from a "senior administrative official." Then I got a phone call from Tynesia, who was beside herself: "It's POTUS!" she yelled into the phone. "It's POTUS!"

It was an amazing moment, on June 19, when President Obama walked into our facility on Wilson Boulevard. All the security preparation and disruption of some classes was worth it, seeing our students' reception. As some press filed in and a tour of the classrooms was about to start, I was surprised to find myself in a room alone for a few minutes with President Obama. He asked me, "So, Gerald—why'd you start this?" How many thousands of times over the last decade had I given my own elevator speech? I kept it brief; I knew I didn't have to school a former community organizer from Chicago about the Opportunity Divide.

The message from the White House advance team had been clear: The president wanted to speak with our students on a specific issue. Press and other observers were ushered out when he sat down for a quiet word with the class before inviting their questions. He wanted to talk seriously about fatherhood, and he was frank: "A lot of young people are growing up without fathers in their houses, and as a consequence, without direction. I'm some-body who didn't have a father in my house."

Here he looked around to speak directly to the young men in the room. "Even if your father was not there, you can be there for your child—when you have one." He paused and smiled. "And it's not a bad idea to *wait* to have one until you've got your act together."

A very excited but poised student guide led President Obama on a tour of our facilities. Our guest peered into computers disassembled for study and made jokes about his own technophobias. In a couple of classrooms, the president noticed our "stop walls" and asked about them. These walls are decorated by students with much laughter and enthusiastic participation. Stop walls are another form of diversity training—a lighthearted, nonjudgmental look at the requirements of accepted workplace language. Around a red cardboard stop sign, students pin up index cards with expressions they should avoid in professional situations: *OMG. Grill. Ya mean? Booyah. Conversate. Forreal. 'Sup! Dude. Whuz good! Ax. Braw, bruh, bro. Dawg. Yo.*

A wide grin spread across President Obama's face as he read the entries. Reginald Love, then his "body man," got an admonition from his boss: "That's it, Reggie. You've got to stop calling me dawg."

CHAPTER FOURTEEN
"I Think That Woman Saved My Life"

"**H**EY, IT'S *DAVID!*"

In the hallway at our Bay Area site, students surrounded David Heredia, who had come from his home in Los Angeles for a quick visit when I was in San Francisco. They must have recognized him from a Year Up orientation video that features pictures of the two of us together over the course of twenty-plus years. The wide, expressive brown eyes are still unmistakable. So is the smile. At thirty-four, David is fit, muscular, and healthy. He and his wife, Sandra Valdovinos-Heredia, are the parents of a little girl, Josefina, now two and a half. In June 2011, they welcomed a son, David Jr. Prior to his birth, Sandra worked as the director of a residence for pregnant teenagers.

David stood chatting and completely at ease with the students who came up to him wanting to shake his hand. I smiled like a proud father when he gave a short, impromptu talk to the whole class about the power of networking and paying opportunities forward. He connected in an easy, natural way. As ever, he seemed a little embarrassed by the attention. I'm not above teasing him about his living-legend status at Year Up.

At the time, David was working through a career adjustment as an animation artist. Over the years, he had moved away from the pressured and unpredictable commerce of big studios and electronic gaming companies. He left Disney's animation department "when I was still making fifteen dollars an hour after four years, with no raises or promotions in sight." It seemed clear to him that his opportunities for advancement were limited there.

During our visit, we did a lot of talking about his career options. David assessed a few of his animation jobs after Disney. "I was doing character design for a Mel Brooks animated series. It was something that I really wanted to do, and it gave me a huge sense of accomplishment. But the project only lasted a year." He loved his stint as character designer at an electronic gaming company. "It was a sweet job. Then seventy-five percent of the company was laid off."

Most cartoon characters do have a short shelf life, and the electronic gaming market is as jumpy and unpredictable as its products. David reconsidered his ambitions. "I started thinking, 'This animation industry is brutal.' With a family, I felt I should have a backup plan. I'm interested in staying in the art field, but as an educator." He found that many teaching positions require a master's degree, which is tough to pursue at the moment with two little ones. David opted for a hybrid solution, keeping his freelance design business and teaching basic Web design skills, Photoshop, and "urban art"— graffiti style and cartooning. For a time he was also an instructor at a nonprofit called South Bay Center for Counseling. There he worked with inner-city young adults in Los Angeles, ages sixteen to twenty-four. When he was the age of his youngest students, David had no outlets for his ambitions—at least none that were sanctioned, nurtured, and supported. Back then he was busy keeping his most inspired art—that graffiti "black book"—as far as he could from teachers' eyes.

Our visit was all too short. The three thousand miles between us make it tough to arrange real face time, and I'm always glad to hear that familiar voice on the phone: "Yo, G." When I'm missing him, I sometimes go to his design Web site, which showcases his many enterprises: children's books, murals, T-shirts, and custom caricatures.

David isn't one to brag about himself, but on his site I did come across a testimonial from the director of the Boys and Girls Club of East Los Angeles, which serves young people in the largely Hispanic district long known as *el barrio*. A few years back, David painted two murals on its walls in a fresh hip-hop style. When the L.A. Lakers and the NBA contributed labor and supplies to redecorate the center, the director wrote to David, "The teens did not want the murals covered, so the Lakers had to move their wall graphics to the hallway. Your murals are still the highlight of the room."

One of these days I'm going to have the joy of sliding into a studio or classroom to watch David teach. I have no doubt he's as engaging as Year

Up's instructors—dynamic, inspired, and completely connected with his students.

Let me be clear: I wish we didn't have to exist at all. In the end, Year Up is here because of systemic failure elsewhere. We have all seen and heard the stats—the bottom line is that the United States is slipping on the international educational stage and, in so doing, reducing our level of global competitiveness. The United States has one of the highest high school dropout rates and the lowest postsecondary completion rate of any industrialized country. Combined, this has resulted in a growing skills gap and a serious mismatch between the skills our citizens have and the skills our businesses need.

If America's education and workforce-development systems functioned better, there would be much less need for what we do. We wouldn't have a situation where only a third of high school students who manage to graduate are prepared to go to college and over 40 percent are unprepared for entry-level jobs. Those statistics won't get better until we ensure that more children arrive at kindergarten ready to learn, until we prevent so many students from dropping out of high school and reduce achievement gaps between poor children of color and wealthier, largely white children. We need to realign the requirements for exiting high school with the requirements for entering college. We have to sync job-development efforts with education reform.

The college system needs an overhaul as well. Our postsecondary education system has wholly outlived its original intent, which was to educate a select few high school graduates and leave the rest to mainly low-skilled, blue-collar jobs. It was never fair, but now it's worse, since many of those jobs—from manufacturing to farming—just don't exist anymore. Millions of high school graduates are lacking the hard and soft skills to fill the entry-level jobs that are available today.

As they exist today, community colleges just can't bridge the gap. Enrollment is way up as fewer Americans can afford private schools. Yet community college students are dropping out in droves from overcrowded institutions still struggling—or unwilling—to bring relevance and applicability into their courses of study. We should be appalled that the schools providing postsecondary education for close to half of all undergraduates have a 30 percent graduation rate—and that's in three years instead of the expected two. So many students funneled into that system need resources as well as academic and personal support—the very things that large, overburdened community colleges cannot give them.

The four-year, fixed-term, residential college model is becoming more outmoded as well. More Americans now have to work while they go to school and often take much longer than four years to complete a degree. Here's a fact that I often remind people of: By age twenty-two, only one in ten adults have received a bachelor's degree. That means that *90 percent* of Americans did not follow the "standard" model in getting a four-year degree immediately following high school.

Stalemate? Hopeless? I don't think so. Nor am I going to play the blame game here. There are too many fine, dedicated educators in this country to point fingers. So many Year Up students—including Malik, Thom Moa, Greg Walton—can cite one teacher or guidance counselor who refused to give up on them or dispensed some life-changing attention and advice. I have met quite a few of these quiet heroes, especially since I accepted Governor Deval Patrick's 2008 appointment to the Massachusetts Board of Elementary and Secondary Education for a five-year term.

It was an opportunity I couldn't afford to pass up. If Year Up is going to work toward viable systems change, it made sense to look upstream and inside the complexities of a school system that serves almost a million K–12 students—in almost four hundred school districts! For an entrepreneur used to running lean, rapid-growth businesses, the glacial pace of state bureaucracy can be frustrating at times, but I have learned a good deal. As a board member I have had a seat at the table—and a voice—in conversations that hit all of the hot-button educational topics today, from the funding and operation of charter schools to union issues to the controversial legacies of No Child Left Behind.

We do field trips. Usually when board members head to a school, students and staff are on their best behavior—with the exception of one event I recall all too vividly at a school in Dorchester. Governor Patrick was with us. We were taking a tour, visiting a science lab, and speaking with students and teachers. As we were walking from the classroom to the auditorium, the bell rang. Within fifteen seconds all heck broke loose. The halls were jammed wall to wall with a rising tide of very loud, somewhat threatening, jostling students.

I had visited plenty of high schools in the same area since the start of Year Up, but that moment made me stop and think. It was clear that the students didn't know or care who we were—the chief executive of their state was trying to maintain his footing and his composure with the rest of us. I couldn't imagine why the adults in charge would allow that kind of intimidating, chaotic hallway culture to persist. I was reminded of Kweku Forstall's comments on the lack of accountability that his nonprofit tried to counter in the Atlanta public school system. Since then, I've asked many Year Up students if they ever enjoyed that hallway culture. Every last one of them has said no, and that they wished it hadn't been that way.

Cut to a scene of tremendous academic privilege a few miles from that Dorchester school. Almost two decades after I graduated from Harvard Business School, I crossed its campus on a frigid December day to receive a Year Up report card of sorts. Our program was being analyzed as a business case in Professor Allen Grossman's class on social entrepreneurship. It would be feedback writ large. Allen is a professor of management practice and a leading thinker on scaling nonprofits. He has been an adviser to Year Up for several years. Allen thinks in terms of large-scale models, but I knew that morning he and his students would sweat the details as well.

It was encouraging that Year Up was positioned as a "capstone case," intended to highlight an organization that uses effective practices taught in the course. Students would evaluate and critique our performance on some key areas: vision, sustainability, board composition, operational performance, and leadership. Kate—rightly introduced by Allen as Year Up's cofounder—took a seat beside me at the front of a perfectly lit, acoustically engineered classroom with three mechanized chalkboards, tiered seating, and high-end recording equipment for documenting lectures.

Managing those devices and their software was Edgardo "Eggy" Rodriguez—a Year Up intern! It was another of those sweet, affirming moments that sustain the long-haul social entrepreneur. Before he set up for class, Edgardo had told me how he came to Year Up: Greg Walton. They go way back, to school and ball fields. His friend Greg's incarceration had grieved Edgardo, but they had reconnected afterward, and soon Edgardo watched the transformation and success of his friend doing so well across the river at MIT.

"I told Greg I'd sure like some of that. And here I am."

Edgardo was monitoring digital sound levels in the control room as class began. It didn't take Allen long to get to leadership evaluations. "Gerald keeps saying that his goal is to replace himself. What is evidence to you that Gerald manages his ego? This is an important element in leadership. I want to unpack this."

As the class unfolded my professional laundry, they didn't hang me out to dry. Their evaluation pretty well matched my own job description: I'm no savior and never set myself up as one. Nobody can claim authorship of a movement that has its roots in historic injustice. Smart social entrepreneurs understand that they are just relay runners. I hope I'll recognize the precise moment to pass the baton. I'm fortunate to do work that I love, but I will also knock myself out to build a strong, sustainable organization that can render me redundant.

I was relieved when the class focus shifted from Gerald's ego—adequately managed, thank you—to the more critical area of team management. One young man offered: "There's a strong culture of performance. I think they're hiring really exceptional people with strong business backgrounds. They're also incentivizing people based on performance."

It was a civil, enlightening hour—no huge negatives, no big surprises for me, until another student volunteered how she found Year Up distinct from some other nonprofits they had studied: "I think something that's important here is the ability to create a sense of urgency—the mission to close the Opportunity Divide rather than just providing the services. You can see that when they were going out to raise the eighteen million dollars of capital. Gerald is dissatisfied with the way traditional nonprofits go about it. He feels it's necessary to achieve the mission in as timely a way as possible, actually saying, 'We're going to close the Opportunity Divide,' in very specific terms."

That was the key takeaway for me. Critical minds had pored over spreadsheets, staff and student interviews, our IPO, and prospectus, and they heard us: We're not kidding—we're really going to do this.

The good professor summed it up: "Embedded in this organization at all levels: We're going to go after root causes and redefine what success looks like. Serving three thousand? They say no. They say it's called the Year Up revolution—that they're actually going to shift what's happening in America. This is a really *presumptuous* kind of statement for a nonprofit to make."

I'm proud to hang on to those presumptions. I was even more gratified when the last word in the class went to Edgardo, who was called on to address the class and take their questions. Our intern let it be known that six months earlier, they would have seen him dive through one of those sleek, double-glazed, noise-reducing windows rather than face a room full of top-flight grad students. "They get you to come out of your comfort level and be able to speak in front of different people," he told them. "I could *never* have done public speaking."

Applause.

His dislikes? Edgardo wasn't keen on dressing up at first and just hated the infractions—until he decided not to earn them. "Also, I did *not* like getting feedback. That was one of the hardest things, but you adjust to it. I was taught that feedback would make you grow. I use it now, not just for Year Up but in life, with my coworkers, friends, family.

"The staff does a good job on placing you in internships, as to your personality, your work ethic, motivation. I worked very hard. I've seen the success of people coming out of this program. I see how hard they work. I see them buying a house, car, getting a great job. Students that fire themselves probably didn't see what I got to see."

He was speaking of Greg Walton, of course. I wish Greg had been there to see his friend holding forth. The students gave Edgardo more warm applause, and several came up to him afterward with congratulations and more questions. Then he went back to work, checking on the recording and sending it to a digital archive. At a button's touch, the chalkboards rearranged themselves silently and a maintenance worker erased Allen's Year Up dissection before the next class. Jottings on "Founder and CEO Gerald" vanished, as they should.

As I watched the students leave, I thought of the Year Up leaders who had found their way to us from this campus and wondered if anyone in this class would hop the divide and join us.

I drove downtown to work feeling pretty good about Edgardo's prospects. I would learn later that Harvard was able to hire him only as a contract worker after graduation, and for a limited period. Since he had a family, Edgardo was working a second job as well, until a serious car accident took him out of commission in the fall of 2011. He recovered but had to begin his job search again. We've had a number of successful students temporarily derailed by illness, downsizing, redundancies, "last hired first fired." Most land on their feet quickly.

But what if they don't? Where can they turn?

Our doors are always open, but we can't know where all the jobs are.

For some time I've been concerned about our underutilizing what could be a tremendous resource for graduates like Edgardo. By 2010 there were almost a thousand Year Up alums in the Boston area. Many were well employed and would have been more than willing to reach out and help Edgardo reconnect. There's no reason our students and graduates can't have a matrix like those generous Harvard alums in the Partners of '63.

The networking potential of our alums was very much on my mind the first time I spoke to Alan Weiss on the phone from his Florida home. Al is a tech pioneer who led the team that built the largest and fastest part of the Internet. He took his business profits and invested them in social entrepreneurs who he feels can make a lasting impact on society. He had a pretty basic question for me: "What do you *really* need money to do?"

I told him, "We need funds to invest in building an alumni association called Life After Year Up." Al came to Boston to speak with our students and consider our plans for building this alumni engine. He committed half a million dollars to develop postgraduation support and services. Already, in Boston, an online newsletter supervised by Nicole Hart, our higher-education specialist, is helping students, interns, and alumni connect. The first edition of that newsletter, *Higher Ed News,* featured recent Year Up college graduates, listed upcoming scholarships to apply for, and announced a free multilevel math class open to all—especially those wishing to avoid remedial math requirements in college. The newsletter also lists visits by college representatives, along with their profiles. At a time when the question *Now what?* looms more ominously for graduates everywhere—from the most prestigious private colleges to our own urban workforce—postgraduate services and networking simply have to improve.

Where do we go from our current nine-city presence? At the end of 2009, long before those graduate students picked up on Year Up's "urgency of mission," we had begun an extended process to plan the next phase of our strategy with a single question in mind: What can we do to maximize our social impact? Our next five-year plan (spanning 2012 to 2016) was the result of a year's collaborative process. We had input from our local and national boards, major donors, and the pro bono services of Monitor Group, a top-flight strategy consultant. Our entire staff was invited to share ideas in conference calls with me directly and with the rest of our team. We talked with more than fifty experts in the field. By the end, we had Year Up and its stakeholders aligned around a clear strategy. We also had our next IPO document and an increased price tag—$55 million.

Over the next five years, Year Up has committed to three major initiatives that include growing our core model, piloting more scalable alternative models, and continuing to influence systemic change. At this writing, we are more than halfway toward raising the $55 million, thanks in large part to a core of loyal donors like Jon and Joanna Jacobson, Josh and Anita Bekenstein, and the Jensen family, who have kept the wind in our sails with generous, catalytic gifts at critical points in our growth. Despite the economic downturn, almost everyone who invested in our first growth capital campaign has stepped forward to help us in our next stage of growth. They have seen our past and current results. They were presented with a detailed prospectus on exactly how their capital would be invested. With their help, we intend to push harder at closing the divide in the following ways.

Grow and Strengthen the Core

Through growth at existing sites and the opening of new sites in Chicago and Seattle, we raised the number of students served to over thirteen hundred in 2011. Once again we stuck to our guns and waited until we found the right person to launch and lead each site. In Chicago we hired Alan Anderson, a former Motorola engineer turned education reformer, who had distinguished himself as a leader in the Chicago public school system under Education Secretary Arne Duncan. For our Seattle site (called Year Up Puget Sound), we found Lisa Chin, whose background includes a PhD from UCLA, twenty years of program management experience, most recently at Amazon, and a stint as the executive director of a transitional housing provider for homeless women.

As in all cities, our success was fueled by local individuals who decided to put their Rolodexes and reputations on the line to help us get started. What Tim Dibble did for me back in 2000 these local board members do for our executive directors today. John Stanton is one of the world's top wireless entrepreneurs. As board chairman for Seattle, he picked up the phone for us and put together a powerful board that includes, among others, that city's former mayor, the founder of Expedia and Zillow, the Pacific Northwest chairperson of JPMorgan Chase, and the King County sheriff. By 2016 we will deepen our presence in our existing cities and open programs in three more, allowing us to serve a total of twenty-five hundred students per year.

Develop a Million-Person Model

We are in the process of designing and piloting, in partnership with community colleges, alternative program models that can ultimately scale to serve more than one hundred thousand students each year. We see ourselves partnering closely with those colleges to provide students with what they need most—academic, financial, and social/emotional support and local labor market attachment. Through these efforts we will increase graduation rates and create more successful transitions into the labor market. We have college partnerships in all of our host cities now, with transferable credits for course work completed satisfactorily at Year Up.

In June 2011 we presented one incarnation of the Million Person Model at the Clinton Global Initiative America conference. We call it the Professional Training Corps (PTC), and it will be modeled after the Reserve Officers' Training Corps (ROTC). The main differences are that PTC will be housed in our nation's community colleges and students will swap fatigues for business dress. As a school within a school, PTC can tailor curriculum, internships, and guidance/support services in a way that the larger community colleges often cannot.

Simply put, PTC will connect young adults with living-wage employment and professional training *while they attend college*. During their first year, PTC students will take classes full time. The following summer and fall, they will transition to part-time school while they gain work experience with PTC employer partners paying for their services. They'll get everything that our current students do: professional skills training, stipends, direct connection to the local labor market. It's a big idea and it is gaining traction in some very influential circles nationally.

Work Toward Systems Change

Access to career and college opportunities is still out of reach for far too many young adults. We will continue our work to influence systems at both the national and local levels. One example: Year Up is promoting a tax credit for employers who provide internships and job opportunities to disconnected young adults. We are also currently involved in shaping broader coalition-building movements with other like-minded nonprofits.

So there it is. We will put our shoulders to the Million Person Model, build out more sites, and continue to dream big. We will do so in partnership with the most forward-thinking organizations in this country. We will measure our results carefully and support our graduates as they build and expand their own alumni network.

Already our graduates are becoming leaders in business and in their communities. They will record the legacy of their own years up in deeper, richer ways than I have here. There are poets in our ranks, young men and women who have the drive and the talent to fill notebooks—stacks of them—with their reflections, aspirations, and struggles. Some of them reduce us to cheers and tears in class and at graduation through spoken word. You can also meet representatives of Year Up Nation, just talking, online. They look squarely into YouTube lenses and describe their journeys. They dream out loud. Better still, they have begun to pay it forward.

We've never had any doubt: Our students will become an increasingly powerful force for economic and social justice. We have such exceptional graduates willing and able to turn on the power. Grassroots change happens at a community level. The first time I really understood this was when a group of Year Up students decided on their own to teach a ten-session course called "How to Use a Computer" to elderly residents in a housing project.

Grassroots change will come from our students. They will take the best of Year Up with them back into their communities and the nation. I see it happen every day.

This is the last story I'm going to tell, because I think it shows the direction of our future. Kern Williams is someone who might have been counted out—way out—by conventional standards. Kern was twenty-two when he was admitted to Year Up in March 2009. He certainly seemed motivated; he applied three times before he finally obtained the documents we require. When he was eight, he and his brother had come to Boston from their native Trinidad to join their mother and sister. As he grew up, there were long-standing documentation issues. His family was in deportation proceedings when he first tried to apply to Year Up.

The matter was finally resolved, and Kern showed up again on Summer Street the very day he got his Social Security number. He had heard about the program through a friend and fellow graduate, Adtuwne Kelley, who interned at Brown Brothers Harriman and is now a senior fund accountant there. I have to smile when I look at Kern's admissions photo in our database. His head is tilted back, chin up, making for a somewhat cocky effect.

Kern had very little money to step up to professional dress, and he was glad for the donated suits, jackets, and shirts we keep in stock at Year Up.

He was assigned to me as a mentee. I can still see him in the sharp navy double-breasted pin-striped suit he was most fond of wearing. The shoulders and cuffs were a bit large for his slim frame, but Kern had the presence to carry it off. When we sat down for the first time, he convinced me that he was hypermotivated to make a change. He talked about making a difficult turn in his young life.

"I had that dilemma of choosing between the right and wrong path in high school," Kern says. "I had experiences on both sides. Okay, the wrong one's not going to work in the long run, but it's not easy to transition to the right path."

With his immigration issues, he knew his career opportunities would be severely limited. In his first two years at Brighton High School, Kern had been trending toward the wrong kind of street commerce. "With no Social Security number, I was going to make money any way I saw fit. I got involved in street life, staying out late, partying, drinking, all those crazy things. My mom was torn up by it. I put her through a lot. My mom, she's my heart. I'm working all the time now to try and repay all that I put her through. I can't take all those times back."

Then came Ms. Monica J. Smalls.

As a junior at Brighton, Kern was in Ms. Smalls's business education class on entrepreneurship. Kern threw himself into an assigned project, creating a theoretical start-up company. He built a business plan for an agency providing services to aging baby boomers, from grocery shopping to home companionship. He had researched his demographics and anticipated their needs. Ms. Smalls saw some natural talent. She also convinced him of a possibility he hadn't dreamed of.

"She made us realize that you can make money doing something you really love," Kern recalls. "And I was in love with *that*. Business and entrepreneurship just looked so much more promising than the other little hustles."

Ms. Smalls's class was part of the NFTE (Network for Teaching Entrepreneurship) program, a nonprofit that works with schools in low-income communities. As its mission statement explains, when young people are given the opportunity to learn about entrepreneurship, basic street smarts can easily develop into academic and business smarts. Students discover that what they are learning in the classroom is indeed relevant to the real world.

"You may not want to start a business," Ms. Smalls explains. "But we want to teach you how to be entrepreneurial, how to look at a problem and see a business opportunity. Can you turn the change that's going on around us into an opportunity? And Kern learned how to do that."

She noticed a huge change in him by midyear. "He placed first in the business fair competition, and I often used him in working with other students on their business plans because he was so zealous in doing his, doing the research, talking with the business mentor the program connected him with. His classmates saw a transformation as well. They saw that he was serious. They started asking him for suggestions and help."

Part of the NFTE program sends students to wholesale markets—in this case, in midtown New York City. They buy goods at wholesale prices, bring them home, and learn to market them. By permit, NFTE students are allowed to sell the likes of hats, gloves, and scarves to dashing commuters at Boston's South Station. Kern found the exercise so engaging and lucrative, he took to doing it on his own. Picture him, glistening with sweat as he struggled to tote huge plastic bags of sneakers, bags, and clothes in Manhattan's garment district back to the bus stop. "One way was fifteen dollars on the Chinese bus. You gotta do what you gotta do."

He and Ms. Smalls got to know each other well. They talked on the long bus rides to New York and when she gave him rides home. "At the point I met her," Kern recalls, "it was 'What are you going to do?' I'm involved in all these other things. Business and entrepreneurship just came along and looked so much more promising than what you'd call street commerce. She helped me make the turn. Ms. Smalls, she's Mama. Her kids are like my little brothers. I think that woman saved my life."

His teacher recalls one especially difficult day on the job, about midway through the class that Kern was in. She has taught at Brighton High for nearly twenty years, and she has always believed that practical, entrepreneurial skills were *exactly* what low-income urban students needed. So many of them had such odds stacked against them. She was having "one of those discouraging moments" when she checked her e-mail before leaving work.

"Kern sent me an e-mail, just to say thank you. He did say, 'You saved my life.' One of his friends had just been murdered, and he was thinking about where he would be if he hadn't had the class and hadn't had a change of mind-set. It had been a tough, tough day, and I said, 'That's why I'm here;

that's why I do what I do.' Oh my *goodness.*
that day."

Even after Kern's graduation, he was a willing
field trips. On the bus to New York one day, he stunned
out a photo of his baby daughter.

"You have *what?*"

When she recovered from the surprise, they discussed
tions. The pressures on him—being a new father, contributing to
support, fretting over the deportation issues—were much greater. He
have made some quick money in "alternative" commerce. But he to
Ms. Smalls, as he later told me, he had finally made his turn and said "later"
to the wrong kinds of neighborhood entrepreneurs.

Kern tells me he had made the mental turn well before he entered our
program. I could see that was true. "I had been working on myself a lot, reading, thinking. I had already decided I'm not going to be a regular student at
Year Up, just doing enough to get by. I'm going to knock this thing out of the
park and take advantage of everything they put in front of me."

He did just that, and I'm not sure how he managed, given his obligations
at the time. "I was also working at a shoe company doing customer service.
I'd be at Year Up from eight to three thirty, leave, get to work for a four-
thirty-to-midnight shift. I'm answering the customer service phone, doing
my Year Up homework. It was crazy. I slept four or five hours—for months.
And I still had to be a dad." Kern did his internship at State Street and was
hired immediately afterward as a fund analyst. He is still there and doing
well. He referred two other friends to Year Up who have graduated and are
employed. Imare, his daughter, is now three and has him "totally wrapped"
around her tiny finger. Her daddy is also now on the board for Year Up
Boston, the first graduate so appointed.

A project Kern has been passionate about for some time—mentoring in
urban areas—has now been brought to fruition as Mentor Corps. It's part of
our new commitment to capitalizing on our ever-increasing new resources:
Year Up Alumni Association. In 2010 a Year Up donor, Phill Gross, challenged us to mobilize the Boston alumni network of more than one thousand
young adults to help younger members of their community make positive
choices. If we developed a viable program, he would fund it. In January 2011
a group of alums, including Kern, and staff members, guided by Executive

...ro, worked on a format that would match alumni
Director Cas... ...ouths twelve to fourteen years old through a partner-
mentors wit... ...others Big Sisters and the Year Up Boston Alumni Asso-
ship betwe... ...our alums to run and sustain the program.
ciation. It... ...orps is a more powerful version of something Kern had
Me... ...to fine-tune on his own. "For a while, with a few friends, I've
been t... ...toring three youths, ages fourteen, fifteen, and sixteen. We were
just ... ...ching them to think in a different way about 'What do I want to do
w... ...h my life?' I wanted to take my peer mentoring program and really grow
...t. I worked a bit with Linda [Swardlick Smith] here and started recruiting
mentees, trying to create a pilot with a little more structure. I wanted to
bring the age down and focus early on building wealth through positive
means.

"Look, these kids understand money. We use it every day, yet schools
never teach us about it. They see and hear me now—good job, in the suit
and all—and say, 'You must have grown up in Brookline or Newton or
something.' I tell them, 'No I didn't. I understand where you're coming from.
I was there a few years ago. So let's really *talk* about your options—right
now.'"

Kern's friend Adtuwne Kelley is a part of Mentor Corps as well. They
both appear in a Year Up video about their start-up. I was knocked out the
first time I watched it. Kern's well-cut suit fit him perfectly. He can buy them
himself now. His shoulder-length hair is impeccably braided, looped, and
tied back. Talking straight into the camera, Kern could easily be a telecom
CEO—something he's still got in mind. Sometimes, when a work colleague
or a thirteen-year-old mentee asks why he wears a suit so much, he has a
ready answer: "I'm dressing for where I want to be, not where I am today."

EPILOGUE
Wheels Up for Opportunity

Wednesday, July 27, 2011

It was Class Nine's last morning together in Brooklyn—ever. No more PDW, *later* on those PowerPoints. Infractions? *¡Adiós!* There was a brief rehearsal for graduation, followed by a reassuring mingle with Class Ten, about to head off on their internships.

"AmEx is the bomb. You'll be fine."

"You got Bloomberg too? We need to talk. No, don't worry. It's all good."

Outside, in the growing shadow of a huge condo building going up on DeKalb Avenue—the "new" downtown Brooklyn had been rising around us all these months—there were fierce hugs and some tears behind hastily slipped-on shades.

Marisol's ivory chiffon graduation dress was ready on its hanger at home; her son, Manuel, was excited about being taken out of day care to attend. The twins were planning travel logistics for the 8:00 a.m. ceremony. (The early hour works for a lot of Wall Street folks.) Their aunt would be there, along with their younger brother Jean-Luc, their father and his new wife, and maybe a mentor or two. Taleisha was looking forward to graduation as well. Of necessity, she was already looking past the celebration, scanning the online job listings and tweaking her résumé. Jared would be starting prekindergarten in a public school in a couple of months. She needed to line up doctor checkups for him, a job for herself, and an after-school program to make it all work. "It's a little hectic," she said.

For the last couple of weeks, as his plans finalized, Malik had carried a creased, much-perused printout of his financial aid package—a combination of Pell grants and loans—along with a list of his first semester's courses at an upstate branch of the State University of New York. To help defray expenses, UBS had extended his paid internship until late August when it was time to leave for school. Provided he kept his GPA up in college, the bank would have him back to work in the summers in its fellowship program, a big help toward tuition, books, and expenses.

As his plan came together, Malik was feeling very glad that he had paid close attention in pro skills for all its cues on workplace behavior, networking, follow-up e-mails, and elevator chat. He had listened closely to Tiffany Cummings, the outstanding Year Up graduate at UBS who counseled interns on "branding" themselves. In his six months on the job, Malik had acquired a college ID number, the opportunity for continued employment, and his own polite brand of workplace diplomacy. Shaking his head at his good fortune, Malik dropped another of the trademark sayings that always cracked up his colleagues: "If you don't learn the soft skills, you fall hard."

That same Wednesday morning, I was out of the house at 4:45 a.m. for a predawn flight from Logan Airport, the start of my weeklong, coast-to-coast marathon of Year Up graduations. I planned to attend most of them: First I'd drop in at our pilot community college program in Baltimore for its first graduation, then D.C., New York, and Boston in a single day, then on to our new site in Chicago, and finally San Francisco. The logistics were a bit punishing, but it always reinvigorates me to applaud and congratulate the students I've met at the outset of their year up. I'll be honest: I need it. Twice a year, graduation week is a chance for me to enjoy a full portion of absolute emotion. I cry at every graduation, but I'm not ashamed. As Tim Dibble always says, "Gerald, if we ever stop crying, it's time for us to step down."

As my plane boarded, I tapped at my BlackBerry for our latest numbers as these graduating classes headed toward their futures. By September 2011, we had served over five thousand students since our beginning in 2001. Not exactly McDonald's "billions served." But I also like to mentally click through a set of postgraduate "exponentials" that have now been set in motion. Think about it: How many of those five thousand have—and will have—children who will now grow up in a home above the poverty line? How many brothers, cousins, sisters, and friends will apply in their footsteps? How many hearts and minds have adjusted their perception of our urban young adults? How many businesses, some of which are still employing Year Up graduates ten years out, will come back to us again and again with those heavenly words: *We want more?* I am optimistic enough to ask myself now: In five years, how close will Year Up be to realizing our Million Person Model?

Scanning the early headlines that morning, I was brought back to earth by the unsettled economic climate that our new graduates were heading into. Job growth had been weak in May and June. Greece was teetering on bankruptcy, and Italy, Spain, and Portugal were threatening to follow suit. The tense, ugly standoff in Congress over raising the national debt ceiling had come to a furious partisan boil. The deadline for an agreement to avoid historic national default was August 2—Class Nine's graduation day.

My first stop was Baltimore, where seventeen thousand disconnected young adults need a Year Up. Just a few weeks earlier, I had asked a staff member to hop in a cab with me for a quick tour of East Baltimore, where some of those thousands live. If you were a fan of that gritty HBO series *The Wire,* you might have some idea of the devastation there: block after block of trashed and abandoned row houses, some pocked by bullet holes, with no viable commerce, just a liquor store or sad, bare-bones deli. Wary-looking residents walk briskly between doorways. It's so much like a war zone, I was reminded of news footage from Baghdad or Kandahar.

Over two hundred Baltimoreans showed up at a downtown hotel to cheer the fifteen students graduating from our first College Based Pilot Program in partnership with the Community College of Baltimore County (CCBC) and ably led by the pilot's director, Hamid Elaissami. The graduates had aced their internships at the likes of Johns Hopkins University and Morgan Stanley. Final college grades were in: Year Up students performed better overall than the rest of the students in their CCBC classes. Eighty percent went on to employment and/or college; one was offered a position with a salary potential of sixty thousand dollars at a high-security financial institution. The other 20 percent were still looking for employment and enrolling in college for spring 2012. For us, that's more than enough reason to persist; we have begun a partnership with Baltimore City Community College and plan to serve many, many more.

Standing at graduation, the men wearing bespoke Year Up ties, those fifteen were trailblazers for our Million Person Model. I was tweeting photos like mad.

Friday, July 29

As my taxi headed toward Arlington, I was thinking of the memorable spring day I had had in Washington with members of our national board, Tynesia, and some of our NCR staff. We'd enjoyed a White House tour in the company of Julius Black and Tiara Palmer, two Year Up graduates who were then working as White House interns. I couldn't stop smiling. I could hardly believe it. I'd love to say that Year Up placed them, but we have no affiliation with the White House, and these aren't corporate internships. Julius and Tiara won their spots entirely on their own. Neither even knew the other had applied. As part of the application, Julius wrote the required policy statement on an education issue; his personal essay was about serving in homeless shelters with his grandfather, a church deacon. Julius had been working in the office of First Lady Michelle Obama on her Let's Move initiative for children's fitness. When the internship was over, he had an IT job waiting for him at Acumen Solutions, a leading technology consulting firm. He had done his Year Up internship there; his manager was fine with releasing him a couple of weeks early to take the White House spot.

A class of fifty-six was graduating that steamy summer day. As the ceremony began, I looked over at Tynesia as she watched the final graduating class under her leadership. She was all smiles, though not in her customary front-and-center spot. Two months earlier, Ronda Harris Thompson, her second in command, had transitioned smoothly into the ED position. I couldn't have been happier for Ty, who was taking our mission to the next level.

Call it enlightened capitalism. She has started a HUBZone business called Reliance Methods that will place Year Up graduates and other qualified workers in technical positions. "HUB" stands for "Historically Underutilized Business" Zones, areas where many of our students live. HUBZone is a Small Businesses Administration program for companies that operate and employ people in those underserved areas.

Tynesia's new company has a well-designed Web page emblazoned with a self-defining motto: *Sustainable Solutions . . . Sustaining Communities.* The firm will use Year Up graduates as manpower in a for-profit enterprise, selling desktop support to government offices and other civic-minded businesses looking for skilled, prescreened, workplace-tested technical personnel drawn from their own communities.

It makes such perfect sense. You'd better believe that Ty has crunched the data, built a rock-solid business plan, and, after her hundreds of corporate meetings on behalf of our interns, accrued the respect and connections that any smart start-up needs. She will make it work, brokering more jobs for more of our graduates. I wouldn't be surprised if she expands, as Year Up has, to other cities in need of such vital connections. A direct job pipeline in every Year Up city would be fantastic.

Tuesday, August 2

Finally it was Class Nine's big day. Kate and I caught the 6:00 a.m. shuttle from Boston to New York. Some of our students would start out earlier than we did to make it to the eight o'clock start time. That morning our graduates were coming by commuter rail, bus, and subway from Ridgewood, New Jersey, and East Flatbush, Brooklyn; from Harlem; Astoria, Queens, and Pelham Parkway in the Bronx. It was the last time for their very familiar commutes.

Graduation was at Cipriani on Wall Street, just two blocks from Year Up's offices. That grand old bank building has been converted into a tasteful party space. We have held most of our ceremonies and some fund-raisers there. I love seeing students' families and friends walk in and smile as they look around at the vaulted ceilings and massive chandeliers. It's a venue respectful of their children's achievements, and it's a sweet repurposing: Where old money prospered, a skilled and diverse new workforce goes forth.

A volunteer usher from Class Ten handed us the day's printed program with student profiles and photos. The booklets had a reassuring thickness; 90 of the original 126 had made it through L & D and internships—more than twice the 30 percent average graduation rate for community colleges nationwide.

Class Nine looked terrific—even better than on their first day in September when our photographer caught their expectant smiles on the steps of Federal Hall. Some students were too keyed up to sample the fruit, pastries, and coffee set up on the balcony during the meet-and-greet period before the ceremony. Others dove into the buffet, as voracious young adults will. Students chatted easily with power-suited men and women wearing name tags from JPMorgan Chase, UBS, Google, American Express, the National Football League, Bloomberg, Deutsche Bank, GE Capital, and Bank of America.

Up on the balcony, Malik rushed over when he spied Dr. Tait, the Harlem community organizer who had steered him to Year Up. Malik shared a little fact that Mariah Peebles, our FAO Schwarz Fellow in charge of outreach, had just passed on to him. "Dr. Tait, Mariah checked her calendar— it's exactly a year *today* that I was at the Year Up outreach session you sent me to." That worthy gentleman, perhaps remembering his dismay when Malik had shown up in shorts and a polo shirt as "proper attire," took in the graduate's suit, the expertly knotted tie.

"Some difference a year up makes, hmm? And I *don't* just mean the suit."

Shortly it would be Mariah's honor to present Dr. Tait and his Harlem Commonwealth Council with our Community Ambassador Award for their continuing effort to connect neighborhood youth with education and job-development programs. They cast a wide and sometimes lifesaving net for us uptown. Malik built his college application essay around the stages of a butterfly's chrysalis. An internship colleague had counseled him to write the essay about his privations and his brother's death. "He was trying to help me," Malik says, "but I wasn't going for the sympathy vote. To me, making the mind-set turn, the transformation, was the right thing to focus on."

At eight thirty on the dot, Giovanna Serrano, the morning's mistress of ceremonies, stepped up to the podium to deliver her welcome. She is a graduate of Class Eight. After graduation, she worked at American Express, then at New York University Medical Center. She introduced Kenneth Austin, the newly hired executive director of Year Up New York.

Lisette had given us her promised five years; we had held a farewell party with staff and students back in February. We had been looking for her replacement for four months, since the night Lisette called to tell me that she would be leaving for a set of new challenges. She had been appointed to the White House Initiative on Educational Excellence for Hispanics. She has also accepted a visiting professorship teaching public policy at the City University of New York at Brooklyn College.

Class Nine's ceremony was a joyful, friends-and-family celebration, as it always is. There are always student speakers, and they are always the stars. I've seen steely CFOs and traders lose it and families group hug until their graduates could barely breathe. Mentors and white-haired *abuelas* dissolve as young women cradle infants in one arm and reach for their diplomas with the other. A towering six-and–a-half-footer lifts his petite mother off the ground in a bear hug.

We did it. We really did.

As the proceedings came to a close, camera flashes haloed the family groups clustered around their graduates in the aisles. Jean-Luc, the twins' younger brother, was standing arm in arm with his aunt—their late mother's sister. They agreed, Odette would have been dancing down the aisle to see this day. As Devon had said during his Milestones recitation, Jean-Luc was the one who had harangued his brothers to try Year Up. "I almost had to put them in a double headlock and shove their faces at the Web site," Jean-Luc said. "I love them too much to see them drift off to . . . nothing." Told that Devon had given his "little brother" an emotional shout-out during Class Nine's Milestones, Jean-Luc was quiet for a moment. "It helps me to know that," he said. "It helps me a lot."

Taleisha came to graduation alone. Her brother had moved away. Jared stayed in day care, since there was no one to watch him before and during the ceremony. She stood smiling amid a tight circle of friends.

Earlier, Malik's father had done a quick drive-by in his cab. He wanted to manage at least a curbside salute to his son's achievement, since he could not take time off from work. His mother, just back from Gambia, was a bright spot amid all the dark suits, dressed in flowing pink robes beneath a crown of braids and a beautiful smile.

"All these months, I hear 'Year Up,' 'Year Up.' It was hard to know exactly what it is. But I saw my son, so changed. I watched him work. He showed me on the computer what UBS is, where he went on the train every day." She remembered all too well the barrage of calls from elementary school teachers, her fears for him during high school. She looked over her shoulder at Malik, surrounded by classmates in the aisle. "These are *good* friends he has now," she said. "They only want success for each other."

During the ceremony, when Malik had stood with four other classmates to receive a thousand-dollar scholarship from the Partners of '63, his mother had craned to see that wide smile she knew so well. "I cannot find words for that moment. It was a mother's happiness. It was very deep for me."

Marisol's mother was smiling too, as she unfolded her grandson's stroller. Manuel had already begged to change out of his shiny dress shoes. He was exhausted and a little dazed by the proceedings, and she would take him home to Washington Heights so that Marisol could celebrate afterward with a group of her friends. They would end up at IHOP—after all, it was early. "The place doesn't matter," Marisol said. "I love these people. I still can't believe I won't be with them every day. I know we'll be in touch. I was so nowhere, just drifting. They lifted me."

Tyrone, a fellow graduate, had tickled Manuel into a fit of giggles. "Marisol, what a cool little dude."

Jarrod Lacks, Damien's magazine editor mentor, had him by the shoulders. "Stay in touch—or I'll hunt you down. You know I will."

When Kate and I got back to Boston a couple of hours later and regrouped for that graduation, I ran into Kern Williams. He had come to this graduation as a member of Year Up Boston's board, and just to enjoy. We caught up and surveyed the size of the event; over nine hundred Bostonians came to celebrate in a huge hotel space at Copley Place. Another decade and we might need to rent Fenway Park.

August 4–5

The final lap: Chicago's first graduation. The late-afternoon ceremony was another beautifully disproportionate event. A dozen and a half graduates and a couple of hundred proud supporters in another fine "old money" club room for our new workforce. Same time, next day: San Francisco. Outside the ballroom at the Merchants Exchange Building, students and families were milling around waiting for the ceremony to start. I struck up a conversation with one graduate and asked him how his internship experience had been. He hesitated for a moment. I had introduced myself, and I think he might have been reluctant to disappoint the founder.

"Really, tell me. I'd like to know how it went."

"Kinda bittersweet," he told me, and explained. He was getting a tour of the office on his first day on the job when he overheard one employee say to another: "Look who's coming. Better watch your wallet." That's more than an ouch—it's an ice pick to the heart.

The student said that he found it hard to go there every day afterward. He persevered. It turned out to be a terrific company despite one imbecile. I was still thinking about the strength of that intern that night as I headed east on a red-eye flight toward sunrise in Boston. I had a full schedule of meetings when I landed, but my part is easy. From coast to coast, the week's graduates, who had worked so hard for so long, were waking up in varying stages of "Now what?"

Like any other, Class Nine has had its share of terrific outcomes and quieter, ongoing searches. On average it takes four months past graduation to see the majority of a class settled in school or employment. We were thrilled when two young men from the class were enrolled in Syracuse University on the JPMorgan Chase scholarship program.

Two months past graduation, Taleisha's life had gotten a bit more complicated. When school started, Jared was classified as a special-needs child, with some language and behavioral issues. School administrators wanted to put him in a smaller class of only special-needs students in another school. Taleisha thought it might help—but that class was for only half days, with no after-school program. How could she work? While she pondered her options, Charmaine connected her with a staffer whose child had undergone similar issues.

By late September, Damien was networking as best he could, sending out résumés and scanning online job sites. In late October, a friend informed him that JPMorgan Chase, the bank he had interned with, was interviewing for jobs at a Brooklyn hotel. Damien suited up and took his place in the long lines at the appointed time. He made it to the second round. "I did thank God for Year Up," he said after the first interview. And when he called me a few days later with the good news—he got the job as a research specialist—Damien wanted me to know how he deployed his pro skills.

"May I be bold?" he asked his interviewer afterward. "Would you mind giving me some feedback on how I handled that?"

She laughed and said that she was happy to oblige. She told Damien, "You stayed on topic. You had great eye contact. And it's clear you've got a good head for this work."

Of course he aced the test for his IT skills and financial knowledge. Once it was known that he had interned with the company, his former manager provided an enthusiastic endorsement. When he got the call saying he was hired and needed to report for his "onboard," Damien said, "I'll admit it, I was crying. I said, 'Thank you, God.'" The location was another gift. He is working at Metrotech Center in downtown Brooklyn, an easy commute and very close to our Year Up site and some community colleges. "I'm doing it all," he told me. "I'm going to settle into work and try and start school in January."

Damien watched with interest, pride, and some concern as his brother gathered the documentation and submitted to a battery of tests and interviews to qualify him as a U.S. Marine. Devon passed all with ease and must have sounded properly motivated in the Corps interviews, which are notoriously tough. Then surprising news came from the recruiter; new inductions were temporarily frozen. Devon regrouped and began a job search.

In early October Marisol e-mailed that finally "exciting things" had begun to happen. She had begun work as a desktop support technician at EmblemHealth, a New York State insurance company; its downtown offices are very close to Year Up. She hopes to enroll in college once she and Manuel have been able to move to a safer neighborhood. "And I've met someone," she reported. He works for a law firm and does IT work there as well. They started talking in a movie line and have not stopped.

Malik had settled into his upstate New York dorm with two roommates. His branch of the state university system was three hours north of Manhattan. He tried to plan his move-in by bus or gypsy cab—no way was that working. Finally his mother and her husband were able to drive him up and join the sets of nervous parents unpacking and making beds. He found a regular place to study, in a dorm lounge, and so far his grades were good.

"I am a little worried," he said, "that algebra might bite me—hard." Despite the fact that Malik could run complex software tests and hold forth coherently on inflation caps, he feared that algebra might be a bear. It's such a common issue for many of our students that we have begun teaching algebra in some Year Up classes to help students avoid dull and expensive remediation courses in college. Malik would have to take basic algebra when it was given in the second semester to get the dreaded math requirement over with. "I didn't have any math at all my last two years of high school," he said.

Could he defenestrate *that* weakness?

"Watch me try."

He was enjoying all his classes, though he ventured, "Sometimes college is a bit abstract. I admit it—I miss the Year Up way of teaching. I miss the hands on. And the instructors. And the laughing." He said he was learning a lot but occasionally found himself drifting a bit in a course called

"Introduction to Business." Participants were expected to dress in business attire; they were learning to draft proper e-mails and work on time management.

"It's not even Pro Skills 1.0."

Malik was hoping it would be an easy A. By midfall, he said that he and his roommates had become "like brothers." One weekend, Malik took the bus back to Manhattan to be interviewed by a scholarship committee at Dr. Tait's organization. Soon after, they notified him that he had won another thousand-dollar grant. On his lean budget, it would go a long way toward second semester books and expenses.

And Cassandra? We had all been concerned about Cassandra, out of the program, out of touch, but still in our thoughts. Solange, the friend she had directed to Year Up, was in contact with her sporadically via Facebook and a series of cell numbers. Charmaine had heard she might be back in Jamaica. One Saturday evening, as I was looking over this nearly completed manuscript, Cassandra called. I was startled; I had just been reading one of her quotes.

"It got kind of crazy for a while, a little bit grim. Such a hard, hard winter. But I'm okay. Really, I am."

She was back in New York and had indeed been in Jamaica for two months after her maternal grandfather died there. She had tried to ignore some health issues for lack of funds until a friend helped her get treatment. She had recovered. Cassandra said that she had agonized over leaving the program, but at the time she felt it was her only choice. "I had been so worn out trying to commute from Connecticut. I'd get up at five to get to Grand Central, then the subway was a mess. Variables, there were too many variables still—trains, weather, where I might find to stay next. I didn't think I could inflict that on an employer. It wasn't fair to them, or Year Up. I felt I had to go."

"Variable" is how she would describe her general state these last few years, but she had gotten used to it. "I still get to church when and where possible. I am in touch with people from Class Nine, yes. We were strong together. I take them with me in my heart—and my laptop. Yes, I still have it. And I still have the family it helped me to find."

With a cousin, Cassandra had decided on a fresh start in a resort city in Florida. I heard from her again shortly after they arrived there. Could I help out with a recommendation? She was applying for jobs "all over town." Charmaine and I both sent our endorsements and I have no doubt that Cassandra handled herself very well in interviews. Within five days, this resourceful young woman was hired by AT&T as a customer representative. She sounded relieved and upbeat as she began her training program. Maybe once she was settled in, she told me, she might think about college. Might she ever try us again? "With me you never know." She laughed. "Meanwhile, you have my godsister. How I bothered her to come. She needed Year Up, I knew it. I almost dragged her to see Charmaine."

We talked a bit more and Cassandra promised to stay in touch. She offered another new e-mail address, another phone number. "Address? I can't remember when I've had one. I'm not worried—someday I will."

Solange, Cassandra's legacy, was enjoying her internship at American Express, in the same downtown tower where Marisol's friend Jonathan continues to excel. She reported that her coworkers were friendly and helpful and she was doing well in desktop support, setting up workstations for new hires, reimaging their laptops, installing software, and managing the queue of help requests. Solange wasn't letting herself think too much about getting hired directly from her internship. Nobody should these days, she reasoned. "It's all so volatile." Asked what she expected from her own year up, Solange was thoughtful for a moment.

"I'll be able to say, 'I've done this. I've been through this.' My future career goals may have nothing to do with technology, but now that I have this opportunity, I can use it in so many ways. I can work in a hospital, wherever. Tech is always around. It's an open door for me, a gateway to something."

Solange paused. "Yes, that's it, so simple—that's what I want from Year Up. I want a door. Just one open door."

Acknowledgments

When I think back over the last decade, there were a few people who steadfastly encouraged me to pursue my dreams and to begin this journey. Highest on the list is of course my wife, Kate, without whom Year Up would not exist. She has been my partner throughout this journey, and in so many ways has been the quiet cofounder of Year Up. Year Up is as much a reflection of her caring and commitment as it is mine, and I am deeply grateful for her unconditional love and support. I would also like to thank my children, who have had to share their dad, in their words, "with other kids who might not have had a father." Cameron, Casey, and Callum have always been there to welcome a multitude of students, staff, and stakeholders to our home, and on many occasions had to put up with my constant phone calls, e-mails, and pleas that "this will just take a minute."

I am deeply grateful to have had the support of my father and late mother, Levon and Joyce Chertavian, as well as my in-laws, Guy and Valerie Smallwood—each of whom, in their own way, put a hand on my shoulder and said, "We believe in you, go for it!" The extended Chertavian and Small-wood families have all been so helpful, and I would like to give a special thanks to my brother Lee and his wife, Elaine, as well as to Edward Small-wood and Charlotte Houghteling.

Of course, this book, indeed this organization, would not exist if it were not for my little brother, David Heredia. David is and will always be my best teacher, and through our relationship I have learned some of life's most valuable lessons. I will always be grateful to his mother, Cornelia, for trusting me to care for her youngest son.

Although my name happens to be on the jacket of this book, I can admit to only having the initial idea for Year Up, and the willingness to provide the spark to get it all going. Our start-up team—Tom Berte, Linda Swardlick Smith, Nikki Patti (now Nikki Patti Berte), and Richard Dubuisson—were the ones who breathed life into the essays that I wrote in 1989 about starting Year Up. They took an idea, shaped and improved it, and Year Up was born. Since that beginning, we have been propelled forward by one of the most capable and caring staffs for which a CEO could wish; I am deeply thankful for the high support and high expectations that these individuals bring to our students each day.

I have always believed that leadership is a team sport, and I am deeply honored to have had the great fortune to assemble an extraordinary group of senior colleagues to build and lead Year Up during its first decade of growth and impact. I cannot adequately thank or recognize them all in this book, or even begin to list what they have done over this past decade to build Year Up into what it is today. Their commitment to serve our young adults is an inspiration, and I am humbled each day by the leadership, passion, and skill that they bring to our program. My views on what we are doing and how to do it have been dramatically enhanced by the wisdom and tenacity of each of these peers. I am deeply indebted to their service and leadership, and know we will be partners in the movement for social justice throughout the rest of our lives.

To the individuals who provided Year Up with the initial wind beneath our wings, Tim Dibble and his colleagues at Alta Communications, we will always be grateful. Tim, his wife, Maureen, and Alta believed in us at the very beginning and generously incubated our efforts from high atop Boston's streets in the Hancock Tower. Without question, we could not have wished for a more genuine, capable, and committed founding chair than Tim Dibble.

Leading us into our second decade is our current chair, Paul Salem, who, along with his wife, Navyn, championed our initial replication seven years ago in Providence and now inspire us to expand our vision for the impact that Year Up can have on the nation.

In addition to Tim and Paul, we have been fortunate to assemble an extraordinary group of national and local board members across the country. These individuals have taken tremendous responsibility for the growth and success of Year Up and provided the advice, resources, and support that we needed to realize our vision. I would like to list them here:

National Capital Region

John King (chair), Shirley Marcus Allen, Burt Baptiste, Larry Fullerton, Garland Hall, Dave Joubran, Nazzic Keene, John King, Bruce Rosenblum, Norean Sharpe, Jill Smith, Nazzic Turner.

New York

David Salomon (chair), Michael Bogdan, Charles D. Ellis, David Fike, Brian Frank, Bethann Hardison, Trace Harris, Alexander Klabin, Glen Macdonald, Avinash Mohan-Ram Richard Ramsden, Phil Schneidermeyer, Cynthia Rivera Weissblum.

Providence

Ted Fischer (chair), David Casey, Oneyda Escobar, Ted Fischer, Katharine Flynn, Barbara Goldner, Dolph Johnson, Chuck LoCurto, Brandon Melton, Anel Perez, Kay Phillips, Paul Salem, Donna Sams, Don Stanford, William Wray.

Puget Sound (Seattle)

John Stanton (chair), Robbie Bach, Rich Barton, Phyllis Campbell, Debora Horvath, Sue Rahr, Norman Rice, Jon Runstad, Judith Runstad, John Stanton, Jacky Wright.

LEADERSHIP COUNCIL MEMBERS

Atlanta

Archie Jones (chair), Alex Avendano, April Breeden, Jason Brown, Joe Crouthers, Rebecca Crumrine, Andrew Day, Trarie Durden, Alex Garrison, Adam Klein, Alecia Maclin, Thomas P. Smith, Tyre Sperling.

Bay Area (San Francisco)

Daniel Hayes (co-chair), John Kobs (co-chair), Ime Archibong, Katie Baynes, Colin Billings, Bakari Brock, Sunil Daluvoy, Abby Rubin Davisson, Matt Farron, Tiffiny Furdak, Chris Herndon, Ana Homayoun, Charles Hudson, Dominique Jones, Renuka Kher, Kate Mendillo, Rama Sekhar, Rebecca Shapiro, Jacobs Sorensen, Stephanie Ting.

Boston

Stephen Davis (co-chair), David Grossman (co-chair), Deborah Barry, Lucy Campbell, Reginald Champagne, Michael Farrell, Peter Grave, Saleel Kulkarni, Matthias McGuffie, Lacy Garcia Roosevelt.

Chicago

Michael Spector (chair), Sumit Chadha, John Clese, Stephanie Hall, Trista Hannan, Denise Turner.

New York

Michael Bogdan (chair), Josh Crandall, Nick Elliot, Cherrelle Goss, Makiko Harunari, Philip H. Hsia, Emily Janney, Bilal Khan, Zeev Klein, Shari Reichenberg, Jemi Shieh.

Puget Sound (Seattle)

Jeffrey Spector (chair), Ariel Dos Santos, Anthony Miles.

MILLION PERSON MODEL ADVISORY COUNCIL

John Galante, Lance Mansfield, Robert Templin Jr., Cynthia Rivera Weissblum.

I consider it one of life's greatest gifts to have the opportunity to both serve and get to know our students. Not a day goes by that I do not have the pleasure to interact with one of our students or graduates. They are indeed the real story here. Through the many hours we have shared together, through orientations and graduations, through tears of joy and tears of pain, I have been so fortunate to know them. We have taught one another in so many ways, and I know that they are the future leaders of not only Year Up but also the wider movement that we aspire to help lead. It has been an honor for me to carry the torch a few steps down the road and to know that true success will involve handing it off to our talented graduates. When that happens, I will rest easy knowing that Year Up's future could not be in any more capable hands.

As with all successful nonprofits, there is a group of stakeholders who commit, often quietly and without recognition, to invest in a mission. Our donors, internship partners, college partners, volunteers, mentors, and community partners complete the circles of support that we seek to wrap around our students. There are so many folks who were there at critical moments in our history, each one providing what they could because they cared about our mission and believed in our students. The following list is not meant to be exhaustive by any means and refers in many cases to individuals with whom I have had a personal interaction. All of you will know what you did, so please excuse the rather informal listing. I'd like to express my personal thanks to: Tony Abbiati and Alicia Collins, Jon Abbott, Iman Abdulmajid, Karen and Bill Ackman, Sarah Ahn and Chris Moody, Min and Marcus Alexander, Angie and Sam Allen, Shirley Marcus Allen, Kris Ann and Dave Andonian, Joe and MaryLynn Antonellis, Chet Atkins, Lucy Ball, Doug Band, Maura Banta, Gary Beach, Steve Belkin, Rachel Bello, Anita and Josh Bekenstein, Lynne and Marc Benioff, Senator Michael Bennet, Jeff Berndt, Paul Bernstein, Doug Borchard, David Bornstein, Phoebe Boyer, Kris Bradley, Benjamin Bram, Nadia Brigham, Paul Brountas, David Brown and Suzanne Muchin, Ron Bruder, Buzz Burlock, Paul Burton, Jonathan Bush and Mandi Dean, Catherine and Paul Buttenweiser, Geoff Canada, Missy and Marsh Carter, Dr. James Ireland Cash Jr., Dick Charlton, Ted Chen, Karen Clark, Congressman David Cicilline, Ed Cohen, Priscilla Cohen, Mimi Corcoran, Mary Jane and Glenn Creamer, Pierre Cremieux, Patrice Cromwell, Mike Danziger, Kim Davis, David Dechman, Nora Devlin and Jim Sloman, Maureen Dibble and the Dibble family, Suzanne DiBianca, Jamie Dimon, Ray Di Pasquale, Sarah DiTroia, Sarah and Al Dobron, Dave Dodson, Stephanie Weinstein Dodson, Amory Donohue, Suzy and Jim Donohue, Sandie Dorman, Jennifer and Chip Douglas, Mike Douvadjian, Bill Drayton, Denise Dupre and Mark Nunnelly, Sandy and Paul Edgerley, Mark Edwards, Jackie and Bill Egan, Mark Elliott, Flora and Doug Ellis, Bob Embry, Tammy Erickson, Katie Everett, Todd Faber, Michael Feller, Sandra Fenwick, Pryan Fernando, Nina and David Fialkow, Cathleen Finn, Melissa and Michel Finzi, Kelly Fitzsimmons, Mindy and Lee Foley, Clare and David Forbes-Nixon, Hilary and Chris Gabrieli, John Galante, Bob Gallery, Mark Gallogly and Lise Strickler, Attorney General Doug Gansler, Doug George, Chris Gergen, David Gergen, Joe Gervais and Bonnie Brown, Geoffrey Gestetner, Martin Gill, Sue Goldberger, Kristen Grannis and the team at Latham & Watkins, Alan Greene, Paul Grogan, Amy Gross, Liz and Phill Gross, Allen Grossman, Corinne and Wyc Grousbeck, Greg Gunn, Wendell Gunn, Chuck Hamilton, Gloria and Ray Hammond, Maria

Handrinos, Russ Hardin, Senator Tom Harkin, Chuck Harris, Mike and Sue Hazard and the Hazard family, Kerry and Sean Healey, Daisy and Bill Helman, Amy Herskovitz, Nancy Hoffman, Barbara and Amos Hostetter, Marci Hunn, Cheryl Hyman, Joanna and Jon Jacobson, Joanne Jaxtimer, James Jensen, Gladys Jensen, the Jensen family, Cassius Johnson, Michele Jolin, Allan Jones, Maria Jones, Tripp and Robin Jones, Blake Jordan, Wendy and Marty Kaplan, Richard Kazis, Robert and Nicole Keller, Mike Kendall and the team at Goodwin Procter, Angela and David Kenny, Julie King, Sean King, Susie King, Vanessa Kirsch and Alan Khazei, Seth and Beth Klarman, Donna Klein, Matt Klein, Zeev Klein, Amy and Rich Kohan, Wendy Kopp, Eva Labouisse, Lori Laitman, Congressman John Lewis, Marjorie and Danny Levin, Amy Lieb, Linda and Ralph Linsalata, Milton Little, Marjorie and Michael Loeb, Alistair Lumsden and Dee Simon, Daniel Lurie, Maria McDonald, Gary McGaha, Holly McGrath, Margaret McKenna, Congressman Buck McKeon, Michael McMahon, Margaret and Brian McNeill, Elizabeth and John McQuillan Jr., Shari Malin, Steve Mandel Jr., Molly and Mike Manning, Tristin and Marty Mannion, Melinda Marble, Chris Mathias, Mayor Thomas Menino, Madge Meyer, Barry Mills, Eric Mindich, Henry Moniz, Pam Moore and Charles Rose, Mary and Garrett Moran, Mario Morino, Meg Morton, Mindy and Reuben Munger, Orhun Muratoglu and Tonya Orme, Senator Patty Murray, John Muse, Andrea Nagel, Jane Oates, Susan and William Oberndorf, George Overholser, Patricia Palacio, Kim Pallotta, Cynthia Parker, Governor Deval Patrick, Anne Peretz, John Phelan, Stanley Pollack, Michael Price, Peter Quinn, Alison Quirk, Hannah Ramsden, Pat Randall, Aron Ranen, Juan Rave, Senator Jack Reed, Kristin and Paul Reeder, Tom Reis, Susan Retik, Mercedes Restrepo, Paul Reville, Bruce Rosenblum, Elyse Rosenblum, Sue and Daniel Rothenberg, Trish and Mike Rotondi, George Russell, David Sachs, Bill Sahlman, Navyn Salem, David Salomon, Richard Salomon, David Saltzman, Alicia Sams, Marlene Seltzer, Jeff Shames, Millie Shepard, Jemi Shieh, Rosemary Jordano Shore and Billy Shore, Sue and John Simon, Peter Sims, Deidre Smialowski, Diana Smith, Rob and Dana Smith, Susan Smith, Kiki and Patrick Smulders, Jennifer Snyder and the team at WilmerHale, Stephanie and James Sokolove, Jack Sommers, Ramez and Titziana Sousou, Stephanie Spector, Wendy and Dan Springer, Diane and Will Stansbury, Jill and Michael Stansky, Theresa Stanton, Adria Steinberg, Norah and Norman Stone, Dave Sylvester, Kim Syman, Kim Tanner, Andrea Taylor, Greg Taylor, Jeff Taylor and

Anna Sweitzer Taylor, Moya and David Tosh, Eileen McCarthy Toti and Stephen Toti, Pamela and Alan Trefler, Patty Underwood, Jeanne Ungerleider, Netty and Ries Vanderpol, Alicia Verity, Gerry Villacres, Bina and Philippe Von Stauffenberg, Herb Wagner III and Charlotte Cramer Wagner, Liz Walker, Senator Mark Warner, Bill Weidlein, Donn Weinberg, James Weinberg, Allan Weis, Tona and Bob White, Tiger Williams, Kathleen Yazbak.

In addition to the many individuals who have supported our journey, there have been a number of foundations that have believed in our mission and provided much-needed capital to fuel our growth. Specifically, I would like to thank:

Abell Foundation, Altman Foundation, Amelia Peabody Foundation, The Annie E. Casey Foundation, The AT&T Foundation, Bank of America Foundation, Barr Foundation, Blue Ridge Foundation New York, BNY Mellon Charitable Foundation, The Boston Foundation, Clark Foundation, The David E. Retik and Christopher D. Mello Foundation, FAO Schwarz Family Foundation, Fidelity Foundation, Goldman Sachs Gives, Harry and Jeanette Weinberg Foundation, Highland Street Foundation, Ira W. DeCamp Foundation, James Irvine Foundation, The Jenesis Group, JPMorgan Chase Foundation, Lloyd G. Balfour Foundation, Lone Pine Foundation, The Lynch Foundation, The Moriah Fund, New Profit, Inc., New York Life Foundation, New York Stock Exchange (NYSE) Foundation, Open Society Foundations Special Fund for Poverty Alleviation, Paul and Phyllis Fireman Charitable Foundation, Peery Foundation, Pershing Square Foundation, Philip L. Graham Fund, Pinkerton Foundation, Price Family Foundation, Regis Family Community Fund, The Rhode Island Foundation, Richard and Susan Smith Family Foundation, Robert W. Woodruff Foundation, Robin Hood Foundation, Rowland Foundation, Salesforce.com Foundation, Sartain Lanier Family Foundation, Inc., State Street Foundation, Inc., Strategic Grant Partners, Sun Trust Bank of Georgia, Tiger Foundation, Tipping Point Community, TowerBrook Foundation, The United Way of Rhode Island, Venture Philanthropy Partners, W. K. Kellogg Foundation, and Walmart Foundation.

Clearly the organizations with which we have partnered to place our interns have made a major impact on our success and provided our students with the opportunity that they need to realize their potential. These companies are leaders in the long struggle for economic justice, and it is with great appreciation and pride that we list them here:

Aaron's, Inc., AARP, ABCD Dorchester Neighborhood Center, Abt Associates, Accenture plc, Acumen Solutions, Acushnet Golf, Advantage Technical Resourcing, Advent International, Aerotek, African Continuum Theater Company, American International Group, Inc. (AIG), AIPSO, Akamai, Alaska Airlines, Allegis Group, Alnylam Pharmaceuticals, Altera Corporation, Amdocs, American Council on Education (ACE), American Dryer Corporation, American Express, American Power Conversion (APC), American Red Cross, American Safety Insurance, American Systems, American Tower Corporation, AmericasMart, Ameriprise Financial, AmeriVault, Amica, AOL, AON Corporation, Aquent, Arthritis Foundation, AT&T, athenahealth, Atlasian, Atrion, Atrion SMB, Atrius Health, AutoTrader.com, AvalonBay Communities, Avectra, Bain & Company, Bain Capital, LLC, Baltimore City Public Schools, Bank of America, Bank of the West, Bank Rhode Island, Barclays Capital, Baupost Group, L.L.C., Bay State Milling Company, Beacon Mutual, Bechtel, Berklee College of Music, BET Networks, Big Fish Games, Bingham McCutchen LLP, Biogen Idec, BITHGROUP Technologies, Black Box Network Services, BlackRock, Blackstone, Bloomberg, Blue Cross Blue Shield of Massachusetts, Blue Cross Blue Shield of Rhode Island, Blue Shield of California, BNY Mellon, Booz Allen Hamilton, Boston Celtics, Boston College, Boston Consulting Group, Boston Financial Data Services, Boston Medical Center, Boston Public Schools, Boston University, Boston Ventures Investment Partners, Boys & Girls Club of Boston, Boys & Girls Clubs of Metro Atlanta, Brigham and Women's Hospital, Bright Horizons Family Solutions, Brisard & Brisard, Inc., Broadridge Financial Solutions, Brookings Institution, Brown Brothers Harriman, Brown Rudnick LLP, Brown University, Building Educated Leaders for Life (BELL), Byte Back, CA Technologies, Cabot Corporation, California Pacific Medical Center, Cambridge Associates, Cambridge College, Canaccord Adams, Capgemini, Capital Hospice, Capital One, Capitol Asset Recovery Corporation, Cardlytics, CARE USA, Carlyle Group, Catapult Technology, Cbeyond, City of Baltimore, BiddingForGood, CBS4 Boston, CDW, Center for American Progress, Centerline Capital Group, CGI, Chat Sports, Chicago Event Management, Children First, Children's Hospital Boston, Citadel, Citi, Citizens Bank, City of Boston, City of New York, City of Seattle, City Year, CitySoft,

Inc., ClusterSeven, Cognizant, Collette Vacations, Comcast, Commonwealth of Massachusetts, CompuCom Systems, Inc., Computer Sciences Corporation (CSC), Computers For Youth, comScore, Inc., Concessions International, LLC, Co-Nect, Concur Technologies, Inc., Consigli Construction Co., Constellation Energy, Corporate Executive Board Company, County of Dekalb, Covidien, CRICO/RMF, Cubist Pharmaceuticals, CVS Caremark, Cyveillance, Inc., Dana-Farber Cancer Institute, Dassault Systèmes, DC Chartered Health Plan, Inc., Delta Dental of Rhode Island, Deltek, Inc., Deutsche Bank, Digitas, District of Columbia Children and Youth Investment Trust Corporation, District of Columbia Housing Authority (DCHA), Domino Foods Inc., DotWell, Dow Lohnes PLLC, Draper Laboratory, DreamBox Learning, DTCC, Dunkin Brands, Inc., Eastern Bank, Eaton Vance, eBay, Edwards Angell Palmer & Dodge, EF Institute for Cultural Exchange, EIS, Inc., Electronic Arts, EMC Corporation, Emerging Health Information Technology, Emory University, Empire BlueCross BlueShield, EPAM, Equifax, Ernst & Young, Euro RSCG Worldwide, EveryNetwork, Expedia, F.W. Webb Company, Facebook, Facilitating Leadership in Youth, Family Service of Rhode Island, Fannie Mae, FBR Capital Markets, Federal Reserve Bank of Atlanta, Federal Reserve Bank of Boston, Federal Reserve Bank of Chicago, Fenway High School, Fidelity Investments, First Marblehead, FM Global, Fred Huthinson Cancer Research Center, Freddie Mac, FTI Consulting, Inc., Future Foundation, Inc., GE Capital, GEICO, Gentle Giant, Genuine Parts Company, Georgia Public Broadcasting, Georgia-Pacific, Gilbane Inc., Gillette, Goodwin Procter LLP, Google, Graduate Management Admission Council (GMAC), Grady Health System, Granite Telecommunications, Greater Washington Hispanic Chamber of Commerce, Groundwork Inc., GTECH, Hanger Orthopedic Group, District of Columbia, Harvard Business School, Harvard Graduate School of Design, Harvard Law School, Harvard Management Company, Harvard School of Public Health, Harvard University Faculty of Arts and Sciences, Harvard University Health Services, Harvard University John F. Kennedy School of Government, Hasbro, Hearst Ventures, Hewlett-Packard Company, Highflelds Capital Management, Hill Holliday, Hilton Worldwide, Hinckley, Allen & Snyder LLP, Hogan Lovells, Holder Construction, Houghton Mifflin, iBiquity Digital, IDG, iFactory, Income Research + Management, ING Group, Inova Health System, InQuest Technologies, InScope Solutions, Institute for the Study and Practice of Nonviolence, Intercontinental Exchange, Inc., InterContinental Hotels Group plc, Ipswitch Inc., IRB Investments, ITS Group, Jackson Healthcare, Jewish Family & Career Services, JMP Securities, John Hancock, Johns Hopkins University, JPMorgan Chase, Juma Ventures, Jumpstart, Kaiser Permanente, Kaseya, Latham & Watkins LLP, Latin American Youth Center, LeasePlan USA, Leerink Swann LLC, Liberty Mutual Group, Lifespan, LinkedIn, Liquid Machines, Litl, Lockheed Martin Corporation, Lucile Packard Children's Hospital at Stanford, McKesson, M. Block and Sons, Inc., Mar-ketAxess, Marriott International, Inc., Marsh & McLennan Companies, Inc., Maryland Motor Vehicle Administration (MVA), Massachusetts Eye and Ear Infirmary MDI Group, MedAssets, Medical Sales Management; Inc., Meeting Street, MFS Investment Management, MicroMenders, Micro-soft, Millennium Pharmaceuticals, Inc., mindSHIFT Technologies, Mas-sachusetts Institute of Technology (MIT), Massachusetts Institute of Technology (MIT) Sloan School of Management, Mitre, Momenta Pharma-ceuticals, Momentum Worldwide, Monitor Group, Monsoon Commerce Solutions, Morgan Stanley, MorganFranklin, Mount Sinai Hospital, Mozilla, National Employee Benefit Companies (NEBCO), National Fire Protection Agency (NFPA), National Football League (NFL), National Public Radio (NPR), NaviNet, NBC10 WJAR Providence, NetApp, Network Health, Neustar, Inc., New Signature, New York City Housing Authority (NYCHA), New York Life Insurance Company, New York Life Retirement Plan Ser-vices, New York Presbyterian Hospital, New York University Langone Med-ical Center, New York University Stern School of Business, Newell Rubbermaid, Nintendo of America Inc., North Highland, Northern Virginia Community College (NOVA), Noth Shore-Long Island Jewish Health Sys-tem, NPower Greater DC Region, Omnicom Group, Orrick, Herrington & Sutcliffe LLP, Partners Healthcare, Patni Computer Systems, Paul Cuffee School, PC Troubleshooters, Inc., Pegasystems, Inc., Pepco Holdings, Inc., Perkins + Will, Perot Systems, PHH Corporation, Pioneer Investments, PopCap Games, PricewaterhouseCoopers (PwC), Primus Software Corpo-ration, Printpack Inc., PROMETRIKA, LLC, Prosper, Providence Equity Partners, Publicis, Putnam Investments, Quality Technology Services, Radio One, Inc., Raffa, P.C., Raytheon BBN Technologies, REI, Reit Man-agement & Research, LLC, Reneida Reyes, D.D.S., Responsys, Rhode Island Economic Development Corporation (RIEDC), Rhode Island Foster Par-ents Association, Ring2, Rock-Tenn Company, Rohde & Schwarz, Inc., Royal

Bank of Scotland, RPC, Inc., Rush University Medical Center, SAIC, Salesforce.com, Sapphire Technologies, Seattle Children's Hospital, Seattle City Light, Secretary of the Air Force Technical and Analytical Support (SAFTAS), SendMe, Inc., Sentinel Benefits & Financial Group, Share Our Strength, Shire Human Genetic Therapies, Inc., Sidley Austin LLP, Siemens AG, Simpson Thacher & Bartlett LLP, Slalom Consulting, Sodexo, Southern Company, Sovereign Bank, SRA International, Staples, Starwood Capital Group, State of Maryland Motor Vehicle Administration (MVA), State of Rhode Island, State Street, Stop & Shop, SunTrust, Swarovski Crystal, T. Rowe Price, Teach for America, TechBridge, Ted Leonsis, Textron Financial Corporation, The APEX Museum, The Charles Hotel, The Coca-Cola Company, The Corporation for Enterprise Development (CFED), The Dimock Center, The George Washington University, The Home Depot, Inc., The MENTOR Network, The United States Holocaust Memorial Museum, The Washington Post, The Weather Channel, Thompson, Thomson Reuters, Thrive Networks, Time Warner Inc., Timothy Smith Network, TNT Vacations, Tower Research Capital LLC, Travel Channel, Travelport, Treasury Wine Estates, Troutman Sanders LLP, Tufts Medical Center, Turner Broadcasting, Twitter, UBS, United Way of Metropolitan Atlanta, University of Massachusetts Boston, Upromise, US Department of Agriculture (USDA), US resources, Vanguard Health Systems, Inc., Veritude, Vertex Pharmaceuticals, Warnaco Group, Inc., WCG Management L.P., Weil, Gotshal & Manges LLP, Wellington Management Company, Wells Fargo, WGL Holdings, Inc., Whittier Street Health Center, WilmerHale, XL Group, Year Up, Yelp, Zane Networks, LLC, Zynga.

I'd like to say a special word to the students and staff who helped create this book. Since this is above all else our students' project, I have relied upon them to help tell their stories. Across our sites nationwide, current students and alums have proved themselves unfailingly generous, honest, and courageous. I'm especially grateful to the students in Class Nine in New York City who helped us illustrate exactly how our program works day to day. They always found time to stay in touch and share their thoughts throughout their rigorous journey, from orientation through their internships and on to that joyous graduation. It was a lot to ask—and believe me, it made all the difference.

Our staff—already giving 100 percent every day—surely went the extra miles to help with this book, answering endless questions, sharing their expertise, and reaching out to students and alumni who might help tell our story. To all of you who stood up to the flood of e-mails, the interviews, the classroom visitations, my deepest thanks. I hope you recognize yourselves in these pages with pride. I would also like to express my thanks to Elise Ford, David Pineros, Aaron Schutzengel, Dan Adler, Chris Thorson, and Moises Cohen for the research that they conducted to ensure the accuracy and completeness of this work.

Through the kindness of my friend Billy Shore, who encouraged me to write this book, I met my literary agent, Flip Brophy of Sterling Lord Literistic. Flip and I share a similar style of swinging for the fences, and within a few weeks of our meeting we were sitting in front of Clare Ferraro and Wendy Wolf, respectively the president and associate publisher of Viking. Thank you, Flip, for believing that our students' voices needed to be heard and finding us the right home. Thanks also to Gina Anderson at Viking for her sage counsel and caring advice.

And finally, about Gerri Hirshey, who is in a category all to herself. In addition to her business smarts, Flip Brophy had the good sense to make one small detour before we went to see our future publishers—to introduce me to Gerri Hirshey. It was clear to me at this first meeting that Viking's interest in this unpublished social entrepreneur was dramatically increased by the deeply talented author sitting next to me, Gerri Hirshey. For the past year and a half, Gerri has provided the steady guidance to bring this project to life and to ensure that our story and our students' stories are properly told. I cannot thank Gerri enough for all that she has done to help write this book. It would not have been possible without her. Our evening and weekend editing sessions are ones that I will always cherish, and I am deeply grateful for the ongoing partnership that we have enjoyed. Although I knew that our book would benefit greatly from Gerri's gift for the written word, I had no idea that her passion and depth of caring for our students would qualify her to be a lifelong member of the Year Up family. Her understanding of our work, our students, and the underlying social and economic justice that we seek was what pulled it all together.

A Message from Gerald Chertavian Founder and CEO of Year Up

BECOME A PART OF THE OPPORTUNITY MOVEMENT!

Empowering all of America's young adults is a worthwhile and monumental ambition that has the potential to transform our great nation. To achieve this mission, we need the involvement of readers like you who understand the magnitude of the obstacles we have to overcome and the fulfillment that comes with enabling others to realize their potential. There are many ways in which you can help Year Up close the Opportunity Divide:

Volunteer

Creating opportunity for our students requires multiple layers of support. As a professional *mentor*, you can help prepare our students to navigate the business world. As a student or professional, you can become a math or communications *tutor*, impacting students' academic performance during the program and beyond. Each of these commitments involves just about an hour a week, and our students rate their relationships with tutors and mentors as some of the most influential to their development. There are other ways to become involved, including *guest speaking* and *conducting mock interviews*.

Invest

Thousands of individuals and organizations have invested in our program because they believe in our mission and because we deliver on our promises. Year Up is one of the fastest growing nonprofits in the country, and this growth would not be possible without the financial contributions that support our program. About half of our revenues come from fees that organizations pay to have access to our talented students through internships. Most of the other half comes from individual and foundation donations. I invite you to join a group of committed individuals and organizations by *donating* to our program or *hosting an intern*.

Advocate

Year Up alone cannot create opportunity for over five million disconnected young adults. This is why we advocate for effective means of empowering young people to help themselves, as well as for systemic changes that will help close the Opportunity Divide. You can help us by *raising awareness* about the divide and by *supporting policies* to close it. Our policy views grow out of our experience working with young adults across the country; they are practical and have bipartisan support. Fundamentally, we believe in *investing in social innovation* and in *supporting the expansion of models with proven results*.

With so many ways to engage, perhaps the first thing you should do is make an appointment to visit a Year Up site in your vicinity.

Fair warning: Meeting a Year Up student can transform your life.

To help shape the Opportunity Movement, please visit:

www.yearup.org

Notes

The information in this book is derived largely from interviews, observations of events, and analysis of Year Up program data. Listed below are the sources for information obtained from newspaper and journal articles and third-party reports.

Prologue: Honk for Opportunity

Page

1 **an estimated 5.2 million young adults:** 2010 statistics by The Annie E. Casey Foundation, *KIDS COUNT Data Book*, 2011.

7 **12 percent of Ivy League graduates:** Teach for America, "Teach for America Fields Largest Teacher Corps in Its 20-Year History," May 24, 2010.

8 **the racial wealth gap *quadrupled*:** Thomas M. Shapiro, Tatjana Meschede, and Laura Sullivan, "The Racial Wealth Gap Increases Fourfold," The Institute on Assets and Social Policy, The Heller School for Social Policy and Management, May 2010.

8 **A recent Pew study:** Rakesh Kochhar, Richard Fry, and Paul Taylor, "Wealth Gaps Rise to Record Highs Between Whites, Blacks, Hispanics," Pew Research Center, July 26, 2011.

8 **40 percent of employers:** Jill Casner-Lotto and Linda Barrington, "Are They Really Ready to Work? Employers' Perspectives on the Basic Knowledge and Applied Skills of New Entrants to the 21st Century U.S. Workforce," The Conference Board, Corporate Voices for Working Families, Partnership for 21st Century Skills, and Society for Human Resource Management, 2006.

8 **the average expense to house a prisoner:** National Institute of Corrections, U.S. Department of Justice, "Correction Statistics by State," 2010.

9 **structural mismatch:** Jinzhu Chen et al., "New Evidence on Cyclical and Structural Sources of Unemployment," International Monetary Fund, May 1, 2011; and Robert J. Samuelson, "The Great Jobs Mismatch," *The Washington Post*, June 19, 2011.

9 **Research by the labor economists:** Anthony Carnevale and Donna M. Desrochers, "Standards for What? The Economic Roots of K-16 Reform," Educational Testing Service, 2003.

11 **The U.S. Government Accountability Office reports:** U.S. Government Accountability Office, "Multiple Employment and Training Programs: Providing Information on Colocating Services and Consolidating Administrative Structures Could Promote Efficiencies," January 2011.

12 **Compare that with community colleges:** James E. Rosenbaum, Julie Redline, and Jennifer L. Stephan, "Community College: The Unfinished Revolution," *Issues in Science and Technology*, Summer 2007, 49–56.

Chapter 1: "Yo, God. What Are You Doing?"

19 **The New York State Education Department reported:** Sharon Otterman, "College Readiness Low Among State Graduates, Data Shows," *The New York Times*, June 14, 2011.

39 **"Crack steered fathers to jail":** Sandy Banks, "The Crack Epidemic's Toxic Legacy," *Los Angeles Times*, August 7, 2010.

Chapter 5: "You Don't Have a Chance in Hell"

97 **Forty-one trillion dollars in wealth:** John J. Havens and Paul G. Schervish, "Why the $41 Trillion Wealth Transfer Estimate Is Still Valid: A Review of Challenges and Questions," Boston College Social Welfare Research Institute, January 6, 2003.

111 **42 percent of high school graduates:** Susan Aud et al., "Indicator 22: Remedial Coursetaking," *The Condition of Education 2011*, National Center for Education Statistics, U.S. Department of Education, May 2011.

Chapter 9: Guilty by Association

188 **chronic, uncontrollable stressors result in hopelessness:** Dana Landis et al., "Urban Adolescent Stress and Hopelessness," *Journal of Adolescence*, 30.6 (2007): 1051–70.

189 **a 2003 study:** John Bolland, "Hopelessness and Risk Behaviour Among Adolescents Living in High-Poverty Inner-City Neighbourhoods," *Journal of Adolescence*, 26.2 (2003): 145–58.

197 **2011 comparison done by *Time*:** Ada Calhoun, "Grammy Nominees Put Full Sail University in the Spotlight," *Time*, February 11, 2011.

Chapter 10: "I'm Having an Intern Moment"

210 **over seventeen thousand children and teenagers:** Coalition for the Homeless, "Basic Facts About Homelessness: New York City," November 2011.

210 **the city's eighteen- to twenty-four-year-olds:** Covenant House Institute, "Youth Status Report: New York, New York," November 2010.

210 **26 percent of homicide victims:** Covenant House Institute, "National Youth Status Report," November 2010.

Chapter 12: The Soul of a New Machine

269 **industry norm for youth-serving organizations:** Opportunity Knocks, "Nonprofit Retention and Vacancy Report," 2010.

269 **recognized by the *NonProfit Times:*** The *NonProfit Times,* "2011 Best Nonprofit Organizations to Work For," April 2011.

278 **3.7 million disconnected young adults:** 2001 statistics by The Annie E. Casey Foundation, *KIDS COUNT Data Book*, 2011.

Chapter 13: "We Are One Year Up"

286 **"English learners":** Andrea Ramsey and Jennifer O'Day, "Title III Policy: State of the States: ESEA Evaluation Brief: The English Language Acquisition, Language Enhancement, and Academic Achievement Act," U.S. Department of Education, May 2010.

286 **fifty-five languages:** Educational Demographics Office, California Department of Education, "Statewide English Learners by Language and Grade," 2011.

289 ***The New York Times DealBook* column:** "Wells Fargo Chief Sees Job Cuts After Wachovia Deal," *The New York Times,* January 8, 2009.

292 **A 2011 study published in *The Harvard Educational Review:*** Carola Suárez-Orozco et al., "Growing Up in the Shadows: The Developmental Implications of Unauthorized Status," *Harvard Educational Review*, 81.3 (2011).

293 **A *New York Times* editorial:** "California Dreaming," *The New York Times,* September 3, 2011.

Chapter 14: "I Think That Woman Saved My Life"

302 **highest high school dropout rates:** Harvard Graduate School of Education, "Pathways to Prosperity," February 2011.

302 **a third of high school students:** Jay Greene and Greg Forster, "Public High School Graduation and College Readiness Rates in the United States," Manhattan Institute for Policy Research, September 2003.

302 **over 40 percent:** Jill Casner-Lotto and Linda Barrington, "Are They Really Ready to Work? Employers' Perspectives on the Basic Knowledge and Applied

Skills of New Entrants to the 21st Century U.S. Workforce," The Conference Board, Corporate Voices for Working Families, Partnership for 21st Century Skills, and Society for Human Resource Management, 2006.

302 **postsecondary education for close to half of all undergraduates:** Harvard Graduate School of Education, "Pathways to Prosperity," February 2011.

303 **By age twenty-two:** U.S. Bureau of Labor Statistics, "Youth at College and Work," February 19, 2010.

Epilogue: Wheels Up for Opportunity

317 **seventeen thousand disconnected young adults:** 2010 statistics by The Annie E. Casey Foundation, *KIDS COUNT Data Book*, 2011.

319 **30 percent average graduation:** Harvard Graduate School of Education, "Pathways to Prosperity," February 2011.

Index